Copyright © 2019 by Tom Weaver
All rights reserved.
No part of this book may be reproduced in any form or by any means, electronic, mechanical, digital, photocopying, or recording, except for inclusion of a review, without permission in writing from the publisher or Author.

Published by BearManor Media
P.O. Box 71426
Albany, Georgia 31708
books@benohmart.com

Softcover ISBN 978-1-62933-473-8
Case ISBN 978-1-62933-474-5
Printed in the United States
Text designed by Robbie Adkins, www.adkinsconsult.com
Cover art by Kerry Gammill
Back cover designed by Mary Runser

Photo previous page: "If I am the Creeper, it is because man's hatred has made me so!": Following in Universal's grand tradition of put-upon monsters, the Creeper joined the lineup in 1944, played by Rondo Hatton.

Dedicated to Rondo Hatton

Many of the illustrations in this book are from...

Table of Contents

Acro-knowledgments vii

Introduction by Lewis Rex Gordon 1

"Rondo Hatton: A Biography" by Scott Gallinghouse 3

***The Brute Man*: Production History** by Tom Weaver 82

"Look at my face!" A Release History of *The Brute Man* by Dr. Robert J. Kiss . 106

***The Brute Man*: Fun Facts** by Tom Weaver 125

The *Brute Man*: Reviews 135

The *Brute Man*: Continuity and Dialogue 137

The *Brute Man*: Trailer Script 226

"Storm Chaser!" – Rondo Hatton and the Great Miami Hurricane 230

"'Oxton 'Orror, I Called Him!" — The Screen Bow of 241
    Rondo Hatton's Hoxton Creeper by Tom Weaver

Rondo Hatton's *The Old Dark House*: Dwight V. Babcock's Story Idea 253

"Hollywood's Strangest Love Story": 1946 *Pageant* magazine article 255

"The Brute Men: Medical Marvels! Giants of the Genre! Monsters of .. 258
    the Ring! And Other Awesome Brutes!" by George Chastain

"He Made a Star Out of Rondo Hatton!" by Andrew J. Fenady 272

Fears New and Old: The Postwar American Horror Film by Gary D. Rhodes .. 275

The Face That Launched the Rondo Hatton Awards by David Colton ... 284

The *Brute Man* Pressbook (from the Ronald V. Borst Collection) 289

All gave some, some gave all 296

Endnotes 298

Acro-knowledgments

Ron Adams · John Antosiewicz
Mike Bannon · Marty Baumann
Charlie Bodishbaugh
Sue Bodishbaugh
Margaret Borst
Ron Borst · John Brunas
Mike Brunas · Ned Comstock
James Cusick · Jan Pivar Dacri
Darlene Fabelo · Drew Friedman
Katie Gallinghouse
Mark Gallinghouse
Tracy Gallinghouse
Kerry Gammill · Lewis Rex Gordon
Jack Gourlay · Sandra Grabman
Martin Grams · Joe Indusi
Steve Kronenberg · Hal Lane
Dario Lavia · Cory Legassic
Scott MacQueen · Leonard Maltin
Mark Martucci · Gary Prange
Fred Rappaport · Fred Olen Ray
Thomas Reeder · Alan Rode
Mary Runser · David Schecter
Rich Scrivani · Laura Wagner
Brian Weaver
Lucy Chase Williams
Valerie Yaros

Introduction

By Lewis Rex Gordon

As the historian for Hillsborough High School, one of the oldest high schools in Florida, I have heard my fair share of legends. Tales of ghosts in the hallways, cries from the clock tower and even doors unlocking by themselves have crossed my desk.

But one story stands tall above the rest. The tale of Rondo Hatton, a 1913 graduate from our gothic-styled school. No one in Rondo's high school senior class could have envisioned the twists of fate that Rondo had in store for his future, and neither could he. A popular and handsome football and track star in a secret society, he became Hollywood's "monster who needs no makeup," and this has served as a cautionary and an inspiring saga for generations of Hillsborough students, staff and alumni.

Rondo is finally in the hands of great horror film historians Scott Gallinghouse, Dr. Robert J. Kiss and Tom Weaver, and new light will be shed on this iconic horror movie star. Enjoy!

– Lewis Rex Gordon
Hilsborean Historian
Hillsborough High School Alumni Association
Tampa, Florida

Rondo is front and center in this high school yearbook photo of the members of "Ye Royal GG," which Hillsborough High's historian Lewis Rex Gordon says was the school's "Skull and Bones" society in 1913: "It wasn't a huge class and everyone listed went on to some form of fame or fortune." A black cat was its mascot.

A Note from Biography Author Scott Gallinghouse

Rondo Hatton's unusual life and film career have attracted several previous biographers. However, their essays are marred by inaccuracies *that were largely the result of limitations on research sources at the time they were written.* Nevertheless, each prior biography contains important information and insights that contribute significantly to our understanding of Rondo Hatton, the man. As such, each prior biographer's unique contribution will be incorporated into the following narrative where it is appropriate, and duly acknowledged. While some errors may lurk in the ensuing record, I can assure the reader that my sole aim throughout has been to do justice to an extraordinary man.

"Rondo Hatton: A Biography"

By Scott Gallinghouse

On the screen, he was a thug, a bouncer, a convict, a leper and a psychopathic killer. Off-screen, he was the son of respected educators – a shy, devout man who had been an exceptional athlete, an esteemed journalist and above all, a beloved friend and husband. In the field of film, and in the crucible of a life marred by an inconceivably cruel disease, Rondo Hatton achieved a distinction that survives to this day. That Hatton portrayed his signature role of the Creeper at the tail end of the second Hollywood horror cycle makes his accomplishment, and the cinematic immortality that accompanied that feat, all the more noteworthy.

A conventional approach to a biographical sketch would begin with a recitation of the subject's date and place of birth, and those facts concerning Rondo Hatton will certainly be set forth in due course. However, in order to get a sense of Rondo Hatton's early life, some introductory information regarding his parents is necessary. While it is fair to say that the early lives of most children are largely the products of the lives and careers of their parents, that notion is particularly relevant to Hatton's formative years. Even the place of his birth was a direct result of the professional pursuits of his parents, Stewart Price Hatton and Emily Lee Zaring. They were in the forefront of the movement to improve higher education for women in the late 19th and early 20th centuries.

Born in July 1862, Stewart Price Hatton was the third of seven sons born to Reverend William Ashley Hatton and his wife Sarilda Ann Bishop Hatton. Surviving records establish that in the late 1880s, Stewart and several of his brothers attended the University

His face was his *mis*fortune until Hollywood helped him turn things around: This is Rondo Hatton's story.

of Missouri. Subsequent events make it plain that the brothers intended to move into the field of education after the completion of their college careers.

By the early 1890s, the Hatton brothers had bought the campus of McGee College at College Mound, Missouri. They intended to revive what had been, in the years leading up to the Civil War, a premier institution of higher learning in Missouri. Stewart was among a small coterie of instructors under the "Hatton Bros." banner. Advertisements in newspapers from the period confirm that over 100 students enrolled at McGee in its

Photo left: By *Brute Man* time, even Rondo's once-snappy-looking hats looked ready for retirement. This one looks like he wore it through a car wash.

first year of operation under the presidency of Stewart's brother, John H. Hatton. An item in the June 3, 1892, *Macon Times* painted an encouraging picture: After outlining McGee College's history, the article continued:

> Last year the Hatton Brothers, six in number, and all graduates of the state university at Columbia, took charge of the school and in a short time ran the roll of students to the remarkable number of 150. The faculty is headed by Prof. J.H. Hatton, ... a gentleman of refinement, culture and talent. He is ably assisted by Professors S.P. Hatton, M.W. Hatton, R.E. Hatton, L.M. Hatton, W.D. Hatton, W.T. Merrill, E.S. Luce, C.W. Newman and Misses Hattie Perkins, Kate Gillespy and Mrs. Mabel Stamper.

Stewart married Emily Lee Zaring in Columbia, Missouri, on June 6, 1893. A graduate of the University of Missouri, "Emma" was ten years his junior. She also intended to be a teacher.

Despite the seeming success of McGee College under the Hattons' management, it was clear that Stewart wanted to strike out on his own. The April 28, 1893, *Macon Times* reported, "Prof. S.P. Hatton started last week to Hager's town, Md., on a business trip. He expects to return this week." Hagerstown was home to Kee Mar College, an institution devoted to women's education. It offered courses and teaching diplomas in a variety of disciplines. Thanks to the research done by Julie E. Greene for a 2008 newspaper article on Rondo Hatton, we know that Stewart quickly accepted a position with Kee Mar. According to Greene, Stewart was listed as a teacher at the college for the 1893 summer school session. Catalogues published by the college during the mid–1890s included both Stewart and his wife (listed as Emma L. Hatton) among the roster of instructors for the 1894 and 1895 sessions. In addition, Greene reported that *Randall's General Directory of Hagerstown, Md. 1895-1896* listed the Hattons as "teachers who resided at Kee Mar College's dormitory."

Based upon the above, we can conclude with some assurance that Emily L. Hatton gave birth to Rondo K. Hatton in Hagerstown, Maryland. According to almost all available sources, Rondo was born on Sunday, April 22, 1894. Film historian Barry Brown stated in an article on Hatton that Rondo was born in the girls' infirmary on the Kee Mar campus.

Before Rondo was even two years old, his father set his sights on a loftier goal than teaching: Stewart Hatton aspired to become a principal at a college. He approached the administrators of Claremont Female College in Hickory, North Carolina, to assume the presidency of that institution. *The Charlotte Observer* for January 5, 1896, reported:

> Negotiations are pending with the trustees of Claremont College, and Mr. S.P. Hatton, of Hagerstown, Md., for the lease of that property for a term of years. Mr. Hatton is said to be an experienced and successful teacher.

Claremont College was located in the "noted health resort" of Hickory, North Carolina. The local newspaper, *The Hickory Press*, expanded on the discussions between Hatton and the administrators in its January 9, 1896, edition:

> S.P. Hatton ... has been in the city the past week negotiating with the trustees of Claremont College for a lease of that institution for a term of years. The manifold duties of Rev. J.L. Murphy, the present president of the college, have proven too onerous and he wishes to withdraw his attention from the institution. We are pleased to state that all arrangements have been concluded, and Professor Hatton will assume control of our famous female college at the beginning of its next term. Professor Hatton comes endorsed in the highest terms as an instructor and as a citizen and we welcome him to our town.

The same day's *Hickory Press* included this item regarding the town's newest citizen: "Prof. S.P. Hatton left for Hagerstown, Md., last Monday evening to resume his duties as professor in a college. He will be back here in the summer."

Even as Stewart returned to his wife and infant son, his hiring as the new president of Claremont College was apparently viewed as such a coup that it made news around North Carolina. Typical of the reports is the announcement in *The Charlotte Observer*:

> The lease of Claremont College to Prof. S.P. Hatton of Kee Mar College, Hagerstown, Md., has been concluded, and the contract entered upon. Prof. Hatton takes charge of the property July 1, 1896, for three years, with an option of extending the lease for five years more.

Newspapers in Raleigh, North Carolina, followed suit in reporting the news; *The North Carolinian* added: "Prof. Hatton has been very successful as an instructor and a manager of schools, and his coming will be a valuable accession to [Hickory]."

While Stewart finished his final semester at Kee Mar College, one of his siblings was also embarking on a change in his career that would ultimately have an impact on the life of Rondo Hatton. Stewart's younger brother, Linius Monroe Hatton (nicknamed Larry), had also left McGee College, relocating to Florida. In the spring of 1896, after Linius organized a business college in Ocala, he moved his family to Tampa. There he began an association with the Tampa Business College that eventually led to his assuming the presidency of that institution. The convergence of L.M. Hatton's relocation to Tampa with the lives of Stewart Hatton and his family was still years in the future.

In the meantime, Stewart embarked on the next phase of his career. According to the June 11, 1896, *Hickory Press*, he and Emily "arrived in the city last Friday, from Hagerstown, Md. Prof. Hatton has leased Claremont College, and will conduct a big school there in the future."

While the infant Rondo settled into his new surroundings in Hickory, his parents set out to put their stamp on Claremont Female College, and improve on that institution's modest success since its establishment in 1880. Besides assuming his duties as college president (including equipping the college with new furniture), Stewart taught a course in English and Anglo-Saxon Languages. At the same time, Emily handled the commercial branches of study for young ladies seeking higher education. Stewart also recruited his brother, Moses Wesley Hatton, a postgraduate of Harvard, to teach mathematics and astronomy.

By September 1897, local newspapers were reporting on the bright prospects of Stewart's new venture. According to the *Hickory Mercury*:

> President Hatton will have about 300 pupils this year and will begin at once to provide accommodations for more boarders.... Young ladies are here from Texas, Tennessee, South Carolina, Virginia and other southern states, besides a large number from all sections of this state. Claremont is an institution of which Hickory may well be proud.

Whatever high spirits that Stewart and Moses enjoyed with the initial weeks of their tenure at Claremont College broke down with the news that their mother, Sarilda Ann Bishop Hatton, 58, had died on November 2, 1897, at the family home in Columbia, Missouri. Mrs. Hatton was buried in nearby New Providence Cemetery.

After a brief period of mourning, Stewart and Moses returned to their Claremont teaching duties. A lighthearted column devoted to doings at the institution reported the following exchange:

> Prof. Hatton – in American Literature Class – "Can any girl in class tell me who is North Carolina's greatest writer?" Pretty girl – "Shakespeare."

This easygoing bit of gossip provides an opportune moment to look further into the type of people that Rondo Hatton's parents were. Since a child is often a reflection of his parents, such an inquiry seems reasonable.

A reporter with the *Newton Enterprise* spent some time with Rondo's parents early in their careers at Claremont, and came away favorably impressed: "We had the pleasure of meeting Prof. S.P. Hatton and wife recently and a great pleasure it was. They are pleasant and kind and full of enthusiasm for Claremont's future."

The Biblical Recorder, a Baptist newspaper published in Raleigh, emphasized another facet of Stewart Hatton's interests in reporting on baptisms in the Hickory area:

> Several of the girls in Claremont College were enabled to claim the Christian hope. The whole number of pupils seemed deeply interested in the meeting. Few colleges in the South have equaled this in steady and rapid growth during the past four years. The building is full to overflowing. In this number we find about fifteen Baptist girls. The president, S.P. Hatton, is an active member of our church here.

Again and again in the local newspapers, journalists emphasized the "favorable impression" that Stewart and Emma made upon all around them, while the Baptist newspaper focused on the "excellent work" that "brother" Stewart Hatton was accomplishing for Hickory's Baptist congregation. As we shall see hereafter, the friends, associates and fellow performers who came in contact with Rondo Hatton in later years consistently remarked on his (Rondo's) kindness, sensitivity and deep religious convictions. Clearly, Rondo came by these qualities honestly.

The North Carolina newspapers also featured reports of Stewart's travels throughout the region; these trips were consistently aimed at increasing the enrollment at Claremont College. While the numbers of Hatton's academic family were increasing, so were the numbers of his actual family. In April 1899, Emma gave birth to the couple's second child, Stewart Price Hatton Jr. Shortly afterward, Claremont College celebrated one of its most successful sessions, marked by commencement exercises spread over a five-day period from May 19 to May 23, 1899. As the *Hickory Times-Mercury* noted,

"On Tuesday, the last night, the chapel was again filled to overflowing. The order was good because President Hatton will have nothing else."

The first mention of Rondo Hatton in official records came in the 1900 federal decennial census: He is enumerated with his parents and younger brother as residents of the Hickory township.

Despite Stewart's achievements at Claremont, it is clear in hindsight that his ultimate goal was to found his own school. From late January through early February of 1900, items continually surfaced in newspapers around the region outlining his newest plans. A report from Charles Town, West Virginia, was typical:

> Prof. S.P. Hatton, president of Claremont College, at Hickory, N.C., has leased from the Charlestown [*sic*] company the large Powhatan Hotel property at this place for a term of 10 years and will conduct therein a college for girls and young ladies. The school will be known as Powhatan College and will open in September next.

Charles Town's local newspaper, *Spirit of Jefferson*, provided a great deal more detail in its January 30, 1900, edition:

> Transactions have lately been made which will mean much for Charles Town and community. It has for some time … been the desire on the part of many of our citizens to have at Charles Town a college of high grade for girls and young women. With this in view a stock company was formed and the magnificent property known as Hotel Powhatan was purchased. The stockholders at once placed the work of organizing a college in the hands of a Board of Trustees. … The first work of the Board was to secure a suitable man for the presidency and management of the institution. After considerable negotiations S.P. Hatton, President of Claremont College, Hickory, N.C., was invited here. After looking over the field he was much pleased with the outlook, accepted the presidency and began at once to make arrangements to open a school next September. President Hatton comes with the highest endorsements. … He bears the reputation of being among the very highest and most successful educators and proposes to build in Charles Town a college second to none in the Virginias.

The news of Prof. Hatton's decision eventually worked its way around to the locals in Hickory, who evidently found it hard to believe. A *Hickory Times-Mercury* writer devoted some space to the story in the March 14, 1900, edition, treating Hatton's possible departure with a good deal of skepticism:

> We see it going the rounds of the press that Prof. S.P. Hatton of Claremont College of this city, "is going to take charge of a Woman's College in West Virginia." We have not talked with the Professor on the subject but are of the opinion that there is a mistake about it – at least, he will not leave here. His school here is growing too popular for him to give it up and leave it. He has built it up till it is second to no female school in the State. His brother may take the school referred to in Virginia, under the advice and co-operative assistance of Prof. S.P.

Despite the doubts of the local press, Stewart Hatton did leave Claremont College to open the Powhatan College for Young Women in Charles Town in the spring of 1900. *Spirit of Jefferson* marked the event in its "Personal Mention" column for June 19, 1900: "Prof. S.P. Hatton, principal of the new Powhatan College, has arrived in town."

Stewart Hatton selected his brother, Wesley Moses Hatton, to succeed him as president of Claremont College.

So we now know that Stewart Hatton uprooted his young family twice in the space of a few years in order to further his professional ambitions. Perhaps this was not an altogether bad thing for his young son Rondo: He may have developed a sense of self that would have been more difficult to achieve had his early years been spent in one place.

Whatever the impact of these relocations may have been on Rondo Hatton, his parents fell quickly into the daily efforts involved in starting a new school. By October 1900, *Spirit of Jefferson* was reporting:

> Powhatan College, which has been established in the Hotel Powhatan Building, and began its first session recently, is conducted by Prof. S.P. Hatton, who is president and promoter. … It is his purpose to establish a high-grade female college, and he has employed first-class assistance. The college began under favorable circumstances and has students from five different states.

This focus on education leads to a question concerning Rondo Hatton: What was *his* early educational background? His enumeration in the 1900 federal census does not include an entry that he was "at school," which offers strong evidence that his parents had not enrolled him in an official school prior to the family's departure from North Carolina. That fact would argue that Rondo first entered school in Charles Town. The Hattons had lived in Charles Town almost a month when the city's school board met on the evening of July 9, 1900, to determine the opening date for the upcoming school year. *Spirit of Jefferson* reported the next day that "the schools were ordered to be opened Monday, September 10th." The article listed the nine schools located in the Charles Town area at that time. Of those schools, it is most likely that the young Rondo Hatton and his brother Stewart attended the Charles Town Graded School. By 1897, the school had added seventh and eighth grade, under the leadership of principal Wright Denny. According to an 1898 *Spirit of Jefferson* article, the Charles Town Graded School had "grown in usefulness and popularity each year of its short existence until it is now universally patronized by all alike, and ranks with the stable and progressive institutions of the State." That reputation could hardly have escaped the discerning eyes of teachers such as Stewart and Emily Hatton. Moreover, according to the March 1976 volume of *Jefferson County School News*, a great deal of the subject matter taught at the Charles Town Graded School was actually beyond the elementary level, allowing many of the school's pupils admission to college. Such a progressive approach to education would have been a plus to Rondo's parents. Nevertheless, the absence of available lists of pupils attending the Charles Town schools of the period ultimately makes the early schooling for Rondo Hatton a source of speculation. Given that both of his parents were teachers, it is entirely possible that Rondo and his brother Stewart were schooled at home. Wherever Rondo received his early education, subsequent events make it a safe bet that the youngster must have shown an exceptional aptitude for athletics as well as for writing.

The first few years of the twentieth century represented a great deal of success for Stewart Hatton's Powhatan College. Author W.O. Speer, writing in the 1907 volume *The History of Education in West Virginia*, described it as a "first-class college," meeting "one of the greatest needs of the age – more real colleges for women." According to Speer, the college was housed in a beautiful building that had been erected at a cost of about $70,000. The entire structure was "heated throughout by steam and lighted by both gas and electricity." In regional newspapers, advertisements emphasized the college's 15 schools, able faculty and its favorable location in the very mouth of the Shenandoah Valley. Yet for all of Powhatan's seeming success, there is evidence that Stewart Hatton was once again restless. According to the *Baltimore Sun* article "Hatton to Stay in Charles Town?" (August 25, 1904):

> The statement published from Frederick, Md., today to the effect that Prof. S.P. Hatton, president of Powhatan College, had accepted the presidency of Frederick City College, is denied by him.

Despite his denial, Stewart Hatton maintained ties with Frederick College: Based on contemporary reports, he delivered at least one address to its graduates at the close of the college year.

Perhaps Stewart's uneasiness had been increased by the July 6, 1904, death of his father, the Reverend William A. Hatton. The venerable minister passed away at the age of 68, undoubtedly proud that his sons had all entered into the teaching profession. He was buried in Boone County, Missouri.

How Stewart Hatton's restive nature may have affected his domestic life can never be known, but his wanderlust would assert itself more than once in the coming years.

Whatever doubts that Stewart Hatton may have entertained about his future (or the future of Powhatan College), he was a consistent speaker at educational conferences in West Virginia, usually touting Powhatan's special advantages. At other times, his topic was more general in scope. One speech that gained attention at a 1909 educational conference provides an insight into the man – and by extension, into the attitudes and philosophy that shaped Rondo Hatton. His topic was "The What and How in Teaching." A *Clarksburg Telegram* reporter provided details:

> The speaker opened his address by telling what is not teaching. He declared that telling or lecturing is not teaching. He said the mere hearing of a recitation is not teaching. He asserted that education and teaching are not synonymous terms – that one is broad and comprehensive and the other narrow and restricted.

> Dr. Hatton stated that the teacher must cause three things. First, he must cause the pupil to know his lesson, that is to understand it; he must cause the pupil to use skillfully the knowledge acquired; and third, he must cause the pupil to develop mental power in the acquisition of knowledge. He declared that the teacher is merely the guide.

Teachers today would be well-advised to adhere to the precepts advanced by Stewart Hatton more than a hundred years ago.

The 1910 federal census enumerated Stewart and his family in the Charles Town magisterial district for Jefferson County, West Virginia. Rondo is accurately listed as 16 years of age, occupation: "none." His 11-year-old brother Stewart is similarly described. Some census enumerators would have included the designation "at school" or "attending school," but the census taker for these entries entered "none" as the occupation for every school-age child listed, so that no conclusion regarding school attendance by either Rondo or his brother can be drawn.

A few months after this census enumeration, tragedy struck the Hatton family. The Washington D.C. *Evening Star* for August 6, 1911, reported the devastating news: "Stewart Price Hatton Jr., son of Prof. S.P. Hatton of Powhatan College, died Wednesday at Charles Town, W. Va., from the result of an operation for appendicitis, aged twelve years." The boy was buried in Edge Hill Cemetery in Charles Town.

Rondo's grief at his brother's death must have been tremendous, but he carried on. Within a few weeks, he enrolled as a freshman at the North Carolina College of Agriculture and Mechanical Arts (now North Carolina State University) in Raleigh. It is at this point in our narrative that Rondo begins appearing in existing records independently from his parents. The North Carolina A&M catalogue for 1911 lists "Rondo K. Hatton" among its roster of students. Rondo's course of study: civil engineering.

It is clear that, from the outset of Rondo's freshman year in college, he intended to make a name for himself. Indeed, it is not too fanciful to suggest that he set out to honor his dead brother by achieving goals that Stewart Jr. did not live to accomplish. Whatever Rondo's motivations may have been, he wasted little time in distinguishing himself. Early in his freshman year, he was elected to the position of class historian for the Class of 1915. The 1912 Yearbook for North Carolina A&M includes a Class History entry for the Class of 1915. Although its author is unidentified, it is virtually certain that Rondo was the writer, since his duties as class historian would include that task. If Rondo was in fact the author, the resulting account represents the first published example of Rondo Hatton's writing. Considering that he would later make his living as a writer for a number of years, this item takes on increased significance.

The 1912 Yearbook for North Carolina A&M provides more information about Rondo's plunge into college affairs. In addition to pursuing his duties as class historian, he joined the school chapter of the Sigma Nu Fraternity and became a member of the YMCA. He also landed a starting position as center fielder for the freshman baseball team.

Rondo Hatton was mentioned a number of times in Raleigh newspapers at the conclusion of his freshman year. Both the *Raleigh Times* and the *Raleigh News and Observer* took note of his position as one of seven marshals supervising the week of commencement ceremonies for the graduating seniors. Those same papers also included glowing reports of the annual dance of the Kappa Alpha and Sigma Nu fraternities, which brought a "brilliant close" to "the most successful commencement" in the college's history. Rondo is listed as one of the attendees, dancing with "Miss Emily Brown of Chocowinity."

The 1913 North Carolina A&M Yearbook makes it clear that Rondo was expected to rejoin the school as a member of the sophomore class. Yet a combination of forces worked to set him on a different path. Financial difficulties had beset his father's tenure at Powhatan, and Stewart was forced to relinquish his position as principal of the embattled institution before the start of the session. With no contingency plan in place, he was forced to turn to his brothers for employment. As noted earlier, Stewart's brother Linius had established himself in Tampa as a faculty member at the Tampa Business College prior to the turn of the century. By 1912, Linius had ascended to the presidency of the school. In the meantime, Bartlett Hatton, another brother, had joined Linius in Tampa. Together they started Hatton Bros., a firm devoted to real estate development and insurance sales located in the American Bank Building. The venture must have represented a godsend to Stewart. The September 16, 1912, *Tampa Times* reported:

> Prof. S.P. Hatton, president and proprietor of the Powhatan College, Charlestown, W. Va., for the past twelve years one of the leading female colleges of the state, arrived with his family last evening, coming direct from Washington D.C. Mr. Hatton has given up educational work and will devote his entire time to the real estate business in Florida. They will occupy their home at 1007 Grand Central Avenue.

The family's financial difficulties put an end to Rondo's attendance at North Carolina A&M. Surprisingly, Rondo enrolled as a junior at the local Hillsborough High School, where he was immediately accepted by his new classmates. They gave him the affectionate

In 1912-13, Rondo (see arrow) was third baseman for the Tampa Gas company's baseball team. Standing in front of him is his cousin John W. "Jay" Hatton, one of the team's outfielders.

nickname "Krum," and later wrote of him in the class yearbook:

> We admire the good judgment of "Krum" in coming to Hillsboro [sic], even if he didn't get here until the last year. The bunch took him in at first sight, for they saw he was of the right kind. He has recently decided to study a little for he has found out that grades are not given away here.

Even as Rondo settled into high school, there were signs that his father's foray into the real estate business was not wholly successful. By December 1912, Rondo's mother was seeking to supplement the family income, while also establishing ties with her brother-in-law's business college. Local newspapers began carrying the following advertisements:

ELOCUTION

MRS. E.L. HATTON, who has, for the past five years, had charge of the elocution department of Powhatan College, near Washington D.C., will give private lessons in elocution to a limited number. For particulars phone 476 or address Tampa Business College.

Meanwhile, Rondo's focus was on achieving distinction on the athletic field. In April 1913, he took part in an interclass track meet held by Hillsborough High School at the Tampa fairgrounds. He took third place in the first event, a 50-yard dash. In the feature event of the day, the 880-yard dash, he placed second. He won the high jump event outright, leading up to the finale. A *Tampa Times* writer reported:

> The pole vault, the best exhibition of this kind ever held in Tampa, and in which there seemed to be the keenest interest, was won by Rondo Hatton, who handled himself like a bird. He went seven feet, eight inches.

Within a month, Rondo was again making headlines – this time on the baseball diamond, as a member of the Tampa Gas Company team in the Cigar City Baseball League. In a May 11, 1913, article, "One More Scalp for Tampa," *The Tampa Tribune* tossed superlatives his way:

> Rondo Hatton hurled a masterful game of ball against the Knight & Wall bunch yesterday afternoon ... [T]he final score was nine to six.
>
> Only one earned run was chalked up against Hatton, poor support being responsible for the other five....
>
> Besides hurling "some game" himself, Rondo leaned against the pellet most opportunely and frequently. Five times did the "crum" [sic] saunter to the plate and four times did he smite it lustily.
>
> Twice did the bingle echo two sacks and Rondo obediently failed to haul in the main sheets until the midway station had been reached. He scored

Hatton and the other baseballers of Hillsborough High School, 1913 (notice the fancy Gothic-style H on their jerseys).

CAN THIS HUSKY BUNCH BEAT THE RED & WHITE JERSEYED HEROES FROM JACKSONVILLE THIS AFTERNOON IS NOW THE QUESTION OF THE HOUR

Top row, from left to right: Coach George Sparkman, Lester, L. M. Hatton, Zimmerman, James Sparkman (captain), Rondo Hatton, Rief, Freeman.
Second row: J. W. Hatton, McPherson, Culbreath, Clark, Holtsinger, Turner, Winn.
Bottom row: Wilsky, Crosy, Adams.

three tallies himself and towed three stranded Terriers into port.

Rondo was also starting to appear more frequently in public records. The Tampa City Directory for 1913 included a listing for Rondo as a student residing with his parents at 1007 Grand Central Avenue. According to the Directory, his uncles Linius and Bart lived nearby. Rondo's cousin Linius M. "Larry" Hatton Jr. was listed as a student residing at 1001 Grand Central Avenue. Larry and his brother John W. "Jay" Hatton also attended Hillsborough High School and clearly were extremely close to Rondo. Larry and Jay were comrades with Rondo in many of his most memorable athletic endeavors at Hillsborough High.

By late summer of 1913, local newspapers were predicting that Rondo would attend the University of Florida and add luster to that institution's accomplishments in athletics. Rondo was hardly content with his previous successes, however. His achievements on the football field in his senior year at Hillsborough are the stuff of legend for Tampans – a legend that Rondo's cousins, Larry and Jay, helped to create. Rondo was the quarterback, Jay an end and Larry a halfback for a Hillsborough team that justly won a place in the history of Florida sports. Representative of the exploits of the "Hatton boys" is an October 25, 1913, newspaper report recapping the highlights of Hillsborough's 32-0 trouncing of Bradentown High School. Excerpts regarding the contributions of the "Hatton boys" follow:

One spectacular forward pass after another … proved the downfall of the Bradentown eleven in their game with Hillsborough High at the Tampa Bay Athletic Field…. The Hatton trio, Rondo, J.W. and L.M. Jr., worked the forward pass for everything that was in it and the gains paved the way for or were responsible for every touchdown made by the Terriers….

When he got the ball, R. Hatton began the brilliant open play which netted the locals the game.

On a fake kick R. Hatton made 10 yards around his right end…. J. Hatton took a 10-yard pass and raced 15 yards for the first score…. Time was then called for the first quarter. Hillsborough 6, Bradentown 0.

In the second quarter, Rondo ran ten yards around right end for a touchdown. The score at halftime was 13-0.

Early in the third quarter, Rondo completed a pass to cousin Larry that netted 15 yards. A pass to Jay moved them 12 yards closer but Hillsborough turned the ball over. After Bradentown failed to move the ball, Hillsborough took over. Rondo threw a pass to Larry, who ran 60 yards for another touchdown.

Besides his duties as quarterback, Rondo was the place kicker and punter as well. The newspaper accounts describe at length his ability to keep his opponent hemmed in by punting more than 40 yards on several occasions. But Rondo had even more to give. With the score 25-0, he threw a long forward pass to Jay for 30 yards and another touchdown just as time was called: Hillsborough 32, Bradentown 0.

On Thanksgiving Day, November 27, 1913, the Hillsborough High Terriers played Jacksonville's Duval High School for the Florida High School football championship. That game was also played on the Tampa Bay Athletic Field before a crowd numbering near to 1000. The final score: Hillsborough 48, Duval 0. The *Tampa Tribune* reporter emphasized that Hatton, "seemingly bearing charmed protection, skirted Duval's ends almost at will." When Duval was forced to punt early in the game, Rondo again answered the call:

Dowling punted thirty yards and R. Hatton took the ball. Dodging and squirming he cleared the entire field and raced thirty-five yards for the first score of the game. The crowd went wild. R. Hatton also kicked the goal and eleven minutes after play had begun saw the Red and Black leading 7 to 0.

In the second quarter, Rondo added to his résumé impressively. After being penalized for offside, he

> called for a forward pass. He got the ball only to be able to find neither end open. The Duval forwards [*sic*] were dashing for him and he backed off until finally standing on his own forty-five yard line he heaved the oval to J. Hatton on his forty-five yard line. "J" stumbled across the goal for the second touchdown. It was one of the prettiest passes ever seen on the local field. The score was 14 to 0 and the wave of enthusiasm that swept the field gave vent to cheers which echoed for several minutes.

Rondo was hardly finished.

> On the next play, R. Hatton kicked to Vincent who started to return the ball. He was tackled and fumbled the ball. R. Hatton racing up the field stopped and picked up the ball on the dead run. He dodged and stiff-armed four would-be tackles and dragged one who reached him the remaining two yards to the goal before he fell. R. Hatton kicked the goal amid thunderous cheers.

The score was 21 to 0.

Larry and Jay Hatton also made significant contributions, but it was clearly Rondo's day. Besides continually completing passes on offense, he made his presence felt on the defensive side of the ball as well. With the score 42-0, Duval seemed to be threatening for its first score. Several pass plays had moved Duval to Hillsborough's 20-yard line. Duval's end, a player ironically named Maull, had caught a pass and dodged Hillsborough's primary defensive back, and for an instant it looked like a Duval score. But R. Hatton was still to be reckoned with. He dashed up the field from behind and

The arrow points to left guard Rondo, one of Hillsborough High's finest footballers in 1913.

dropped Maull with a beautiful tackle from behind.

The Hillsborough defense held firm and Duval turned the ball over on downs. Larry Hatton scored the last touchdown for Hillsborough on a thrilling 25-yard run. Rondo proved he was human by missing his final extra point try. By the time the whistle blew, Rondo had personally accounted for 24 of his team's 48 points.

> "R. Hatton kicked the goal amid thunderous cheers." – *The Tampa Tribune*

It was no surprise that Rondo, Larry and Jay were awarded football letters by the Hillsborough High School Athletic Association in December 1913. The accolades did not end there. The *Tampa Tribune* sports reporter was tasked with selecting a statewide high school All-Star football team by position. When he got to quarterback, the writer observed, "This is another stretch of comparatively easy riding. There are only two contestants, loud enough to be heard, for the position. McCarthy of Fort Meade and R. Hatton of Hillsborough."

After giving McCarthy some well-earned praise, the journalist turned to Rondo:

> Rondo Hatton, who is my choice for the position, has nearly every qualification that can be desired in a quarterback. Fast and agile, he is almost a perfect man in running through a broken field. He keeps his feet exceedingly well for a 136-pounder and is a past master of the stiff-arm. He runs forcefully yet apparently without much effort and hurls himself forward when tackled. He is an admirable man to run

back kicks.

Besides this he gives excellent interference and is a deadly tackler. He drives himself low and when he connects with a runner's ankles, that individual feels it. He hurls a forward pass with the best of them and can take one with ease and regularity. His passes are wide and his ability to control the pigskin had much to do with Hillsborough's success in this line.

As a general he is always cool and calculating and while his judgment is not as good as that of McCarthy, the difference is too slight not to be offset by the many advantages he has. He keeps a level head and that is worth a lot.

It is his right toe which gives him a large part of his prominence. In the Duval game his two punts averaged 37 yards, and it was the poorest day's kicking which he did during the year. As a drop kicker he has no equal in his class and his performance of booting six out of seven placements after touchdowns in the Duval games speaks for his ability and value in this line.

Taking all in all he is the most versatile man on the eleven. The one man on whose shoulders the greatest part of the work, aside from the duties as a general, would devolve.

The reader may question the space devoted to Hatton's athletic accomplishments to this point. The reasons are simple. First, it is important to emphasize just what a stellar athlete he was, and how those abilities defined his school years. More significantly, the qualities that an individual displays in the arena of sports are often the same characteristics that he displays in daily life. The cool, calculating judgment and leadership which were noted features of Rondo's on-field performances likely served him well off the field.

The December 16, 1913, *Tampa Tribune* devoted some space to Hillsborough High's forthcoming baseball season. Rondo's cousin Larry was chosen as captain; Larry was described as a versatile player popular with his teammates and sure to make a good leader. The article went on to praise the squad (which had won the previous Florida championship), while reserving particular plaudits for Rondo – not only as an exceptional pitcher, but as a third baseman. Predicting that Rondo would be a star, the writer added, "Hatton is particularly being considered by many to be the best third sacker in the league."

Once the Tampa City League baseball season was underway in late May 1914, that assessment was confirmed. In appraising its chances for success in City League play, the team's manager commented that Rondo rounded out the infield to a perfect "T." Reviewing Rondo's year with Hillsborough, he added,

> Before the Terrier season was over, [Hatton] was recognized as the best high school third sacker in the state. He is absolutely fearless and comes in on the hardest hit balls. He is a sure judge of a bound and gets the ball away from him quickly, and his peg is remarkably accurate. He is speedy and handles bunts well and tags a run-

RONDO HATTON

"Yon Cassius hath a lean and hungry look; Such men are dangerous."

Football (4); Baseball (4); Athletic Association (4).

We admire the good judgment of "Krum" in coming to Hillsboro, even if he didn't get here until the last year. The bunch took him in at first sight, for they saw he was of the right kind. He has recently decided to study a little for he has found out that "grades are not given away here."

From Rondo's 1913 yearbook.

ner in faultless style. He batted 270 last year.

After graduating from high school,[1] Rondo continued to play in various city baseball leagues around the state through the summer of 1914. While he was on one of the teams outside of Tampa, a *Tampa Tribune* sportswriter intimated that there was more than baseball on Rondo's mind.

> Rondo Hatton, ex–Tampan, is with the invaders. Looks like every team in this neck of the woods has to nip some Tampa talent. Rondo brought in two suitcases with him yesterday and though we don't know what he had to put in them, one of the wise boys on the club tipped us off that Rondo has been a regular burner on for the mailman wherever he has been. "They couldn't have been letters from home not twice a day, anyhow," murmured the informer.

The spring of 1914 represented another turning point of sorts for Rondo. In April, he was given a tryout at third base in the Georgia-Alabama D Baseball league. When that opportunity failed to yield a commitment, he returned to Tampa and went to work as a salesman for Knight & Wall Company, a prominent hardware-department store located on East Lafayette Street. At the same time, he joined the Tampa baseball team in one of the local leagues. The conjunction of events was the subject of a May 26 *Tampa Tribune* item:

> Rondo Hatton, the crack third sacker who has been signed up by the Tampa team, is possibly the only player in the Cigar City league who is not going to get any money for his performance on that corner. Rondo is working for Knight & Wall Company, and will play ball just when he can get off. He is one of the best little players that has ever been turned out of the Hillsborough High School, and will be a strong factor on the field of the Tampa team.

By mid-summer, Rondo had to change his plans again. The Tampa team disbanded, and Hatton caught on with another team in Loughman. According to a July 14, 1914, *Tampa Tribune* article, Hatton "has made good with the Loughman outfit and is now considered a regular at the midway sack, where he is making monkeys of them all in the sticks."

Presumably, Rondo's stint with the Loughman baseball team required his resignation from Knight & Wall. Even if he was able to shuttle between Loughman and Tampa sufficiently to retain his job through the summer, his next move would have still called for him to resign: In the fall of 1914, he enrolled as a sophomore at Davis and Elkins College in Elkins, West Virginia.

Very little is known about Hatton's stay at the private college beyond his exploits on the football field. Years ago, at the request of a *Tampa Tribune* reporter, Davis and Elkins' director of alumni relations verified that Hatton attended as a sophomore and junior. Yet no news items from the period address any of his activities during his sophomore year.

The fall of 1915 was quite a different matter. According to a *Tampa Tribune* sportswriter, Rondo "went away from [Tampa] and starred on a West Virginia team." In what was apparently an up-and-down season for the Davis and Elkins football team, Rondo was outstanding as the starting quarterback. Even in defeat, he could be counted on to score a touchdown to keep the outcome of a game in doubt until the final seconds. On defense, he often intercepted a pass to keep an opponent out of the end zone. By the end of the season, Rondo's teammates held him in such high regard that they expressed that appreciation directly. When the Davis and Elkins team held its annual banquet at the college dining hall on December 4, 1915, not only did Hatton letter in football, he was elected captain of the 1916 football team.

Hatton returned to Tampa for the Christmas holidays, a homecoming that was noted in several local newspapers. Before he left West Virginia, he made a decision that would have a profound effect on the course his life would take thereafter: On January 11, 1916, he enlisted in the Florida National Guard.

Rondo's spring semester at Davis and Elkins was apparently uneventful. He returned to Tampa after the end of his junior year and joined the West Tampa baseball team in one of the City Leagues. There he was reunited with his cousins Larry and Jay, who were also starters for West Tampa. By June, however, the three "Hatton boys" were reuniting on a different team altogether. Responding to a duty call, the young men were called up to join Company H of the Tampa National Guards, known as the Tampa Rifles. Within days, the recruits were subject to new orders. On June 20, 1916, *The Tampa Tribune* reported:

> Company G and H of the National Guard of Florida, the Hillsborough Guards and the Tampa Rifles, were ordered to the colors yesterday morning at 9 o'clock and by a few minutes after 2 o'clock in the afternoon every available member of the two organizations had assembled at the City Hall, ready to leave for the State camp,

where the second Infantry of the Florida National Guard will mobilize for service on the Mexican border. They will leave tonight at 9 o'clock.

These orders were hardly surprising, and were a direct result of attacks launched at the southwestern United States by the paramilitary forces of Mexican revolutionary Pancho Villa. By June 1916, raids by Villa's forces on American soldiers numbered over three dozen, leading to the deaths of 26 U.S. soldiers and 11 civilians.

There were additional casualties during a June 15, 1916, raid near Laredo, Texas. That led to President Woodrow Wilson taking advantage of the recently enacted National Defense Act, which had created the U.S. National Guard. Under that legislation, Wilson mobilized Guard units from across the country for border duty on June 18, 1916.

As a result, Rondo and his cousins traveled by train with their company to the training facilities at Black Point, Florida, for basic drills, with an anticipated arrival in El Paso, Texas, by August 1, 1916. Regular reports from the Black Point training camp kept families of the soldiers informed of camp activities. Within the first month, Rondo received a leave of absence that made the newspaper back in Tampa:

> Corporals Robert M. Hicks and L.M. Hatton arrived yesterday for a three days' furlough, with Private Rondo Hatton. They are highly pleased with their service at Black Point, and the effect of their strenuous outdoor life has left them browned and healthy-looking.

Of course, whatever patriotic fervor was generated in the locals was leavened by their concerns as football fans. The following item is not only amusing, but also documents Rondo Hatton's tentative plans for the fall of 1916:

> One of the questions that is bothering a bunch of sport lovers throughout the country is how long Uncle Sam is going to keep our militia-footballers in State camps. The University of Florida eleven will be hit rather hard if the Second Regiment is kept in camp with a quartet of Tampa boys who are being counted on at Gainesville to form the nucleus for a Southern Championship eleven. Sim and James Spark-

TAMPA LADS AS "KITCHEN MECHANICS"
Left to right: Gettis Henderson, Rondo Hatton, Hale Hampton

man are both with the Rifles as is Bushnell, a sub last year, Rondo Hatton, who was figuring on attending the 'Gator stronghold and whose ability was figured on to make him a regular, and one or two Hillsborough cracks who were figured in on the "pudding" this fall.

The anticipated move by the Florida National Guard to the Mexican border by August 1 failed to occur. By late August, the commanding officers at Black Point were issuing official apologies to the citizens of Florida that their troops had not yet been deployed. Politicians were blamed for the delay.

This long wait did allow for the Tampa papers to feature a special column, "What's Doing at State Camp," that kept readers current on the events and gossip at Black Point. Rondo was mentioned regularly in this column; one item refers to a romantic relationship: "Private Rondo Hatton's Queen of Hearts takes him joyriding every Sunday afternoon. Why did Rondo want a twelve-hour pass?" One column included a photograph of Hatton with two other Tampa guardsmen. The 22-year-old Rondo's lean good looks are striking.

Eventually, the Tampa Rifles were transported to Laredo, Texas, as guards for border crossing points. Their patrols occasionally encountered smugglers and refugees. One such nighttime meeting was described by reporter John W. Biggar in the November 9, 1916,

Hatton (top left) and the other sergeants of Company H at Camp Wheeler in Macon, Georgia.

Tampa Tribune:

> The Tampa Rifles are having their full share of excitement right now. The section we have been instructed to guard contains two fords across the Rio Grande, and these seem to be favorite crossing places for smugglers....

An outpost squad at the ford nearer the encampment spotted, about 500 yards from their position, a group of men crossing the river. A sentry was sent back to camp to report the incident. One of the smugglers noticed the patrol and opened fire. Shots were traded as the smugglers, who were in midstream, returned to the Mexican side of the river. At that moment,

> Captain Lowry arrived with a visiting patrol consisting of Sergeant Bushnell, Corporal J.W. Hatton, Private Rondo Hatton and Private Roger Drew. When they learned the circumstances, the patrol proceeded over the river to the point across from where the smugglers lay in hiding. Here they located several sacks of garlic, upon which a duty tax of two cents per pound is charged.

What little can be determined about Hatton for the next few months must be gleaned from his military records. He apparently responded well to continued training; on December 6, 1916, he was promoted to the rank of corporal of Company H. The leadership qualities that Rondo had exhibited in his athletic activities were being recognized by his commanding officers.

The war in Europe had dragged on for more than two years, deteriorating into prolonged trench warfare. Accompanying the stalemate was the development of what the German forces saw as a quicker route to victory, and one which would later mean a great deal to Rondo Hatton: poison gas.

By the spring of 1917, troop shortages for British and French forces led to an urgent call for aid from the United States, and America responded by declaring war on Germany in April 1917. The officers and troops of the National Guard were inducted into federal service. Rondo's unit became Company H of the 124th Infantry.

Rondo was viewed as having superior leadership potential; he was among the Floridians sent to the officers training camp at Camp Wheeler in Macon, Georgia. On August 18, 1917, the Tampa newspapers noted that Capt. Lowry of Company H, Second Infantry, announced the promotion of Corp. Rondo Hatton to sergeant.

While Rondo continued his advancement within the army, changes with his family in Tampa were also underway. Rondo's father had never given more than half-hearted efforts to the Hatton Bros. real estate and fire insurance business. It was clear that Stewart's heart was in education. At about the same time that Rondo was called up to National Guard duty in June 1916, *The Star Press* of Muncie, Indiana, announced that Dr. Stewart P. Hatton "of West Virginia" had been added to the faculty of the Muncie National Institute. According to the June 4, 1916, article, Dr. Hatton was "on the ground organizing the department of education for the new term's work." By September 13, 1917, the *Waterloo* (Indiana) *Press* was announcing that Dr. Hatton had been "elected president of the Marion Normal Institute." Yet despite what seemed a solid future with this Indiana institution, Stewart soon returned to Tampa seeking other opportunities. What is clear is that Dr. Hatton was away from his home on Central Avenue for extended periods, leaving his wife Emily increasingly to her own devices. His absence is implicit in a March 6, 1918, *Tampa Tribune* update on Rondo's military training:

Rondo Hatton, former Terrier football and baseball star, is in the city on a short visit to his mother.... Rondo is now a first sergeant and was recently detailed for a special course in bayonet training and bomb-throwing, which he has completed. If the former Terrier shows the same accuracy and skill in throwing bombs at the Kaiser's forces that he displayed while cavorting around the third cushion for teams in the Cigar City baseball league, the Huns will have a bad day when he begins hurling these powerful balls of explosives into the enemy trenches.

Rondo returned to Camp Wheeler in Georgia and continued his advancement in rank. At a special ceremony on August 28, 1918, he was among 43 Florida soldiers who received commissions as second lieutenants in the infantry.

The late summer of 1918 represented a turning point in the Great War: The French and British allies were now certain of American help. At that point, hundreds of thousands of Americans were being sent to the front every month. Rondo's call-up was inevitable.

According to available records, Rondo Hatton traveled to New York and from there embarked for England on the ship *Olympic* on October 17, 1918. He is listed in transport records as a second lieutenant, Company H, 124th Infantry, Thirty-first Division. Hatton was among a number of officers who departed Southampton, England, for France on October 25. He sailed on the ship *Charles*.

Rondo was joining the conflict at a point when German forces were falling back in the face of Allied forces bolstered by the increasing American presence. Yet while the Germans retreated, the intensity of the fighting increased – and Hatton suffered a devastating personal loss.

Rondo's cousin Jay had joined the war months earlier as a first lieutenant with Company C, 328th Infantry. During August, Jay had received a flesh wound in heavy action in France. Despite his injury, he insisted that he had recovered sufficiently to return to the conflict. After being wounded a second time on October 5, Jay was killed in the battle north of the Argonne forest on October 19, 1918, while Rondo was en route to the fighting. A fellow Tampan and mutual friend, Lt. John W. Hampton, penned a letter to his (Hampton's) sister that appeared in *The Tampa Tribune*:

> Night before last I went out on another sad mission. I found the body of one of my very good Tampa friends on the field after a long search.... This hero's name is J.W. Hatton, whose father owns the Tampa Business College. He was one of my best friends and in the same regiment, and although very young, he was considered one of the best officers in the entire brigade, and was also a fearless soldier....

Lt. Hampton continued by describing the circumstances of Jay's death:

> One of the many boche machine guns was holding up the advance of his men, so I was told by one of them who was fighting by his side at that time. J.W. raised up a bit to get a line for better shots at the boche gunner and a machine gun bullet found his stomach.

John W. "Jay" Hatton was 21 years old. Lt. Hampton was among the party who took his body back behind the lines and buried it in a churchyard. Hampton himself first wrapped the body in an American flag.

Whether Rondo learned of his cousin's death once he (Rondo) was "on the ground" in France is unknown. What we can now say with certainty is that Rondo was involved in the bloodiest, most extensive operation for the American Expeditionary Forces during World War I: the Meuse-Argonne offensive.

Piecing together any details regarding Hatton's World War I military service takes into account a variety of sources. Although his military service records are somewhat general, we do know that he was a member of the 31st Infantry Division, composed of National Guardsmen from Alabama, Georgia and Florida. That division began deployment in France in late September 1918, mere weeks before the November 11, 1918, armistice that ended the hostilities. As we have seen, Rondo was in the last wave of soldiers from that division arriving in Europe in late October. Yet it may be that last two and a half weeks of the war that changed his life forever.

Hatton and his fellow officers arrived at Southampton and spent a brief period in rest camps before moving to France through Cherbourg and Le Havre. The division was then largely skeletonized and the men used as replacement troops, a move prompted by heavy casualties suffered in the Meuse-Argonne fighting. By the time of Hatton's arrival at the front, U.S. troops had advanced ten miles and cleared the Argonne forest. At that point, American forces reorganized into two armies. The First Army continued to move toward the Meuse River and the village of Sedan in northeast France, while the Second Army moved eastward toward the town of Metz. In an article written years after the conflict, Hatton confirmed that he was among the forces near Sedan when the news of the armistice arrived, so we know that he was in service with the First Army in those last weeks of the war. By November 6, French forces had captured Sedan and its crucial railroad, while the American forces captured the surrounding hills.

With that basic matrix of time and place settled, what else can be inferred or deduced about Hatton's World War I service? The question is no idle one aimed at merely fleshing out biographical details of his life. Profound consequences hang on whatever particulars about the Meuse-Argonne Offensive can be confirmed. The reason will be obvious to longtime fans of Rondo Hatton and his films. For more than 80 years, writers have stated as fact that Rondo Hatton developed the pituitary disorder acromegaly from exposure to mustard gas during World War I. That notion demands examination from several directions before it can be considered conclusive. The first question concerns the probability that Hatton was exposed to mustard gas in the short time he was part of the offensive.

This question is easily answered in the affirmative. Newspaper reports in early November 1918 confirm that by November 3, the American forces were in Belval wood, six miles directly west of a vital point in the German line along the Meuse River and 14 miles south of Sedan – the center of the whole German railroad system in Eastern France. German resistance against American pressure was furious; the Germans were employing artillery against American machine guns. The Germans were also using another weapon on the "Sedan front," as reported in the *Orlando Evening Star* for November 6, 1918:

> Gas barrages for some time have been one of the principal factors in German warfare. Their mustard gas, with its horrible aftereffects, is one of the worst atrocities of the war. Even now, in their retreat, the Germans are using a non-exploding, perforated gas shell which they fire into marshlands and which makes the entire district into which they are thrown a "section of death" for days afterward.

An article in *The Maine News* provides additional confirmation of the repeated use of mustard gas in the area of Hatton's service:

> Whenever the Allied troops come into contact with the enemy, they report bitter fighting on the part of the Germans who are stubbornly holding back the line from Sedan. The woods which they have evacuated are left filled with mustard gas so that they cannot be occupied for days after by the Allied troops.

The location for Rondo Hatton's World War I service made exposure to mustard gas a virtual certainty. Availability of gas masks was a problem for the American forces, increasing the possibility of inadequate protection from gas attacks. Ointments and special protective suits were only sporadically effective. Since hot, soapy water could lessen or even eliminate the effects of mustard gas, "mobile degassing units" were deployed for each division in the line of battle. In effect, these units (carried on tank trucks) provided portable shower baths for soldiers exposed to mustard gas.

These protective measures make it possible that Hatton's exposure to mustard gas was minimized, although such a conclusion is far from certain. What is much more of a certainty is the range of effects produced by exposure to mustard gas. Reports in newspapers at that time are consistent with later descriptions:

> Mustard gas is a powerful producer of tears. After several hours the eyes begin to swell and blister, causing intense pain. The nose discharges freely, and severe coughing and vomiting ensue.
>
> Direct contact with the spray causes blistering of the skin, and the vapor penetrates through the clothing. Gas masks, of course, do not protect against this. The symptoms are similar to pneumonia – high fever, heavy breathing and often stupor.

These symptoms certainly sound unpleasant, but this dry recitation does little to convey the shocking nature of the consequences of mustard gas exposure in World War I. The following excerpt from a letter written by an American officer to his family appeared in a Pennsylvania newspaper from 1918, and it provides much more of an exact description, however grisly:

> In a little field hospital west of Montdidier I stopped at the bedside of an American boy, one of those victims of the German mustard gas, with which the Huns are making all of their present gains. His eyes were matted with yellow pus and he could not see. His face was terribly burned. His lips were swollen and purple. His whole body had been turned the color of an Indian, and portions of it looked like melted flesh as though it had been liquefied.
>
> The fighting had been renewed all along the American lines, and German wounded had begun coming into our hospitals. I said to this soldier:

"The boys are getting their revenge for you fellows tonight."

He smiled through his seared lips, and in a voice so faint that I had to bend down to listen, he gasped, "God! I wish I was back there with 'em."

As horrific as the above description is, it represents the typical account of the symptoms resulting from extreme exposure to mustard gas, all the way from World War I to contemporary times. What is missing in all these accounts is one shred of evidence that mustard gas could cause the disease that afflicted Rondo Hatton: acromegaly.

To fully appreciate just how improbable it is that a mustard gas attack caused Hatton to develop acromegaly, we must first examine both the symptoms and the causes of this chronic affliction. For that investigation, we need not turn to contemporary sources. Acromegaly was being discussed in print as early as the late nineteenth century, when it was the "disease of homeliness." An article from a newspaper in the 1920s detailed the effects of the condition to an anonymous reader who had been diagnosed with acromegaly:

> This is not strictly a disease, but a series of symptoms which are the expression of a definite disease. It is distinguished by enlargement of the hands and feet, the bones of the nose, cheek and lower jaw.
>
> There is also outward curvature of the upper portion of the spine, causing hump back and changing the dimensions of the back and chest.
>
> It is more common in women than in men and begins between 18 and 25, and may last four or five years, or as many as 30. It ends in fatal exhaustion unless cut short by acute disease or by accident within the brain.
>
> First, the ends of the fingers and toes are thickened, and then the entire hand and foot are enlarged, the enlargement consisting in increase of the connective tissue which binds the muscles together. Though the hands are large and clumsy, the forearms are unchanged.
>
> The toes become enormous and the legs are enlarged to the knees, the feet like the paws of an animal. The face is elongated, the lower jaw projects, the forehead is narrow and receding, though the brows are enlarged.
>
> The eyes are small but protruding and expressing, and one or both may squint.
>
> The nose is flat and broad, lips and tongue enormous, ears protuberant, and face repulsive. The skin of the face is brownish yellow and may have warts upon it, the hair is coarse and stiff, the voice is deep and metallic. In some cases the knee, wrist and elbow joints are enlarged and crackle painfully when moved.
>
> The heart is enlarged, its action irregular, and there are various enlarged veins in different parts of the body.
>
> As the condition develops, the patient becomes sensitive to cold and complains of neuralgia or rheumatism.
>
> Acromegaly is due to an enlargement or tumor of a structure on the undersurface of the brain called the hypophysis or pituitary gland....
>
> Its secretion is similar to that of the thyroid gland, it is supposed to be useful only during fetal life, and if it continues after that period it causes acromegaly.
>
> The enlarged gland may reach the size of a cherry or a small orange and causes headache by pressure upon the brain.
>
> It may also cause facial neuralgia, dizziness, vomiting, also changes in the mental condition and in taste, hearing and sight.

Other articles mentioned additional symptoms: wider spacing between teeth, high blood pressure and lung disease. These newspaper items again identified the most common cause of acromegaly as a benign tumor of the pituitary gland which, in some rare cases, resulted from an inherited gene mutation. The items also emphasized that acromegaly progresses very gradually, making it easy to miss the early, subtle symptoms marking its onset.

The parallels between the thorough listing of symptoms and what we know of Rondo Hatton through his films and previous biographical material is uncanny. It is equally clear from the enumeration of symptoms that there is virtually no correspondence between the causes and effects of acromegaly and the effects of mustard gas exposure.

Nonetheless, the story persists that Hatton contracted acromegaly as a direct result of exposure to mustard gas. Perhaps this yarn originated with Hatton himself, who may have sincerely believed it. Let's examine some facts. We have seen that the onset of acromegaly normally occurs in an individual between the ages of 18 and 25. Rondo had turned 24 months before he was sent to France as a member of the American Expeditionary Forces. Initial symptoms of acromegaly are apparently so obscure that they are easily missed. Fred Olen Ray reported in his Hatton biography that Rondo was hospitalized "for an indefinite period" after the November Armistice "with damaged lungs," and that "military doctors suspected that the acromegaly directly resulted from the poisonous gas." That information may have derived from Ray's interview with Tom Kaney, a friend of Hatton's from whom we shall learn more hereafter. Yet on logical grounds, that supposition is difficult to support. Statistics set the number of American casualties in World War I at over 26,000 men. According to articles at the time, fully one-third of those casualties were the result of mustard gas exposure. That would yield a figure of almost 9000 American casualties caused by mustard gas. One would certainly expect a reported sharp increase in acromegaly among returning World War I veterans – yet no report of a spike in such cases appears to exist.

A more plausible explanation is that Hatton was already in the initial stages of acromegaly by the time he was sent to France, and the progress of the disease moved from subtle symptoms to more noticeable characteristics around the same time as his exposure to mustard gas near Sedan. Military doctors found a cause-and-effect relationship between the two events in juxtaposition that simply did not exist.

Still, there are difficulties with that premise as well. While Fred Olen Ray reported that Hatton was hospitalized with "lung damage for an indefinite period" (presumably running beyond the November 11, 1918, Armistice), Hatton's World War I Service Card includes a notation that he was "0 per cent disabled on date of discharge, in view of occupation." Perhaps this means nothing more than that Hatton had achieved maximum cure in the eyes of the military medical authority by the time of his discharge. Even so, the anomaly is troubling, particularly since Ray stated in his Hatton article that Hatton "received a medical discharge and a monthly disability allowance of $106.26."

Nor can we infer anything concrete about Hatton's condition based on the length of time he remained in Europe after the end of the war. While that information might suggest a protracted convalescence in a military hospital, the fact is that America was ill-equipped to bring the doughboys home, so that most Americans did not depart from Europe until 1919. The Expeditionary Forces were moved to France by degrees for transport home. Hatton departed Brest, France, on the ship *Koningin Der Nederlanden* on June 26, 1919, bound for Camp Hill, Newport News, Virginia, as one of the "Brest Casual Officers Company No. 896."

Hatton was honorably discharged from the Army on July 9, 1919; according to his Service Card, his services were "no longer required." He returned home to 1007 Grand Central Avenue and his family.

Rondo came home a changed man, but he was not alone. Many returning soldiers found civilian life difficult. There was a sudden rise in violence and drunkenness in the cities in 1919, as veterans tried in vain to wipe out ghastly memories. Yet Hatton suffered as much, or more, than most, since the more obvious effects of his acromegalic condition must have begun asserting themselves. Years later, he commented,

> Facing the people you know, seeing the shock and pity and horror ... that's tougher than anything that ever happened at the front. To any casualty, the hardest part of war is coming home.

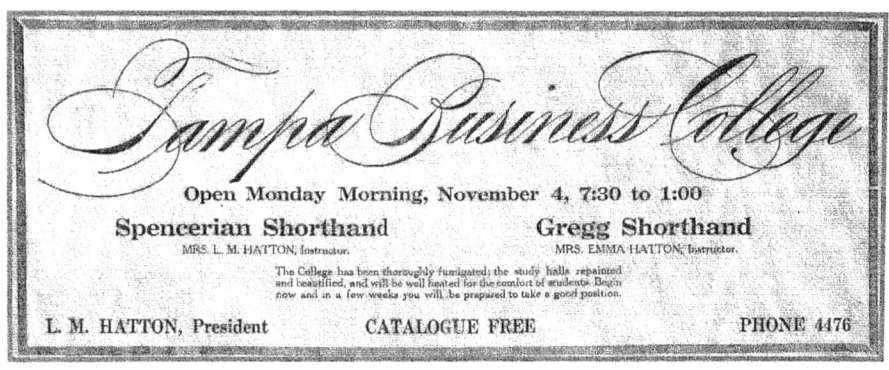

Rondo's family had also undergone changes during his overseas service. His mother Emily had taken a teaching position with the nearby Tampa Business College run by her brother-in-law Larry Hatton (see a 1918 ad above). Rondo's father Stewart had moved to Atlanta, Georgia, to go into partnership with educator Thomas Lenoir Bryan to establish the Bryan-Hatton Business College. Atlanta city directories from the period show that Stewart established a residence in Atlanta.

Whether this apparent upheaval in his home life caused Rondo further agitation is unknown, although the changes could hardly have been an emotional benefit. Nevertheless, Rondo persisted in moving forward.

One of what must have been several prospective courses of action was reported in the September 14, 1919, *Tampa Tribune*:

> Rondo Hatton, star quarterback on the Terrier eleven of 1913, will take charge of the candidates of Hillsborough High School this week when they take the field for their first practice. There has been some criticism of the late start the Terriers are getting, as it is thought that in spite of the hot weather they could have profitably spent a week or two in getting limbered up, in passing and falling on the ball, and in improving their wind.

Maybe the late start for the Hillsborough Terriers football team was due to negotiations with Hatton dragging through summer, while Rondo hoped for other situations. At any rate, a September 23, 1919, *Tampa Tribune* item was a bit more enthusiastic:

> One of the most welcome bits of news we read while mingling with the denizens of the deep and Sir Neptune himself was the selection of Rondo Hatton as coach for the Terrier eleven. Hatton played quarterback on the greatest eleven old Hillsborough ever had and his great quarterbacking was one of the things that contributed to its greatness. He went away from here and starred on a West Virginia college team and what he don't know about football mighty few high school coaches can teach him. Of course Rondo may not be a coach – that is he may know it and not know how to teach it – but it's a slim possibility. The ole boy has got lots of pep, he put it into the [1913] Terriers and he ought to be able to put it into the [1919] outfit, and if he doesn't do a bit more, he represents a wonderful improvement and certainly Principal Robinson is to be commended on his choice.

Previous biographers have stated that Hatton, after the onset of acromegaly symptoms, was unable to achieve his goal of becoming a high school football coach in Tampa because his "pain-racked body couldn't stand exertion." That may have been true at some later point — although Hatton continued to be involved in competitive athletics in Tampa well into the 1920s. But he gave up the Hillsborough High School football coaching position in September 1919 because it was only one of several options, or "irons in the fire," that he was pursuing.

What appears to have been his major focus bore fruit late in September 1919. Hatton, at the age of 25, wanted one last hurrah on the college gridiron, and the University of Florida gave him the chance. In anticipation of the decision, *The Tampa Tribune* carried a short announcement of a change in plans:

> THOSE TERRIERS ARE PLUGGING along getting ready for the Oscar Daniels outfit in the football curtain raiser Saturday afternoon and are looking better each day. Rondo Hatton, former Terrier, who has been coaching them, left yesterday for the state university, but Professor Robinson expects to have a successor on the job right away.

That tentative notification was followed almost immediately by a formal declaration in the *Tribune*:

> 'Gator hopes are boosted a bit with the announcement that Rondo Hatton, Hillsborough quarter in 1914 [*sic*], all–Florida quarter that year, and perhaps the greatest scholastic quarter the state has turned out, has cast his lot with the Blue and Gold. Rondo is a general who can nurse a team along and get it primed for a scoring drive that will count if possible – and in addition the boy is one of the best runners in the state, has a toe good for fifty to sixty yards regularly, and one of the best forward passing arms we have seen anywhere. And he weighs about 170, pretty much all where it ought to be.

Rondo apparently had little difficulty with "late enrollment" at the University of Florida, quickly settling into a routine that represented his main reason for heading to Gainesville. On the eve of the opening football game between the University of Florida and Georgia A&M (Saturday, October 4, 1919), *The Tampa Tribune* revealed that

> Rondo Hatton, ex–Terrier player, reported in a Florida uniform this afternoon. He ran the team through a few paces and after an intensive study of the plays and formations tonight it is possible that he will see action in Saturday's game.

Hatton was projected as a back-up to starting quarterback Bryan Anderson in the season opener. Apparently, Rondo's initial performance as a Florida 'Gator in a 33-2 defeat of Georgia A&M was impressive enough that pundits were expecting a change in the "rotation" at quarterback for the next contest – an October 18 meeting with Mercer College. An October 9, 1919, *Tampa Tribune* article, "'Gators Back at It Once Again – First

RONDO HATTON (Crum) (Left Guard)

Hillsboro's dependence as a punter—and Hillsboro never had cause to regret this dependence. He played a strong game in his position and tackled well. He was late in starting the season as he was a newcomer, but his work on the squad was such that he soon attracted the attention of the coach and Captain Asp. On the defensive he was strongest, securing the jump on his opponent nearly always.

From Hatton's 1913 Hillsborough High School yearbook.

Scrimmage Since Aggie Game Finds Hatton Looking Good at Helm," heaped especial praise on Rondo:

> A light scrimmage today lasting about thirty or forty-five minutes was the first rough workout that the 'Gators have had since the game with Georgia A&M Saturday....
>
> Rondo Hatton is certainly rounding into perfect shape in record time. The few minutes that he played in the game Saturday was sufficient time to demonstrate that he is a pigskin chaser of merit. There is little doubt on the campus but that he will receive the first call in the next game in which the 'Gators participate. Bryan Anderson, who started the game at quarter Saturday afternoon will probably be held in readiness on the squad, but Hatton has it on him in weight, and as weight coupled with a personal ability to cover the ground hides a multitude of sins on the football gridiron he should be the choice....

Despite this prediction, Anderson started at quarterback for Florida in a rain-soaked 48-0 defeat of Mercer.

In hindsight, it appears that these first two games were mere preamble to an October 25 showdown between the 'Gators and the University of Georgia, a game scheduled to be played at Plant Field in Tampa, Rondo's "hometown." That fact could hardly have been lost on members of the Florida coaching staff, who seem to have been bringing Rondo along in preparation for this particular game. The contest was viewed by the University administration as so significant that a special train was commissioned to take the student body from Gainesville to Tampa as a unit. As the "big game of the season" approached, *Tampa Tribune* sportswriters placed extra emphasis on Hatton's value to the 'Gator team:

> The addition of Rondo Hatton, quarter of the famous Hillsborough eleven in 1913, when Duval was smothered 48 to 0, has added new pep to the squad, which has been sadly missing an "old head" as helmsman. Hatton is one of the greatest broken field runners and punters seen in action in this state and when he went to Davis & Elkins after leaving Hillsborough, he kept up his reputation there....

This article is notable for two reasons. It went on to suggest that this particular 'Gator team would be the "heaviest" as a group to play the Georgia team since the two schools began their football rivalry. A listing of the weights of the 40-odd members of the Florida team included in the roster the following: "Rondo Hatton, 180." This listing of Hatton's weight in 1919 is significant, because in a *Pageant* magazine article written in 1946 after his death, writer Erma Taylor claimed that Hatton's "weight went up to 204 pounds" as a result of the progressive enlargement of his hands, feet and face from acromegaly. Certainly, Hatton's described weight in this and other articles – 170 or 180 pounds – was well beyond his earlier playing weight of 136 pounds, which was often mentioned in pre-war newspapers.

The mention of Rondo's earlier playing days at Davis & Elkins also assumed importance in the days leading up to the game with the University of Georgia. Apparently, the reference stirred up questions concerning his eligibility to continue to play college football. The matter was brought up to the Southern Intercollegiate Athletic Association, the conference to which the University of Florida belonged. It went unanswered until the very evening preceding the "big gridiron battle" at Tampa:

> Priming for the battle of their career, confident that a fighting team of 'Gators can beat Georgia this year, though they admit that it will take time and hard football, thirty husky young Florida Crackers—real crackers, every one of them—reached Tampa at 10:30 last night from Gainesville to get in the finishing touches for the clash with Georgia Saturday afternoon. The train was two hours late.
>
> Coming with the outfit was a piece of welcome news—a telegram that arrived just before it left announcing that Rondo Hatton, the 'Gator general, is eligible. They had ruled Hatton ineligible, claiming he had played on a first-class college team before going to Florida…. The S.I.A.A. officers have ruled that Davis and Elkins, where Hatton went to school, is a prep school, and Hatton plays Saturday…. The entire squad is ready for the game, and fit for the fight.

That kind of eleventh hour drama is ordinarily reserved for the movies, with the suddenly eligible star leading his team to an improbable win. But real life rarely follows the script. Hatton's availability for the game didn't produce a storybook result, although the 'Gators couldn't be faulted for effort. Even though the Florida squad was outmanned in the face of a much larger Georgia team, the two squads battled to a scoreless tie at halftime. True to expectations, Rondo started at quarterback on his hometown field before 3000 fans. Florida kept the game close for three quarters, before Georgia's superior size eventually wore the 'Gators down. Georgia downed Florida 16-0.

Such a debilitating loss after a maximum effort often produces a letdown in the next game, and so it was for the 1919 University of Florida football 11. Eight fumbles by the 'Gators produced a stunning 7-0 loss to Florida Southern. Hatton was not in the starting line-up; it is unclear whether he played in the game at all.

This humbling loss to a lesser opponent reportedly led to some internal dissension among the team members, according to a November 2, 1919, *Tampa Tribune* article. A spirited pep rally seemed to "right the ship" for the 'Gators as they left Gainesville for a November 8 game with Tulane in New Orleans. Rondo started at quarterback once more, and drew special praise from sportswriters for his efforts in a 14-2 loss. The *Pensacola News Journal* (November 10, 1919) carried representative comments: "[Rondo] Hatton shared the [star] honors with [Sparkman] the Florida captain, doing most of the passing and punting, but failed to get across the Tulane goal line."

Rondo was again the 'Gators starting quarterback in a 64-0 romp over Stetson at Gainesville on November 15. The game "was such a one-sided affair as to be a farce," and back-ups played the entirety of the second and fourth quarters, accounting for 30 points themselves.

Bryan Anderson started at quarterback for Florida in a 13-0 win over South Carolina on November 22. The list of substitutions contained in *The Tampa Tribune* confirms that Rondo did not play in that game at all. The Florida 'Gators closed out their 1919 season on Thanksgiving Day with a 14-7 homecoming victory over Oglethorpe University. None of the available newspaper reports indicate whether Hatton played in this last game.

Hatton's collegiate athletic career ended on November 27, 1919, at Gainesville's Fleming Field. None of the available newspaper articles includes a word about any discernible changes in his appearance (beyond the mention of his weight, if that counts); any such reference would have been both tasteless and unnecessary. Yet if acromegaly symptoms were already becoming evident, some dime-store psychology may not be completely out of bounds. If Rondo was going through a completely understandable emotional upheaval at that point, isn't it equally understandable that he would turn to something at which he excelled, in order to ease the move into a new chapter of his life – particularly if he could be around large numbers of people behind the partial mask of a 1919 football helmet?

Whatever reasons beyond the joy of athletic competition that may have spurred Hatton to play one last season of collegiate football, some last comments are appropriate in relation to his time at the University of Florida. First, it is notable that his attendance there, however brief, means that he attended a college in every state in which he had lived except for his birthplace, Maryland. Secondly, it does not appear that Hatton obtained a degree from the University of Florida, or that he remained there after the 1919 fall semester. Whatever earlier plans he may have had to pursue a career as an engineer seem to have been discarded.

Hatton's next move represented another turning point in his life – a change that had more significance than he could have anticipated. He decided to seek a career as a newspaper reporter.

According to Erma Taylor's 1946 *Pageant* article, his decision was not easily reached; it may have a determination born out of self-preservation. In describing that time in Rondo's life, Taylor commented, "It seemed that everyone [Hatton] passed on the street made some remark. What hurt most was the furtive whisper, 'I'd hate to meet him in the dark.'"

Hatton's reaction to this painful situation was thoroughly understandable. As he told Taylor,

> Finally you get to where your only impulse is to hide, run away, stay out of sight in hospitals, forever.... However, you can't stand yourself for long, running away. It's the sympathy that gets you, most of all self-sympathy. It's an insidious poison that gets into your soul, as this thing I've got gets into your bones.

Consequently, according to Taylor,

> Rondo had a long talk with himself one day, and he decided the best thing he could do was the hardest thing he could think of – to face people, new people, all the time. That's exactly why he chose reporting as a career.

Previous writers have stated that Hatton began his newspaper reporter career prior to World War I. Patient research has failed to produce any published articles in Tampa newspapers with Hatton's byline from that period. Additionally, Hatton's activity level during the years between Hillsborough High School and his time overseas was such that it is highly unlikely he could have pursued an actual career as a reporter before 1919. Finally, the reason that Hatton told Taylor he chose newspaper reporting as a career did not exist before the war.

Taylor also suggested in her article that Rondo worked as a reporter for some time before he was named sports editor of a Tampa newspaper. While that is a possibility, available evidence again suggests otherwise. The 1920 federal census enumeration for Rondo took place between January 16 and 17, 1920. This listing of Hatton occurred less than two months after Rondo's final football game with the University of Florida, yet the column on the census enumeration devoted to each party's occupation lists Hatton's job as "sporting editor – newspapers."

This 1920 census enumeration also provides further information of value. Rondo was living with his mother Emily at the 1007 Grand Central Avenue address. Emily's occupation is listed as "teacher – business college," which is consistent with previous data showing Emily as a teacher at the Hatton Business College. It is interesting to note that the head of the family residing at 1007 Grand Central Avenue is Emily's mother, Mary E. Berry. Notable by its absence is the name of Rondo's father Stewart, who was still apparently spending the bulk of his time in Atlanta, furthering the interests of the Bryan-Hatton Business College.

If newspaper reports from the early 1920s are any indication, Rondo's new career as a reporter allowed him to achieve some measure of peace within himself as his condition progressed. Indeed, if that peace was achieved by constantly facing new people, Hatton tackled his goal with a passion. Beyond his position as *Tampa Times* sports editor, Rondo also became an ardent, highly visible member and spokesman for U.S.S. Tampa Post No. 5 of the American Legion. (The American Legion is a veterans organization chartered by Congress in September 1919 to represent the interests of wartime veterans.) Hatton repeatedly served on committees organized by American Legion executives to bolster attendance at special events as well as increase active membership.

Rondo also continued his athletic pursuits. The fledgling reporter became an avid golfer with membership in several local clubs. (Hatton was reported to have a 27 handicap!) He initially attempted to manage the Tampa American Legion baseball team for the 1920 season, but he was forced to resign the position "as he could not look out for that work because of his duties as sporting editor of *The Times*."

It was around this same time, May 1920, that Rondo began writing the sports column "From the Game's Dust" over his byline. His writing style in these early efforts is conversational, lean, witty and straightforward. In a way, he was fulfilling the promise which his Hillsborough High classmates had seen in him years earlier: In the school yearbook, the class prediction for Rondo was: "Many famous books will come from your pen." (This, however, was followed by the teasing postscript, "[T]he most widely read one will, perhaps, be entitled 'Advice to H.S. Pupils,' or 'How to Keep Out of Detention Period at Least Once a Month.'") Even if Hatton's talents as a writer were not directed toward writing books, he was making good on those expectations.

A persistent depiction of Hatton during this time is of a person wrestling with increasing debility. Erma Taylor's comments are characteristic: "For a long time [Hatton] was blind, and the ache in his bones, he once said, was like a migraine headache all over his body." It is no longer possible to say to what degree Taylor's statements represented Hatton's reality – or when. If they are at all accurate in reflecting Rondo's physical situation in the early 1920s, then his triumph over those issues is more testimony to his unconquerable

A typical Rondo sports column, from the May 11, 1920, *Tampa Times*.

In addition to his pitching duties for the Legion team, Rondo maintained his public profile. He served on publicity committees for a number of athletic organizations, and also volunteered his time as an umpire or judge for various events. In October 1920, he was named vice-president of the Florida West Coast Winter Baseball League, a four-club circuit playing games from November through the latter part of February.

At some point during this period, he also worked a brief stint as a reporter for *The Tampa Tribune*; by the spring of 1921, he was back on staff with *The Tampa Times*. One of Hatton's *Times* articles appeared on June 8, 1921. That same day, an article appeared in *The Tampa Tribune* that was entirely more foreboding than Rondo's sports item:

> Rondo Hatton, well known Tampan and member of the staff of the *Times*, and formerly of *The Tribune*, left Tampa last night for Baltimore, Md., where he will enter Johns Hopkins Hospital to undergo an operation. En route to Baltimore, Mr. Hatton will spend several days in Atlanta. He is expected to be gone about three weeks.

This item appears to represent the first mention in print of Hatton's entering a hospital for any kind of surgical procedure. According to Erma Taylor's *Pageant* article, it would not be the last. Taylor wrote that Hatton spent fully ten of the last 28 years of his life "in hospitals from Connecticut to California." Based upon the July 1946 date of Taylor's article, as well as the date of Hatton's death, that would put the start of Rondo's time in hospitals at 1918—a date which is consistent with Fred Olen Ray's earlier references to Hatton's initial medical procedures.

Taylor's article also included a brief but harrowing description of some of these procedures:

> In one series of operations his cheek bones were taken out and replaced with metal. The lower jaw grew out so far his lower teeth extended at least an inch beyond his uppers, and it required several more operations and four sets of teeth before Rondo could chew again. No number of

spirit. Not only did Hatton continue playing in competitive golf tournaments through the summer of 1920, he returned to the baseball diamond as well. According to the August 20 *Tampa Tribune*:

> The Tarpon Springs American Legion baseball team is scheduled to arrive in Tampa this morning for a game this afternoon with the Tampa Legion team, it was announced last night by Assistant Manager Eddie Bond. The game will be played at Plant Field and will be called at 4 o'clock.
>
> Bond said last night it has been decided that Rondo Hatton will take the mound for the Tampans....

Joys Chase Away Glooms As Goodfellow Rallies To the Aid of Old Santa

Rondo and The Times Are Confident That Saint Nick Will Not Overlook a Single Little Boy or Girl In This Big City of the South.

Today is the last call—almost.

Or shortly it will be the year that Santa Claus went on strike.

That's the way this year 1921 is going to be remembered throughout the world. But isn't going to be as bad as all that in Tampa. And the reason is you, Mr. Goodfellow. You are certainly going to step to the front and center in gallant style.

Now Is the Time.

And if ever a Goodfellow were neeeded, he is certainly needed now. From the city officials, American Legion officials, Salvation Army officials, from everywhere—comes the opinion that never before has a Yuletide seen the extraordinary number of poverty cases as have come to light this year.

These cases include those of the poor children, the grownups, the disabled service men and others who are walking the streets jobless.

Which means, army Goodfellows, that you've got to hustle in line to put the happy Christmas-for-all stunt over today. Sunday is Christmas. But the army is increasing. In the last few days the Many Mr. Goodfellows and Mrs. Goodfellows and little Tommy Goodfellows and little Susie Goodfellows have simply rolled into the ranks.

Joy to Win.

Old General Industrial Depression and Old Man Gloom are trying their best to keep ahead of you, but we're out to get those birds and get them right. Santa Claus goes on no strike in Tampa, though he may elsewhere, if the Goodfellows can help it. Let him lay down on the job in points, east, west and north, if he will. Mr. Goodfellow's home is in Tampa, and in spite of the poverty abroad this year, Mr. Goodfellow is going to talk up loud and sassy to this Santa Claus fellow and "All right, let's go, a merry Christmas to everybody in Tampa."

A Mrs. Goodfellow walked into The Times office the other day and asked how she could help keep Santa Claus on the job. She was told of the Empty Stocking Fund and the list of needy kept by local charity organizations. She also asked if the office boy knew some of their names. He replied, "Yes, there is a Widow Legion, with little Tommy Legion and Esmeralda Legion and Julie Legion, all looking for roast duck and dolls." Tommy is a smart boy, he is.

Off She Flies.

"Lead me to them," Mrs. Goodfellow replied. And Mrs. Goodfellow disappeared in a trail of dust.

And Mr. Goodfellow, don't you wait until the day before, or until Christmas itself.

Hustle up and find out who needs help. Go out and get acquainted. Talk to them and find out the true condition of affairs. Discover just how far you can go in doing the things necessary to help.

If you can't swing it alone, put the case up to your friends. Tell them you are going to give them a great opportunity. Talk to them like a life insurance agent. Sell them part of your Christmas good will.

This is the age of salesmanship. If people can sell furs in Florida in the summer, and oil stock and things of that sort, you ought to sell a case of poverty that you yourself have looked on and probed into, and understand and sympathize with.

The Strong Fight.

One soldier of the army of Goodfellows said after he read of the idea, "I know a man who has more money than a federal reserve bank. He is a hard boiled egg and says that if people don't work of course they'll starve, and they ought to. I'm going after that bird. I pretty nearly got him last year. I told him about my centipedes and I poured it into him. I told him about a little girl with big blue eyes who kept calling me 'dada' and that she had clothes made out of an old shawl. I pretty near sold him that little girl. But he was sitting in his car and he yelled: 'Shut up, you're breaking my heart,' and he stepped on the gas and, blooie, he was gone.

"But, as they used to say in church during revival time, 'he's under conviction'. That little girl with the big blue eyes is going to haunt him. I'll bet he'll take the contract of shoeing my centipedes all himself. And the rest of the syndicate will take care of the clothes and coild boiled this and that and the toys."

All right, Mr. and Mrs. Goodfellows, let's go. Hunt up the needy. It's a merry Christmas for all in Tampa. Don't let Santa Claus lay down on the job a particle in the Cigar City. RONDO.

Ho-ho-Hatton: Rondo wants to make sure even needy kids have something under their tree on Christmas morning (*Tampa Times*, December 23, 1921).

operations, however, could wholly alleviate the appearance or the excruciating pain.

The incidental reference to Hatton's spending "several days in Atlanta" surely means that Rondo took some time to visit his father Stewart at his Atlanta residence at 16 West Hunter before Rondo traveled on to Baltimore. Perhaps it was this procedure, with its lengthy convalescence, to which Erma Taylor referred: "Rondo was still young when he came home from an early hospital siege and his parents did not recognize him. That was a special kind of excruciating pain."

Nonetheless, Rondo persevered. A September 1, 1921, *Tampa Times* article reported that he was among the attendees at a dance party held by his Sigma Nu fraternity at the Tampa Yacht and Country Club. Yet within mere days, the *Times* was providing this sobering report:

> Rondo Hatton, a member of the reportorial staff of *The Times*, underwent a minor operation by Dr. J. Brown Farrior Friday. He was resting easily Saturday at his home at 1007 Grand Central Ave. and is expected to completely recover by the first of the week. His ten thousand friends are pulling for him.

Whatever pain Hatton endured, perhaps the last sentence in this item lessened his torment. For it is clear from this item and others that Rondo Hatton was beloved by all who knew him, and that his fellow Tampans remained keenly interested in him. Even the following brief item (*The Tampa Tribune*, September 19, 1921) attests to Tampans' concern for every event in his life: "Rondo Hatton, who has been ill, is able to be back at his post as sporting editor of the evening paper."

Rondo immediately stepped back into more than his duties at the *Tampa Times* sports desk. He joined several other former Hillsborough High football players as assistant football coaches for the Hillsborough football team.

The end of 1921 saw Hatton remain in the public eye. He was a central force in urging the incorporation of the Tampa American Legion Post under Florida law, and functioned as a captain of a committee to sell tickets to a Legion-sponsored Christmas football game between ex–college stars and the St. Petersburg Tigers. Rondo maintained his visibility by refereeing the game before a crowd of 2000. He continued as

OVERSTREETS HAVE ALIBIS FOR MURDER

Defense Contends Paul Was in Lakeland.

STAR WITNESS CONTRADICTED

Impeachment of Testimony Is Feature of Day.

By RONDO HATTON.
(Staff Correspondent The Times.)

Dade City, Dec. 16.—Paul Overstreet, on trial for the murder of A. F. Crenshaw, deputy sheriff, and J. V. Waters, federal prohibition agent, declared on the stand this morning that he spent the day on which the murder occurred in Lakeland, and the defense offered several witnesses to prove this alibi. The defense rested at noon and the state started rebuttal arguments when court reconvened this afternoon. It is believed that the case will go to the jury tonight.

Paul denied point blank the conversations with John Trautman and Perry Hayes, which these two state witnesses testified to. He said that he was in Lakeland the greater part of the day and told in detail of his movements there. Witnesses who testified to his being in Lakeland were Jamie Collins, Lakeland; Steve Reynolds, Lakeland; Sam Pinkston and R. L. Beck of Zephyrhills, Preston Overstreet and Marvin Gaskins. Harmon Johnson testified that he saw Overstreet and Connell in Plant City on the day in question.

Connell Testifies.

Wilson Connell, who is under indictment as an accomplice in the case, testified that he drove Paul to Lakeland on November 4. With them were Ivy Overstreet and J. Paul Brown, both of whom remembered seeing and speaking to Paul on that day in Lakeland.

After scoring Friday afternoon by securing on an instructed verdict the release of Preston, the defense during the afternoon and three-hour night session marshalled a stream of witnesses who contradicted testimony of the state, particularly that given by the two star witnesses, Hayes and Trautman.

As to Trautman's declaration that Paul Overstreet admitted the killing by saying, "John, I got them," and that Paul told Trautman that he soon would "see something" while on their way to the scene of the murder, the defense put on the stand the other occupants of the automobile, who testified that they had heard no such conversation between Paul and Trautman.

Offer Alibis.

Alibis to account for the movements of the Overstreets during the the day and night of the killing were offered by the defense in the direct examination of witnesses yesterday and last night. The defense contended that members of the Overstreet family were in Dade City on the day in question and several witnesses testified to the truth of this.

Witnesses testified further that Bascom Overstreet's truck, in which Hayes declared he had ridden with Bascom to Preston's house on the day of the murder, had been left in a garage early on the same day for the replacement of a broken spring. The defense laid stress on the claim that both Hayes and Trautman hoped for financial reward for their testimony.

Hold To Testimony.

Under severe cross-examination, the defense witnesses held to the direct testimony. The witnesses included K. G. Burch, R. B. Sturkie, Luce Overstreet, Rollie Ward, Jesse Lyons, Mrs. J. L. Overstreet, Bird Overstreet, George Overstreet, Preston Overstreet, Bascom Overstreet, George Downing, Taft Overstreet, Josie Overstreet, Rabe Overstreet, J. L. Skipper, Charles Browing, Jack Coleman and Morris Redding.

The courtroom was crowded throughout the day, with an increasing number of women present.

It was predicted last night that the defense had practically closed its case and that the jury will retire this afternoon or night.

By 1922, Rondo was chasing crime stories in Tampa. Here's his coverage of the trial of a man accused of the murder of a pair of law enforcers.

a vocal member of the Tampa American Legion Post into 1922, spearheading a membership drive while urging membership dues remain at $2 per year. He also continued to compete in various local golf tournaments.

A notable event in his professional life also occurred in early 1922. Rondo's reporting assignments for *The Tampa Times* were expanded beyond the sports desk into the realm of crime reporting – an interesting change, considering his later film career. His writing style in this new arena shows maturity: It is incisive, vigorous and informative, with none of the conversational tone of his sportswriting.

Reading some of Hatton's stories creates the impression that he was one of those reporters who dashed to crime scenes with his photographer, arriving with or even ahead of the police on occasion.2 For example, in 1931, The *Tampa Tribune* carried the story of three men who had secretly turned a 12-foot vault under a residential garage into a liquor storehouse – and then, descending into the pit one night, found themselves unable to breathe. By the time neighbors hoisted their bodies from the pit, they were dying. Rondo accompanied the city's chief of detectives to the garage and, while the chief and a constable remained safely above, it was Rondo who descended into the lethal chamber to investigate! He inspected the vault's contents for a minute or so and then returned to report that it was filled with sacks of liquor. A coroner's jury later determined that Paul Antinori, Jimmy Valenti and Nick Midulla had come to their deaths from inhalation of marsh gas generated from the decay of the straw and sacks in which the liquor was packed.

Returning to 1922: Reports from later in that year hint that Rondo was feeling better and enjoying options that came along with that wellbeing. A July 1922 article noted that he had returned to some old haunts: "Mr. Rondo Hatton is enjoying a visit in Hickory, N.C., and other points in that state."

Playing in golf tournaments, Hatton manifested his ongoing efforts to maintain himself physically in the face of acromegaly. A series of articles in Tampa newspapers bear witness to the degree to which he was willing to test himself in athletic competition. Tampa's American Legion post planned an October 21 football game with the University of Florida at the city's Plant Field. Daily workouts were planned to start on September 27, to run until game day. Among the Legion "gridmen" named as prospective starts in the backfield is "Rondo Hatton at full." The prospect that Hatton would play football again in front of his hometown crowd generated quite a buzz among local sports fans. One sportswriter waxed rhapsodic about the possibility:

> The unofficial reports that Rondo Hatton is to appear in an American Legion football uniform this fall, is joyful news—if true. Here's one who long has been hoping to see those yard-across shoulders plowing through some crumpling defense.

Whether Hatton actually played in the contest is not known; the most significant aspect of this sequence of events is that Rondo felt good enough to try his luck on the football field again. A short item in October 14, 1922, *Tampa Times* – a week before the contest – suggests his frame of mind:

> Thursday last was a gray still day; the kind of a lookout that betokens a snow storm up north. Old Timer Rondo Hatton opined it made him kinda yearn for a bout with the pig-skin.

Hatton kept up his crime reporting in *The Tampa Times*; the articles under his byline by the end of 1922 are both lengthier and more frequent, reflecting the increasing confidence that the newspaper leadership had in his reporting skills. Much of 1923, Hatton appears to have split time between his work as a reporter and his expanded duties with the Tampa American Legion Post. In the fall of 1923, his contribution to *The Tampa Times* was formally recognized in a lovingly crafted article that appeared in the *Times* as part of a series of compositions devoted to various members of its editorial staff. Not only does the article provide a short Hatton biography, it expresses the esteem in which he was held by his fellow workers. The article includes a portrait of Hatton which shows evidence of the extent to which his appearance had been altered by acromegaly as of September 1923. What is more chilling, in hindsight, is the degree to which his appearance was distorted still further by acromegaly in the years afterwards.

A few excerpts from this "get to know Rondo" article should suffice to show the regard in which he was held, and the kind of man he was:

> Rondo Hatton is probably the most widely known member of *The Times*' editorial staff. Everyone knows Rondo, from the newsie to the bank president. He is Rondo to all of them, and this acquaintance makes him one of the most valuable assets....
>
> A keen sense of humor has made him a versatile writer and news gatherer. Many of the best stories of murders, fires, etc., appearing in *The Times* during the past few years have been his. He has always injected into his work a spirit of reliability and faithfulness....
>
> Asked whether or not he was married, Rondo said "Exposed but never took."

This last remark likely masked a great deal of pain. Hatton had told Erma Taylor that "former girlfriends crossed the street for fear he'd ask for a date."

However discouraged Rondo was about his personal life, events suggest that he continued much as before over the next couple of years. In September 1924, he was one of five delegates from the Tampa American Legion Post to attend the national convention in St. Paul, Minnesota. His *Tampa Times* co-workers continued to extol his contribution. One writer for the newspaper singled Hatton out:

> Hatton! Now we're getting down to the fellow who bring[s] in the thrills. Fire! Murder! Help!

LETTERS SENT BY IRENE ARE READ AT TRIAL

Girl Companions On Stand in Death Case.

By RONDO HATTON.
Staff Correspondent.

Bushnell, April 5.—The trial of Mrs. Ida M. Whittington and her daughter, Irene Whittington, 16-year-old school girl, of Webster, on charges of manslaughter in connection with the alleged killing of an infant, whose body was found in a pond several miles from here early in March, began in earnest today.

The trial, which opened on Tuesday, was delayed but little in getting under way, the selection of a jury having required but about si...

Police! Ah! The engines and the patrol wagon – and Hatton – there they come, thank goodness. Now it'll go in the Home Edition, sure nuff. This man Rondo is a husky lad; they say he was a football star, and a Hun-killer. His hobby is swimming – keeps you fit, and he is noted for always being on time in the morning, providing some one gives him a hitch in. Rondo is kind of a fixture here. … We'd hardly know how to get along without the big boy, for a fact.

Nonetheless, his newspaper colleagues had to do without Rondo – if only for a limited time. A column published in *The Tampa Times* on the occasion of Rondo's 31st birthday in 1925, "Who's Who Today," provided further biographical details on Hatton, and also revealed that he had forsaken employment with *The Times* in favor of a job as a publicity man for the local Mabry-Hall Realty Company. The article also mentioned that Rondo had maintained his membership in the Rocky Point Golf Club, and that he remained unmarried.

But Hatton's marital status was about to change. According to *The Tampa Times*, Miss Elizabeth Immell James, a native of Lawson, Missouri, had relocated to Tampa in January 1926. She made a number of friends in Tampa in a very short time due to her "charming personality."

One of those ardent devotees must have been Rondo Hatton, and something like a whirlwind courtship must have ensued. They were married on Thursday, April 15, 1926. The next day's *Tampa Times* carried an article describing the modest ceremony:

Miss Immell James and Rondo Hatton Quietly Married Yesterday Afternoon

Miss Elizabeth Immell James and Rondo Hatton were united in the bonds of matrimony yesterday afternoon at 4 o'clock at the home of the Rev. George Hyman, 603 South Willow Avenue. Dr. Hyman, who served as chaplain in the same company with Mr. Hatton during the World War, performed the ceremony.

Those attending the wedding were Mrs. J.A. James, mother of the bride; Mrs. Emma L. Hatton, mother of the groom; Mr. and Mrs. George James, Kenneth McPherson and Ernest L. Hall.

Immediately following the ceremony, Mr. and Mrs. Hatton left for a month's honeymoon trip to points in Tennessee and Georgia to visit friends and relatives. They are traveling by motor.

Publicity Director

RONDO HATTON, OF MABRY-HALL REALTY COMPANY

The *Tampa Tribune* society writer expressed surprise at the wedding, a surprise shared by "many friends and relatives," according to an item which appeared in that newspaper on April 18. The *Times* staff kept up with the couple's travels: The next week, the paper carried the following piece: "Mr. and Mrs. Rondo Hatton are now the guests of Mr. Hatton's uncle in Hickory, N.C. They expect to return to Tampa about the first of May."

Suiting action to the word, the newlyweds returned to set up housekeeping at their new matrimonial residence early in May 1926. The *Tampa Times* for May 8, 1926, recounted that the Hattons had returned from their honeymoon trip "and are now at home at 1930 DuBois Street."

It seems wholly appropriate at this point to provide some details on Elizabeth Immell James, Rondo's first wife. Previous biographers have said little or nothing about her, and what has been written contains inaccuracies. She was born on January 21, 1906, near Lawson, Missouri, the daughter of William Arthur James, a prominent Missouri physician from Lawson, and Josephine Culver, a socialite from nearby Grayson, Missouri. The family always referred to their daughter as Immell, which was the surname of her paternal grandmother.

Immell and her older brother George Washington James grew up as members of the more privileged class of Lawson, if we can believe the number of articles in the *Plattsburg Leader* detailing the many social events hosted by their parents. By 1919, Dr. James had moved the family to Kansas City, Missouri. Immell attended Central College in Lexington, Missouri, and Howard-Payne College in Fayette, Missouri. The divorce of her parents in the early 1920s led Immell to take a job as a stenographer for the National Candy Company. It appears that George moved with his father to Colorado, while Immell remained with her mother. By January 1926, Immell and Josephine had moved to Tampa and taken up residence at 208 Grand Central Avenue. Josephine had obtained work, and was claiming she was the "widow of W.A. James."

One can speculate on the reasons that the 20-year-old Immell married a man nearly 12 years her senior. One hopes that love had blossomed between Rondo and Immell in so short a time, but there's also the possibility that the prominence of Hatton's extended family in Tampa led Immell and Josephine to mistakenly conclude that Immell's marriage to Rondo could restore their social status – and their economic wellbeing.

At any rate, Immell began her marriage by repeating what she had experienced growing up in Missouri. Newspaper articles described her activities hosting a variety of social events; usually her mother was among the guests. By July 1927, Rondo and Immell had moved to new lodgings at 717 South Orleans Avenue. Rondo had left his position in the Mabry-Hall Realty Company advertising department and returned to work as a *Tampa Times* reporter. Within the year, Rondo and Immell moved again, to 215 North Boulevard.

In November 1928, he was one of eight war veterans on the *Tampa Times* staff asked to contribute thumb-

> **Southeast of Sedan.**
> **By RONDO HATTON.**
>
> The "Frogs" and "Joe Latrino" boys had been "whispering" the fini la guerre for so long that when the news did reach us, we didn't believe it. The official report caught us just about midnight along the main drag southwest of Sedan which had been reached by some of the units of the outfit in competition with other American divisions and the French. The only thing we had to celebrate with were grenades, rockets, rifles, etc., and everybody did. The bedlam wore off about daybreak. The waffle boys of the staff drove up in their big limousines and shiny uniforms and boots and demanded: "Where are your men?" The captain pointed. Here and there in a rain-soaked field and out in the open in the steady drizzle, there were the men, sleeping singly, coiled up like a dog, or in twos or threes, anything to keep warm.

nail reminiscences of their whereabouts ten years earlier on Armistice Day. Hatton's sketch, reproduced below, is representative of his lean, expressive writing style. (Note: The title that *The Tampa Times* gave the sketch, "Southeast of Sedan," must be a typo, as the story specifies that these events took place south*west* of Sedan.)

The year 1928 also brought with it another event that would have a significant impact on Rondo's marriage. On February 29, Immell's mother Josephine made the marital leap with Samuel Bucklew Sr., an insurance adjuster with the Southern Adjustment Bureau. Josephine's marriage meant financial security – and a new refuge for Immell that had been unavailable before.

Where do a "funny money" ring and a firebrand ex-governor meet on the graph? Hatton of the *Tribune* brought Floridians answers!

More and more the local newspapers carried reports of Mrs. Rondo Hatton and Mrs. Sam Bucklew attending Tampa's signature social events in tandem, and without Rondo.

While Rondo's marriage moved closer to collapse, he doggedly pushed forward. He maintained his staff correspondent position with *The Tampa Times*, but also rejoined the staff of *The Tampa Tribune*. He penned important *Tribune* articles, including lengthy items about political corruption (an ex–Florida governor tied to a counterfeiting ring) and illegal immigration. Hatton endeavored to further supplement his modest income as a reporter by working as an on-air personality for local radio station WDAE.

Radio pioneer Don Thompson, a WDAE engineer, recalled that Hatton was involved in a program stunt for the station. It was announced that Rondo would render a vocal solo as the next broadcast number, and then the station instead aired the canned music of some famous singer. Hatton received "all kinds of compliments from admirers who had no idea [he] could sing and play so well," according to Thompson. Hatton even received requests "to appear outside the studio for churches and private recitals," Thompson disclosed.

At the same time that Rondo was struggling to remain solvent, other events were combining to produce another turning point in his life: Hollywood was arriving in Tampa. In late August 1929, local newspapers proclaimed that carpenters were preparing nearby Rocky Point as the location set for United Artists' *The Little Pirate*, an adaptation of Rida Johnson Young's novel *Out of the Night*. Set on a Caribbean island, the Lupe Velez–Jean Hersholt–starrer was being touted as the first all-talkie to be filmed entirely on location. By the time filming began at 7:30 a.m. on Monday, September 9, it had been given a new title: *Hell Harbor*. It was originally slated for eight weeks' shooting, but it was stated again and again on the first day of production that at least 10 and probably 12 weeks would be necessary. A *Tampa Times* reporter noted at the end of that first day that *Hell Harbor* would be

> the first all-sound production of [director–executive producer] Henry King, and from his meticulous insistence on perfection in taking the scene this morning, it may be assumed he will not rush work to a degree that might endanger the artistic merit of the picture.

On the fourth day, Thursday, September 12, 1929, fate took a hand. That morning, *The Tampa Tribune* dispatched Rondo to interview King about the film. The shrewd director saw that Hatton's acromegalic features made him a unique "type" and offered him a small but showy part as the proprietor of a shabby dive in which much of the activity plays out. The next day, Rondo was one among 120 Tampa locals who began work in the waterfront dance hall set. A *Tampa Tribune* reporter described the scene, as King set the stage:

> Forget you are in Tampa; Mr. King said. "You are patrons of a waterfront den, assembled for a

OFFICERS HERE EVER ALERT TO DEPORT ALIENS

Help Legal Immigrants; Fight Smugglers

By RONDO HATTON

Uncle Sam has put up the "go" sign for undesirable aliens and Tampa immigration officials, turned traffic officers at the command, are seeing that it is obeyed.

Last week several aliens who heard the word "go," were put aboard northbound trains and started back on the long trip to their native lands.

There are others in the county jail, men who have sailed the high seas without a country, and who now are behind bars for attempting to enter the land of the free. Stowaways, these men are. Just those who never seem to get under the quota laws of their countries.

Now awaiting deportation, they may never return, for under the new ruling that went into effect a month ago, they are forever barred from re-entering this country.

During the last fiscal year, which ended June 30, a total of 12,908 persons were deported from the United States, according to Immigration Commissioner Harry Hull at Washington. Of this army, Tampa contributed its quota of 100 or more.

Enter U. S. Illegally

The principal of all reasons for deportation of this alien host is because they entered the country illegally. There are numerous other reasons for their expulsion; namely, they are criminals, have overstayed their leave, have become public charges and what not. In Tampa and Florida, though, one word is descriptive of the vast majority of deportations and that word is "smuggled." Florida's nearness to Cuba, particularly to Havana—the haven for aliens seeking illegal entry in the United States—is the reason.

"Stowaway" also is written across numerous immigration deportation records. Attempts to stowaway are countless and ingenious but seldom successful.

Keeping track of the invading alien army and running down countless tips on those who are located here and there after being smuggled in is a never ending job for Tampa and Florida immigration inspectors. Around the Tampa office there has grown up among Chief Eugene Kessler, his assistant, S. B. Hopkins, and the other officers and inspectors a slogan similar to Canadian mounted police's: "Always get our man," and the records of their office, showing in some instances arrests and deportations after a trail has been followed for years, substantiates how well the force has lived up to the slogan.

It has been only in recent weeks that a young alien shiek of the modern hard boiled, smooth talking type learned this.

He, like hundreds of others, was smuggled into Florida from Cuba and eventually came out of hiding to live in Tampa. As the days passed and he was not molested he became bolder and bolder. He entered the liquor racket. Even an arrest and his having to make bond for appearance before a federal grand jury failed to instill any fear in him.

Finally Captured

Out of jail on bond, he boldly resumed his bootlegging, but there came a day when it was "curtain" for him in the United States. All along the immigration officials had kept close on his trail but all unknown to him. While he was boasting about it among his comrades, immigration men were completing their chain of evidence.

Then one day he was re-arrested on another liquor charge and boldly went to the third floor of the postoffice building to make another bond. But this time, there was no bond. An immigration inspector had followed him into the elevator and another was waiting when he left the cage on the third floor. He was arrested this time and manifested surprise that immigration officers knew him or anything about his activities.

After the arrest, the remainder was only routine procedure, a deportation hearing, an order fom Washington and the trip to Ellis Island, and under the new law, the alien is now on the high seas enroute to his native land and permanently barred from ever returning.

Records at the Tampa immigration officers show that thousands of cases go through that office. For example, during the last federal fiscal year, inspectors here examined a total of 12,391 alien seamen and 7347 American seamen, employed on foreign vessels. The Tampa officers handled 149 deportation warrants and investigated in all 899 cases for warrants purposes. Then intermittently during the year, they examined 1564 aliens who applied for legal admission into this country and deported a number of these who were found undesirable.

The Tampa office detains its immigrants and aliens as short a time as possible, for officials are extremely busy and are as anxious to help qualified aliens enter as the visitors are themselves, but the officers are equally and more anxious to speed traffic at the "go" sign for the undesirable aliens.

Sounds like Rondo's ready to "Build the wall! Build the wall!"

---

wild party, to laugh, to drink, dance and have a good time. Lose yourself in your characters. Act naturally. Let your feelings guide your expressions, your voices and your actions. Listen to the throb of the music and catch the spirit of the surroundings. All set? Let's go!"

The music starts and the couples sway to the strains of the barbaric dance. Waiters scurry from table to table, serving cold tea in whiskey glasses. Rondo Hatton, scowling from his vantage point at the head of the bar, contemplates big profits and watches for budding brawls. He swaggers away to punch the checks of the dancing girls. Three sailors argue over schooners of near beer about the relative merits of blondes and brunettes. A tipsy senorita flirts with a steamboat engineer, pointing suggestively to the stairway leading to private rooms on the balcony.

RONDO HATTON, Tampa newspaperman, who has turned cinemactor temporarily, and has an important role in the picture, "Hell Harbor," at Rocky Point. Hatton, in the picture, is proprietor of what is euphemistically described as a honky-tonk.

Boom-boom-boom! The drums beat a faster rhythm while perspiring musicians, toiling in a blue fog of tobacco smoke, approach the frenzied climax of the dance.

"Cut!" cries Director King. The music stops and the extras snap back from the land of make-believe to the mundane parts of ordinary Tampans. Shooting the scenes in the honky-tonk will continue during the remainder of this week and all of next week, Director King said....

Although King expressed himself as more than satisfied with the Tampa extras in general, he reserved particular compliments for Rondo Hatton after the first day of shooting, according to the September 14 *Tampa Tribune*:

Rondo Hatton, the *Tribune* reporter who has been cast as the proprietor of the honky-tonk, won the praise of the director-producer for some splendid work in the bar and dance hall. Mr. King isn't given to lavish commendation but he likes Rondo's work and said so....

"He is ideal in the part," Mr. King said. "I like him, too, because he is intelligent, listens to instructions and seems to get the feel of his part much quicker than the average extra!"

It was a great day for Rondo, who went to Rocky Point Thursday morning as a newspaperman and walked away with a part in the picture....

The selection of Hatton as the proprietor of the honky-tonk gave other extras incentive for greater effort. They saw one of their number hoisted from the rank and file. Consequently, the action yesterday was even more satisfactory than on the first day the supers entered the picture.

King commented further on the local talent in another interview early in the shooting. Although he did not refer to Hatton specifically, his remarks are so consistent with the points he made that were particular to Hatton that his observations are still worth noting:

I am surprised and gratified at the intelligent way these people take hold of the job.... By the time this picture is finished, my group of extras will be far superior to any I've ever been able to round up in Hollywood. Not only are they willing and quick to pick up the characterizations desired of them, but they are almost entirely without self-consciousness and make no effort to "hog" the scenes – two qualities directors would like to find among extras on the coast.

King also remarked that the aptitude of the Tampa extras was such that he was able to speed up work and keep on the schedule originally planned for the production. A prominent newspaper ad taken out by the Tampa Chamber of Commerce urged the locals to extend every cooperation to the *Hell Harbor* company; the organization obviously sought "motion picture work" for Tampa.

By the third week of filming, King was focusing on dramatic scenes between principals Lupe Velez and John Holland. The break in Rondo's involvement allowed him to take part in planning a reunion of his old Company H, the Tampa Rifles. Any activity that took

How many Classic Horror stars began their movie careers on a Friday the 13th? Rondo did: Friday, September 13, 1929, was his first day on his first picture, the Florida-made *Hell Harbor*.

Rondo away from the increasing turmoil in his marriage must have been a relief. He was therefore eager to volunteer his services to the "*Hell Harbor* Night" organized by the U.S. Tampa Post of the American Legion for Thursday, October 3. The festivities, held at Davis Island Coliseum, included "a miniature honky-tonk built all in *Hell Harbor* style, with Rondo Hatton, the villainous proprietor, at the bar, and Henry King's Cuban Orchestra playing native music." Proceeds from the event went to the Disabled Veterans of the World War.

By late October, Jean Hersholt, who had portrayed the "close-fisted island trader Horngold," had already returned to Hollywood to work on another film. The October 24 *Tampa Times* reported:

> Many Tampa extras are being used in scenes on the lot these days, and more will be called in as soon as the big honky-tonk fracas is staged. Rondo Hatton, Tampa newspaperman, ... will be back in the scene next week.

That same day, the *Times* repeated King's vow that the last shots on the production would be finished "within three weeks."

The eighth week of *Hell Harbor* production (Monday, October 28–Saturday, November 2) was split between the dance hall fight scenes filmed at Rocky Point and scenes shot Thursday, Friday and Saturday in the deep water off the municipal pier in St. Petersburg. These "concluding scenes" took place aboard a schooner. A *Tampa Bay Times* reporter visited the Rocky Point dance hall set on October 29 and his detailed account ran in the next day's paper. Amid brief meetings with King, John Holland, Lupe Velez and Al St. John, the unidentified reporter ran into Rondo – who is not identified by name in the article. Nevertheless, the subject of the reporter's brief remarks is obvious:

> Over behind the bar is as tough a looking customer as you ever laid eyes on. He is a cross between Lon Chaney in his worst makeup and Bull Montana *à la* natural. You think you would dislike to meet him alone in a dark alley. As a matter of fact he is one of the most gentle of human beings – a Tampa Times newspaperman drafted for the part. But he is frank to admit that while the movies are fine as a change, he would rather have the thrills of being a reporter as a steady diet.

That last remark attributed to Hatton may have been an indirect comment on an offer that King made to Rondo. According to Erma Taylor's *Pageant* article,

King "tried to persuade Rondo to come to Hollywood" after the completion of *Hell Harbor*. At the time, Hatton demurred. Taylor wrote, "Rondo figured Tampa was used to his face; there was no point in pushing his luck."

Perhaps Hatton was also hesitant after seeing some of the downside of motion pictures. King's insistence on realism during the climactic dance hall brawl produced some harrowing moments – moments to which Rondo was a witness:

> Featured players and extras of *Hell Harbor* ... made generous use of arnica and bandages as a result of a free-for-all which is part and parcel of one of the big climaxes in the production. Many Tampans who had been agog with excitement at the prospect of having a film company in their midst contrived to get themselves cast as extras in the big dance hall scene where the catch-as-catch-can battle took place. Despite bruises and cuts none of them has lost any enthusiasm for picture production.
>
> Among those to be temporarily incommoded because of bangs and hurts was John Holland, leading man in *Hell Harbor*, who went to the local osteopath to ease the pain of a wrenched neck and back incurred during the melee taking place in the honky-tonk.
>
> Despite keen pain, Holland returned to the location, where Director Henry King drove his company to the limit by having them exchange real punches. The blows struck landed with a convincing thud. Chairs and bottles whizzed across the dance floor and one large flask crashed into the mirror back of the bar...
>
> To build up the situation, Director King engaged many local Tampans to act as habitués of the honky-tonk. When the brawlers were going full tilt, a number of dancing girls ran screaming across the scene as a crowd of angry villagers closed in on the two principals and eventually engaged in the quarrel themselves.
>
> Rondo Hatton, reporter for *The Tampa Tribune*, playing the part of the dance hall proprietor, leapt over the counter to get into the thick of the battle. Al St. John, the film comedian, who is featured in a whimsical role in the story, showed that he has not forgotten the acrobatics that first brought him fame in pictures, for he mounted a swinging chandelier, described a wide arc and let go to fly through a shattered window.
>
> Holland, beset by three husky extras, was finally knocked headlong out of a latticed sidewall.

As befits a pirate village dance hall, *Hell Harbor*'s was often short on dancing, long on fighting and rioting. And Rondo (right) was always in the thick of things. With the set superheated by a battery of 2000-candlepower floodlights, everyone must have sweltered.

The above description is no publicist's exaggeration. The *Tampa Bay Times* reporter who visited the set on October 29 provided confirmation:

> There are blows struck and there are no stage blows either; they are resounding whacks. Holland topples over among the iron standards of the big lights. There is no playing in this. It is real. The crack Holland takes hurts, but he comes up smiling. It takes a half dozen retakes to satisfy King, but eventually it is finished.

With the completion of filming on *Hell Harbor*, Rondo Hatton returned to the "thrills of being a reporter." Along with Erma Taylor, other writers have

Hell Harbor was popular with reviewers, the *Hollywood Spectator* critic gushing, "Pictorially, I think it is the finest thing given to us in black and white."

January 1930 brought what must have been some cause for elation to Rondo. Hollywood returned to Tampa for the world premiere of *Hell Harbor* on Friday, January 24, at Tampa's Victory Theater. Henry King attended the initial showing of the film, which *The Tampa Times* reported was "more than the mere showing of a picture" – it was also a cornerstone event for the fledgling sound feature film, and a bellwether for Tampa as a potential location for future films. A "thundering wave of applause" swept through the Victory at the film's conclusion, and reviews were unrestrained in declaring it a "great picture." Speakers at the event encouraged "citizens to get out and hustle" Tampa for more film work. Telegrams from luminaries such as Harold Lloyd, Mary Pickford and Douglas Fairbanks were read to the crowd, attesting to Tampa's success as a location.

Then, according to *The Tampa Tribune*,

> There was a little thing which was a surprise to King and which took him off his feet. He was presented with a beautiful gold watch from the city and the citizens of Tampa … and it took King a little time to steady himself. He was touched by the gift….

In the midst of unstinting praise for the "superb photography," the "splendid" sound recording, and the "action and suspense" in the story, Rondo Hatton came in for particular praise from his brethren at *The Tampa Tribune*:

> The honky-tonk scenes were especially of interest, and good. Tampa saw Rondo Hatton first, with a cigarette in his lips, glaring at Peg Leg. It saw him use the clipper on the dance tickets of his customers. And it saw him smash a bottle of liquor over the head of the big black negro, a Tampan, in the honky-tonk fight, which was a fight.

> I have noted that none of our motion picture critics has given our own Rondo Hatton a review. So, it must be up to me. In his first screen appearance, in *Hell Harbor*, Rondo did his bit with the ease, aplomb and ability of a seasoned movie player. In this verdict, I have the concurrence of none other than Henry King. Moving among the motley mob of the dance hall, Rondo is the "spot" of the scene. His posture is perfect,

also stated that, despite King's urging, Hatton was reluctant to pursue a Hollywood career. There is no reason to doubt the assertion, since Rondo remained in Tampa. Yet subsequent events indicate that Hatton's initial exposure to filmmaking kindled some degree of interest in him. Over the next few years, he made more than occasional efforts to establish ties to the motion picture industry – at least in Florida.

On the face of things, the remainder of 1929 passed smoothly for Rondo and Immell. They were among the attendees at the annual Christmas Ball given by the Alpha Tau Omega fraternity at the Forest Hills Country Club. Behind the scenes, however, their relationship was increasingly strained.

Hell Harbor director Henry King. He put Rondo's feet on the path to Lotus Land (Hollywood); once Rondo got there, King cast him in three *more* pictures.

Service with a scowl: *Hell Harbor* cabaret proprietor Rondo prepares to crack open a cold one…over somebody's head.

his movement eye-compelling; and he bashes a bozo's bean with a bottle with the artistry of a Wallace Beery or a George Bancroft. King said Rondo took to the part with greater adaptability and understanding than any amateur he had ever tried out.

But Rondo "couldn't be bothered" with the lure of Hollywood.

He has lived in Tampa too long and likes it too well to answer the call of the cinema.

Within a few years, Henry King's unqualified praise of Rondo's performance would be the foundation of Hatton's entry into a film career.

Whatever high spirits Rondo experienced from these commendations were dashed almost immediately by the extreme pain of his personal life. On February 6, 1930, Immell left Rondo and moved in with her mother and stepfather at their 236 Plant Avenue residence. Rondo was left with virtually nothing – a fact confirmed by *Tampa Tribune* reports on suits filed in local courts. The listing in the April 26, 1930, newspaper includes "Rondo Hatton v. Elizabeth Immell James" among the circuit court filings. Even more telling: On the same day, Rondo filed a voluntary bankruptcy proceeding in federal court.

Rondo's divorce action was concluded relatively quickly; Hatton biographer Fred Olen Ray apparently reviewed the suit record and determined that Immell was awarded $15 a week alimony from Rondo for a pe-

Scenes From Tampa's Talkie "Hell Harbor"
Showing at the Victory Theater

Rondo was prominently featured in one of the *Hell Harbor* photos run by *The Tampa Times* the day after it played at the city's Victory Theater. Pictured: Ruth Hall, Harry Allen, Hatton.

riod of one year. She was represented by her stepbrother, attorney Samuel Bucklew Jr. (not his father, Samuel Bucklew Sr., as previously suggested by Ray). Immell's stepbrother obtained her divorce from Rondo on June

This ad for the Bryan-Hatton Business College, picturing Rondo's father Stewart Hatton, ran in the *Atlantic Constitution* in 1928.

9, 1930. Ray also determined that Rondo was earning $50 a week as a reporter.[3]

Although Hatton's divorce had been completed, his bankruptcy dragged on. Hatton's reduced circumstances forced him to move back in with his mother and grandmother at their Grand Central Avenue residence. The 1930 federal census does not list Hatton's father Stewart among the residents; Stewart had bought out his partner in the Atlanta-based Bryan-Hatton Business College and apparently spent the majority of his time away from Tampa supervising the newly dubbed Hatton Business College.

While Rondo continued working as a *Tampa Tribune* reporter, the continuing financial demands to which he was subjected forced him to look at other options. He continued supplementing his income with disc jockey work, and also looked at other newspaper opportunities. Years later, Hatton's friend R.C. Hilton recalled that time in a *Tampa Tribune* article:

> [Rondo] was one of the nicest guys I ever knew and had a wonderful sense of humor about his features. He and I were best buddies as he took me on to teach me the newspaper business. ...
>
> Rondo acted as a disc jockey for a while for the WDAE radio station. When he got an opportunity to work for a newspaper called the *Jacksonville American*, he took me with him as a cub reporter. ...
>
> Regarding his ability not to worry about his facial disfigurement: Rondo and I were in an elevator in an office building in Jacksonville. While we were standing there quietly, a little old lady kept staring at his face.
>
> Rondo politely removed his hat and went "Boo!" at her. She did not know what to do or say and finally laughed with him.[4]

For whatever reason, the job with the *Jacksonville American* did not eventuate, and Rondo returned to Tampa. He was elected to the executive committee for the Tampa American Legion Post in November 1931.

The year 1932 saw the conclusion of Hatton's personal bankruptcy with the forced sale in November of three parcels of real estate that he had purchased years earlier. His spirits were further brightened when he received a letter from *Hell Harbor* star Jean Hersholt. According to a short item in *The Tampa Tribune*, Hersholt asked Hatton to remember him to "his Tampa friends."

Continuing financial difficulties forced Hatton to abandon his newspaper reporter job in late 1932. He obtained employment with the Celo Company of America, a Tampa bottling company.

Then, in 1933, another opportunity presented itself: The motion picture industry returned to Tampa. T.C. Parker Jr. of Baltimore had a film industry background and he partnered with developer Fred Blair in conceiving Sun Haven Studios to rival Hollywood. Blair and Parker enticed Hollywood director Aubrey Kennedy to join the venture; Kennedy obtained commitments from

A shot from the voodoo sequence of the St. Petersburg-lensed *Chloe*. According to one local press report, Hatton appeared in these scenes - although one wonders quite *where* in these scenes (which pointedly feature only black performers) any footage of Rondo could conceivably have been used.

directors Marshall Neilan and George Melford. Kennedy purchased 500 acres in nearby St. Petersburg and built a large soundstage on Weedon's Island. Contracts were signed for an ambitious slate of 36 pictures.

Filming on Kennedy's first production, *Chloe*, began on May 22, 1933. An adaptation of the novel *Bar Sinister* according to contemporary accounts, it told the story of a girl, kidnapped as a child by a black slave, who grew to adulthood believing herself to be the slave's child. More than 175 people were cast in the film; $14,000 in salaries and other costs were paid out weekly during production.

One of the performers on the payroll was Rondo Hatton. A casting bureau office had been set up in St. Petersburg, and Hatton was quick to seize the opportunity.

According to a *Tampa Tribune* article on the production:

> [O]f those already registered [at the St. Petersburg bureau], more than half have been used as extras. Among the first to register was Rondo Hatton, who had a part in *Hell Harbor*, produced in Tampa some years ago, and Hatton has appeared in a number of scenes.

Another *Tribune* article reported that Hatton appeared "in the voodoo scene" in *Chloe*. Without more information, it may be to some degree speculation, but it seems entirely possible that Hatton enacted his first "horror role" in *Chloe*. That conclusion seems all the more likely when one learns that some of the extras portrayed "zombies" with "expressionless faces" – or, in the lingo used by the film crew, "dead pans."

The production was troubled from its inception; retakes on several scenes were required after a shipment of film was lost in the June 4, 1933, crash of an Eastern Air transport plane near Bowling Green, Virginia. Director Neilan and a game cast (including Olive Borden, Reed Howes, Molly O'Day and Philip Ober) forged on, working late hours until the filming was completed late in June.

Production on Kennedy's second feature, *Playthings of Desire*, began the first week of July under the direction of George Melford. However, the basis of the venture was already starting to unravel. The two distributors that had been contracted to release the pictures, P.A. Powers Inc. and Adolph Pollock's Eagle Distributing, backed out under pressure from the major studios. A planned production intended to star Buster Keaton collapsed in the face of broken promises made by Aubrey Kennedy to Keaton. Then, the failure of negotiations in New York in early August 1933 to obtain alternate distributors forced T.C. Parker Jr., the venture's major financier, to buy out Aubrey Kennedy just as the third film, *The Hired Wife*, was starting production. According to reports, Parker's investment already had totaled close to $100,000. Parker announced that Kennedy's various companies would be absorbed by a new company, Sun Haven Studios.

Part of the reorganization involved a tie-up with a New York company, Florida Pictures Corporation, being organized at the same time to distribute the St. Petersburg studio's films. Parker's purchase specifically included any and all interest that Aubrey Kennedy held in *Chloe* and *Playthings of Desire*. Sun Haven Studios planned to continue producing "the best pictures possible for $50,000."

By November, this initial surge of optimism had vanished. Even though filming on *The Hired Wife* had been completed, it appears that the intended distribution wing, Florida Pictures (to be headed by Adolph Pollok), failed to materialize. On November 16, 1933, T.C. Parker Jr. was interviewed by a *Tampa Bay Times* reporter concerning the results of a trip which Parker made to New York in connection with the sale of the three completed films. Not only did Parker refuse to announce the results of his trip, he stated that he had no plans for a resumption of work at the studio before the first of 1934.

Parker sought new partners in the troubled enterprise. Tampa newspapers reported in December 1933 that Sun Haven Studios had merged with the Beecroft-Florida Studios, a production company that had lately been established in Tampa by Chester Beecroft, former production manager for the Cosmopolitan Company. The new firm stated that it would begin production of eight pictures "at once." After confirming the management of the enterprise, the newspaper reports concluded with the announcement that Rondo Hatton and William A. Dawson would be in charge of public relations for the new company. On some level, Rondo was willing to cast his lot with the film industry.

For years, it did not appear that the company ever completed any films, although a feature comedy, *She Lived Next to the Poor House*, was announced for production "at once" under the direction of Sydney Allcott. For the moment, Rondo's ties to the motion picture industry were severed. The fate of *Chloe*, Hatton's second film credit, was initially unclear; over the ensuing decades, various accounts stated that the film had been impounded by the Internal Revenue Service, that it had been destroyed, or that it had been lost after being exhibited at the Capitol Theatre in St. Petersburg. In 1999, film historians George E. Turner and Michael H. Price announced the re-discovery of *Chloe* – with the subtitle *(Love is Calling You)* – in their 20th anniversary "Definitive Edition" of *Forgotten Horrors*. Yet watching the available print does not make the speculation about Hatton's participation in this "voodoo romance" any clearer. Neither Hatton nor the "zombie extras" can be spotted in the climactic sacrificial ritual.

The failure of these Florida-based film companies left Rondo at loose ends once more. He sought to once again combine his love of sports with his journalistic abilities and obtained employment as publicity director for Downing's Sports Syndicate, a Tampa-based corporation formed to promote wrestling and other sporting attractions on Florida's west coast. The new syndicate began its operations in late June 1934.

While Hatton pursued his newest job, he continued to attend local social events, seemingly feeling that his Tampa friends had adjusted to his increasingly odd appearance. If prior biographical narratives are accurate, he also supplemented his income by returning to freelance journalism. These two circumstances would converge to produce another major development in Hatton's life.

Some time in the summer of 1934, Rondo was assigned by one of the local newspapers to cover a masquerade ball. By some serendipity, he noticed an attractive blonde sitting on a stairway, apparently nodding off to sleep. Years later, Rondo told *Pageant* magazine's Erma Taylor, "She looked like a tired little angel."

Starting a conversation with the "angel," Hatton learned that her name was Mabel Housh, and that she was the dressmaker for the hostess of the ball. She was exhausted because she had "been up all the night before sewing costumes." Hatton and "Mae" (Mabel's nickname) talked non-stop for hours. (Note: In *Pageant*, Taylor spelled Mabel's nickname "May." Rondo spelled her nickname "Mae," so that spelling has been adopted herein, except when the *Pageant* article is quoted.) Rondo learned that Mae was a Tampa native, the daughter of Sylvester and Minnie Housh. (Sylvester was an engineer with a local ice company; he and Minnie had produced six children before Minnie's premature death in 1918.) Rondo also discovered that Mae was twice-married (first to Mack Semse, secondly to James Kaney) and twice-divorced; she had been divorced from Kaney mere months earlier. According to Erma Taylor, Mae's prior failed marriages to conventionally "handsome" men had led her to "value more than looks." As they talked, Rondo's gentleness, spirituality and character kindled an immediate response in Mae. Their mutual devotion increased; they married on September 29, 1934. The *Tampa Tribune* for October 4 reported:

> Miss Mabel Housh, daughter of S.R. Housh, of 106 West Fern Street, and Rondo Hatton, son of Mrs. Emily L. Hatton, of 1007 Grand Central Avenue, were married quietly Saturday night. The ceremony was performed by the Rev. E.C. Nance, pastor of the First Christian Church, at his home, 906 Fremont Avenue, in the presence of friends.
>
> The bride was born in Tampa and received her education in Florida, having lived in Tampa virtually all of her life.
>
> Mr. Hatton is a native of Hagerstown, Md., but he has lived in Tampa for many years. He was on local newspaper staffs for many years but is now connected with Downing's Sports Syndicate.

In contrast to his first marriage, Rondo did not move away from 1007 Grand Central Avenue after marrying Mae; the couple established their matrimonial domicile at his family home. By all accounts, Rondo and Mae were completely devoted to each other from the outset of their marriage. Erma Taylor wrote in *Pageant* that Rondo never wavered in his belief that Mae "was an angel"; Mae always "felt Rondo's love was a miracle."

Within the first few months of their marriage, the couple's fortunes suffered the first in a series of trials. Rondo's employer, Downing's Sports Syndicate, was forced into bankruptcy by its creditors on March 27, 1935, less than a year after the venture started. A federal court enjoined company head James R. Downing, and all persons dealing with him, from promoting any sporting events in Tampa or other Florida cities. Hatton found himself out of work once more.

Whatever distress Rondo and Mae suffered as a result of Hatton's unemployment, their next trial was

Members of the Dramatic Club of the First Christian Church, including Mae Hatton (right).

more painful by far. The newspaper announcement in *The Tampa Tribune* for Wednesday, July 17, 1935, is deceptively routine in reporting the situation:

> Rondo Hatton, 1007 Grand Central Avenue, is a patient at the Veterans Hospital at Bay Pines.

Behind this simple statement lay a much more serious reality. Rondo had been stricken with a severe attack of arthritis, another symptom arising from his advancing acromegaly. He entered the new Bay Pines hospital facilities where doctors tried their best to combat his worsening condition; he was in and out of the hospital a number of times during this period. In January 1936, *The Tampa Tribune* announced that Hatton, "who has been suffering from an infected hand, entered the Veterans' hospital at Bay Pines for treatment yesterday."

Meanwhile, Mae busied herself with volunteer work at First Christian Church – as well as something more. In May 1936, *The Tampa Times* reported that the Dramatic Club of the First Christian Church would present three one-act plays in the Sunday School Auditorium on the night of May 27. "Mrs. Rondo Hatton" was announced as performing one of "the leading roles" in the one-act play *King Sàrgon's Jars*. It seems that, to some degree, Mae was familiar with the lure of acting.

Meanwhile, Rondo's battle with acromegaly's side effects took a significant turn: According to Erma Taylor, He was so incapacitated by mid-1936, "he couldn't even walk." Finally, the Bay Pines doctors advised Rondo that relocating to a drier climate might retard some of the symptoms. In the early 1970s, Hatton fan Robert A. Burns interviewed the actor's wife Mae in California, and learned that it was she who persuaded Rondo to select Hollywood as the "drier climate" – and indicated that Hollywood would also offer him the possibility of employment as a film actor. Rondo initially balked at the notion, observing that Hollywood would just exploit his appearance, and Mae quickly agreed – but she added matter-of-factly that Hollywood exploited the looks of *every* performer.

The decision was made; Rondo would try his luck in films.

According to Erma Taylor, Rondo wrote to director Henry King, who had tried to persuade him to go to Hollywood years earlier. Rondo asked King if the director really believed that a film career was a viable option for him. He supposedly received an affirmative reply that convinced him. A *Tampa Bay Times* reporter recounted a slightly different version of events. The unnamed reporter stated that King had visited St. Petersburg in late 1937 and "took Rondo back to Hollywood with him." There may be some accuracy to this account; Henry King had returned to St. Petersburg on *several* occasions since filming *Hell Harbor*.

There may be additional implicit support for the reporter's account. Previous biographers asserted that Rondo and Mae left Tampa together and moved to California as a couple when Hatton decided to cast his lot in Hollywood. Available information suggests otherwise: Rondo wisely hedged his bets and made the initial trek to California alone, Mae remaining in Tampa with his mother and grandmother at the Grand Central Avenue residence. Why uproot Mae from Tampa if Rondo's film career didn't take off?

In an interview, Hatton alluded to the combination of reasons for his relocation. He said he left Tampa for Hollywood "to see if a change wouldn't benefit my health and also to look around and try this movie business."

The timing of his arrival in Hollywood remains somewhat uncertain. Newspaper articles place the time that Hatton reached the film capital as anywhere from late 1936 to the spring of 1937. Whatever the timing, Hatton described his circumstances:

There was a strike on when I got [to Hollywood], and this added to other things made the business of "crashing" the movies doubly hard. So I just kept plugging away at it and I admit with no success.

Presumably Rondo is talking about an actors' strike that was actually *avoided* in the spring of 1937. If so, then he has told us, over all of the intervening years, that he arrived in Hollywood in late April or early May 1937.

In another interview, Hatton said simply, "I was out here and barely hanging on."

Henry King had promised to help Rondo get his start, but there "was no spot available" in a current King picture: The production of King's *In Old Chicago*, one of the biggest films on the 20th Century-Fox schedule, had been delayed as a result of the death of Jean Harlow, who was set to star. Then Alice Faye signed to play the role intended for Harlow, the film started shooting in June 1937 – and King made good on his promise to Hatton. Rondo told an interviewer that, just as his spirits were at their lowest ebb, he got the call:

Weeks and months went by until late one afternoon I received a telephone call from the 20th Century-Fox studio that Mr. King wanted to see me there as soon as I could get there. You can imagine how I felt and although I was about 12 miles from the studio I am sure I got there by bus and making three transfers in record time.

King needed a character actor for the part of villain Brian Donlevy's bodyguard, and called Hatton. As Rondo recalled:

They took me to the stage set where Mr. King was working with several hundred extras. And was I nervous, because that was the first time I had ever really been in one of these big studios on a working set.

I had hardly become accustomed to the setting before they called me for a scene. There was another of these moments when I found the scene was to be with the star, Tyrone Power, and before an audience of hundreds to whom movie-making was just "old stuff."

Hatton also told the interviewer about the "monkey suit" he wore in the film – pearl derby spats, checkered suit and diamond horseshoe stick pin – before describing his reaction to being told to come back the next morning:

Boy, that was a swell feeling. I was a country yokel, but I got used to things and everybody was swell. They played some tricks, like putting the "hot foot" on you, but we had a great time.

In interviews, King claimed that the film was "the best picture" that he had ever made and reported that the total cost of the production was $1,700,000, with almost a third of that amount devoted to its climax, a painstaking recreation of 1871's Great Chicago Fire. A 270-acre golf course next to the studio was purchased in order to reproduce Chicago. Full-size structures and streets were built. Streetcars, wagons and fire engines were gathered from around the country. When the studio property department asked King if three fire engines would be enough, the director calmly replied, "Seven, at least … and they had to be exactly like those used in Chicago in 1871 and all had to be in working condition to pump water."

As for the climax, King felt it was the "greatest fire ever filmed," and described the scene thusly:

> The special effects department did itself proud on it, and had flames leaping 150 feet in the air. We had to wait for a day that was just right with the atmosphere clear and the wind in the right direction.

> Then we set fire to the city, and it was very cleverly organized. It had to be. Otherwise, it would have burned too fast. They used a pressure pump system through the whole set that covered three square blocks. I yelled "Camera" and in the 11 seconds it takes for a camera to get up the proper speed they had the thing going like wildfire.

Rondo Hatton: Screen Actors Guild member #11,139

Yet King felt that the best part of the production wasn't the fire – it was the simple story of the life of an Irish family that anchored the film. And amid his plaudits for his three "favorite players" – Tyrone Power, Don Ameche and Alice Faye – he provided special praise for Rondo Hatton to a reporter for *The Tampa Tribune*:

> [Y]our own Tampan, Rondo Hatton, comes into his own in the picture. He worked for five weeks in it as a bodyguard and political henchman of [Donlevy].

Hatton's stint on *In Old Chicago* was apparently enough to convince the fledgling actor that he could make a go of a Hollywood career, and he communicated his feelings to Mae. On September 11, 1937, *The Tampa Times* noted:

> Mrs. Rondo Hatton left this morning for Hollywood where she will join Mr. Hatton who has recently completed a movie there. They will make their future home in Hollywood.

In the short term, at least, Hatton's confidence was

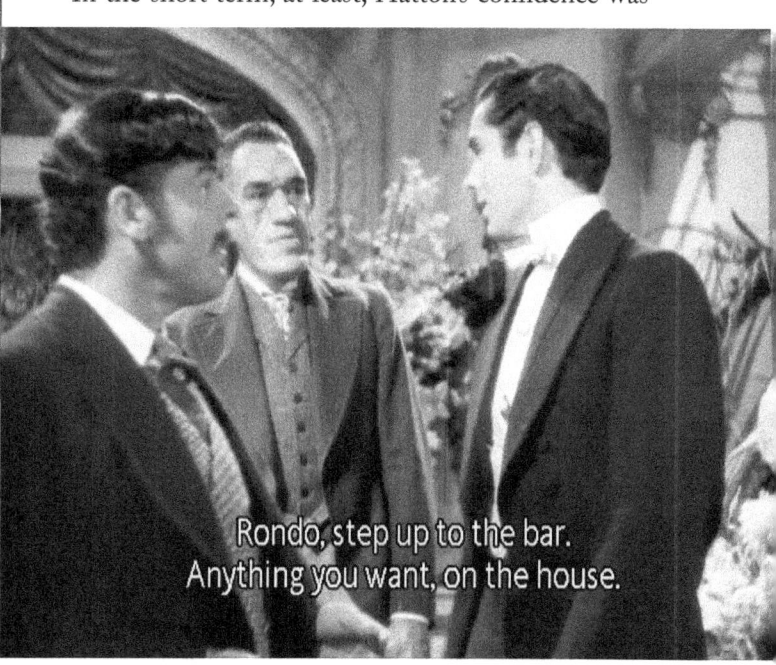

Rondo Hatton made his Hollywood bow (20th-billed) in his director pal Henry King's *In Old Chicago*, a Best Picture Oscar nominee. The frame grab on the right features Brian Donlevy, Hatton and Tyrone Power plus a closed caption which shows that Hatton's minor character was named Rondo. Toward the end of the movie, it's Hatton who shoots co-star Don Ameche.

Rondo phones home.

justified. When *In Old Chicago* had its Hollywood premiere in early January 1938, it received rave notices – and Ed Sullivan directed some of the praise at Rondo in one of his columns:

> Rondo Hatton, who plays the gargoyle-bodyguard of Brian Donlevy in the flicker, is a Tampa, Fla., newspaper man who was gassed during the war…Result, elephantiasis…He'll get plenty of character parts as a result of clicking in this picture…

By the time *In Old Chicago* opened in Tampa on March 19, 1938, local Tampans had already enjoyed a *Tampa Tribune* story in which staff writer Bill Abbott recounted a long distance telephone interview he had conducted with Rondo the previous Sunday (see photo above). After exchanging banter about their mutual friends, Abbott asked him about the film. Rondo's responses say a great deal about him as a man:

> The picture – oh yeah – it's really swell. I mean it. You can't go wrong on that one… Lissen, Bill, I'm not saying that just 'cause I'm in it. I've got only a small mug part, but it's really great.

Abbott then asked, "How many scenes are you in?" Hatton modestly replied,

> Oh, I never counted 'em. Not many, and I stick out in only two or three. But lissen, Bill, if you write something about it, please say that Henry King is one swell guy. He's a grand fellow. He's a prince and he likes Tampa.

Hatton went on to tell Abbott that he had a "stack of fan mail from Tampa," and he added,

> Lissen, Bill, thank 'em all for me. They're mighty kind, and I get homesick every time I get mail from Tampa.

At that point, Abbott asked, "Well, how are you getting along now, Rondo?" Hatton responded,

> Oh, pretty good – fair to middling. I got a day's work yesterday [Saturday, March 12, 1938] in *Alexander's Ragtime Band*, and I'm going back tomorrow. That's another of Mr. King's pictures and it's going to be a knockout, too.

It's got the same stars as *Chicago*, Alice Faye, Tyrone Power, Don Ameche and a whole flock of others. They're just giving me a little atmosphere part in this one. But things are looking pretty good out here. Everybody says they're getting better. I'm gonna stick a while longer anyway, and see what happens.

Hatton ended the interview with a simple request:

Lissen, Bill, do me a favor. Call up my mother and tell her you talked to me.

Perhaps no other statement attributed to Rondo Hatton in print goes as far in summing up the essential character of the man. In the first blush of celebrity, his mother was uppermost in his mind.

According to a *Motion Picture Herald* item, local boy Hatton's presence in the picture was played-up by the Tampa Theater. Its manager Vincent Wade also arranged for moviegoers to send congratulatory wires to the actor in Hollywood: "Through tieup effected with local Western Union officials, booth was set up in lobby, background of which was oversize telegraph blank addressed to Hatton. Folks were handed previously prepared form messages of greeting which they could send at very small cost." At Rondo's request, a friend of his, an invalid war veteran, was brought to the opening show in an ambulance.

Tampans demonstrated their appreciation of their hometown boy when *In Old Chicago* began its local run. Mayor R.E.L. Chancey declared the week of March 20 as Rondo Hatton Week in the city. In his proclamation, the mayor praised Hatton as "an old Tampa boy who has made good," and expressed the hope that the people of Tampa "will give Rondo the big hand he deserves." Tampa's Western Union chief followed up with a wire to Ed Sullivan that same week saying that Tampa was "raving over Rondo Hatton's performance" in *In Old Chicago*. When Hatton learned of Mayor Chancey's proclamation, he responded in typical fashion: After thanking the mayor, he focused on how Tampa could benefit from his connections with Hollywood celebrities. As Rondo made the rounds of the film studios, he discovered that Tampa had "many warm friends" in Hollywood – "wonderfully good, boosting friends, like Henry King." After recounting other Hollywood types who viewed Tampa fondly, Hatton concluded by advising Mayor Chancey that

[s]omehow, Tampa does get under one's skin, and I believe Tampans would do well to take more time to see that these visitors enjoy themselves. I believe more and more "big shots" would be attracted to Tampa and find it a haven of rest and recreation preferable to many spots that are so much in the limelight.

Mayor Chancey was hardly finished in voicing Tampa's support for Rondo. Ed Sullivan's "Hollywood" column for March 28, 1938, was devoted to letters from his readers, including one from Chancey:

My dear Mr. Sullivan: You were good enough recently to give Rondo Hatton, an old Tampa boy, a boost in your column as the result of his splendid performance in *In Old Chicago*. I thought you'd be interested to know that when the picture played here, we set aside the week as Rondo Hatton Week, to express our pride in a local boy who made good in Hollywood. We want you to know that we appreciated very

Rondo's name is bigger than the stars' names … in Tampa, anyway.

much your recognition of him in the column. Best wishes always.

Sullivan's response was simple and complimentary: "Dear Mr. Mayor: If you have any more down home as good as Hatton, send 'em along."

Rondo had already expressed his gratitude to Sullivan in an earlier column:

> Dear Mr. Sullivan: If I ever amount to anything out here I'll have you and Director Henry King to thank for it. Regards, Rondo Hatton

"Rewinding" this biography a few months: In September 1937, around the time *In Old Chicago* wrapped at Fox, Hatton got work on an outright oddity: *Wolves of the Sea* with Hobart Bosworth, Jeanne Carmen and Dirk Thane. Publicity releases described it as "the most sensational melodrama of the season." According to promotional material, the film

> deals with the casting-away on a desert island in the tropics of a young and beautiful heiress, who is the sole survivor of a great ocean liner wrecked nearby. She is rescued by the first mate of a ship which has come to secretly salvage a collection of valuable jewels from the sunken vessel, and is plunged at once into a maze of startling adventures, which includes a mutiny, a second shipwreck, and a love affair with her rescuer that ends happily for both. The film is unique in that its atmosphere is partly that of exciting events upon the high seas, and partly that of the tropical jungles, where thrilling encounters with wild beasts that threaten the heroine's life lends nerve-cracking zest to the fast-moving action.

The film falls somewhat short of the publicist's hyperbole. Insofar as Hatton's involvement is concerned, film historians suggested for years that his appearance was limited to the insertion of *Hell Harbor* stock footage. Film researcher Tom Weaver sacrificed an evening to view *Wolves of the Sea* and discovered that

> this shockingly low-budget flick features a café scene made up of (a) stock footage from *Hell Harbor*, (b) *Hell Harbor* stock footage rear-projected behind the *Wolves* actors, and (c) new footage. Rondo is seen in the old *Hell Harbor* footage – including a couple shots that may not have been in that 1930 movie – and in *new* footage, as a loutish waiter who takes Jeanne Carmen's order, and who plots to rob Dirk Thane.

At some point in the early months of 1938, Hatton appeared as a barfly in Henry King's *Alexander's Ragtime Band*, which King said was "bigger and better" than *In Old Chicago*, and Fox production head Darryl F. Zanuck called "the best picture" his studio ever made. *Los Angeles Times* columnist Edwin Schallert was less effusive after attending the premiere at the Cathay Circle Theater:

> To be sure there are words to be said both for and against *Alexander's Ragtime Band*. Against the picture is its length, and the fact that it is almost too persistently a cabaret show, and further that the ending tapers off.

After acknowledging the film's merits as a "remarkable song cavalcade," Schallert recognized the "singular and beautiful serenity of the episode where [Don] Ameche surrenders [Alice] Faye," concluding that "this particular climax is the making of the picture"; but he went on to observe

> …naught seems anywhere near as impressive afterward, despite the excellence of John Carradine toward the end of the picture in his impersonation of the taxi driver.

Schallert's mention of Carradine merits comment. Besides Carradine, the cast of *Alexander's Ragtime Band* also included 20th Century–Fox contractee Lon Chaney Jr. in a bit as a photographer. It is notable that Carradine, Chaney and Rondo Hatton appeared in this film, when each would achieve lasting fame later at another studio: Universal.

Even while Hatton labored to gain a Hollywood foothold, he never forgot his friends. The June 28, 1938, *Tampa Tribune* reported:

> Tampa Shriners, recently returned from their convention at Los Angeles, got a peep at the inner workings of Hollywood under the guidance of Rondo Hatton, Tampa character actor. Rondo had his biggest part thus far in Henry King's *In Old Chicago* and when the picture was shown here the Shriners reported that Rondo's fan mail for one day exceeded that of Shirley Temple.

Rondo's next mention in *The Tampa Tribune* noted a sorrowful occurrence: the death of his maternal grandmother. According to the October 9, 1938, edition:

> Mrs. Mary E. Berry, 91, grandmother of Rondo Hatton, former Tampan who recently appeared in the movies in Hollywood, died last night at

the home of her daughter, Mrs. S.P. Hatton, 1007 Grand Central Avenue.

Shortly after Mary's death, Rondo's mother Emily moved to California to live with him and Mae. City directories for 1939 indicate that Rondo's father Stewart Hatton initially remained in Atlanta supervising the Hatton Business College.

Early 1939 saw Rondo secure a small role in the Hal Roach production *Captain Fury*. Roach had abandoned his *Our Gang* comedy shorts in favor of full-length features, and after completing the first two *Topper* films, the shrewd producer began casting about for other material – material with a "maximum of action and a minimum of talk." According to Roach,

> In the old days, when there was no talk on the screen, there was plenty of action. Things happened. Now it seems to me that with stage performers coming to Hollywood, and Broadway producers trying their hands at pictures, there is entirely too much dependence on the loudspeakers and not enough on the picture itself.

Roach apparently found the elements he was seeking in a swashbuckling tale of colonial Australia penned for the screen by Grover Jones, Jack Jevne and William deMille. Brian Aherne was cast as Captain Fury, a 19th-century Robin Hood sent to Australia on a convict ship to work out his penal servitude under the brutal conditions imposed by a sinister land baron (George Zucco). The film began production in early January 1939, with producer Roach himself functioning as director. Barracks to house and feed over 200 persons were constructed on Santa Cruz Island, 40 miles off the California coast from Santa Barbara; the lonely island functioned as the film's primary location. Victor McLaglen, Paul Lukas, June Lang, Virginia Field, John Carradine and Douglass Dumbrille had prominent parts and Margaret Roach, Hal's 17-year-old daughter, had a small role. Early in the production, Hatton's role as a convict in the film was apparently viewed as important enough that it generated publicity in the January 23, 1939, *Tampa Tribune*:

> Rondo Hatton, former Tampa newspaper reporter who [played] a political hanger-on in Henry King's *In Old Chicago*, is now an Australian convict in Hal Roach's new picture, *Captain Fury*.

On the set of *Captain Fury*, Hatton, in prison clothes with broad arrows, poses with the movie's technical director Frank Baker.

> The Roach studios announced yesterday that Hatton created such a vivid impression in his *Chicago* part that he was sought out by Joe Collum, casting director for Hal Roach, for a character role of similar significance in *Captain Fury*.
>
> The picture, now in the second week of shooting, depicts on a mammoth scale the colonization of Australia in the 1840s, laying special dramatic emphasis on the plight of prisoners, many of them jailed for difference of political opinion, made to work out their sentence under the cruel lash of Australian land barons of the period.
>
> …Huge sets have been erected under the supervision of Frank Baker, motion picture expert on Australian customs, representing authentic backgrounds for life on the vast ranches. In addition, many days are to be spent on locations in southern California which duplicate to a startling degree the physical attributes of the continent "down under."
>
> Throughout the picture Hatton wears rough prison garb and is one of the most browbeaten of the unfortunate convicts. The advance publicity on the picture did not say whether he leads a rebellion or if he kills anyone.
>
> His mother recently went to Hollywood to live with him and his wife at 228 South Tower Drive, Beverly Hills.

Although this early publicity indicated that substantial footage was devoted to Hatton, such was not the case when *Captain Fury* premiered at Radio City Music Hall on May 25, 1939. Rondo wrote friends in Tampa that his part was not big because many of his scenes were cut during the editing of the film.

The summer of 1939 found Hatton making another brief appearance, this time as a peasant contending for the crown of King of Fools in RKO's lavish version of *The Hunchback of Notre Dame*. Rondo is seen during the film's first few minutes, which transpire on the principal set, a five-acre reproduction of a section of 14th-century Paris, complete with "the marketplace before the cathedral and the stone houses and narrow, winding streets that surround it," as reported by columnist Paul Harrison. Harrison visited the RKO lot early in August 1939 and filed a report that suggests that Hatton's time on the set may have involved some discomfort – a discomfort likely shared with the remainder of the hundreds of extras:

> First thing you see upon entering the set from the mess tent and makeup room is a whole beef being turned on a spit over a bed of real coals. It's a real beef, too. Only trouble is that at this writing it has been cooking for three days and is fit only for burying. Chickens also are roasted over the pit, but the extras see to it that they don't get old enough to spoil.

When [director William] Dieterle started the picture he asked the studio to buy him six loads of city garbage to give authentic atmosphere to the notoriously unclean Paris of that day, but the health department nixed the idea. A realistic stench pervades the place though, because the sun has gone to work on the merchants' vegetables and defunct fowl, the sausages and dried fish. Otherwise the area is full of milling citizens who, assisted by a trained bear and troupes of acrobats and clowns, are doing their best to simulate a holiday mood.

In 1939's *The Hunchback of Notre Dame*, men and women compete to be crowned the King of Fools (the ugliest face wins); the first hopeful is Rondo, and he's booed by a raucous crowd. King Louis XI (Harry Davenport) observes of said crowd, "The ugly is very appealing to them. One shrinks from the ugly, and wants to look at it. There's a devilish fascination in it. We extract pleasure from horror." This might explain why you—yeah, I'm talkin' to you—are holding a Rondo Hatton book.

Columnist Frederick C. Othman reported that Dieterle achieved a compromise when he was denied cobblestones strewn with garbage. RKO technicians bought 7200 cases of celery in order to scatter chopped celery stalks on the set pavement. So much for reducing the stench: The weather was so hot that the company went on a night schedule to reduce the number of players suffering from heat prostration.

It does not appear that Hatton received any publicity for his modest participation in *Hunchback*. Even if he had, it would have been overshadowed by the merry-go-round of publicity regarding the casting of Quasimodo. Before the selection of Charles Laughton for the role, the following actors were considered, pursued or tested: Richard Whorf, Luther Adler, John Garfield, Bela Lugosi, Joseph Calleia, Orson Welles, Robert Morley and Lon Chaney Jr. What newspaper ink that wasn't devoted to this "Quasimodo War" was devoted to the selection of Laughton's protégé Maureen O'Hara to portray Esmeralda after Ginger Rogers had tested for the role.

Several items which appeared in print in 1939 did suggest that Rondo was making some inroads in Hollywood. He was the principal subject in a Ripley's *Believe It or Not* column which appeared in newspapers across the country in late July. A large sketch of the actor served as a contrast to a photograph professing to represent Hatton's appearance in high school. The caption accompanying the two images not only further promotes the notion that Rondo's acromegaly was the result of exposure to poison gas, it also identifies Hatton as a "movie actor who played horror parts without make-up." What is odd about that reference is that Hatton's "horror parts" were still years in the future. Altogether more accurate is an article which appeared earlier in the summer in the weekly *Pic* magazine: "Soft-Boiled Yeggs" highlighted Hatton and five other actors who specialized in "heavy" roles. The majority of the article focused on Rondo, devoting half a page to the novice actor's outside pursuits:

> Rondo Hatton's hobby is writing prose and poetry. For many years he was a Florida newspaperman and has since found his experience covering the police beat in Tampa valuable research for his "mug" acting. He has been killed in scores of films – most unusual death came when he was crushed in the collapse of a building in *In Old Chicago*.

(Actually, we do *not* see Rondo killed in *In Old Chicago*.) The statement that Rondo had been "killed in scores of films" initially seems quite an exaggeration – yet Erma Taylor stated in her *Pageant* article that he was in 23 pictures "in his first three years in Hollywood." Taken together, these assertions argue that Rondo's filmography is significantly greater than hitherto thought.

An August 2, 1939, *Tampa Times* article emphasized Hatton's willingness to go out of his way for old friends – while perhaps more correctly identifying the extent of his film work to that point:

> The Beverly Hills home of Rondo Hatton, former Tampa newspaper reporter now engaged in motion picture work, has become the mecca for scores of South Florida visitors to Hollywood.
>
> This is the report of Mr. and Mrs. B.T. Prell, 803 E. North St., who have just returned from a six-weeks' trip to California. Mr. Prell, who knew Mr. Hatton when he lived in Tampa, called on him and found that to be the usual thing for all South Floridians, especially Tampans, whether or not they are personally acquainted with the former Tampan.
>
> Mr. Hatton said at least 200 visitors from South Florida had called on him this Summer. Most of them know of him only by what they have read of his motion picture work, and call to get his advice on what to see in Hollywood. The former Tampan's friendly interest leaves not one of the visitors disappointed, according to Mr. Prell.
>
> Mr. Hatton also has great bundles of mail sent by persons throughout the South wishing him well in his new work. He has had no big roles – his most important being *In Old Chicago* – but is "doing nicely and is making a lot of friends at all of the studios," Mr. Prell reported.

Among the visitors to Rondo's home that summer were Mae's parents, Mr. and Mrs. Sylvester Housh. Around this same time, Rondo had a permanent addition to his Beverly Hills home. His father Stewart Hatton, now 77, left Atlanta and his Business College to reunite with his wife and son. It is unknown whether Rondo's parents were able to contribute to the support of the modest household once he arrived; perhaps one can draw an inference from the various means by which Rondo and Mae attempted to supplement Hatton's earnings as a film actor. Erma Taylor reported that Rondo paid the rent by reporting for the *Inglewood Daily News*. Fred Olen Ray mentioned in his Hatton article that Mae added to the family income by fashioning little Santa Claus figures which she sold at local department stores. Ray also reported that Mae marketed a brassiere for which she held a patent.

We can now add another source of income: Rondo maintained a mail-order business (which he advertised in *The Tampa Tribune*) called "Shop in Movieland," for which he charged a $1 shopping fee. (On Rondo's letterhead, he called this service "Let Rondo Do It For You.")

However limited the family resources might seem from this vantage point, the sum total income must have been sufficient; the more so since the 1940 federal census enumeration for the Hatton household at 238 South Tower Drive shows that Rondo's family members were among 18 different people living at the same address. Clearly, Rondo, Mae, Stewart and Emily lived in a Beverly Hills apartment building.

Making the rounds of the studios paid off for Hatton. His next documented film part was another convict role in the penitentiary drama *The Big Guy*, starring Victor McLaglen as a prison warden caught between the desire to keep a fortune in stolen money or give it up in order to save the life of a wrongly convicted youth (Jackie Cooper). According to Fred Olen Ray, Rondo's appearance is limited to scenes in which he mills around the prison yard. What makes *The Big Guy* notable Rondo-wise is that it represents the first known film in which he appeared for Universal, the studio which later catapulted him to minor-league fame. Paramount awarded him a small role as a sailor in Dorothy Lamour's *Moon Over Burma*, which went into production in the early summer of 1940. Another Lamour vehicle with a South Seas locale, the film was based on a novel by Wilson Collison, author of *Red Dust*. *Tampa Tribune* movie critic Ruth Alden thought little of the results but noted, "Rondo Hatton, former Tampan, makes a brief appearance in one scene on the river boat, although he is not mentioned in the cast."

Lamour was also featured prominently in 20th Century–Fox's *Chad Hanna* (1940). Title character Hanna (Henry Fonda) is an awkward country bumpkin who joins Guy Kibbee's traveling circus as a stable boy. He eventually becomes part-owner of the circus, all the while juggling the typical romantic entanglements between Linda Darnell and Lamour. Rondo's old friend, Henry King, directed the film, and found a spot for Hatton as a canvas man setting up the circus tents.

The summer of 1940 produced a series of events that focused attention on the essence of Rondo Hatton, the man behind the visage. MGM was enthusiastic about filming *The Yearling*, Marjorie Kinnan Rawlings' touching story of a young Florida boy's attachment to a pet deer. MGM selected Spencer Tracy to play the boy's father, but then elected to conduct an extensive talent search throughout the South to find the right 12-year-old to play son Jody. After eighteen hundred screen tests were made in the South, one of the two finalists was John Kelton, a 12-year-old from Tampa. He was offered a trip to Hollywood for five weeks of screen tests, as was Atlanta boy Gene Eckman. Before Kelton and his family (his father, druggist Floyd Kelton, his mother Mary and his two sisters) even left on their cross-country train ride to Hollywood, they received a letter from Rondo: He had read about John's being a finalist and offered his assistance to the family. Once the Keltons arrived, John was turned over to an acting coach at MGM to prepare for hours of appearances before test cameras; each day, the tests were interspersed with three hours of school in order to comply with California law. In newspaper articles from 1940, Floyd Kelton remarked briefly on Hat-

SHOP in Movieland
HOLLYWOOD, California
by MAIL
for YOUR Christmas, Birthday, Anniversary, or whatever YOUR NEEDS
SHOP BY MAIL in Movieland
at cost plus one dollar shopping fee
Write:
Rondo Hatton
238 S. Tower Drive
Beverly Hills, California

ton's support during the family's time in Hollywood: "Rondo gave us a lot of help and showed us around, and the studio provided every convenience for us."

The full extent of Rondo's help was disclosed by Mary Kelton in a 1983 *Tampa Tribune* article. More than 40 years later, Rondo's kindness was still fresh in her memory:

> We stayed [in Hollywood] several weeks, and [Rondo] was just wonderful to us while we were there. We became well acquainted with Rondo and he came to the hotel every evening to have dinner with us.

According to the 1983 article, Rondo took John Kelton's sisters to play in a nearby Beverly Hills park while John was at the studio making screen tests. The Keltons were also frequent visitors at the Hatton home. Mrs. Kelton summed up Rondo movingly: "He was so kind and humble, and we didn't even think about his appearance. He was a nice friend from then on."

MGM casting director Billy Grady apparently took note of Hatton's kindness. Floyd Kelton disclosed that Rondo was being considered for a part as one of Jody's five brothers.

Yet neither the role nor the film eventuated – at least not at that time. After John Kelton lost out to Gene Eckman for the role of Jody, production was abruptly halted, and *The Yearling* was not made until 1945-46, with Gregory Peck, Jane Wyman and, as Jody, Claude Jarman Jr. Nonetheless, when John Kelton returned home in September 1940 and delivered an account of his Hollywood experiences to the local Rotary Club, he included a special acknowledgment to Rondo Hatton, who helped him "through the maze of Hollywood wonders."5

Rondo's generosity was never spread too thin. In the same week that John Kelton delivered public thanks to him, the national convention of the Veterans of Foreign Wars took place in Los Angeles. The Tampa members of the Florida delegation were quick to report in *The Tampa Tribune* (September 8, 1940) that Rondo had taken the delegates on a tour of Beverly Hills and several of the principal movie studios. Hatton carried the Florida banner in the VFW parade.

A little over a month later, Rondo contributed an article to *The Tampa Tribune*, reporting in his typical crisp, lucid writing style on the motion picture future of Tampa's Jayne Hazard, one of the 13 "Baby Stars of 1940" chosen by Hollywood directors. In late October 1940, Tampa newspapers told the tale of Mrs. Albert Moody, 18-year-old bride of a WPA worker: She was saved from a mysterious paralysis by a nine-day stint in an iron lung. Mr. and Mrs. Moody received a large number of gifts and letters, but it was the "encouraging letter" from Rondo that the couple mentioned specifically.

The year 1941 presents a challenge in documenting the life and film career of Rondo Hatton. There is a puzzling absence of documented film roles for 1941 in Hatton's accepted filmography. In addition, there are very few mentions of Hatton in 1941 newspapers. Both circumstances may be the result of Rondo's focus being elsewhere than his career during the early part of that year. His mother Emily developed a serious medical condition (the nature of which was undisclosed) that required surgery. The situation was grave enough that the Hatton family sent for Emily's younger sister Elizabeth, who had resided with Emily in Tampa from 1931 (after the death of Elizabeth's husband Carroll Shuford) until Emily's move to California. The February 25, 1941, *Tampa Tribune* reported, "Mrs. Elizabeth C. Shuford of the Crescent apartments, left yesterday by airplane for Beverly Hills, Calif., where her sister, Mrs. S.P. Hatton, mother of Rondo Hatton, is seriously ill."

By the middle of March, *The Tampa Tribune* carried the welcome update that Emily "is reported to be improving after a major operation in a Hollywood hospital. Mrs. Elizabeth C. Shuford …, who flew to California to be with her sister, will remain for several days."

Beyond his mother's medical emergency, there are other circumstances that superficially argue that 1941 represented a slack period for Hatton in front of Hollywood cameras. Tampa newspapers were ordinarily quite diligent in keeping their readers abreast of his screen work, yet there were no such items in those

---

> **Fish Face**
> Martha Raye can really howl
> And Ned Sparks has a mean scowl;
> Tampa's Rondo Hatton is tops in horror
> And Greta Garbo can register sorrow,
> But for a look that's commonplace
> You can't beat a fish's face!

Tampans might find Rondo's name *anywhere* in their local newspapers. Tucked away inside the *fishing column* in a May 1940 *Tampa Morning Tribune* is a poem in which he's name-dropped!

papers whatsoever in 1941. These papers did, however, carry more articles *written by* Hatton that year, perhaps suggesting that he had resorted to supplementing his income by returning to journalism. With the start of war in December 1941, *The Tampa Tribune* gave special recognition to another of Rondo's literary efforts. On December 21, the newspaper proclaimed the following in its "Blurbs" column:

> Announced by Publisher E.S. Johnson for publication in the next issue of that sprightly Tampa magazine, *Literary Florida*, is a special story by Rondo Hatton, Tampan in the movie colony, entitled "Hollywood Goes to War."

The sum of these facts can certainly be viewed as establishing that Hatton obtained no film work in 1941, consistent with the actor's accepted filmography. Yet one should be careful about jumping to that conclusion. Rondo's work on screen has traditionally been listed as encompassing approximately two dozen films. But, as we have seen, Erma Taylor asserted in *Pageant* that Rondo was in 23 pictures in his "first three years in Hollywood." If one reviews his traditional filmography for that same period, no more than a half-dozen credits are listed. Even more telling is Taylor's positive statement that Hatton's appearance as the Creeper in *House of Horrors* was his "100th role." Since this information presumably originated from interviews conducted by Taylor with Hatton (or Hatton's wife Mae), it must be accorded a great deal of weight. If Taylor's statements are accurate, this means that Hatton appeared in more than 70 films between 1940 and September 11, 1945 (*House of Horrors*' starting date). Since Hatton's "authoritative" filmlist for that period tops out at a small fraction of that number, it seems quite likely that Hatton's film work is dramatically understated in standard filmographies.

Hatton's next documented appearance was in the all-star *Tales of Manhattan* (1942), an indie made for 20th Century–Fox release. One of its several episodes starred W.C. Fields as a con man who inveigles his way into Margaret Dumont's ritzy home and lectures a soigné high society–type audience on the evils of drink. Blink and you miss seeing Rondo, dressed to the teeth, as a front-row listener. He worked either in late January 1942 when the sequence was shot or, more likely, on March 2, a day spent doing retakes. The segment was cut before release, either because it was too "slapstick" and not in keeping with the rest of the movie, or because it stole the show (sources differed, and *still* differ).[6]

Rondo was again the Face on the Cutting Room Floor when *The Pride of the Yankees* (1942), producer Samuel Goldwyn's brilliantly realized biography of baseball giant Lou Gehrig, was released. Confirmation that he worked on the film came from the actor himself, as reported in the March 27, 1942, *Tampa Tribune*:

> Our old friend Rondo Hatton recently did a little movie work in the Lou Gehrig movie that Sam Goldwyn is making with Gary Cooper, Babe Ruth and others. "We were doing a New York street in connection with some scenes of Lou Gehrig as a youth (1914) and around Amsterdam and 126th," Rondo mentions in the course of a quite long letter from Beverly Hills; seems he got a bit homesick when glancing in the store fronts along the movie-built streets and seeing a real display of cigar boxes with "Made in Tampa" labels…

In his Hatton biography, Fred Olen Ray maintained that Rondo appeared as an extra in Republic's *The Cyclone Kid*, an unconventional Don "Red" Barry western with Barry as Johnny Dawson, a hired gun for a cattle rustler. Dawson's criminal activities generate the funds necessary to pay his brother Bill's (John James) way through medical school in the East. When Bill unexpectedly arrives in town, he shames Johnny into siding with ranchers against Johnny's former gang.

Hatton's next documented appearance was in Albert Lewin's directorial bow *The Moon and Sixpence* (1942), an adaptation of the W. Somerset Maugham novel loosely patterned after the life of 19th-century French painter Paul Gauguin. George Sanders' Charles Strickland is first seen as a London stockbroker who heartlessly abandons his family to go to Paris to paint;

Facing Page: In the movie version of the novel *The Ox-Bow Incident*, Hatton (top) played the minuscule role of townsman–posse member Gabe—a character who *is* found in the novel. In Chapter 2, we learn that Gabe is a hostler (a man who takes care of other people's horses), "a big, ape-built man, stronger than was natural, but weak-minded; not crazy, but childish, like his mind had never grown up. He was dirty too; he slept in the stables with his horses, and his knees and elbows were always out of his clothes, and his long hair and beard always had bits of hay and a powder of grain chaff in them." Gabe has "one meanness": He hates blacks, and shows it later in the chapter. Pictured, top to bottom: Hatton, Anthony Quinn, Leigh Whipper, Francis Ford. (Art courtesy Mike Bannon.)

the outrageous cad causes similar turmoil there before his artistic muse takes him to Tahiti. That primitive Polynesian island is the sepia-toned setting for the final third of the movie, as we see Strickland attracted to a young native girl (Elena Verdugo) who brings a plate of food to a leper (Hatton). Strickland: "I was just thinking how much more fun it'd be to paint [the girl] than that dreadful old leper."

Rondo is heard before he is seen, his leper's bell softly ringing to warn people of his approach. As called for in the Bible, his clothes are torn and his light-colored hair (undoubtedly a wig) disheveled; we also get a look at his stick legs. The moviemakers probably featured this character to establish leprosy in their story, as a prelude to the later scene where a doctor (Albert Bassermann) examines Strickland's face, makes a snap diagnosis and asks Strickland to look in a nearby mirror:

> Don't you see anything *strange* in your face? Don't you see the *thickening* of your features?

And the "look"… how shall I describe it? The books call it "lion-faced." My poor friend … must I tell you that you have a terrible disease?

Strickland's disease is leprosy, but if Rondo ever saw the finished film, this scene surely would have brought him back to the day of the corresponding episode in his own life.

Then Hatton was back at Fox for the Western drama *The Ox-Bow Incident*, director William Wellman's grim indictment of mob violence. Hatton is a member of a large posse that sets out after a rancher's killers. In the middle of the night, they find the rancher's stolen cattle in the camp of Dana Andrews, Anthony Quinn and Francis Ford, who have no bill of sale, and the posse men take the reins of justice into their own hands in this land of rope law. Rondo is just a deep-background, non-speaking

"face in the crowd" throughout, but it's rewarding to play "Where's Rondo?" (the Monster Kid equivalent of "Where's Waldo?") and keep an eye out for him, because he creates as much of a character as any extra could: While Anthony Quinn cheerfully digs a bullet out of his own leg with a knife, Hatton watches for a few seconds and then turns and walks away, apparently unable to endure seeing the full procedure. When the "rustlers" sit on horseback with nooses around their necks and death looming, everyone gapes expectantly except Hatton, who lowers his head, unwilling to watch the triple lynching. And at the end, in a saloon, as Henry Fonda reads aloud a letter the innocent Andrews wrote to his wife as he waited to have his neck stretched, all his listeners (the guilt-ridden posse men) look stoic except for Hatton, who rubs his face with his hand in a way that suggests wiping away tears. [7]

At this point in his film career, Rondo Hatton was very likely frustrated. After a promising start in *In Old Chicago*, five years in Hollywood had yielded him little more than a succession of uncredited bit parts. And there was a darker undercurrent to his stalled professional life: The specter of an early death could never have been far from his thoughts. There was no effective treatment for acromegaly, and the conventional view of the medical community was that death would result from the condition around 30 years after the initial onset of symptoms. This was due in large part to the increased risk of cardiovascular disease as the acromegaly progressed. All available information argues that Hatton's acromegalic condition began to manifest itself in 1918 – which means that Hatton was now up to Year 25 in dealing with the disease. Worse yet, not only was acromegaly threatening Hatton's life, the disease was threatening his ability to provide for Mae and his parents. Hatton clearly needed a significant change in his film career while he could take advantage of it.

While he hoped for better roles, he continued to find other ways to supplement his income. Besides his "Shop in Movieland" service, he also conducted tours to the homes of Hollywood stars, according to researcher Robert Houston.

Surviving records establish that Hatton was neither making the rounds of the studios nor conducting celebrity tours on Saturday, April 25, 1942. Along with millions of other men born between April 28, 1877, and February 16, 1897, he was registering with his local draft board as part of what became known as the "Old Man's Draft," aimed at collecting information on potential U.S. manpower resources for help on the homefront during World War II. Each man was required to complete a two-page registration card along with an extensive questionnaire intended to generate data on the industrial skills of each registrant. Unfortunately, the questionnaires were not preserved.

But many of the registration cards have survived, including Rondo's (see left), which he filled out at his local Draft Board in the Beverly Hills Post Office. The first page lists his place of residence as 308 North Maple Drive in Beverly Hills. The card also confirms the date and place of his birth: April 22, 1894, in Hagerstown, Maryland. His wife Mae is listed as a contact who would always know Rondo's address. Rather than list an employer's name and address, Hatton entered "freelance actor." Most interesting is the second page of the registration card, which focuses on the physical characteristics of the registrant. Besides listing "acromegaly" as an obvious physical characteristic that would aid in identifying him, Hatton declared that his eyes and hair were both brown. What is most striking is the listing of Rondo's height and weight. According to the information provided, Rondo's "approximate" height was 5'11" and his "approximate" weight 182 pounds. Both representations seem at odds with his stature and extremely thin appearance in all of his films, excepting his roles as the Creeper (in which he wears varying amounts of body padding). Most of his film roles suggest that Hatton's weight was closer to the 136 pounds listed as his weight in college. Erma Taylor's *Pageant* article provided a weight for Hatton that seems even less believable – although she provides an explanation that is grounded in Rondo's acromegaly:

> [Hatton's] face bones increased to nearly double their normal size, distorting his features into

In *Sleepy Lagoon*'s amusement park funhouse scene, Judy Canova and Joe Sawyer encounter come-to-life figures of a wolf man, a mummy and more. Rondo (left) is much more prominent in this photo than in the movie.

frightening proportions. His weight went up to 204 pounds, and much of the gain was in the extra bone and cartilage that deformed his face and feet, his head and hands.

Rondo's fans know of no movie in which he appeared between *The Ox-Bow Incident*, shot in the summer of '42, and Republic's *Sleepy Lagoon* (1943), which commenced in late May 1943.[8] Could he have been out of (movie) work all those months? *Sleepy Lagoon* was a vehicle for comic actress–singer Judy Canova to play one of the bumpkin types in which she specialized. Here, as a coffee shop owner in a small town ruled by corruption, she runs for mayor and wins. Her reforms include closing all the bars and re-opening an old amusement park. When she and lowbrow goof Joe Sawyer visit the park's funhouse, a trap door unexpectedly opens under them and they slide down into a torch-lit, castle-like Chamber of Horrors with a giant swinging pendulum. All about are stationary figures of monstrous characters: A wolf man in a sailor's suit talks back to them, as does a cannibal (played by *I Walked with a Zombie*'s Darby

Jones in leg irons), and a Mephisto-like character pokes Judy. She and Joe break into song, and the wolf man and Mephisto join in. Also getting in on the fun are a mummy and a gorilla (Emil Van Horn in his *Ape Man* suit). *Not* getting in on the fun: Rondo, playing a ghoulish stationary figure visible in the blurry background. If he did more than stand stock still in the background, that footage didn't get into the movie.[9]

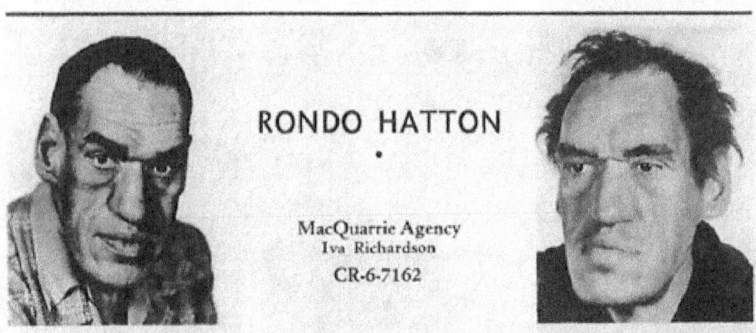

From the June 1944 Players Directory.

Newspapers around this time contain only minor references to Rondo's personal life, beyond blurbs in Tampa papers that he and his wife continued to entertain Tampans visiting Hollywood. California voter registration lists confirm that Rondo and Mae still resided at 308 North Maple; both were registered Democrats.

On the film front, Hatton contributed an amusing vignette as "B. Graves, Undertaker" to Monogram's *Johnny Doesn't Live Here Anymore* (1944), a King Bros. production directed by Joe May. Based on a story from the pages of *Liberty* magazine, this wartime comedy deals with the housing shortage in Washington D.C. Hatton's segment lasts less than 90 seconds, yet May's use of Rondo could serve as a model, in capsule form, of how to present Hatton most effectively on screen. In a street scene set at night, Simone Simon, trying to avoid sailors James Ellison and Chick Chandler, spots a chauffeur-driven sedan with the initials "BG" on its door. Simon asks the chauffeur where "BG" is, and the chauffeur invites her to wait for "BG" in the back seat. Simon arranges herself comfortably in the sedan and waves Ellison and Chandler away; the sailors start to walk off, assuming that Simon has a date.

At this point, the viewer has been enticed into wondering just who this "BG" is – a perfect set-up for generating audience interest. The scene shifts to a nearby building; the placard over the entrance reads "B. Graves, Undertaker." The door is completely in shadow, so that the features of the formally attired man who emerges are shrouded in darkness. When Graves appears at the back door of the sedan, we see that it is Hatton, dressed in top hat and cape, with his features lit from below. His appearance frightens Simon, who exits the car screaming and runs down the street to Ellison and Chandler. Hatton chases Simon and catches up with her as she cowers behind the sailors – but only so he can tip his hat and return Simon's purse, which she left in his car.

Hatton delivers his one line – "You forgot your purse, miss" – in the metallic voice that was another characteristic side effect of acromegaly.

This short incident in a 77-minute comedy is worth describing in detail because it demonstrates just how impressive Rondo's on-screen presentation could be, if a modicum of thought were devoted to utilizing his unique "gifts." Building expectation, initially depicting the actor as a showy outline, artful lighting to emphasize Hatton's face, limiting his dialogue – all are on display in *Johnny Doesn't Live Here Anymore*.

Hatton's presentation in this madcap comedy prefigured the brilliant expansion of that approach in his next appearance – in the film that signaled the crucial turning point in his film career. *The Pearl of Death*, the seventh film in Universal's Basil Rathbone–starring Sherlock Holmes series, presents Hatton in his seminal role as the Hoxton Creeper, the homicidal henchman of criminal mastermind Giles Conover (Miles Mander).

Everything works in Bertram Millhauser's loose adaptation of Sir Arthur Conan Doyle's "The Adventure of the Six Napoleons." Particularly effective under Roy William Neill's assured direction is the suspenseful manner in which Hatton's character is introduced in a series of well-designed steps. Dialogue in the film's first 30 minutes puts audience expectations on high regarding the unseen Creeper. Tension builds as, close to the 45-minute mark, we see the back-breaking maniac's silhouette as he commits a murder. Just short of the hour mark, Neill tantalizes us with glimpses of his shadow, his gloved hands, and views of his back as he follows Conover into the house of the next intended victim. It is close to 65 minutes into the 69-minute film before the audience gets its first good look at Hatton's Creeper: Neill uses artful, atmospheric lighting to enhance the closeup of Rondo's face for maximum impact. Consistent with the earlier references to the Creeper as a monster "with the chest of a buffalo and the arms of a gorilla," Universal's wardrobe department built Hatton up with extensive body padding (as well as likely using lifts to increase his height, since Rondo seems to tower over both others). Holmes tricks the Creeper into

Hey, Rondo ... why the long face? After years on the down-low, your *Pearl of Death* performance will make you a (B) movie star.

Rondo Hatton's horror characters had a habit of either killing their masters, or at least *wanting* to. *The Pearl of Death*'s Giles Conover (Miles Mander), lying at the Hoxton Creeper's (Hatton) feet, was the first to feel the crunch. Sherlock Holmes (Basil Rathbone) wants to avoid that fate.

The real menace in this one is Rondo Hatton who, as the Creeper, displays a very special technique in breaking person's backs. He evidently has quite a future in store for him in horror films since he's really quite good at this sort of stuff. – "R.G.," *Harrisonburg Telegraph*, August 28, 1944

Rondo Hatton [is] the ugliest man you ever clapped an eye on. – Ed Klingler, *Evansville Press*, September 15, 1945

The co-stars' support is very good…. Mander's lethal little playmate is played by heavy-featured Rondo Hatton, and he's a shock to see. – *Cleveland Plain Dealer*, September 9, 1944

killing Conover, then dispatches him with three bullets. Hatton's final scene, as he approaches Rathbone with arms outstretched, is masterfully composed and lighted by Neill, with fine support from composer Paul Sawtell's ominous score. Truly, Rondo Hatton could have hoped for no better realized introduction to audiences as a horror character.

When *The Pearl of Death* was released in the fall of 1944, Rondo found himself listed eighth in the opening credits among the supporting cast -- his first and *only* on-screen credit since *In Old Chicago*. But that was not the most significant benefit to hearten the perennial bit player. Once *Pearl of Death* began playing around the country, a considerable number of newspaper film critics singled him out for particular praise. A sampling of those comments serves to establish the impact of Rondo's performance:

Rondo Hatton is far more frightening than any Karloff or Chaney monster as the pathological Creeper who dotes on [Evelyn] Ankers and always snaps a back at the third vertebrae. –Mildred Martin, *The Philadelphia Inquirer*, February 22, 1945

[*The Pearl of Death*] introduces "The Creeper," whose size and other hideous aspects make Frankenstein look like a kindly nursemaid. In the end Rathbone kills him off; but that probably won't prevent him from staging a comeback in the next of the series. – *Miami Herald*, October 18, 1944

> **Rondo Hatton is a real horror find if he is directed as intelligently as he was in this [film].
> – unidentified 1944 movie reviewer**

Unfortunately, Hatton was fated to never work again with a director as talented as Roy William Neill – and the difference is apparent in his subsequent horror films.

Apparently, Rondo received another benefit from his participation in *The Pearl of Death*: a lasting friendship with dialogue director Ray Kessler. A native of Evanstown, Indiana, Kessler had been coaxed by Universal to take a leave from the Northwestern University drama department and assume the position of "Director of Speech" with the studio. (Universal also led Kessler to believe that he would transition into directing films. That day never came. Kessler functioned as a dialogue coach on Roy William Neill's last seven films – and Hatton's last film, *The Brute Man*.) After working as dialogue director on *Swing Out, Sister* (1945),

Hatton and his friend Ray Kessler, a Universal dialogue director, in 1945.

Kessler turned to writing a screenplay for his newfound friend "Rondo Hatton, that terrible-looking fellow in *The Pearl of Death*," according to *Evansville Press* entertainment columnist Karl Kae Knecht. Knecht included Kessler's concise appraisal of Hatton in his article on Kessler's time in Hollywood – an estimation that was typical of everyone's opinion of Rondo: "Fine chap."

The remaining advantages that Hatton experienced as a result of his *Pearl of Death* role were alternately immediate and far-reaching. The immediate benefit was a paycheck from Universal in the amount of $408.35 (the equivalent of $5826.11 in 2019 dollars) to help support Mae and Rondo's parents. The long-term impact was Hatton's elevation to latter-day horror star. Rondo's ascendancy was inevitable: His appearance in *Pearl of Death* generated such an "avalanche" of fan mail that Universal felt that the character of "The Creeper" warranted a series of films. *The Brooklyn Daily Eagle* reported that

> Ben Pivar, Universal production executive assigned to develop a new series of horror characters, will introduce "The Creeper" to the public in a top-budget picture tentatively titled *The House of Horrors*. The new "chiller" man joins Universal's roster, which includes Frankenstein, Dracula, the Monster [*sic*], the Mummy and the Mad Ghoul.

Pearl of Death's director Roy William Neill didn't want audiences to see the Creeper's face until its closing moments...unaware that an artist would make a big, placid-looking Rondo head shot prominent on the posters!

> Pivar will concentrate his entire activities to a full program of top product. Among the list of pictures he is lining up for the coming year, in addition to *The House of Horrors* is *She-Wolf of London*.

To suggest that Pivar would make "top-budget" films was shameless hyperbole on the part of Universal publicists. Nothing in Pivar's résumé suggested that he was capable of producing a Class-A film, or that he would be trusted with that kind of budget. Yet Universal continued to deceive the entertainment editors on newspapers around the country with overblown claims surrounding Pivar's upcoming productions. Betty French, theater editor for the *Akron Beacon Journal*, was among the gullible. On November 21, 1944, she reported:

Rondo's signature as seen in his 1913 yearbook (top) and on his 1944 *Pearl of Death* contract (bottom). Notice that by '44, Rondo had gotten chichi: Not only does a single line now cross the two "t"s in Hatton, it also completes the "H."

UNIVERSAL, home of the Wolf Man and Frankenstein, is planning to create a whole new set of bogeymen. Ben Pivar, production executive, is working on the problem now and has already devised a new character to be known as "The Creeper." This creature will make its debut in a million-dollar film called *The House of Horrors*!

Universal hadn't devoted that kind of budget to a horror film since the Claude Rains *Phantom of the Opera* (1943), and it was nothing short of shameful to suggest that they had "top-budget" horror films forthcoming. To put it kindly, none of Hatton's horror films could be mistaken for *The Lodger* (1944).

More germane to Hatton's promotion to Universal horror star status is the relative vacancy in that position by late 1944. Bela Lugosi was "out" at Universal after his performance as the Monster in *Frankenstein Meets the Wolf Man* (1943). By the summer of 1944, Boris Karloff had finished a two-picture deal at Universal (*The Climax* and *House of Frankenstein*) and signed a star contract with RKO at a salary of $6000 a week. (Karloff was hopeful for meatier, multi-dimensional roles. He was not getting them at Universal.) Although Lon Chaney Jr. was Universal's biggest horror attraction at the time, his up-and-down relationship with the company deteriorated after the studio heads broke their promise to cast him as the Phantom of the Opera in the 1943 remake of his father's classic. One need only look at Chaney's film appearances in 1944 to see that Universal was probably punishing the volatile Chaney for his on-set misbehavior – or trying to placate his demands for non-horror roles by (mis)casting him in the *Inner Sanctum* series.

Whatever the reason, Rondo Hatton was the beneficiary of an abundance of publicity befitting his new "notoriety." Typifying the promotional material is this item from *The Montreal Gazette*, which provides some biographical details about Hatton for the reader – and an amusing reaction from the unnamed journalist:

> A newspaper is the best training for a wide variety of jobs, it is often stated, and to mull over the list of prominent people who have worked on a newspaper at some stage in their careers, this is easy to believe.
>
> It is, in fact, something of a shock to learn some of the positions for which newspaper work is a foundation. Hollywood offers some fine and mystifying examples.
>
> Take the case of Rondo Hatton, for instance. A former reporter, Hatton has been chosen by the Universal studio for a very important role in a forthcoming film, a role which might develop into a career in itself.
>
> Hatton is to play the Creeper, the latest of the horror characters which the Universal scriptwriters have dreamed up to scare the daylights out of the less sophisticated members of the screen audience.
>
> As such, the Creeper will be following in direct line of succession that noble company of characters which included the Phantom of the Opera, Frankenstein's Monster and the eccentric Count Dracula (all having had literary lives before their screen success). The Ghoul, the Mummy and the Wolf Man are the more purely cinematic creations which have evolved on the Universal lot. Now comes the Creeper, to make his bow in a series of films, the first being labelled *The Brute Man*.
>
> No details are forthcoming about the Creeper, but the name conveys a picture of something loathsome. Just why Universal had to pick a former newspaperman is a little difficult to understand, but it's a disturbing thought.

While those Universal script-writers worked on fashioning a suitable vehicle for Hatton and the Creeper, Ben Pivar moved his new contractee into a supporting role as "Moloch, the Brute" in *The Jungle Captive*, third and final film in Universal's Ape Woman series. Hardly the "top-budget" film promised in publicity releases for Pivar, this sluggish, cliché-ridden film began production on August 31, 1944, and wrapped on September 16. As

A Los Angeles women's group called *The Jungle Captive* "not fit for human consumption" and the *L.A. Times* noted that Hatton's performance "drew only giggles from the audience kids." And no jungle! Pictured: Hatton, Vicky Lane, Otto Kruger.

the assistant to Otto Kruger's stock mad scientist, Rondo's Moloch has the bulk of the first ten-plus minutes of the film largely to himself, and initially establishes an imposing presence – an impression that vanishes almost completely over the remaining 50-odd minutes of film. Deprived of the body padding (and lifts?) which made Hatton so impressive in *The Pearl of Death*, Rondo seems almost diminutive, making it difficult to believe that Hatton weighed 182 pounds, as he indicated on his draft card, or 204 pounds, as Erma Taylor stated in *Pageant*.

But it was not Hatton's stature that was most damaging to his on-screen persona in *The Jungle Captive*. Writers M. Coates Webster and Dwight V. Babcock bestowed upon Hatton's character a good deal of dialogue, the delivery of which seemed to be beyond Rondo's reach as an actor. Hatton speaks his lines in a metallic rasp that may be an attempt to add dimension to his role – or one of the reported side effects of acromegaly. His apparent difficulty with dialogue in *Jungle Captive* seems at odds with his talent as a journalist – his writing always showed every indication of intelligence and perception. Perhaps Rondo was more of an actor than he has been given credited for. Whatever his talent may have been, Phil Brown, Rondo's *Jungle Captive* co-star, remembered him as a "pleasant man" in a latter-day interview.

Rondo earned $1250 for his efforts on *The Jungle Captive* ($18,215.92 in current dollars), more than enough to tide the actor over while he awaited the start of his promised series of Creeper films.

Thanks to Erma Taylor's *Pageant* article, as well as several other sources, we know how Hatton filled his days between films in the mid-1940s. *The Tampa Times* was among the newspapers that reported that he spent his spare time among disabled World War II veterans, demonstrating to them how he had overcome his own handicap "to achieve success and happiness." Taylor expanded on this further example of Hatton's kind-hearted nature:

> Rondo was first and foremost a war veteran; he'd spent his youth in the Army, and what should have been his best years in hospitals among the disabled. Even after he'd become a prominent actor he spent every spare moment among young veterans, making them laugh.
>
> "Look at me, boys – you won't believe it, but I won a beauty contest once," he'd say. And then, when he'd amused them into forgetting themselves, Rondo put every ounce of sincerity and faith he had into – not a lecture, but a heartfelt sermon. Life was still good, he told them. There was still a job ahead for them to do. There was still happiness ahead for them, too.

The arrival of the year 1945 saw Rondo Hatton still waiting expectantly for the beginning of production on his Creeper series. While he probably felt he was in a race against the worsening physical manifestations of acromegaly, an event affecting the entire motion picture industry threatened to obstruct the start of any new productions: A strike stopped movie production at five of the major studios on Monday, March 12. Universal was among the studios that had to call off its shooting schedules when key personnel refused to cross picket lines that had been set up as early as six a.m. Only a third of Universal's 2000 employees reported for work. The focal point of the work stoppage grew out of a jurisdictional dispute between the AFL Set Designers' Local 1421, Painters' International Union and the Local 44, AFL International Theatrical Stage Employees. Each organization claimed to be the legitimate bargaining agent for the motion picture industry's 78 set decorators. Herbert Sorrell, president of the Conference of Studio Unions, forced an escalation of the squabble when he called on 8000 members of nine industry unions to walk off their jobs to force the studios to recognize Local 1421. Among the other unions supporting the strike were the industry carpenters, machinists, painters, electricians and plumbers.

By March 22, Sorrell was ignoring an edict from the War Labor Board to terminate the strike. According to Sorrell, studio executives had urged the set decorators to accept jobs as carpenters and painters in an attempt to wreck the Set Designers Local 1421 Union. Once that effort was rebuffed, Sorrell promised that the strike would continue, even though it was in disregard of labor's no-strike pledge. Although studio heads admitted that production had been slowed by the absence of skilled carpenters, painters, machinists and set decorators, 26 feature pictures were still in the process of filming. Universal achieved a minor victory when 19 plasterers who had refused to work on March 20 were back on the job.

It was during this hiatus from film work that Rondo began splitting his spare time between visits to disabled veterans and serving as host to a particular serviceman from Tampa. According to Fred Olen Ray, naval officer Tom Kaney, stricken with pneumonia during his military service, convalesced at a Los Angeles naval hospital. (Kaney was the nephew of Mae's ex-husband James Kaney. It is a compliment to Mae that she and Tom apparently remained close after her divorce from Tom's uncle.) Whenever Tom was allowed to leave the hospital, he would have dinner with Rondo and Mae. Ray interviewed Kaney about his time spent with the Hattons and found him to be a valuable source of information in relation to the last few months of Rondo's life. A few passages from Ray's article shed light on Rondo's personality and preferences:

> [Kaney] and Rondo would converse for hours about Tom's military experiences, the subject often crossing over into Rondo's own colorful military career and, of course, the world of sports.
>
> Kaney and the Hattons would sometimes eat out at the Brown Derby, a famous show folk restaurant. He remembers Rondo once speaking with child star Margaret O'Brien while there. "He never spoke much about his movies," Kaney recalls. "I asked him to take me down to the studio to have a look around, but he never would." Kaney recalls that Rondo did go down often to check on work, but was generally not very interested in films. "He was a real homebody, very unassuming."

It is quite possible, given Kaney's comments, that he actually resided with Rondo and Mae for a time. If Kaney lived with the couple in addition to Rondo's parents, it is no wonder that those who knew Rondo best were later quoted as calling him "friendly, kind and charitable beyond his means."

During this same period, Pivar reportedly solicited storyline ideas from the public for its new horror character, the Creeper. According to *The Los Angeles Times*,

> Since decision was made about "The Creeper," namely choosing Rondo Hatton for the role, Universal has had no end of letters with suggestions. One was received from a young lad afflicted with nightmares who said that he would be glad to write his experiences while dreaming to aid film. A patient at a sanitarium was willing to submit her hallucinations. A minister feels that religion should be used to overcome the horror phenomena.

Meanwhile, the motion picture strike dragged on. In April 1945, a series of payroll suspensions generated more unwanted publicity for the movie companies:

> The Screen Actors Guild is investigating suspension of seven screen contract players and three directors from film studio payrolls because of the four-week-old motion picture strike.
>
> Universal and Republic Studios suspended Jane Frazee, Dale Evans, a group of western players and three directors.

While the motion picture strike stretched into the summer of 1945, *The Jungle Captive* began playing across the country, reviewers taking note of Rondo's contribution. In the July 12 *Shamokin News-Dispatch*, a critic recommended the film to "entertainment seekers who feel the need of chills and thrills." After commenting favorably on the acting of Otto Kruger as well as Vicky Lane's makeup ("one of the top wonders turned out by Hollywood's cosmetic experts"), the writer turned to Hatton:

> Rondo Hatton, whose face you must see in order to believe there can be one like it, appears in a heavy role. Hatton exerts an eerie spell, and will no doubt become a star soon in horror stories; he's that chilling.

By July 1945, the motion picture strike had moved into its fifth month amid sporadic reports of minor work stoppages and confrontations between studio employees and picketers. At Universal, production on *The Royal Mounted Rides Again*, a 13-chapter serial, was set to begin. The chapterplay dealt with the conflict between outlaws and the Mounted Police in the

Hatton's hometown paper *The Tampa Tribune* reviewed *The Jungle Captive* and mentioned that "[a] number of nervous people got up and left the show before the end...." One wonders if it was actually nerves that forced Tampans to desert the theater before the credits ran!

northwest wilderness, and was intended to focus on "a new screen team," young stars Bill Kennedy and Daun Kennedy. Tragedy struck the production on July 16: The United Press report appeared in the *Knoxville News-Sentinel* the next day:

> Addison Randall, stage and screen actor and husband of actress Barbara Bennett (and the brother of Republic Western star Robert Livingston], was killed yesterday when he fell from a horse during his first day's work on a new serial at Universal Studios.
>
> Randall, who was an expert rider and formerly acted in Western pictures under the name of Jack Randall, was riding fast when he seemed to be losing his hat, a studio official said.
>
> He tried to grab it and fell, striking a tree. He died almost immediately, and the body was removed to a mortuary in Canoga Park.
>
> The accident occurred on his third ride for the cameras. He was making a serial to be called *The Royal Mounted Rides Again*.
>
> Randall, who only recently returned to Hollywood to re-enter pictures after a period in New York,

had not even been to the studio, but had reported directly to location for his first day's work.

Studio contractee Rondo Hatton was set to join the production in a bit part as Robert Armstrong's bodyguard when another disaster struck the Universal lot. Newspapers across the country contained details in their July 19 editions. The report in *The News-Herald* for Franklin, Pennsylvania, was typical:

> Universal Studio officials estimated today that $250,000 damage was done by fire which swept through six acres of sets, destroying irreplaceable stage properties and sending film stars scurrying to safety.
>
> Fanned by a strong wind, the fire started yesterday on the "back lot" and destroyed the historic Tom Mix prop barn housing 70 carriages and other antique vehicles, some more than 200 years old.

Within a short time, studio officials upped their estimate of the damage to $500,000, after determining that other "outdoor sets which figured prominently in early screen history" could not be salvaged. Interestingly, none of the newspapers reporting the fire suggested any connection to the ongoing motion picture strike.

To add to the obstacles at Universal, a heat wave had hit California. Newspapers noted that on August 3, 1945, the heat at Universal reached 104 "and it was feared new costumes would have to be made – everyone was losing so much weight..."

At this late date, it is unlikely that we will ever know if all, or any, of these circumstances were at the bottom of the delays in the start of Rondo's Creeper films. Whatever the reason, the lag in production did allow Hatton to catch up on reading the Tampa papers, and that free time led to another instance of Rondo's considerateness. In 2000, a *Tampa Tribune* article on *Hell Harbor* included a reference to Hatton. That mention generated a letters column response from reader Camille Garcia Reynolds, who said that she graduated in 1945 from Hillsborough High School and was awarded a University of Tampa scholarship by the Elks Club – a bit of news carried by *The Tampa Tribune*. She continued, "Although living in California making movies,

Marcel (Martin Kosleck) helps the half-drowned, bullet-ridden Creeper (Hatton) out of the river and, within a few days and on a $3 budget, makes him good as new. Artist shmartist, Marcel should be a doctor!

Mr. Hatton kept up with the hometown news. I had no idea who he was or what he looked like when I received his letter." In his August 20, 1945, letter to Reynolds, Rondo wrote:

> Congratulations. All good wishes upon winning the new Elks scholarship to the University of Tampa. As a former Tampan, I was reading an old *Tampa Tribune*, hence learned of your splendid record. I am sure you will continue this record in college under directions of my friend, Dr. [Elwood] Nance [president of the university] … Sincerely, Rondo Hatton

According to Camille, "I was so impressed that a celebrity and a perfect stranger had taken the time to write such a nice letter. I wrote back thanking him and wishing him well." As we shall see, Hatton wrote Camille a return letter – correspondence that will appear in its proper sequence hereafter.

Seeing this 1945 correspondence certainly argues that Rondo's writing skills were intact, and runs counter to the prevailing notion in recent years that Hatton was struggling intellectually by late 1945.

By September 1945, Rondo had completed his minor appearance in *The Royal Mounted Rides Again*, and the camera was finally ready to roll on the first film in the long-promised "Creeper" series.

Ultimately released as *House of Horrors* but initially titled *Murder Mansion*, the film began production on Tuesday, September 11, 1945. Hedda Hopper thought the start of filming was of sufficient importance that she led off her September 13 column with this announcement:

> Horrors and whodunits are crowding hard on the heels of musicals in our postwar pictures. Kent Taylor gets the lead in *Murder Mansion* – guaranteed to turn you white. And Universal's very proud of its latest zombie, Rondo Hatton, who plays a character called "The Creeper," and who'll creep through a whole series b'gosh!

(Actor Kent Taylor *was* announced for the film, but radio announcer–actor Bill Goodwin instead played the detective role intended for Taylor.)

In September 1945, when *Pittsburgh Press* entertainment reporter Florence Fisher Parry visited Universal with the specific intention of interviewing producer Walter Wanger, she remained to see what was going on at the studio. Parry noted that Wanger was attempting to give horror pictures "airs" by referring to films such as *Scarlet Street* as "psychological thrillers." Parry wasn't buying the attempted distinction:

> …While right on the same lot *The Royal Mounted (still) Rides Again* and *The Daltons Ride Again* and *Murder Mansion*, a blood-curdling horror class B quickie starring Universal's latest monster, Rondo Hatton ("The Creeper"), give honest testimony to Universal's steady policy of Open Thrills Openly Arrived At.

From Wanger's *Scarlet Street* to Universal's *Murder Mansion* wasn't a far step literally *or* figuratively. The setting for *Murder Mansion* was pretty heeby-jeeby, I must admit – the monstrous "Creeper" (not a bit of makeup, either) hunched over off-set talking baseball scores with a couple of cronies.

Rondo found the time to do more than hash over baseball scores with studio pals during filming. In the waning days of filming his most important role to that point, Hatton took the moments required to pen another letter to his newest fan, scholarship recipient Camille Garcia. An excerpt from this follow-up correspondence again serves to highlight the innate decency of the man behind the face:

> …I know you're happy about winning the scholarship, and although as you wrote it is only for one year, don't be afraid or alarmed. Just remember it's

The Creeper is already a walking crime wave before the start of *House of Horrors*, but he really gets cracking once his benefactor Marcel declares open season on New York art critics.

In this shot from the *House of Horrors* finale, the Creeper (Rondo, on floor in foreground) has caught a police bullet – but he'll live to creep again some other day. And Marcel (Martin Kosleck), dead in the background, waves to his fans! (Courtesy of Ronald V. Borst/Hollywood Movie Posters)

the first step along your way to your goal and that we advance and go forward only step by step.

So keep your chin up, and do your best day by day and you will find all will come out OK, no fooling. …At the moment, I'm working on a new movie, *Murder Mansion*, hence kept pretty busy. Thank you, too, for your good wishes for my movie work.

Every good wish to you and yours, and I wish you a happy and successful school year.

Here we have, in a nutshell, the essence of Rondo Hatton in the twilight of his life – a loving, spiritual man willing to offer encouragement to a stranger, while imparting life lessons learned from experience in an open, accessible fashion without seeming patronizing. Decades after her brief correspondence with Rondo, Camille was still moved to add her opinion of Hatton to those sentiments expressed by so many who were close to him:

"What a nice man he was!"

Three-year-old Lorie Pivar, *House of Horrors* producer Ben's daughter, sat in Hatton's lap and lived to tell the tale! (Photo courtesy Thomas Reeder.)

By the time *Murder Mansion* had concluded production on September 25, 1945, Rondo had made a similar impression on his co-star Martin Kosleck, with whom Hatton shared the bulk of his scenes. Years later, when Kosleck was asked about working with Rondo, he replied simply: "He was a pleasure to work with – intelligent, sensitive and kind."

Late September 1945 saw Hatton preparing for his next feature under his Universal contract – an event noted in the context of another short item appearing in Rondo's hometown paper, *The Tampa Times*, for Friday, September 28:

> Marine C.J. Giler takes time during his journey to the Army of Occupation in China to report that Rondo Hatton, former *Times* reporter turned movie star, is still entertaining Tampans on the West Coast. The Marine says he was a guest at the Hatton home in Beverly Hills two times while he was there and met several other Tampans visiting there. "You can take it from me that Tampa and Florida have no bigger booster in the U.S. than old Rondo. He really sells Tampa," Giler writes. He reports at the same time that Rondo is now working in three pictures.

The second of those three pictures, *The Spider Woman Strikes Back*, had Gale Sondergaard in the sinister title role, Hatton as her mute partner in crime and an unusual setting for a Universal horror: Small Town America, cattle country. Filming began on Monday, October 1, 1945, after months of unexplained delays – a feature common to Hatton's final three Universal films. Again, part of the delay may have been attributable to the motion picture strike which had entered its eighth month. Violence broke out at the nearby Warner Bros. lot that same week as pickets set up a blockade around the studio. Two automobiles were overturned and one man was stabbed before the Burbank police force called in the Glendale P.D. and the Los Angeles County sheriff's department to deal with more than 300 pickets. All the while, Universal executives attempted to divert attention from the strike by focusing on their seven pictures in production: Studio manager David Garber had publicity releases appearing in newspapers around the country emphasizing "business as usual" on the lot. Among them was the following announcement from *The Brooklyn Daily Eagle*:

> Universal has signed Brenda Joyce and Kirby Grant for the romantic leads in *The Spider Woman Strikes Back*, Howard Welsch producing.

The Spider Woman Strikes Back gave Hatton a no-dialogue role as villainess Gale Sondergaard's mute butler..

> Rondo "The Creeper" Hatton will also have a featured role.
>
> Production starts this week under the direction of Arthur Lubin.

During the second week of *Spider Woman Strikes Back* production, Universal's luck ran out. On October 11, an estimated 500 picketers left Warner Bros. to mass at Universal at 6:40 a.m. The announcer in the broadcasting truck for the strikers blared at intervals:

> Universal closed down tight at 7 a.m. We're going to move on every studio in this damn business and do the same.

The October 12 *Los Angeles Times* carried a fairly complete summary of the events at Universal on the 11th:

> One worker who tried to enter the studio was tossed into the shrubbery by the strikers; another worker trying to slip through the picket line was hustled away from the gate.
>
> Character actor Donald Meek drove up to the gate only to be "hooted away." Basil Rathbone arrived in a station wagon to work on the Sher-

lock Holmes film *Terror by Night*, but was "deterred from driving through the gate."

When assistant director William Tummel started to drive through a line of 50 pickets, the strikers grabbed his car and began to tip it over before Tummel backed up his car and drove off. Script girl Dorothy Hughes had a similar experience.

Studio manager Garber was forced to admit defeat. Early on October 11, he announced to the press that "it looks like we won't work today." One of the Universal studio policemen took the news less than gracefully. An Associated Press reporter related that the unidentified policeman dragged one of the picketers into the studio and told him, "If you guys want trouble, you are going to get it," before he released the picket.

Spider Woman Strikes Back was affected: For the tenth day of production, Thursday, October 11, the original plan was for actors and crew to make their third location trip to the Providencia Ranch,[10] this time to shoot farm and pasture exteriors. But they did not go "because of strike conditions," according to a notation on assistant director V.O. Smith's Daily Report. In fact, nothing was shot that day. The moviemakers convened the next morning on Stage 15's Spider Room and Conservatory set but shooting could not commence promptly because, according to the Friday the 12th Assistant Director Report: "No Camera Crew." Up until this date, Paul Ivano was the movie's d.p.; but this day the job was done by a late-arriving Jerome Ash (the *Flash Gordon* serials, *The Phantom Creeps*, *Buck Privates*) and some substitute camera crew members. Cameras finally rolled around 11:30 a.m. The following morning, Saturday the 13th, there was *another* new d.p., Charles Van Enger (*Night Monster*, Sherlock Holmes movies, Abbott and Costello movies), a different substitute camera crew and another late start (they didn't get their first shot until 12:15 p.m.). On Monday, however, Ivano and his crew returned and things got back to normal. Scheduled for 12 days shooting, *Spider Woman Strikes Back* wrapped on its 15th day, October 18.

By this time, a federal conciliation commissioner, Earl J. Ruddy, had been appointed by the Labor Department to attempt a settlement of the strike. As the strike limped toward its end, Universal responded with an immediate solution – one which may have affected Rondo and the *Spider Woman* cast and crew, and offered some levity in the reporting. *The Central New Jersey Home News* disclosed:

Hatton occupies himself in Gale Sondergaard's subterranean Chamber of (Botanical) Horrors in *The Spider Woman Strikes Back*.

> In the closing days of the Hollywood strike, Universal studio stars were ordered to report for work as early as 5 a.m. to avoid the picket lines, which usually formed around 6. One morning a big-name glamor girl was having a cup of coffee in the studio café at 5:15. An electrician came in, sat down beside her and said: "This is wonderful. My wife has always wondered what you looked like at 5 o'clock in the morning. Now I can tell her!"

The prolonged motion picture strike finally ended on Wednesday, October 24, 1945, nearly a week after completion of *The Spider Woman Strikes Back*. Hatton should have been particularly delighted since this meant one potential obstacle to the start of his next film, *The Brute Man*, had been eliminated. It is likely that he was also happy to return to the lead role of the Creeper in this next production, since it should have been obvious that his role as "Mario, the Monster Man" in *The Spider*

Rondo as Mario, the man-of-all-work in the Spider Woman's house of horticultural horrors.

Woman Strikes Back almost plays as an afterthought in the completed film.

The Spider Woman herself, Gale Sondergaard, supposedly once said that, during the making of that movie, she believed Hatton's visage had been achieved by Universal's resident makeup genius Jack Pierce. To be fair to Sondergaard, she may have been influenced by a shameful falsehood that circulated in newspapers around the country after the completion of *House of Horrors*: The unsourced article identified the Creeper as the "newest of monsters" introduced to the screen by Universal, before adding:

> Hours of skillful planning and work went into the daily morning makeup of Rondo Hatton, who portrays this grotesque character, for much makeup was needed to transform this good-looking actor into the hideous, frightening man.

One can only hope that Hatton never saw this disgraceful item in the last months of his life.

While Rondo awaited the start of *Brute Man* production, the *Shamokin News-Dispatch* reported:

> Someone printed a yarn recently that Universal Producer Ben Pivar was looking for more stories to follow [*House of Horrors*] in his horror series. Now he has a letter from a woman patient in a psychopathic hospital reading: "For five years I have been having the most horrible dreams which would be perfectly wonderful for murder movies. I'll try to remember some and send them to you."

Meanwhile, Pivar's star may have undertaken an errand of mercy. What is open to question is the timing of the occurrence, not the fact of it.

In the 1980s, longtime film buff Robert Houston contacted a number of Rondo's friends and associates in an attempt to compile material for an article or book on Hatton. One particular story about Rondo stuck with Houston. In one of his interviews, he learned that Rondo once went to Tampa to help finance an operation for the child of a friend. There is some logic in concluding that this event happened late in Rondo's professional career. His financial resources had certainly improved since he signed his Universal contract, and Rondo would have been in a better position to offer money to a friend. Moreover, the break in filming between *Spider Woman Strikes Back* and *Brute Man* offered Hatton ample time to travel from California to Tampa and back again. In fairness, one must concede that, to some degree, these arguments also apply to the nearly year-long gap between *The Jungle Captive* and *House of Horrors*. Perhaps it is ultimately more important to catalogue another example of Hatton's unqualified generosity than to know when his kind gesture took place.

Los Angeles Times entertainment scribe Edwin Schallert capped off his column for Thursday, November 6, 1945 with the following notice of Rondo's next effort:

> Although not designated as one of the "Creeper" series of shockers at Universal, *The Brute Man* is probably just that, because it has Rondo Hatton in the starring part.

Of course, Schallert was correct, and production on the next Creeper saga began on November 15. As a title, *The Brute Man* may have been a nod of identification to Rondo. Publicity dating back to the production of *The Jungle Captive* claimed that Hatton was "known in Hollywood circles as the 'Brute Man'" and referred to him as "the most fantastically visaged actor." Wherever the title came from, the Universal casting department did its part to insure the success of the film by surrounding Rondo with an abundance of reliable character actors to support the action: Donald MacBride, Peter Whitney, Joseph Crehan, Tristram Coffin, Charles Wagenheim and John Hamilton all lent their talents to the proceedings. Tom Neal and Jan Wiley joined studio contractee Jane Adams in more substantial roles.

With a break for Thanksgiving, filming on *The Brute Man* under Jean Yarbrough's direction ended on Friday, November 30. After a hiatus of almost a year (not counting a virtual bit part in *The Royal Mounted Rides Again*), Rondo had completed three films in less than three months. *Akron Beacon Journal* theater editor Betty French later wrote, "During the making of all these films Hatton was in good health and seemed vigorous, both mentally and physically, his co-workers said. And he was well-liked by his associates."

It is highly likely that the kindly Hatton was "well-liked by his associates" – that assessment was confirmed in later years by castmates Phil Brown and Martin Kosleck. One co-worker, however, cast doubt on Hatton's mental alertness during the production of *The Brute Man*. In Jane Adams' later years, she recounted in several interviews that Hatton was "almost autistic" in his scenes with her – yet she, too, confirmed that Rondo was "a nice, thoughtful person."

Rondo merited a respite from work as Christmas approached, and according to Fred Olen Ray, the family made reservations to leave on a trip to Tampa (Rondo, Mae and Rondo's parents) on Sunday, February 11, 1946. Ray also mentioned that Rondo

> found time in Los Angeles to have a long bedside chat with little Bobby Suarez, a 15-year-old crippled boy from Tampa who had been brought to the city for a serious operation. Hatton and the boy's mother had been newspaper writers together in Tampa and the visit must have certainly impressed the youngster.

Could Bobby Suarez have been the child whose operation was partially financed by Rondo? The basic outline of facts certainly fits, but in Robert Houston's anecdote, reported earlier, the operation took place in Chicago, not Los Angeles. If this was, in fact, the operation that Hatton helped to pay for, it is added support for the conclusion that Rondo had made a prior trip to Tampa in the fall of 1945.

In hindsight, Jane Adams made the more accurate appraisal of Rondo's health by December 1945: His acromegalic condition continued its progression, and its worsening side effects finally manifested themselves during the Christmas holidays. Family friend Tom Kaney told Fred Olen Ray about joining Rondo and Mae at a neighbor's house for a small Christmas get-together:

> Rondo had gone home for a minute to bring over a potted plant that was to be a gift for the neighbors. When he did not return, Kaney went outside to look for him and found Hatton standing on the walk, dazed, the flowerpot smashed at his feet. He said he thought he was all right, but doctors later concluded he had a mild heart seizure.

Despite this foreshadowing of disaster, Rondo continued to look ahead to the trip to Tampa. He also kept up his contacts with Tampans visiting Hollywood. One visitor, Hillsborough High School graduate Peter Conte, had been in the Air Force during World War II. During his military service, Conte appeared in a touring comedy revue that generated favorable critical response. Convinced he could become an actor, he headed for Hollywood after the war. The aspiring actor knew that Rondo, another Hillsborough High graduate, "had made a name for himself in the movies." Conte had also been told that Hatton was known for welcoming visitors from Tampa. In a May 1990 *Tampa Tribune* article, a writer related Conte's plan to meet Hatton:

> Conte was too shy to try a direct approach, and he took a job in a restaurant while he waited for his break. One day, Rondo Hatton walked into the restaurant and Conte summoned the courage to introduce himself.

> They discovered that besides sharing the same hometown and high school, they had both worked on the old *Tampa Daily Times*, Hatton as a reporter and Conte as a copy boy. Hatton did more than befriend Conte; he promised to help him with his acting career by giving him a part in a movie.

Conte concluded his reminiscence by adding sadly that the movie was never made.

Conte's recollections are significant for several reasons. First, his story serves to stress once more just what a decent man Rondo Hatton was. Secondly, it suggests that Rondo believed by that time he could influence casting decisions to some degree. Finally, Conte's anecdote provides strong evidence that Hatton felt

Continued on page 72

Backstage on *The Brute Man*

Brute Man director Jean Yarbrough (right) looks on as Hatton gets rough with JaNelle Johnson. The luckiest member of the cast, Johnson is bumped off in the first reel; the others had to stick around.

Dialogue director Raymond Kessler, Jane Adams and Hatton on the Helen's Apartment set in *The Brute Man*.

Brute Man director Jean Yarbrough gets a hands-free sip from Jan Wiley in somebody's idea of a cute publicity photo.

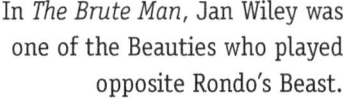

On the Waterfront (or, more accurately, on the edge of the Universal Tank), it's the *Brute Man* crew. In the foreground, script girl Mary Chaffee and dialogue director Raymond Kessler. Turning in his chair to scowl at us, director Jean Yarbrough. Behind him, d.p. Maury Gertsman smokes a pipe.

In *The Brute Man*, Jan Wiley was one of the Beauties who played opposite Rondo's Beast.

that Universal planned to star him in more films. In mid–January 1946, several newspapers carried reports that Hatton's "Hollywood Studio" (i.e., Universal) had named the next picture in which he would appear. At the end of January, *The Tampa Times* reported that Hatton was "slated to start work within two weeks as a star in a new Hollywood thriller, *House of Horrors*." (This was obviously intended to be an entirely different production from the already-completed *Murder Mansion*, which would eventually be retitled *House of Horrors*.) Perhaps this film was to have been based on the script promised in 1944 by Rondo's friend Ray Kessler, who had worked with Hatton again as dialogue director on *The Brute Man*. It is unlikely that we shall ever know – because Rondo's valiant struggle against the advance of acromegaly had come to an end. As Peter Conte sorrowfully stated about his potential role in Hatton's next film, "[B]efore the movie could be started, Hatton suffered a fatal heart attack."

Rondo's friend Tom Kaney provided Fred Olen Ray with the details:

I remember sitting in the living room reading the paper. Dinner was almost ready and Rondo was in taking a shower. I heard him fall and thought he must have slipped getting out. I went in there and he was sitting on the edge of the bathtub, his head hanging down. I grabbed a towel and started drying off his back and shoulders. He said he wasn't feeling well. I told Mabel to call the fire department because that's who used to run the ambulances. When they got there, they stuck their heads in the bathroom door and asked if he was all right. I said I thought so and they went into the living room. When I turned back, Rondo was dead.

Mae called on Dr. Harry Wayne Wagenseller, Rondo's personal physician, to determine the cause of Hatton's death. Wagenseller had attended Hatton previously, from October 26 to November 14, 1945 – or from shortly after final shooting on *The Spider Woman Strikes Back* to the very eve of shooting on *The Brute Man*. It is likely that Rondo was advised by Wagenseller that his condition was worsening, or even that time was running out. If so, Rondo carried that knowledge with him onto the set of *The Brute Man*. In any case, Wagenseller certified that Hatton died of coronary thrombosis, or the blockage of a coronary artery of the heart by a blood clot, caused by chronic myocarditis – an inflammation of the middle muscular layer of the heart wall. That the myocarditis was "chronic" implies that the condition was of long duration – and one that had developed as the result of Rondo's acromegaly.

Even in their bereavement, Mae and Rondo's parents were steadfast in their decision that Rondo should be buried in Tampa, the place that he had always considered his hometown. Nevertheless, they also knew that a funeral in Beverly Hills was necessary, in order to afford all of the friends that Rondo had made in Hollywood a chance to say goodbye. The arrangements appeared in *The Los Angeles Times* for Tuesday, February 5, 1946:

> Funeral services for Rondo Hatton, 51, character actor who died suddenly Saturday, will be conducted today at 1:30 p.m. in Pierce Bros. Beverly Hills Chapel. Following the services, the body will be taken to Tampa, Fla., for burial by his widow, Mrs. Mabel Housh Hatton, and his parents, Mr. and Mrs. Stuart [*sic*] Hatton, who lived with him at 308 N. Maple Drive, Beverly Hills. He also leaves an aunt, Mrs. Elizabeth Shuford of Tampa.

The Pierce Bros. Beverly Hills site was nearby, at 417 North Maple Drive. It appears that no details surrounding the Beverly Hills services have survived.

Rondo's final earthly journey began with the conclusion of the Beverly Hills services. The *Jackson Clarion-Ledger* for February 6 included an item outlining the next leg of the journey:

> STAR DEAD
> Tampa, Fla., Feb. 5 – (INS)
>
> The body of Rondo Hatton, 51, former Tampa reporter and more recently a screen "horror" player was en route today from California to Tampa for burial.
>
> Hatton became a screen actor as the result of his features being distorted as an aftermath of a gas attack in World War I. His first picture, *Hell Harbor*, was filmed in Tampa.
>
> The actor died in California last week after an illness.

Mae and Rondo's parents accompanied Hatton's remains on the cross-country trip, which was apparently via railroad. The *Tampa Tribune* for February 10 announced the particulars for Rondo's burial:

> Funeral services for Rondo Hatton, former Tampa newspaperman and Hollywood movie actor who died last Saturday, will be held Tuesday afternoon at 4 o'clock at the First Christian Church with Dr. E.C. Nance assisted by the Rev. J. Walter Carpenter officiating.
> The body may be viewed at the church from 3 to 4 o'clock.
>
> Interment will be in the Legion cemetery with services conducted by the American Legion at the grave. Pallbearers will be selected from Company H. Arrangements are in charge of Joe L. Reed.

In the space of a few days and in the midst of her own grief, Rondo's widow Mabel had pulled together a funeral that surely would have satisfied Hatton's wishes:

 The American Legion Post No. 5, of which Hatton was a member, was in charge of the funeral;

 The pallbearers were members of Company H, Tampa Rifles, the National Guard Infantry Unit to which Hatton had belonged;

 Burial was in the American Legion Cemetery among veterans;

 Dr. Elwood C. Nance, veteran of both wars, Purple Heart recipient, president of the University of Tampa, and former pastor of the First Christian Church which Rondo had attended, was selected to officiate the services. Nance had officiated at Rondo's marriage to Mabel.

Leaving stones and coins on tombstones is a common practice, done to show respect. Someone (no one knows who) regularly does this at tombstones at Tampa's American Legion Cemetery, including Rondo's.

Scores of Tampans attended, and the local newspapers carried lengthy descriptions. The best article appeared in Rondo's old paper, *The Tampa Tribune*, in its Wednesday, February 13, edition:

> Rondo Hatton, former Tampan and one of Hollywood's outstanding character actors, was buried in a military ceremony yesterday at the American Legion Cemetery.
>
> Members of Company H, Tampa Rifles, with whom he served in World War I, acted as pallbearers and honor guard in the funeral. An American flag was draped over the coffin as the body lay amid the many floral pieces at the First Christian Church.
>
> Dr. E.C. Nance, chaplain of the USS Tampa Post No. 5, American Legion, officiated at the ceremony, assisted by Dr. J. Walter Carpenter, pastor of the church. Dr. Nance paid final tribute to the former Tampa newspaper man in a brief address.
>
> "Rondo's heart will always be in Tampa," he said. "It always was. He was a practical, everyday human being, guided in everyday relationships with other people by principles of Christianity.
>
> "He never let affliction lick him. He was one of the most inspiring examples of what faith can do for you. He was just getting to a place where he might have made a lot of money as an actor, but if he had made a million dollars, I know he would have given it away."

This touching item had been preceded in *The Tampa Tribune* on the day of Rondo's funeral by one of the finest of the dozens of obituaries devoted to Hatton in newspapers across the country. Save for an inaccuracy in misidentifying Universal Studios as Warner Brothers, this death notice (no doubt written by a friend) consistently hits the mark, especially in its insights into Rondo's hopes and aspirations:

> Rondo Hatton converted a war-inflicted affliction into a personal asset. Given an opportunity by Henry King in the Tampa-made film *Hell Harbor*, he decided on a screen career and went to Hollywood. He was a familiar figure around the studios, well-liked by players and producers, but his progress was slow. In only a few pictures was there a role fitted to his unusual characteristics; so he had to be content with a few minor parts, denied the chance to show what he could do in a featured "spot." But Rondo was never discouraged; he stayed on and at last, his big moment came. He was chosen by Warners Brothers [*sic*] for the lead in a forthcoming "horror" series, *The Creeper*. The Tampa man felt that this was to be his opening to better and greater things.
>
> It was the cruel irony of fate that death struck him suddenly, just as he was about to realize the dreams and ambitions of many years. In a letter to a Tampa friend, written the day before his death, he spoke of the assured fruition of his long preparation and waiting. The next day, came the final "fade out" for this Tampan, ultimately the victim of an injury he received while fighting for his country in the First World War.
>
> Rondo Hatton's body, borne across the continent, will be buried in Tampa this afternoon. From Hollywood he constantly wrote Tampa friends cheerful and cheering letters. His pallbearers will be his battle comrades; his mourners a legion of

friends, who watched his career, hoped for his advancement, were shocked and sorrowed when death intervened just at the moment of success.

Even if this obituary perpetuated the notion that Hatton's acromegaly was the result of Rondo's war service, it survives as a sincere epitaph to a man whose impact stretched far beyond Tampa and his coterie of friends.

Rondo Hatton was laid to rest in the American Legion Cemetery in Tampa, among other military veterans. The simple tombstone marking his grave is superficially indistinguishable from those surrounding it – under a glyph of a cross in a circle, the inscription reads:

RONDO
HATTON

———

FLORIDA

———

2 LIEUT INFANTRY
APRIL 22, 1894
FEBRUARY 2, 1946

After nearly 30 years of standing out in a crowd, Rondo Hatton was finally able to blend into his surroundings – surroundings that blurred all distinctions, whether joyful or burdensome.

Aftermath

Rondo Hatton passed away on February 2, 1946, but a number of notable events directly relating to his life and career occurred in the years subsequent. Some of the more prominent happenings follow:

Friday, March 22, 1946: Universal released *The Spider Woman Strikes Back* nationally. It premiered at the ever-reliable Rialto Theater in New York.

Friday, March 29, 1946: *Murder Mansion*, re-titled *House of Horrors*, went into national release, after again premiering at the Rialto. Apparently, Universal executives considered *House of Horrors* to be too good a movie title to waste: It was intended to be the title for the film Hatton was to begin filming in mid–February 1946 when death intervened.

???????: Rondo Hatton's widow, Mabel Housh Hatton, returned to Beverly Hills to live. The exact date of her departure from Tampa is unknown.

With his appearance in *House of Horrors*, Hatton became Universal's newest horror headliner. When it played at the country's unofficial cathedral of the horror flick, the Rialto in Manhattan, *New York Times* reviewer Edmond J. Bartnett called Rondo "properly scary."

Monday, May 6, 1946: Rondo's father, Stewart Price Hatton, died. *The Tampa Tribune* was among the local newspapers to announce his passing in its May 7 edition:

> Stewart Price Hatton, 83, of 3406 Santiago St., father of the late Rondo Hatton, died suddenly yesterday afternoon at the residence.
>
> Mr. Hatton, who was born in Columbia, Mo., recently returned from California, where had had lived with his son, who was an actor. Prior to going to California, Mr. Hatton had lived in Tampa for many years and taught at the Tampa Business College.
>
> He is survived by his widow, Mrs. Emily L. Hatton.

Stewart and Emily sold their previous residence, 1007 Central Avenue, in March 1946.

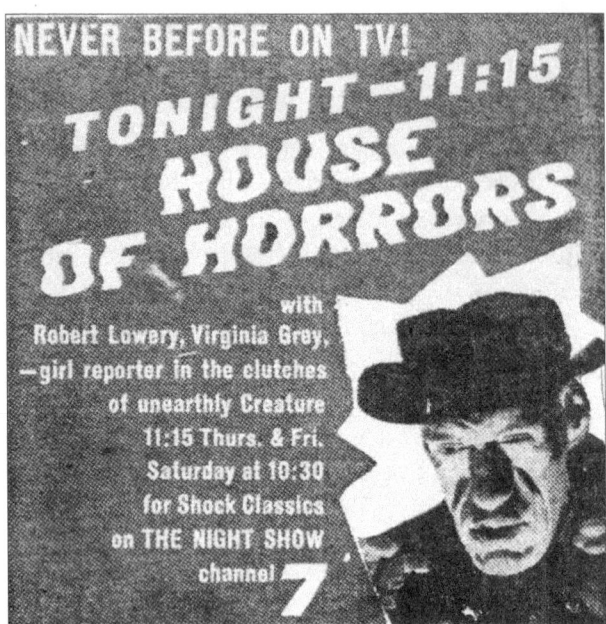

The Baby Boomer generation of Monster Kids got its first look at the Creeper when *House of Horrors* came to TV, running in late-night slots from coast (California's KTLA, left) to coast (New York's WABC, above).

Memorial Day, May 27, 1946: Roses were delivered anonymously to Rondo's grave. Roses would come to Hatton's grave on Memorial Day from an unknown sender every year thereafter until 1974.

October 1946: Rondo's last film, *The Brute Man*, was released by Producers Releasing Corporation. PRC had purchased the film from Universal after that company's merger with International Pictures.

Sunday, December 29, 1946: Fifteen-year old Robert Suarez of Tampa died in a local hospital from bronciectosis of both lungs. He was the child who had undergone an operation in Los Angeles a year earlier – whose family likely received the money to finance the operation from Rondo. The newspaper announcement of his death mentioned that "while in Los Angeles, he was visited frequently by Rondo Hatton, Tampa movie star who died recently."

Wednesday, November 12, 1947: Mabel Hatton's father, Sylvester Housh, died at his home. Obituaries in Tampa newspapers confirm that Mabel was residing in Beverly Hills, California.

Sunday, July 15, 1951: Rondo's aunt, Elizabeth Shuford, died in Tampa. Elizabeth and Rondo's mother Emily had resided together ever since the death of Rondo's father, Stewart. *The Tampa Times* reported in its July 27, 1951, edition, "The estate of Mrs. Elizabeth Christine Shuford … was valued in excess of $50,000, probate papers showed."

1957: Screen Gems made the *Shock!* package of Universal horror and mystery films available to television stations around the country. *House of Horrors* and *The Spider Woman Strikes Back* were included among the 52 features.

Wednesday, March 15, 1961: Rondo Hatton's mother, Emily Lee Zaring Hatton, died in Tampa. *The Tampa Tribune* carried her obituary the next day:

> Mrs. Emily Lee Hatton, 90, 505 W. Lafayette St., widow of S.P. Hatton, died yesterday afternoon at her residence. A native of Columbia, Mo., she had been a resident of Tampa since 1913. Mrs. Hatton was the mother of the late Rondo Hatton, one-time reporter with *The Tampa Tribune* and later a Hollywood movie actor.

The 1970s: Musician-iconoclast Frank Zappa began introducing himself as "Rondo Hatton" at some of his concerts. He often referred to his group of musicians as "The Rondo Hatton Band."

Sunday, March 2, 1974: In San Luis Obispo, California, Rondo's widow Mabel married Dr. Harry Wayne Wagenseller, the physician who certified Hatton's death. That year also marked the *last* year that a bouquet of roses appeared on Rondo's grave.

Monday, May 31, 1982: Mabel died, age 76, in Paso Robles, San Luis Obispo County, California. Her husband Harry Wagenseller died almost exactly five years

Tiny Ron, made-up by Rick Baker to resemble Rondo Hatton, gets rough with Billy Campbell in *The Rocketeer*.

later. Both are buried in Paso Robles District Cemetery.

1986: Rondo is a favorite with award-winning cartoonist and illustrator Drew Friedman; in 1986, his "The Heartbreak of Acromegaly: The Rondo Hatton Story," a two-page encapsulation of the actor's life, ran in a *National Lampoon's True Facts* special (and later reappeared in Friedman's book *Warts and All*). There have been way-out Rondo sightings in other Friedman art over the years. For the love of Rondo, he even volunteered to create a new portrait of the actor for this book's companion volume on Rondo (and he did!). If these books didn't have to be dedicated to Rondo (and they did!), we'd have dedicated them to Drew Friedman.

1991: The release of Walt Disney Pictures' sci-fi–adventure film *The Rocketeer* generated a resurgence of interest in Rondo's life and film career. Former University of California basketball player Ron Taylor (billed as Tiny Ron) played the villain's henchman Lothar in a Rick Baker makeup that made him a dead ringer for Hatton. The picture was based on the 1981 *Rocketeer* comic books by artist Dave Stevens, who had featured the Hatton-inspired character in those publications.

Making Tiny Ron resemble Hatton led to a series of awkward discussions with Disney decision-makers. At first, no one in the front office knew who Hatton was. According to a June 27, 1991, *State Times Advocate* article, director Joe Johnston was amused that these executives had no idea that Lothar was based on a real person; Johnston told interviewer Glenn Lovell, "To them, he was just another scary face." Disney management rejected the oversize head as too hideous, according to Johnston:

Another look at Tiny Ron(do) of *The Rocketeer*.

They said it was over-the-top, too frightening. They wanted me to reduce the size of the nose and chin and pull the ears back. I said, "Hey, this is the guy. This is how he really looked." I stood firm on that.

Makeup artist Baker was a longtime Hatton fan, so he was enthusiastic when he was contacted about working on the project – to the point of doing without his usual contract. By that time, the realization that the Lothar character would involve reproducing the face of an actual person caused Disney management to fear that Hatton's relatives in Tampa would want a piece of the action. Baker told Glenn Lovell about the next round of studio shenanigans:

From the Realm of Unwrought Things: Circa 2000, when a new monsterzine called *It's Alive!* was in the works, artist Basil Gogos provided a Hatton painting, and this cover mock-up was prepared.

They told me, "We don't have all the money in the world." So I didn't make the kind of deal I usually make. I just sent them a simple letter of agreement. I was doing it more for fun, as a fan. They sent back a very elaborate agreement making me responsible if they got sued. I said, "No way. You're asking me to duplicate this guy's face. It wasn't my idea."

Disney eventually relented, and Baker delivered six foam rubber appliances to turn Ron Taylor into a facial duplicate of Rondo. The brief time that Taylor spent embodying Hatton's deformity had an impact on him:

When I had the makeup on, people would frown in pain. They couldn't believe how big and ugly I was. People on the set wouldn't talk to me. It was almost as if they were afraid to. But, you know, it took me into another realm… made me feel better about myself, the way I look.

Thursday, October 18, 2001: Hillsborough High School, Rondo's only established high school alma mater, inaugurated its Football Hall of Fame with a number of living inductees, as well as nine posthumous members. Rondo Hatton was among that initial group. His plaque was presented to Robert A. Burns, an expert on Hatton's life and career. While the inscription listed his athletic accomplishments, it also spoke to Rondo's larger impact. It read:

INDUCTED OCTOBER 18, 2001

Stand-out two-way end and guard in 1912 Terriers run for State Championship * Defensive leader of 6-1 team that lost only to Duval in Championship Game * Was outstanding punter and considered best place kicker in State * Played semi-pro football and baseball * Second Lt. in France during WWI when pituitary disorder infliction derailed coaching plans * Reported for *Tampa Times* and *Tribune* demonstrating strong social conscience * Hollywood beckoned after 1928 role in *Hell Harbor* filmed in Tampa * Renowned horror and suspense film character actor in 17-year feature film career * Lifelong involvement in Veterans Affairs advocacy.

(As beautiful and deeply felt as this tribute obviously is, it is disappointing that the enumeration of Rondo's accomplishments yet omits a significant number of his athletic feats.)

2002: David Colton, moderator of the Classic Horror Film Board, an online forum for Monster Kids, devised and developed "The Rondos": awards for the year's best genre books, magazines, DVDs, commentaries, etc., with the winners determined by the results of an online poll. Colton selected "Rondo" as the name for the awards, and winners received a miniature replica of the bust of Hatton which appeared in *House of Horrors*. Colton tells the full story of the Rondo Awards beginning on page 284.

Circa 2011: Four Baton Rouge, Louisiana, musicians – Bruce Lamb, John Rosetti, Les LeBlanc and Joe Miceli – began an all-instrumental surf-rock band in the mold of the Ventures. When the quartet began talking about names for the band, local music fan and friend Bill Boelens threw out "Rondo Hatton," remembering Frank Zappa concert recordings in which Zappa introduced himself by that name.

The name stuck, and the band members subsequently learned the history behind their namesake. The four added graphics of Rondo to their performance – and an extra touch of devotion. The show emcees first introduce the four-piece band as the Rondo Hatton Quintet. The group adds to the allure by putting an empty chair center stage during their performance. Guitarist Johnny Rosetti added that the prop is "a chair with a mike in front of it. Yeah, Rondo didn't show again. Don't know what we're gonna do with the guy."

The Rondo Hatton Band has released several albums of superior surf-rock in the past few years.

October 2017: Hillsborough High School selected the Halloween season to set up a memorial to Rondo in the trophy case facing the main office of the school. Teacher Rex Gordon, head of the alumni association, arranged for a shelf of the trophy case to contain a display of photos, a poster, a brief Hatton biography *and* – the centerpiece of the display – a Classic Horror Film Board Rondo Award bust. (Earlier in the year, Gordon had approached David Colton about acquiring a Rondo to exhibit as part of the memorial and Colton was quick to provide one, commenting simply, "It should have been done years ago.")

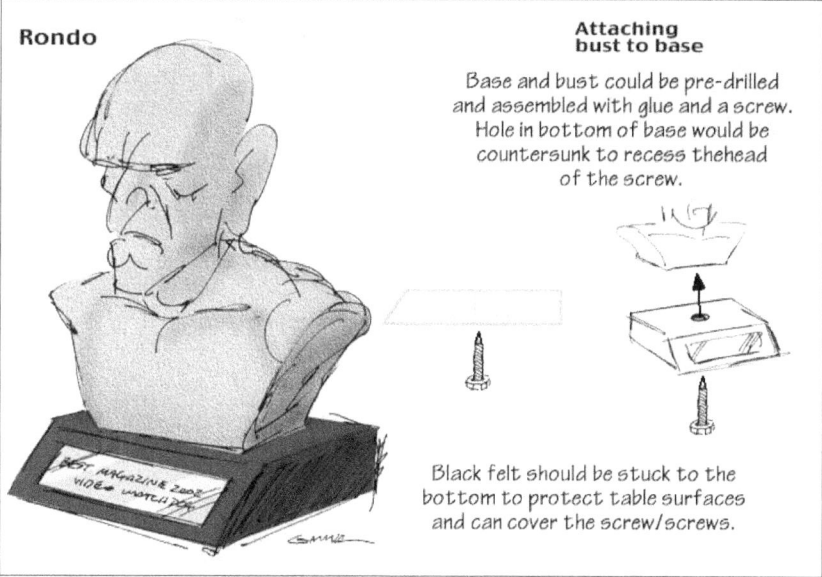

Photo top: Artist-sculptor Kerry Gammill's Rondo Award sketches from 2002. Photo bottom: The first Rondos. The 21st century finds the least of Universal's horror stars representing the finest in genre achievement.

Epilogue and Personal Observations

It is no longer open to question that Rondo Hatton has become an undeniable and lasting presence in popular culture – a part of the American consciousness. It is equally unquestioned that it is Hatton's face that enabled him to achieve that status. His face was his fortune during his film career, and in that regard, he is not at all unlike a significant number of film performers, then or now. The difference between Rondo and most of his contemporaries on screen is obvious, of course:

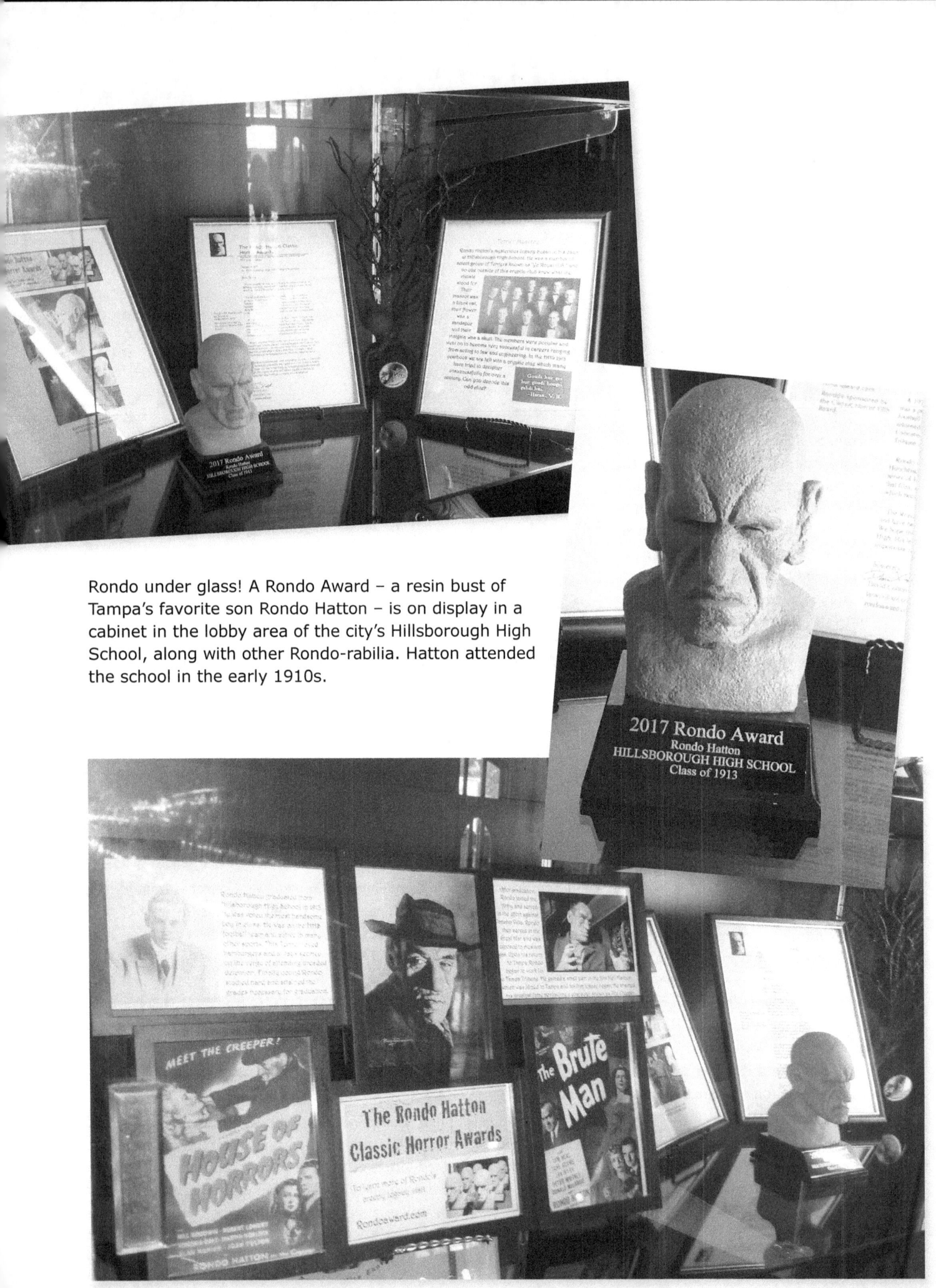

Rondo under glass! A Rondo Award – a resin bust of Tampa's favorite son Rondo Hatton – is on display in a cabinet in the lobby area of the city's Hillsborough High School, along with other Rondo-rabilia. Hatton attended the school in the early 1910s.

While most performers relied upon their attractiveness to advance their careers, Hatton depended on ugliness. In a way, that fact renders any evaluation of his acting ability largely irrelevant: His unique face granted Rondo Hatton a screen immortality denied to performers who almost certainly outstripped his talent as an actor.

There is still another irony in comparing Rondo to the more mainstream, conventionally attractive actors of his era. More than a few biographies devoted to Rondo's more beautiful contemporaries make it clear that real ugliness and moral corruption lay behind those attractive Hollywood faces. In stark contrast, Rondo's "horrible" countenance concealed a tender, kind, charitable soul – an intelligent man beloved by his co-workers, family and friends; a deeply spiritual man who always thought of others while he was engaged in a courageous but doomed struggle against an incurable and ultimately fatal disease. Who, then, is more deserving of the sobriquet "Monster Without Makeup" – Rondo Hatton, or some of his more "conventionally" attractive contemporaries?

On a personal note, I now know more about Rondo Hatton than I ever expected to learn. Rondo has seemed like a lifelong friend since I first encountered him on a television screen as a young boy watching *House of Horrors* one Saturday night on the New Orleans–based *House of Shock* program hosted by Morgus the Magnificent. Now that friendship has been deepened immeasurably. In preparing to write this biography, I discovered that for me, one of the more dismaying aspects of even attempting to write the history of a person's life is an implied evaluation of the subject from a distance – whether for good or ill. As a result, I attempted, wherever possible, to let Rondo or those who knew him speak for themselves, with a minimum of my interpretation. Whether I have succeeded, on this or any other level, is for the reader to decide. If I have provided a glimpse of the soul behind his face, then at least my own intention has been achieved. Then we will all know a Rondo Hatton that was much more than a reporter or one of the most beloved and iconic of those actors who toiled on Hollywood soundstages; we will know someone who exemplifies the very best that the human spirit has to offer – the fight against insuperable odds. Perhaps this is the characteristic that makes a human beautiful. If so, I can think of no better final tribute to Rondo Hatton than the following. As a poet himself, Rondo might appreciate the words of the late Irish poet John O'Donohue:

> Ultimately, it is the soul that makes the face beautiful.

Then we can all be sure, Rondo Hatton is beautiful, now and forever.

> [Rondo] Hatton's famous killer roles only lasted for two years, but he'll never be forgotten.
> – Michael Weldon, *The Psychotronic Encyclopedia of Film*

The Brute Man: Production History

By Tom Weaver

The Classic Universal Monsters era (1931-1946): What was its banner year?

There are a couple likely-sounding answers to that question, but some fans might choose an *un*likely-sounding one, 1944, long after the cycle's glory days. For these fans, 1944 may be attractive as it was the only year that every one of the studio's sequel-worthy creeps and monsters strut their hour upon the stage: Dracula, Frankenstein, the Wolf Man (*House of Frankenstein*), the Mummy (*The Mummy's Ghost* and *The Mummy's Curse*), the Invisible Man (*The Invisible Man's Revenge*) and Paula the Ape Woman (*Jungle Woman*). And, to really stretch a point, also the unblinking spectral head in the crystal ball that welcomed fans to the Inner Sanctum. At one point during that year, *every* feature in production at the San Fernando Valley plant was in the "Universal Horrors" category.

And why *shouldn't* Universal keep milking the cash cow? The company projected in July 1944 that by year's end, their fright flicks would have poured $10,000,000 profits into their coffers in the 13 (count 'em!) years since Dracula bid us welcome and Frankenstein subjected our nerves to such a strain. (Ten million in 2019 dollars: over 144 million.) According to a July 1944 *Variety* article,

> Brood of screen monsters with the U copyright brand—"Frankenstein Monster," "Dracula," "The Wolf Man," "The Invisible Man," "The Mummy" and their eerie satellites and ghoulish comrades, have been paying off at the rate of around $750,000 net annually, with some years showing considerable excess over that figure.

Because of the genre's box office reliability, even the company's Sherlock Holmes mystery series was hijacked by horror: As of July 1944, the newest five ranged from borderline-horror (*Sherlock Holmes Faces Death* and *The Spider Woman*) to horror-heavy (*The Scarlet Claw*, *The Pearl of Death*, *The House of Fear*). Universal even began adding psychological crime-horror titles to their lineup: *Phantom Lady* (1944) with Ella Raines, *The Suspect* with Charles Laughton and *Uncle Harry* (1945) with George Sanders.

It was high time to hatch a new monster in the writing chambers of the Studio That Horror Built.

* * *

With a grain of salt, check out this November 8, 1944, *Variety* blurb:

Ben Pivar Upped to Top Budget Films

Ben Pivar has been upped in his producer status at Universal to handle only top-budget pictures hereafter, after having supervised program material for several years. At the same time Pivar has been assigned to develop new horror pic character under title "The Creeper," to be used in series.

Monster Kids will find the story laughable because then, now and forever, producer Pivar's name was synonymous with B- (and C-) movies and we all know it. The suggestion that the pictures in his then-future (the remaining Inner Sanctums, *She-Wolf of London*, more) would be "top-budget" is representative of the kind of reality-challenged squibs that infiltrated trade papers back in that era (and perhaps to this day). The blurb is, however, historic for heralding the coming of a new horror character...although calling the Creeper "new" again falls short of accurate.

The Washington Evening Star's Jay Carmody quipped, "Universal has the idea that [the Creeper] will be popular enough to outlast even Andy Hardy." Other papers provided additional details about the proposed series, including this from the November 8 *New York Herald Tribune*: "Universal has assigned to Producer Ben Pivar the task of creating an entirely new set of horror characters, the principal one of which will be the Creeper. This latest figure will be introduced to the public in a

Illustrations that accompanied Arthur Conan Doyle's Sherlock Holmes story "The Adventure of the Six Napoleons" when it was originally published: On the left, Holmes takes a bite out of crime when he tackles the apelike Beppo, on the right, he tests his theory that the pearl is hidden within a Napoleon bust.

top-budget feature tentatively known as *The House of Horrors*." Even the stuffy *New York Times* brought its readers this hot news flash from the epicenter of the monster movie world, trumpeting that the Creeper would join Universal's "stock bogey men" Frankenstein, Dracula, the Mummy and the Mad Ghoul.

In 1946, when the first movie in Pivar's Creeper series, *House of Horrors*, came to Shamokin, Pennsylvania, a *Shamokin News-Dispatch* reviewer noted,

> Rondo Hatton portrays "The Creeper." Hatton, it will be recalled, had a small featured role as "The Creeper" in the Sherlock Holmes picture *Pearl of Death* a few seasons ago. The resultant flood of fan mail at Universal convinced Producer Ben Pivar that the character was worth an entire series, and so Hatton was signed for the role.

This has the ring of Universal publicity department nonsense. TV producer Andrew J. Fenady, writing about Pivar in one of this book's appendices, recalls what Pivar told *him* about the start of the Creeper series, and it's a very different story (see page 272).

Whence Crept the Creeper?

What writer or writers were most responsible for the Creeper character? That's not an easy question to answer.

As noted above, a character called the *Hoxton Creeper* had already lurched to horror picture prominence in Universal's best Sherlock Holmes entry, *The Pearl of Death*, shot in the spring of 1944. It was based on Sir Arthur Conan Doyle's story "The Adventure of the Six Napoleons"—and there *is* a loosely corresponding character in the Conan Doyle yarn. In "Six Napoleons," Holmes, Dr. Watson and Inspector Lestrade are on the trail of a nut (or *is* he a nut?) who smashes other people's plaster casts of the head of Napoleon…but only the Napoleon casts made by a particular factory. It turns out that the culprit is Beppo, an Italian ne'er-do-well who once worked at that factory. And at that time, with the police on his heels, he was forced to hide a stolen jewel, the famous black pearl of the Borgias, in one of six newly made, still-drying Napoleon busts. After a stretch in Ye Olde Pokey, Beppo began tracking down the owners of those busts, stealing and then smashing them, often in public, in hopes of recovering the gem.

Pearl of Death scripter Bertram Millhauser expanded the Conan Doyle story: In his adaptation, international crook Giles Conover (glibly played by Miles Mander) is the on-the-lam jewel thief responsible for secreting it in a wet plaster bust and, with the help of confederate Naomi (Evelyn Ankers), he's now locating the busts' buyers. *Pearl of Death*'s Beppo equivalent is Conover's homicidal henchman, the Hoxton Creeper (Rondo Hatton), who walks like a wind-up doll and has the same amount of conscience. At Conover's command, he snaps the spines of the bust owners—even a woman.

Beppo is described by Conan Doyle as a "simian man, with thick eyebrows and a very peculiar projection of the lower part of the face, like the muzzle of a baboon." Holmes, Watson and Lestrade stake out a house Beppo is burglarizing; when he dashes out, he's "a lithe, dark figure, as swift and active as an ape," with "a hideous, sallow face" and "matted hair." A captured Beppo snaps at Watson's hand "like a hungry wolf."

With a gruesome "Man in the Moon" profile courtesy of the glandular disease acromegaly, Hatton as the Hoxton Creeper is certainly ape-like; the actor adds to this effect by wearing body padding and by rocking side to side as he walks. The similarities to Beppo end there. The Creeper is not a resourceful rogue like Beppo, just a backward lout with a Kong-sized crush on Naomi—who's hardly complimented. And unlike the swift, lithe Beppo, Hatton's Hoxton Creeper is more like the Mummy, either sneaking up on his victims or cornering them and then slowly closing in for the kill. The verdict: not much credit to Conan Doyle for the Hoxton Creeper.

But…what about Raymond Chandler?

This is sheer speculation, but I think there's a good chance that Moose Malloy, a character in Chandler's 1940 novel *Farewell, My Lovely*, may have roundaboutly inspired some aspects of the Creeper. Chandler's protagonist, L.A. private detective Philip Marlowe, describes Moose as

In *The Pearl of Death*, baddies Rondo Hatton and Miles Mander die within the space of about 30 seconds. Less than two years later, the two actors died within the space of just a few days.

a big man but not more than six feet five inches tall and not wider than a beer truck.

[He had a] hand I could have sat in.

[Moose's face] was a face that had nothing to fear. Everything had been done to it that anybody could think of.

This huge brute is just out of the Oregon State pen after an eight-year stretch for bank robbery—and the one thing on his simple mind is to find Velma, the girl of his dreams (*à la* the Creeper and Naomi). But Moose may be the boy of Velma's nightmares, because she makes herself scarce.

Where do *Farewell, My Lovely* and *The Pearl of Death* meet on the graph? In the office of Howard Benedict, executive producer of RKO's *Falcon* detective series. In 1942, his last RKO picture was *The Falcon Takes Over*, a vastly altered, mouth-washed-out-with-soap adaptation of *Farewell, My Lovely*. In *Takes Over*, the Falcon, not Marlowe, is our protagonist, an amateur sleuth on the trail of a stolen pearl jade necklace. His companions in adventure are "Goldy," his comedy-relief sidekick, and O'Hara, a gruff police inspector. Also figuring into the plot of Benedict's movie are a criminal mastermind; his

> Read all the *Pearl of Death* script pages featuring the Hoxton Creeper: "Script Excerpts from ***The Pearl of Death***" begins on page 242.

dual-identity partner-in-crime, the beautiful Velma; and the 6'5", 265-pound Moose Malloy (played, sans screen credit, by Ward Bond), a man-mountain recently escaped from prison and now searching for Velma, the object of his obsession. The monstrous Moose's method of murder: He uses his hands to snap the necks of his victims.

Two years later, RKO was counting down the days to the start of production of the A-picture *Murder, My Sweet* with Dick Powell as Philip Marlowe, by far a more faithful rendering of *Farewell, My Lovely* than *The Falcon Takes Over*. At the very same time, Benedict was at Universal shooting his newest Holmes stanza, *The Pearl of Death*—whose story owes a huge debt to *The Falcon Takes Over*. The Falcon film's character lineup of the Falcon, "Goldy," the inspector, the criminal mastermind, his multiple-identity moll and the neck-snapping Moose (who loves the moll) reappears in *Pearl of Death* as Holmes, Watson, the inspector, the criminal mastermind, his multiple-identity moll and the spine-snapping Hoxton Creeper (who loves the moll).

Taking speculation one step further: Could Benedict have been sore at RKO? It seems too coincidental that just as RKO prepared to put *Murder, My Sweet* into production, Benedict was ripping off RKO's previous *Farewell, My Lovely* adaptation *The Falcon Takes Over* (as *The Pearl of Death*). And you wonder if Benedict wasn't giving RKO the finger when, in *Pearl*, practically the first thing Giles Conover does in his first scene is to call Naomi "my sweet."

Credit Hatton's Hoxton Creeper for pushing *The Pearl of Death* into the horror category: He's one of the most frightening menaces in any B-mystery (or A-mystery) of that period. He never speaks, so perhaps he's a mute; Conover taunts Naomi by telling her that the Creeper has prowled around her flat "making wistful little noises like a dog." The Creeper is Conover's right arm when it comes to killing, but between homicides Conover keeps him under lock and key, as though he can't be trusted to roam loose. We hear about him but don't see him until the two-thirds mark, and even then it's just his silhouette…closeups of his hands (in rubber gloves so tight, they look painted-on)…the shadow of his profile…the back of him, as he mounts a staircase.

> Rondo Hatton plays [the Hoxton Creeper] and if he goes to the right Hollywood parties with the right people, Boris Karloff had better look to his horrors. – *New York Herald Tribune*, August 26, 1944

Twice a hand of The Creeper is viewed, which is more hideous than the full-face view of him at the end of the picture. – American Legion Auxiliary, 1944

Even when the Creeper is "at ease," he holds his elbows out from his body and his fingers are splayed so that they resemble claws. Hatton is also made to look king-sized when he was actually of average height, or maybe a bit less. And he might have the eeriest musical accompaniment of *any* of the Universal monsters, especially in the climactic scene where he advances on Holmes. The Great Detective has a gun and the Creeper just his powerful mitts, but the viewer is still frightened for Holmes…and Holmes looks plenty frightened too!

In the spring or early summer of 1944, Hatton played his final uncredited role in Goldwyn's Technicolor production *The Princess and the Pirate*, a Bob Hope spoof of pirate pictures. Funnily enough, Hatton played a part which allowed him to get in some practice for his coming horror roles. At around the half-hour mark, "brave coward" Hope and princess-on-the-run Virginia Mayo find themselves on the lawless island of Casarouge, where there's out-in-public murder and mayhem everywhere they look, including *up*: They hear a woman's scream, look up and see a beauty push open the shutters of a second-story room and try to dive out head-first. But before she can fall, she's grabbed from behind by Rondo in pirate garb (as she continues to scream). He hauls her back in (as she screams), shoves her roughly (as she screams) and pulls closed the shutters. Now, from inside the room, we hear one last scream and then a portentous silence. "I wonder what they *do* around here for excitement," Hope nervously quips as his hand goes to his throat. (The only thing missing: Rondo should have rasped at the girl, "Stop yellin'.") *Pearl of Death* and *Princess and the Pirate* were made at the same time; Rondo played his passionate pirate either immediately before or (more likely) soon after his turn as the Hoxton Creeper.

After *The Pearl of Death*, '40s horror fans next saw Hatton in *The Jungle Captive*'s opening morgue scene. The latter was their first indication that with a director like Roy William Neill (*Pearl*), Hatton was horrifying…but with lesser directors, hilarious.

Ape Interlude

> It was a new menace for [Universal] to exploit—and they didn't need Jack Pierce to do his makeup!
>
> – Fred Olen Ray, discussing Rondo Hatton in the documentary *Trail of the Creeper* (2011)

Someone at Universal must have thought that Hatton's mutated mug would be a welcome addition to their horror division: In the summer of 1944, even before the release of *Pearl of Death*, the actor appeared in his first full-fledged Universal Horror, *The Jungle Captive*. Third and last in the company's Paula the Ape Woman series, it starred Otto Kruger as Stendahl, a biochemist with an office in the city, where he's well-respected, and a house in the country, where he's an all-in member of the Mad Scientist Club. Stendahl is determined to prove he can revive the dead, and for some bizarre reason, he thinks the ideal candidate for a second chance at life is the body of the anthropo-illogical Paula. Toward that end, he has his henchman Moloch (Hatton) steal the hairy corpse from the morgue where she was placed at the end of the previous Ape Woman movie, 1944's *Jungle Woman*.

In *The Pearl of Death*, screenwriter Millhauser and director Roy William Neill collaborated to give Rondo's Creeper a royal roll-out: He's talked-about but not on-camera until almost 45 minutes into the movie, and even then we only get tantalizing partial glimpses. *The Jungle Captive* gives the character no such build-up. In an opening-reel night scene, we see his outsized shadow on the wall of a building, a good start; and seconds later, once he's inside the morgue, his black coat and hat look like Creeper hand-me-downs. But then everything goes downhill at warp speed. "I come for the body," he tells the attendant (Charles Wagenheim) in a raspy voice that sounds like Satchmo after a shoutathon, and grammar no better than the voice. Wagenheim doesn't really react at all to his ugliness; and when Wagenheim stands, we're shocked to see the little fellow come right up close to Moloch's height. *Pearl of Death* gave us a Hoxton Creeper who, even unarmed, struck terror in the heart of a gun-wielding Sherlock Holmes. In *The Jungle Captive*, we get a pint-sized goon who don't much scare Charles Wagenheim.

Stendahl needs blood to resuscitate the Ape Woman so he lures Ann (Amelita Ward), his city office assistant, to the country house; he introduces Moloch as his caretaker. Hatt-on, hat-off: 1940s horror fans here got their first-ever gander at a hat-less Hatton. Yikes. In addition to all the actor's other woes, his barber has done him no favors. And the wave in the hair atop his head calls to mind a brick of Ramen Noodles.

Moloch does a slow'n'creepy job of helping Ann off with her coat, and then he lays it across the back of a couch and starts rubbing it even though she's watching. Never a good sign. Soon she's unconscious on Stendahl's operating table, having some blood extracted. When Moloch shows concern, Stendahl chides him: "Don't be a fool. We're scientists, not sentimentalists!" Then he adds, "No offense, Moloch, but, uh, with that face, you're not exactly a Casanova." Then he points to the corpse of the Ape Woman and zings him a second time: "*This* is more in *your* line, Moloch!" (Shades of bestiality *and* necrophilia.) Mae Hatton must have loved this dialogue.

But Moloch doesn't mind being dissed; in fact, all it takes is for Stendahl to "casually" mention that he'd like to have another scientist's medical records and Moloch promptly fetches them—killing that scientist and wrecking his office in the process. (Upon his return, a looking-for-approval Moloch smiles a sunbeam smile and asks Stendahl, "I done all right, huh?") The resuscitated Ape Woman proves to be a handful, so Stendahl takes more of Ann's blood and uses it to transform the beast into Paula Dupree.

The 70 awkward seconds Moloch spent with Ann (she said "How do you do?" and let him take her coat and hat) has of course made him her love slave. When Stendahl prepares to remove her brain for the Ape Woman's use, the servant-henchman follows in the footsteps of Boris Karloff's Bateman (*The Raven*) and tells the doc, "You ain't gonna hurt her!" Unfortunately for Moloch, Stendahl packs heat even under his surgeon's smock. The unarmed Moloch advances on Stendahl, who expresses his disapproval with three bullets. The scene is a virtual remake of *Pearl of Death*'s Holmes-Creeper confrontation, down to the operating room setting and the shooter in surgeon's smock. As Moloch drops to the floor, *Pearl of Death*'s Creeper music plays. Another minute or two of mayhem precedes the usual happily-ever-after fade-out.[11]

Moloch wasn't much of a part, and yet whoever scripted *Jungle Captive*'s trailer tried to give the impression that he might be the Next Big Thing in Universal's horror hierarchy: It begins with the shot of his super-sized shadow on the wall and the superimposed words

OUT OF THE SHADOWS

STALKS *MOLOCH*...

THE BRUTE

And toward the end of the trailer, he and Vicky Lane get prominent billing, these words superimposed over a shot of Lane, Hatton and Kruger:

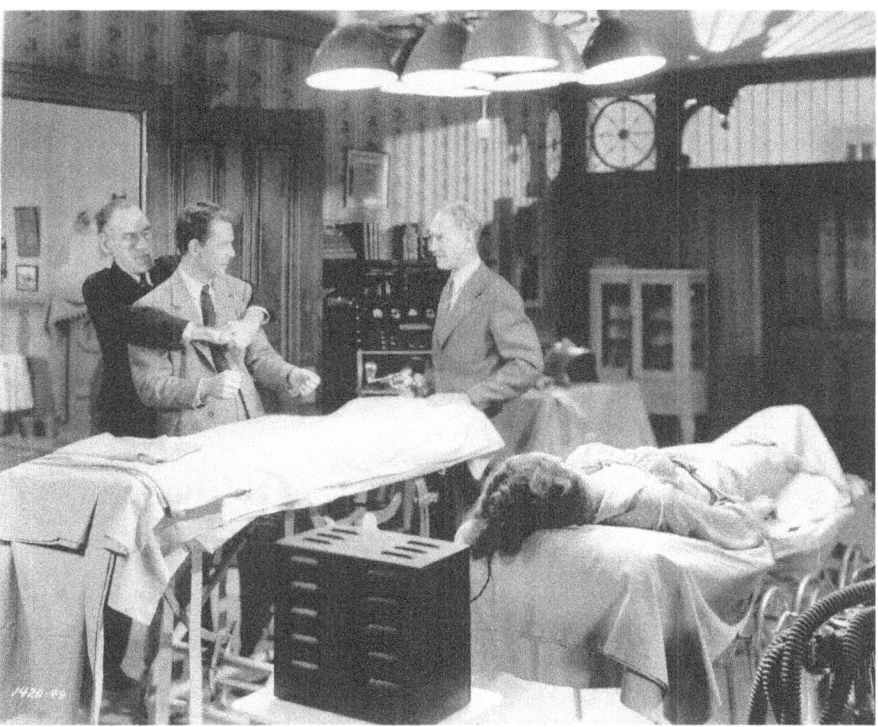

The threadbare charm of Universal's Paula the Ape Woman series had worn *too* thin by the time *The Jungle Captive* rolled around. Even the presence of a second mutant, Rondo as the mad doctor's homely henchman, was no help. Pictured: Rondo, Phil Brown, Otto Kruger and, on lab table, Amelita Ward.

Rondo HATTON as "MOLOCH" *Viky* LANE as *PAULA* THE APE WOMAN

By September 1944, Hatton had two Universal Horrors roles under his belt, his unforgettable Hoxton Creeper (*Pearl of Death*) and his extremely forgettable Moloch (*The Jungle Captive*). As outlined above, November brought the news that the Creeper would get his own series; surely Universal intended right from the giddy-up for Hatton to star, but he was not mentioned in the November announcements. The following month, however, his name could be found in new Creeper squibs, including *Variety*'s December 6 "Hatton Set in Creeper": "Rondo Hatton, former football coach and newspaperman, signed with Universal yesterday to play title role in studio's new horror series, 'The Creeper.'" On that same day, *The New York Times* reported, "Rondo Hatton, a former newspaper man who has been playing bit parts for the last six years, is to be Universal's new horror creation 'the Creeper.' The first picture in a series for this character will be *The

Brute Man."

Three days later, *Variety*'s "Hollywood Inside" column revealed that Pivar was

> using several hundred letters from avid whodunit customers and horror pix experts in setting up the [Creeper] character to be played by Rondo Hatton. Missives of suggestion come from all over the country by customers brought up on Frankenstein, the Wolf Man and other classic monster creations at Universal. Some of them are on the screwy side, but many are careful analyses and creative suggestions toward shaping the identity and behavior of the "Creeper."…First picture in the series will be *Brute Man*.

December 8 is the date on writer Dwight V. Babcock's three-and-a-half–page story "The Creeper #2—Idea: *The House of Horrors*." But it's not the story of the Creeper movie *House of Horrors* (1946) that we know, but a Hatton-starring remake of Universal's 1932 *The Old Dark House*! No such movie was ever made; you can read Babcock's story for yourself, starting on page 252.

Later that December, a Sunday supplement feature titled "Horrors!! Some New 'Faces' to Make Your Blood Run Cold" helped prepare Rosie the Riveter–era Monster Kids for the coming Rondo renaissance. Spotlighting new and upcoming films from "Universal studios—Home of Horrors," it featured stills from *The Mummy's Curse*, *House of Frankenstein* and *The Jungle Captive* plus a suitably shadowy shot of Rondo and the caption "Naturally scary-looking, Rondo Hatton, a new-comer to Universal's horror stable, is no makeup problem."

He Who Waits

After years of bit parts, Rondo Hatton seemed now on the verge of (very) minor-league stardom. In January 1945 came a trade paper announcement that George Bricker, having just put finishing touches on his script for the Inner Sanctum *Pillow of Death*, would now turn his hand to the writing of "*The House of Horrors*, second of the new 'Creeper' yarns." Confusingly, a January 8, 1945, *Variety* squib indicated that Dwight V. Babcock had submitted a *House of Horrors* script; and then on April 9 came news that Bricker had just been assigned to write a *House of Horrors* script. (As Ben tells Mr. Cooper in *Night of the Living Dead*, "It would be *nice* if you get your story straight, man!") Truth be told, I don't know if, in the first half of '45, the proposed (*The*) *House of Horrors* was the abovementioned *Old Dark House* remake, or the Creeper vs. the Art Critics movie eventually made, or a whole 'nother story altogether.

In the spring of 1945, Universal had a record 59 players under long-term contract, Hatton among them. Also two of his future co-stars, *The Spider Woman Strikes Back*'s Gale Sondergaard and Kirby Grant; his future victim Joan Shawlee (*House of Horrors*), and his future leading lady Jane Adams (*The Brute Man*). But as far as the Creeper movies themselves were concerned, the Universal assembly line had slowed to a crawl or perhaps a halt. *The Jungle Captive* finally hit theaters in the summer of 1945, a month short of a full year after it was shot.

Around this same time, Hatton finally got in front of a Universal camera for the first time in perhaps a year—not as a Creeper, but as a sleeper! From the August 9, 1945, *Variety*:

Rondo Rides, Too

Rondo Hatton has inked for a featured role in *The Royal Mounted Rides Again*, serial currently shooting at Universal.

Set in the Klondike's latest gold town circa 1900, *Royal Mounted* is 13 chapters of low-budget boredom and confusion in the long-standing Universal Serial tradition. In fact, it's even worse than their mind-numbing norm. George Dolenz and Bill Kennedy are its lawmen heroes, Milburn Stone the "brains heavy" and Robert Armstrong a saloon operator on the wrong side of the law. Rondo, billed 18th and last on every chapter's castlist, plays Bull Andrews, a shabby-looking

---

> When cinematic monsters play
> A super-duper thriller
> And turn your raven hair to gray,
> It is a chiller-diller.
> Now looms amid the shadows gray
> A demon called "The Creeper."
> And all the flacks arise and say
> He is a creeper-deeper.
>
> —*Variety* humorist George E. Phair in his "Retakes" column, December 7, 1944

Rondo in *The Royal Mounted Rides Again*. To convey being fatally shot, he closes his eyes and slowly leans back in his chair, as if contentedly settling into a warm, luxurious bath.

goon slumped in a chair outside saloonkeeper Armstrong's office door. His hat is pulled down a little over his face, his hands clasped over his belly. He occasionally gets a medium closeup and you often can't tell if he's supposed to be awake or asleep. Is he Armstrong's bodyguard? Is he just pretending to sleep? Who knows. Who cares. It's an "atmosphere part," putting Hatton right back where he started in Hollywood (*Alexander's Ragtime Band*, etc.). If Hatton had died smack-dab in the middle of production, Universal could have stolen his body and featured him in the rest of the saloon scenes and it would be impossible for any viewer to tell the Living Hatton chapters from the Dead Hatton ones. The three Hatton "highlights," such as they are: He stirs slightly at a dramatic moment in Chapter 7 and gets his hat shot off; he draws a derringer and fires a shot in Chapter 10's cliffhanger ending; and he draws the gun again in Chapter 12 and is unexpectedly drilled by Armstrong.

Tuesday, 9/11, 1945: A full ten months after Universal heralded the coming of the Creeper series, the camera at last rolled on its first entry, director Jean Yarbrough's *Murder Mansion* (released as *House of Horrors*). Far from "top-budget," it was scheduled for 12 days of on-the-double shooting (and went 13). Hatton's co-stars: the deeply uncharismatic Robert Lowery, lovely Virginia Grey and Martin Kosleck. *If* there was ever a plan to have the new Creeper movies take place in England (as *Pearl of Death* did, and the *Old Dark House* remake might have), it was dropped; an all–American Creeper, not his across-the-Pond cousin the Hoxton Creeper, is featured in *House of Horrors* and the other Creeper chiller, *The Brute Man*.

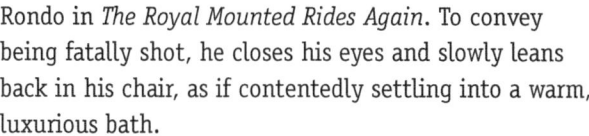

"Universal's very proud of its latest zombie, Rondo Hatton…" – Hedda Hopper, September 1945

On the morning of the first day of *House of Horrors* production, actors and crew congregated on Stage 20 and the movie's opening scene was shot: In his cavernous, candlelit Greenwich Village studio-home, destitute artist Marcel DeLange is hoping to make a $1000 sale of his bizarre sculpture "Surcease from Toil." But the mild-mannered buyer brings along F. Holmes Harmon (Alan Napier), dean of New York's art critics, whose pen (and tongue) come acid-dipped. Harmon belittles DeLange's sculpture (and DeLange) and queers the deal. Brandishing a Norman Bates–worthy bread knife, DeLange wigs out and chases the men away.

The plight of destitute, despondent DeLange would bring a tear to a glass eye: Viewers sympathize as he now makes his way to the dark, lonely riverfront and contemplates taking the plunge. But then the artist sees someone *already* struggling in the water. He fishes the half-conscious fellow (Hatton) out of the drink, gets a look at his face—and proclaims, "*Magnifique*! The perfect Neanderthal man." Intending to use this stranger as the model for a sculpture, DeLange brings him to his studio and restores him to health.

An amusing *House of Horrors* shot of Hatton with his stand-in, Ed Cushing.

Profile of a Serial Killer: Marcel (Martin Kosleck) immortalizes the Creeper's (Hatton) cockamamie kisser in clay. Perhaps part of the reason shorty Kosleck was cast was to make Hatton appear bigger and taller.

Marcel doesn't know it yet, but the man is the Creeper and he has a history of back-breaking murder; New York's boys in blue are under the mistaken impression that he perished in the river. (This is reminiscent of *Pearl of Death* where, initially, Inspector Lestrade is sure that the Hoxton Creeper died in a Devil's Island escape attempt.) Late one night, the Creeper steals out of the studio and follows a woman (Virginia Christine), presumably a streetwalker, who panics at the sight of him. He polishes her off in a snap. Now aware of his houseguest's penchant for predatory behavior, Marcel has the devil of an idea: He will use the Creeper as more than a model. In "idle" conversation, Marcel begins a regular routine of complaining about his art-critic enemies, always happening to mention where they live, and, unasked, the Creeper does the rest; as the *New York Times* reviewer put it, "Five corpses with broken spines litter the screen before things are cleared up." Marcel and the Creeper are reminiscent of *Son of Frankenstein*'s (1939) Monster (Boris Karloff) and Ygor (Bela Lugosi), the latter a whacked-out character with an enemies list and no hesitation to make full use of a giant ogre who, in Ygor's words, "*does* things for me."

During the opening credits, there's a big musical swell as Hatton makes a cameo appearance (walks into a close-up) and gets special "Introducing" billing; one eye is open wider than the other and his cheek visibly twitches to add to the ickiness. Posters featured the lines "Screen's Newest Monster of Terror!" and "Meet the Creeper!" But right from Kosleck's first moments on-screen (describing his current plight to his cat Pietro), the actor makes DeLange an engaging personality—perhaps *too* engaging, in a movie meant to showcase the Creeper. Kosleck is a delight as the devious artist, the worm who terrifyingly turns, whose mind begins playing a nonstop reel of umbrage-taking once he has an avenger. "[Kosleck] holds the show together," according to DVD Savant Glenn Erickson.

In the scenes that Hatton shared with silky snake-in-the-grass Kosleck, guttural Rondo with his Leo Gorcey-level dialogue just couldn't compete. *And* it was again apparent that he couldn't act. You'd think it'd be impossible to judge a performance when the actor speaks infrequently, and his average line is just 2.6 words; it'd be like trying to determine if a guy is a good piano player when he'll only play you 2.6 notes at a time. And yet everyone agrees: It's obvious, Rondo couldn't act.

> [T]here is no getting around the fact that he was a terrible actor with virtually no range ... incapable of mouthing even the most mundane dialogue. Photographer Maury Gertsman's effective use of silhouettes and low angles in capturing Hatton's grotesqueness heighten the chill factor of the picture, but even his efforts are jettisoned whenever Rondo deadpans abysmal dialogue like "You're my friend ... shake," or, "You'd let the police get me, huh?"—John Brunas, *Universal Horrors*

Rondo also has one expression for all occasions, a vacant, not-a-thought-in-my-head look, whether he's posing for Marcel, chowing down, chasing a girl or violating someone's vertebrae. (In *The Royal Mounted Rides Again*, his expression doesn't change when he gets *shot*!) Universal Horrors truly ran the gamut, from Lon Chaney's Man of a Thousand Faces to poor Rondo's Man of *One* Face!

But at least Rondo's back to his *Pearl of Death* look (body padding that makes him ape-like), after looking like a bit of a peewee in *Jungle Captive*. I don't know if the *House of Horrors* folks did anything to actually make him taller (lifts in his shoes, etc.), but at least they were careful with their camera angles so that viewers couldn't tell that he was short. Notice that when the Creeper invades F. Holmes Harmon's Dover Tower office, he kills the critic by grabbing the *sitting* man from behind—a good way to handle the scene, since Hatton surely would have looked ridiculous reaching up to grasp the throat of 6'5" Alan Napier, one of Hollywood's tallest thesps. Another *House of Horrors* victim, Stella the model, was played by showgirl-tall Joan Shawlee, so the moviemakers took the trouble to keep them in separate shots, or on opposite sides of a room, or putting the camera much closer to one than the other. Only for a split-second do we see them together, more or less on the same level.

In its *House of Horrors* review, the *Chicago Daily Tribune* critic opined, "Martin Kosleck [right] gives an excellent performance as DeLange, and is really too good for such flimsy and nonsensical stuff."

Virginia Grey slaps the back of her left hand to make the cigarette atop it fly up into her mouth. Biggum fun with cancer sticks on the *House of Horrors* set. Left-right: Hatton, Grey, Bill Goodwin, Robert Lowery.

House of Horrors uses lighting, shadows and closeups for eerie effects; the sum of its small pleasures makes for a very entertaining hour. In fact, outside of movies featuring Universal's mascot monsters, it might be the

Rondo doesn't look too bad in this sketch seen on-screen in *House of Horrors*. In fact, give him a pince-nez and he'd look ... dare we say it? ... presidential.

best horror flick Universal had turned out in a couple years. And yet a fan should be forgiven for questioning the wisdom of a Rondo Hatton Creeper series. It must not have occurred to anyone at Universal that monster film aficionados might be dissatisfied...might even be put off...by the attempt to add to the Universal Monster Club a powerful retarded (I know, I know) man who kills in bulk. Following *House of Horrors*' 1946 release, the *Harrison's Reports* reviewer grumbled, "[T]here is little about the proceedings to horrify one unless the fact that the murders are committed by a half-witted giant can be considered horrendous rather than unpleasant." The *New York Herald Tribune* carped that the movie

> is not in the best of taste. The menace...is a glandular and mental case, an ugly, Neanderthal-featured brute of a moron called "The Creeper," who goes about strangling people at the drop of a suggestion. ... "The Creeper" is more pathetic than terrifying. The door for sequels is left wide open at the end, since the detective, after shooting the killer, says: "We have to get this man to a hospital." This is one door which should be closed at once.

In the mid-1940s, the heyday of movie series like Sherlock Holmes, the Falcon, Tarzan, Lassie, Dr. Kildare, etc., was the public ready for a B-movie series focused on the escapades of a backward serial killer, one who didn't even stop at women? It was a morbid concept for a series and (with the exception of Dr. Phibes) a concept that wouldn't fly until the late '70s and '80s and the rise of butchery buffs among Monster Kids, the dawn of the era of Michael Myers, Jason, Freddy *ad nauseam*. It's strange to think that the Creeper was the granddaddy of 'em all.

But maybe I, and *Harrison's Reports* and the *Herald Tribune*, are as all-wet as the Creeper on a midnight river swim. *Variety*'s reviewer praised *House of Horrors* up and down and said that Hatton's work "is of a quality to build up a strong following for the series among the shudder-audience."

Along Came a Spider Woman

After a slow year movie-wise, Rondo found himself in demand in the fall of 1945: Just six days after the September 25 wrap of *House of Horrors*, he extended his lengthening résumé of screen mayhem as shooting began on *The Spider Woman Strikes Back*. Universal had estimated the cost (total direct charges) of their next thriller at $117,200.

Look at it *this* way, Rondo: Without ugly in the world, there'd be no beauty. So thanks for your sacrifice! From *The Spider Woman Strikes Back*.

The Creeper began as a character in a Sherlock Holmes movie (*Pearl of Death*), and then in his own series he was a same-name New York killer cut from the same monstrous cloth. Now Gale Sondergaard, who spun her web for Sherlock in *The Spider Woman* (1944), made a similar crossover: Unconnected with her Holmes movie, *The Spider Woman Strikes Back* was intended as the first chapter in a Spider Woman horror series. *Variety* funnyman George E. Phair reacted to the news when it was first announced in March 1945:

> The Wolf Man and Frankenstein were weeping in their beers.
>
> The future of the monster trade was full of doubts and fears.
>
> "The femmes are muscling in on us," they wailed amid their tears.
>
> And in walked dismal Dracula to join the disquisition.
>
> "When monsterettes invade the screen, we're headed for perdition.
>
> What chance have mere male monsters got with female competition?"

* * *

Gale Sondergaard as "The Spider Woman" points to a new trend in horror films. Ghouls with glamour. And how about a line of 20 Delightful Demonettes?

Set in Nevada cattle country near a flyspeck town, *Spider Woman Strikes Back* stars Sondergaard as blind Zenobia Dollard, a woman blessed with gracious manners, a once-gracious manor (Universal's Shelby House from *Man Made Monster*, *The Mummy's Tomb*, *Son of Dracula*, etc.) and a streak of philanthropy. But even first-time viewers in 1946 had to have been aware right from the jump that she had criminal intent in every curve: The movie's title gave away that she was the Spider Woman, the poster proclaimed her "Mistress of Menace!" and her servant Mario was Rondo Hatton. Even Zenobia's hired companion Jean (Brenda Joyce) smells a rat upon learning that Zenobia's past companions all came and (quickly and mysteriously) went.

When Zenobia's forebears were in high cotton, they owned the land in all directions; she's now set her

"Got milk?": Horror movie makers went on a dairy kick for a few months in 1945-46, with drugged milk moving the plots of *The Spider Woman Strikes Back*, *She-Wolf of London* and *Devil Bat's Daughter*. Here "Spider Woman" Gale Sondergaard and Rondo try to force a glass on Brenda Joyce, who's udderly uninterested.

sights (she actually *isn't* blind) on driving out the local residents and then paying dirt-cheap prices for all the property that was once the Dollards'. In a basement botanical lab remindful of *WereWolf of London*'s, she cultivates carnivorous plants and extracts from them a poison with which deaf-mute Mario kills her neighbors' cattle. Every night, Jean is given a drugged glass of milk so that she's zonked when Zenobia creeps into her bedroom to draw blood, which is then fed to the plants. (Zenobia also feeds them spiders, to justify the title.) All of Zenobia's past companions were unwilling donors before their deaths.

Despite the starring performance of the sublimely sinister Sondergaard, *The Spider Woman Strikes Back* is a drag. And Hatton's Mario, like *The Jungle Captive*'s Moloch, looks like the runt in the litter of Universal movie menaces (scarcely taller than the women, and no padding). In fact, when the Brunas Brothers and I interviewed *Spider Woman Strikes Back* director Arthur Lubin in 1988 and asked about Rondo, the veteran director misremembered him as being a dwarf! Here, more than in *Jungle Captive*, the absence of padding on Rondo's body makes the viewer realize how disproportionately big his head was.

Rondo "talks" to Zenobia via sign language. I know nothing about sign language and yet I still feel certain that all of his gesticulations actually communicate nothing. Poor Rondo: Even when he acts (delivers dialogue) via sign language, he stinks! Zenobia describes Mario as an "atrocious servant," but that's a disservice: He's no Mr. French when it comes to household chores but he compensates by preparing Jean's drugged milk, helping Zenobia in the lab and Kevork-ing every passing cow.

During the run-up to production, Hollywood censor Joseph I. Breen communicated back and forth with Universal about the script, repeatedly advising that there be "no suggestion that Mario has any designs upon Jean" (Brenda Joyce). The filmmakers did not heed his admonition and gave us a Mario who would obviously be quite happy to molest her. In one Jean's Bedroom scene, he sits on the edge of the unconscious girl's bed and gets very hands-on, obviously about to make out with her. But Sondergaard unexpectedly appears in the doorway with a gasp of "Mario!" and Sexy Time is over before it even begins.

In the final reel, Mario loses his life trying to save Zenobia when flames engulf the lab and Zenobia is caught in the clutches of one of her own grabby vampire plants. Mario's noble gesture is a nice switch after three Hatton movies in a row in which he killed his bosses (Conover in *Pearl of Death*, Stendahl in *Jungle Captive*, Marcel in *House of Horrors*).

Hollywood's First Prequel: *The Brute Man*

Hatton was now on a movie-a-month schedule: November 15 marked the start of shooting on the next Creeper stanza, *The Brute Man*. This murder thriller tells the Creeper's origin story, and so for years Monster Kids have called it the first prequel. But let's acknowledge the *possibility* that Universal had no such thing in mind: Who's to say that, once *The Brute Man* and *House of Horrors* were in the can, Universal didn't intend to release them in that order (the origin story *Brute Man* first)? Then, after Hatton's February 1946 death, any number of considerations could have changed that plan. All the way back to 1944, Universal was announcing that *The Brute Man* would be "the first picture in a series for this character" (the Creeper).

> [*Spider Woman Strikes Back*] occupies a unique position in the canon of Universal horror movies of the '40s _ right at the bottom of the heap. – Universal Horror historian Michael Brunas

That said, it must be added that when Rondo cameos in the opening credits of *House of Horrors*, the superimposed text reads "Introducing RONDO HATTON as THE CREEPER," while in *The Brute Man* it reads "And RONDO HATTON as The Creeper." So by the time the titles were put on these movies, the decision for *The Brute Man* to go second had already been made. Maybe Universal released *House of Horrors* first simply because it was the better of the two movies, a livelier kick-off for the series.

Regardless of what Universal's original plan may or may not have been, the fact remains that *House of Horrors* did come to theaters first and then *The Brute Man* (following Universal's sale of the latter movie to PRC), and that makes it a prequel. Hollywood's next prequel, commonly called the first-ever, was again a Universal: *Another Part of the Forest*, the 1948 predecessor to the story of 1941's *The Little Foxes*.

A *Brute Man* script dated October 15, 1945, was sent to Motion Picture Producers & Distributors of America (i.e., Joseph I. Breen) and he *very* promptly (October *16*!) responded to Universal's Maurice Pivar (Ben's brother):

> [We] are happy to report that the basic story seems to comply with the provisions of the Production Code.

> Please see the during the murders that there are no sounds escaping from the victims, such as the "gurgles" described in scene 223 [the scene in which the Creeper kills Cliff], in order to prevent unnecessary and unacceptable gruesomeness.

Perhaps the tackiest thing about *The Brute Man* is that at least one of its scripters seems to have known a biographical detail of Hatton's life, and wove it into the story. His character is seen in flashbacks as a handsome young football hero, which is precisely what Hatton *was* before acromegaly set in. If Rondo read the whole script, the fact that the flashbacks feature a "re-imagining" of Hatton's own life could not have been missed by the unfortunate actor.

The Brute Man: Synopsis

Police cars with wailing sirens career along the gritty night streets of a big city following the report of a homicide. Afoot on these same streets is the Creeper, a deformed man in black coat and hat; he looks like Murder looking for a place to happen. He walks to a residential neighborhood and the home of socialite Joan Bemis: Catching her alone outside, he calls himself Hal Moffat. "You're not Hal Moffat!" she protests, as he comes closer. He promises not to hurt her, but the horrorstruck woman starts screaming. The camera itself rises up-up-and-away so that we don't see him break her back. And we're only four minutes into the movie.

Joan's the newest victim of this killer, called the Back Breaker in a newspaper story but known to all the movie's characters as the Creeper. Police surround him in a waterfront tenement district, but he makes an unseen fire-escape ascent and enters the apartment of piano teacher Helen Paige as she plays Liszt's "Liebesträume." The Creeper is surprised that Helen isn't afraid of him. When the footsteps of approaching policemen are heard, he vamooses. Helen now plays Schubert's "Second Impromptu, Opus 142." Helen must dig public domain music.

Under cover of darkness, the Creeper slips a note under the door of Mr. Haskins' grocery store. The next morning, Haskins bags the requested items and gives them to his delivery boy Jimmy, who suspects that the mystery customer is the Creeper. The address "23 Waters Street" in the note is the Creeper's hovel under a wooden walkway at the river's edge. Suspicious, Jimmy tries to spy on its occupant but the Creeper detects him, and he makes short work of the Boy Who Cried Creeper.

Investigating Jimmy's disappearance, Capt. Donelly, head of the homicide squad, and Lt. Gates find his body in the shack, along with an old newspaper clipping depicting Hampton University class of 1930

By 1946, moviegoers knew that Gale Sondergaard's characters were a high risk for lowdown behavior. In *The Spider Woman Strikes Back*, she and deaf-and-dumb butler Hatton put a dent in the local cow population, a key part of their bigger plan. *Hollywood Reporter* called this flick "past rescue by director or cast."

From left to right: Joan has fallen for Hal but Hal has fallen for Virginia but Virginia and Cliff have fallen for each other. A four-sided triangle leads to tragedy.

students Cliff Scott, Virginia Rogers and Hal Moffat. Suspecting that Moffat may be the Creeper, the cops proceed to Cliff and Virginia's fancy Cottage Grove Avenue home (they're now man and wife) to question them. We spend four minutes watching Cliff-narrated flashbacks of four college kids—Cliff, Virginia, Hal and Joan Bemis—as they were in 1930. To get even with

Fred Coby (pictured here with Jan Wiley) plays Hal Moffat pre-deformity in the *Brute Man* flashbacks. He was a good choice looks-wise as he has a face that kinda resembles one that *could* morph into that of the Creeper.

football star Hal for various shenanigans, Cliff tricks him into giving a wrong answer at a verbal quiz in Prof. Cushman's chemistry class. The professor tells Hal to stay after class; Hal gives Cliff an "if looks could kill" look. After class, Hal's temper flares and he throws a test tube of chemicals to the floor at his feet. It explodes, and the glands and nerves in Hal's face are affected. After a head-wrapped-in-bandages hospital stay, a bitter Hal drops out of sight. But he carries a grudge longer than the Count of Monte Cristo and now he's back with a vengeance; just ask Prof. Cushman and Joan.

The Creeper remembers that Helen was not repulsed by him and, tender soul that he is, he enters a pawnshop with an attractive butterfly pin in the window. When the pawnbroker expects to get paid, he gets killed. Returning to Helen's beaten-down corner of the city, the Creeper pays her a second visit. This time, she reveals that she's blind (which explains why she didn't flinch at his ugliness). After Helen asserts, at some length, that blind people are excellent judges of character, she invites the six-time murderer to visit as often as he likes. When the Creeper next comes calling, Helen is playing Chopin's Etude, No. 10, Opus 3. (You don't *get* plot details like that in other books!) Prodded by his questions, Helen says that her sight could be restored by an operation but the cost, two or three thou, is two or three thou too much for her.

The Scott home has a police guard but the Creeper still manages to invade it, and he confronts the Scotts in Virginia's bedroom. (The Creeper to Cliff: "I don't blame you for not reck-a-nizin' me.") Responding to his demand for money, Cliff takes a box of Virginia's jewels out of a wall safe—but he *also* gets hold of a gun with which he shoots the Creeper in self-defense. While Virginia runs to fetch the police guard, the Creeper grabs Cliff and finishes him off.

Heavier by the weight of a bullet or two, the Creeper now gets around at a sub-creep pace. He painfully makes his way to Helen's apartment where he drips blood on her rug and gives her Virginia's jewels, which she can sell for enough money to afford the operation. Helen brings them to a jeweler for appraisal, but he recognizes them as Virginia's stolen baubles and hollers cop. During interrogation by Donelly, Helen collapses into a chair when he reveals that her pal Hal is the Creeper.

The Creeper buys a newspaper and learns that Helen sang to the cops about their friendship. His devotion turns to hate and a desire for revenge. With a reckless indulgence common to characters in the last reels of B-movies, he steals into Helen's apartment as she sits replaying "Liebesträume." From behind, he sneaks up on her, his meat hooks outstretched. He's on the 30, the 20, the 10...*fumble*! It's a police trap! Two uniformed officers pop out of hiding, seize the Creeper and wrestle him out of the room. This too-abrupt, let's-get-this-thing-done denouement leaves the door open for Further Adventures of the Creeper.

Because the Creeper tried to help her, Helen regrets acting as bait on behalf of the police, but Donelly cheers her up by revealing that arrangements will be made for her to have her sight-restoring operation.

> [The Brute Man] proves mostly that spoiled young football heroes used to winning and never losing make dandy manic-depressives.
> – Buffalo Courier-Express

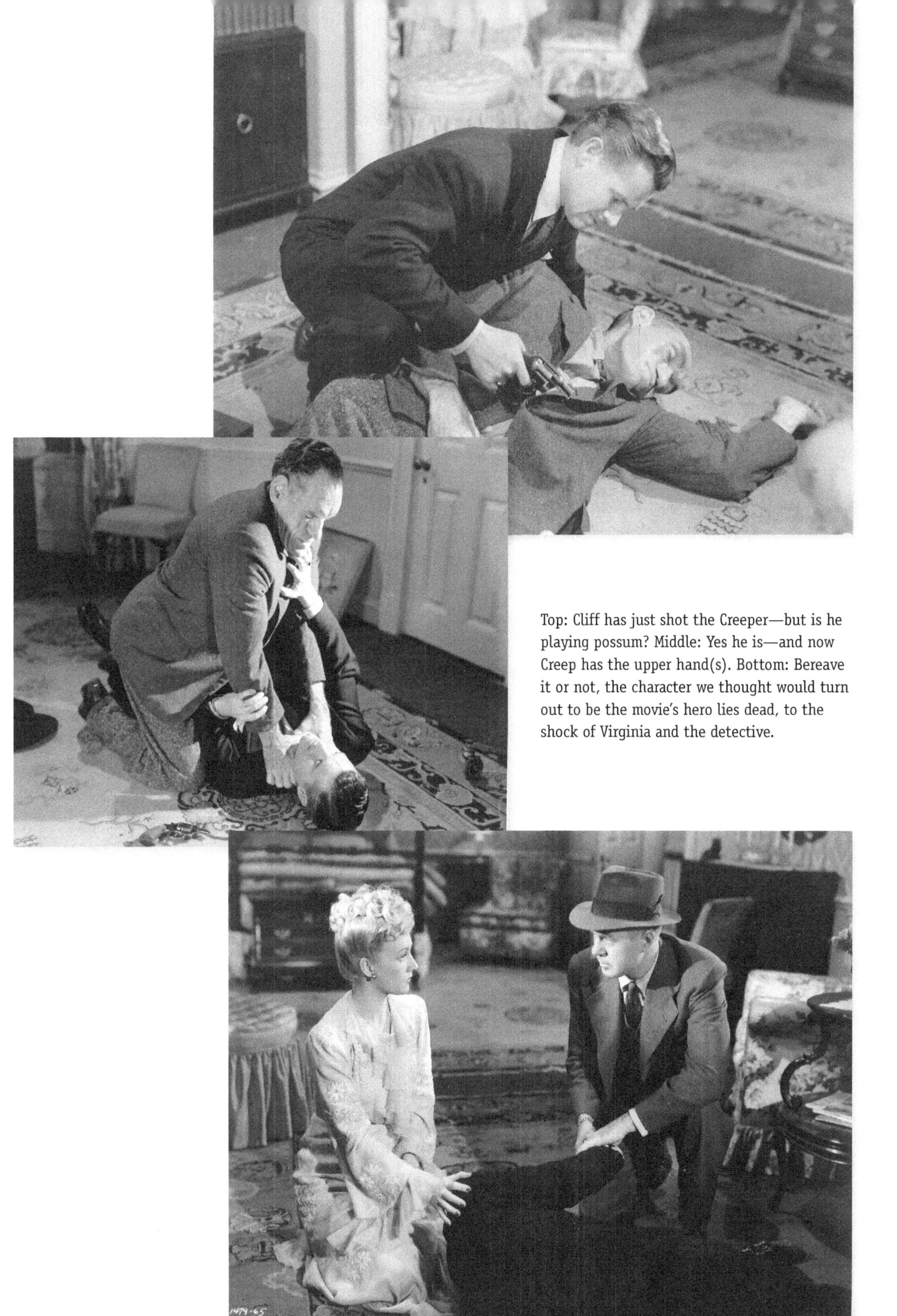

Top: Cliff has just shot the Creeper—but is he playing possum? Middle: Yes he is—and now Creep has the upper hand(s). Bottom: Bereave it or not, the character we thought would turn out to be the movie's hero lies dead, to the shock of Virginia and the detective.

Alan Foster, who plays the jeweler who drops a dime on Helen and her hot rocks, probably got his *Brute Man* bit through his producer pal Ben Pivar. Read about Foster on page 274.

"Treachery, thy name is Helen"—or so the Creeper believes—and affection U-turns to animus.

The Brute Man: Production

There was a company call of nine a.m. on Day 1 of *Brute Man* production, November 15, 1945. Cast and crew congregated on Tenement Street where, one month earlier, the Creeper caught up with Virginia Christine in *House of Horrors*. In *Brute Man*, it represents slummy "Woddel Street, 700 block" (per the police radio announcer) and, from nine in the morning until early evening, Hatton, several bit players and over two dozen extras filmed (day for night) most of the exteriors set in this area. In part of the Tenement Street footage, the police lieutenant leading the Creeper search is veteran movie villain Tristram Coffin.

On Day 2, the company shot more footage on Tenement Street until 4:20 p.m. and then moved to Stage 9 for the pawnshop scene in which the Creeper takes a $12.50 butterfly pin and the life of the pawnbroker. The luckless fellow was played by Charles Wagenheim, already a past victim of Hatton's (*The Jungle Captive*'s morgue attendant).

The next two days of work, Saturday, November 17, and Monday, November 19, were spent in Helen's Apartment on Stage 8. Saturday's to-do list included the scene of policemen searching the apartment for the Creeper; on Monday, they shot the scene where Helen gives little Dorothy a piano lesson. Dorothy's mom was played by Peggy Converse, wife of Universal contractee Don Porter (*Night Monster, She-Wolf of London*). The annoying Dorothy ("Boogie-woogie *is* solid, it really sends me!") is Mary Anne Bricker, who might be related to *Brute Man* co-writer George Bricker. But if she was, a Universal publicist opted not to mention that connection and instead identified her as the seven-year-old cousin of ex–Ohio Gov. John W. Bricker. I doubt that this prompted fans of ex–Ohio Gov. John W. Bricker to see the picture. (I bet it didn't prompt ex–Ohio Gov. John W. Bricker to see the picture!)

On November 20, on Universal's Waterfront Street, the moviemakers shot the movie's pier scenes: the street level above and, down a ramp and practically at the edge of the water (i.e., the studio tank), the door to the shack where the Creeper hangs his ratty hat. Jimmy, the grocery store delivery boy who gets too curious, was played by Jack Parker. Parker was one of several *Brute Man* bit players who had already worked in *House of Horrors*; there he was the elevator boy ogling Virginia Grey.

This was the first day of employment for Donald MacBride as Capt. Donelly of the homicide squad and Peter Whitney as a lieutenant, suit-and-tie policemen assigned to the Creeper case. (*The Brute Man* was MacBride's second Universal genre flick, the comic actor having already played the gangster with designs on kooky inventor John Barrymore's invisibility machine in 1940's *The Invisible Woman*.) In the mid-afternoon, cast and crew shifted to Stage 8, where they shot the shack interiors. Scenes set in Helen's Apartment (Stage 8), the Grocery Store (Stage 9) and the Police Broadcast Station (Stage 9) were shot on the 21st.

A day off for Thanksgiving and then on Friday the 23rd a couple real turkey scenes: the dreadful comic relief sequences set in Donelly's office (Stage 9), as the police captain matches wits with the commissioner (Joseph Crehan) and the mayor's secretary (Lorin Raker). Work started late (a one p.m. company call) on Saturday the 24th and more shooting was done on the Donelly's Office and Helen's Apartment sets. The moviemakers labored right into the night: After dinner, they reconvened on the back lot's New England Street, where the Creeper spies on socialite Joan (JaNelle Johnson), who's escorting departing guests to their car, and waits until she's alone to confront her. The scene is nicely photographed, starting with a tracking shot of the Creeper's legs as he walks down the block toward the house. The camera then cranes back and up as the Creeper conceals himself in shrubbery. After the guests leave, the Creeper (and the camera) menacingly advance on Joan. After a medium closeup of the screaming Joan, she drops below the frame line as the camera rapidly cranes up to the level of a second-story window. And now the screaming stops.

On Monday, November 26, as production headed for the homestretch, Tom Neal and Jan Wiley joined

Police search Helen's apartment for the Creeper, led by suit-and-tie detective Pat McVey, future star of TV's long-running *Big Town* series.

From the *Brute Man* pressbook, we learn that Hatton gives "[what] is described as one of the cinema's most gripping performances." If this is what the writer meant by "gripping," yes; otherwise, no.

the cast playing upper crusters Cliff and Virginia. On Stage 15, scenes inside the Scott home were shot during the day. After dinner, the company converged at the back lot's Shelby House, now being seen for the second time in a Rondo Hatton movie (it "played" Zenobia's home in *Spider Woman Strikes Back*). In *Brute Man*, the Shelby House serves as the exterior of Cliff and Virginia's home, and footage of Hatton

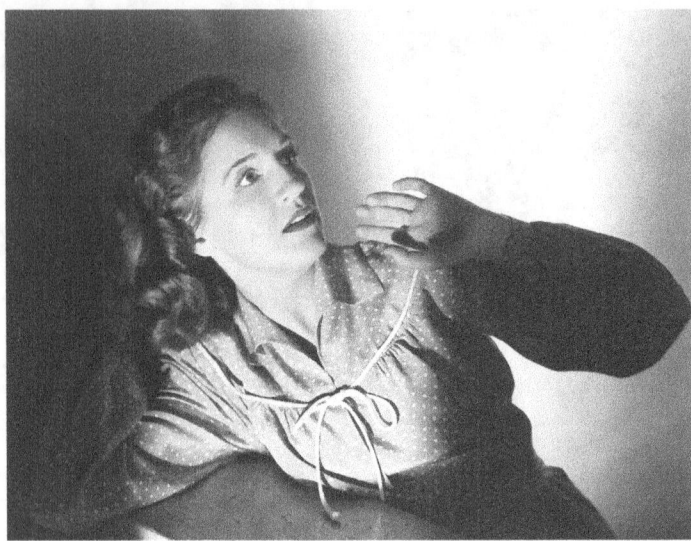

JaNelle Johnson, who played Creeper victim Joan Bemis, was the wife of actor George Dolenz, star of Rondo's serial *The Royal Mounted Rides Again*. Their son Micky Dolenz, eight months old at the time of *The Brute Man*, became a kid actor in the 1950s (TV's *Circus Boy*) and one of the Monkees in the 1960s.

By *Brute Man* time, even Rondo's once-snappy-looking hats looked ready for retirement. This one looks like he wore it through a car wash.

and a police detective (John Gallaudet) prowling around the outside was photographed late into the night. Scott Living Room, Lower Hall and Upper Hall scenes were shot on Stage 15 the whole of the next day.

It's interesting to note that on days that Rondo Hatton did not work, or worked briefly, or worked without much dialogue, there were a lot less takes of each shot. For example, on the two days spent shooting Scott House scenes with Neal, Wiley, Donald MacBride and Peter Whitney, production paperwork reveals smooth sailing; they got many shots on the first and only take. On days when Rondo had dialogue, many shots required multiple takes, on one occasion well over a dozen, with the notation **nga** (no good—actor) revealing the reason for most of the bad takes. Since Rondo Acting Days and Multiple Takes Days coincided throughout production, we seem to have our culprit.

Jane Adams confirms this: She told me that Hatton "had an awful time remembering his lines." She expanded on this for Greg Mank: "The progressive state of Rondo's disease made it very difficult for him to remember his script and always be responsive." To interviewer Chris W. Pustorino: "It was hard working with him, but mainly because I felt so sorry for him.…He would occasionally forget his lines, but he was always extremely polite." She laid it on the line bluntly for interviewer Jack Gourlay: "So pathetic to work with—almost autistic." At this point (late November 1945), Hatton had just over two months to live.

Adams had also observed, "Universal was starring him and exploiting him, which was sort of too bad." But was it really "too bad"? If Hatton enjoyed acting in movies and liked the money, it would have been "too bad" if every studio *refused* to use and exploit him. Imagine having some disability or deformity and wanting to act, but every studio "respects" you too much to hire you…and at the same time, they regularly hire "normal" actors and make them look and/or act like someone with your disability or deformity. Operator, get me the EEOC!

On November 28, Virginia's Bedroom scenes were filmed on Stage 15. The Creeper, Virginia and Scott talk back and

Just weeks after Jane Adams played the hunchback nurse in Universal's *House of Dracula* (top), she tackled the role of another dreary disabled character, *The Brute Man*'s blind Helen. But for *Brute Man* publicity photos, she went from modest to hottest.

Bare-handed back-breaking, the most tactile of murder methods. Just ask Rondo.

Best scene in *The Brute Man*: The Creeper pauses during his late-night ramble and leaves patrons of the Collegiate Cafe aghast.

forth quite a bit, and at a faster pace than the Creeper schmoozed with blind Helen, and the production paperwork again shows that the company kept going deep into multi-take territory. Getting an acceptable Shot 214 took 18 attempts, nine of them "no good—actor," the ordeal stretching from 3:10 to 5:15.

Some short scenes were shot on the 29th: first, on Stage 6, the scene of Cliff and Hal in their college room. (Tom Neal is on the wrong side of 30 to play a college boy.) Then, on Stage 9, Hal's hospital room, the jeweler's shop and more.

Scheduled for 12 days, *The Brute Man* unluckily went over by one: The 13th and last day was November 30, with shooting taking place on Stage 9 (the interior *and* exterior of the Collegiate Cafe) and Stage 22 (the chemistry classroom and the football field grandstand). We don't get a very good look at Prof. Cushman the teacher in the classroom scene but every Baby Boomer Monster Kid should recognize the actor by his unmistakable voice: John Hamilton, *Adventures of Superman*'s dyspeptic Perry White. Between the three settings, over 50 extras worked that day.

On that final day, Rondo was on hand from nine in the morning until 8:10 at night, but all he could have done on film was the opening-reel scene in which the Creeper pauses on the sidewalk to peer inside the Collegiate Cafe, his hangout back in his college days. With Hatton (seen from the back) in the foreground, we too look through the large plate-glass window at the young people inside. One girl, seated at a window table, is the first to notice him, and her smile fades. One by one, other heads turn; one appalled girl rises to her feet. Emanating from the cafe, the pleasant instrumental number "Once Upon a Dream" is heard during this nightmarish interlude. His face a mask of disdain, the Creeper slowly turns and paces away as the kids continue to silently gape. It might be the most effective moment in any of Hatton's horrors (outside of *Pearl of Death*, of course). And it appears to be the last thing Hatton ever did on film.

"Creeper" Series Folds

Recent death of Rondo Hatton, screen actor, caused the death of Universal's "Creeper" series.– *Variety*, February 13, 1946

House of Horrors made its bow in February 1946, while *The Brute Man* waited in the pipeline. Then in late July 1946, Universal—one of Hollywood's oldest production companies—merged with one of its newest, International, and this new Siamese Twin of the industry announced that it was dedicating itself exclusively to the production of high-budget pictures. But like the Creeper brooding in his below-the-boardwalk shack, the completed *Brute Man* lurked in its catacombs, alongside other B pictures left over from the earlier regime. Imagine *The Brute Man* with the glossy new Earth-seen-from-outer-space Universal-International logo!

U-I couldn't imagine it, and with partial success they tried to unload some of these lower-tier flicks on PRC. As reported in the October 23, 1946, *Variety*:

> Aiming to rid its releasing slate for next year of one of its few remaining low-budgeters, Universal has sold the negative of *The Brute Man* to PRC. Price was approximately $125,000, which comprised the negative cost plus interest on the coin U had tied up in the film.
>
> Deal was made about 10 weeks ago, following U's merger with International and the resultant decision to make nothing but top-budgeters. It wasn't revealed until last week, however, when PRC held its trade screening of the film…. Titles on the pic gave no indication of its origin on the U lot….
>
> Two other films were included in original negotiations, it has been learned, but U decided to hang on to them, since they are both in Cinecolor and company figures it could justifiably distribute them under the new policy. They are [*The*] *Vigilantes Return* with Jon Hall and Margaret Lindsay, and *The Michigan Kid* with Hall….
>
> No further sales of U negatives are contemplated, a U exec stated last week.

For years, various captains of Monster Kid fandom have written that Universal palmed *The Brute Man* off on PRC because, once Hatton had died, the movie was an embarrassment to them. But learning that its fellow B-films *The Vigilantes Return* and *The Michigan Kid* were also dangled in front of PRC makes these fans' *Brute Man* "facts" sound more like speculative fiction.

Drab and depressing, *The Brute Man* was a good fit for PRC, a company remembered for its welter of somber horror shoestringers. (William K. Everson wrote in *More Classics of the Horror Film*, "PRC [was] probably delighted to have such a glossy little picture, bad or not.") It's not half, or even one-quarter, the movie *House of Horrors* is. Movies have a lot more life when they tell their stories rapidly and concisely, and *House of Horrors* does a better job of that. A *magnificent* job, in fact, measured against *Brute Man*'s cycle of soporific scenes (Creeper slaying innocent people, awkward Creeper-Helen banter, Donelly and Gates passing the buck). There are stretches where all you can think is that nothing is happening. Blame the fact that Rondo's face could stop a clock, but the movie seems to last a *very* long 58 minutes.

One of the sad things about Hatton's early death: In 1944, Universal signed him to star in his own series but things stalled and *House of Horrors* and *The Brute Man* weren't made until the second half of 1945; and then Universal was in no hurry to release them. Because Universal proceeded at a creeper's pace, Rondo went to his grave without seeing *either* of the only two movies in which he starred.

> [*The Brute Man*] makes *House of Horrors* look like *Citizen Kane*. – DVD Savant Glenn Erickson

> A *Brute Man* "Selling Angle" from *Boxoffice* magazine:
> Have a uniformed "officer" lead a man, heavily chained and with padded chest and shoulders, through the streets.

Cast and Credits: Rondo Hatton's Creeper Series

House of Horrors (1946)

Released by Universal
66 minutes
Produced by Ben Pivar
Directed by Jean Yarbrough
Screenplay: George Bricker
Original Story: Dwight V. Babcock
Photography: Maury Gertsman
Editor: Philip Cahn
Music Director: Hans J. Salter
Art Directors: John B. Goodman and Abraham Grossman
Director of Sound: Bernard B. Brown
Technician: Robert Pritchard
Set Decorators: Russell A. Gausman and Ralph Warrington
Gowns: Vera West
Makeup Director: Jack P. Pierce

Uncredited:
Additional Photography: George Robinson
Assistant Directors: Mort Singer, Ralph Slosser and Phil Bowles
Script Supervisor: Dorothy Yutzi
Camera Operator: John Martin
Assistant Camera: Max Wolk
Still Photographers: George Strock and Art Marion
Gaffer: John Brooks
Best Boy: Murray Rock
Grip: Russ Frank
Second Grip: Bob Daudette
Prop Men: Bob Murdock, Lee Carson, Clarence Baker and Fay Frame
Sound Recorder: Bill Richards
Boom Men: A.B. Roberts and Frank Artman
Makeup: Carlie Taylor
Hairdresser: Dotha Hippe
Men's Wardrobe: Shirley Ware
Women's Wardrobe: Rose Brandi
Painters: Peter Puzzo and Jim Watson
Laborer: Frank Litson
Rondo Hatton's Stand-in: Ed Cushing

Robert Lowery (*Steve Morrow*)
Virginia Grey (*Joan Medford*)
Bill Goodwin (*Police Lt. Larry Brooks*)
Martin Kosleck (*Marcel DeLange*)
Alan Napier (*F. Holmes Harmon*)
Howard Freeman (*Hal Ormiston*)
Joan Fulton [Joan Shawlee] (*Stella McNally*)
Virginia Christine (*Daisy Sutter*)

Uncredited:
Byron Foulger (*Mr. Samuels*)
Syd Saylor (*Jerry*)
Billy Newell (*Tomlinson—Deputy Coroner*)
William Ruhl (*Ellis*)
Jack Parker (*Elevator Boy*)
Oliver Blake (*Janitor*)
Janet Shaw (*Cab Driver*)
Terry Mason (*Clarence*)
Clifton Young, Kernan Cripps (*Detectives*)
Charles Wagenheim (*Walter—Newspaper Engraver*)
Stephen Wayne (*Speed*)
Perc Launders (*Smitty*)
Mary Field (*Nora*)
Tom Quinn (*Cab Driver*)
Unconfirmed:
Danny Jackson (*Office Boy*)

The Brute Man (1946)

Produced by Universal
Released by Producers Releasing Corporation
58 minutes
Produced by Ben Pivar
Directed by Jean Yarbrough
Screenplay: George Bricker and M. Coates Webster
Original Story: Dwight V. Babcock
Photography: Maury Gertsman
Editor: Philip Cahn
Art Directors: John B. Goodman and Abraham Grossman
Director of Sound: Bernard B. Brown
Technician: Joe Lapis

Set Decorators: Russell A. Gausman and Edward R. Robinson
Gowns: Vera West
Hair Stylist: Carmen Dirigo
Director of Makeup: Jack P. Pierce
Dialogue Director: Raymond Kessler
Uncredited:
Tracked Music: Frank Skinner, Hans J. Salter, Paul Sawtell, William Lava, Dimitri Tiomkin, Charles Previn, Lester Pine, Jack Brooks, Franz Liszt, Franz Schubert
Assistant Directors: Ralph Slosser and Harry Jones
Script Supervisor: Mary Chaffee
Camera Operator: John Martin and William Dodds
Camera Crew Members: Walter Williams, Cliff King and Max Wolk
Assistant Cameraman: Walter Bluemel
Grip: Russell Franks
Gaffer: Johnny Brooks
Best Boy: Maury Rock
Assistant Cutter: Mort Tubor
Boom Operator: Jack Bolger
Sound Recorder: Don Cunliffe
Props: Bob Murdock
Wardrobe Man: Maury Friedman
Wardrobe Lady: Margaret Bornman
Hairdresser: Alta Hitchcock
Stand-in: Sally Wood
Still Photographer: Maurice Goldberg
Unit Publicist: Ann Meyers

Tom Neal (*Cliff Scott*)
Jan Wiley (*Virginia Rogers Scott*)
Jane Adams (*Helen Paige*)
Donald MacBride (*Police Capt. M.J. Donelly*)
Peter Whitney (*Police Lt. Gates*)
Fred Coby (*Hal Moffat*)
JaNelle Johnson (*Joan Bemis*)
And Rondo Hatton
as *The Creeper*
Uncredited:
Jim Nolan (*Police Radio Announcer*)
Rodney Bell, Perc Launders, John Roche, Karen Knight, Norma Gilchrist (*Joan's Guests*)
Tristram Coffin (*Police Lieutenant/Voice of Radio Newscaster*)
Cy Schindell (*Policeman*)
Patrick McVey (*Detective in Helen's Apartment*)
Warren Jackson (*Policeman in Helen's Apartment*)
Jack Parker (*Jimmy*)
Oscar O'Shea (*Mr. Haskins*)
Margaret Hoffman (*Mrs. Hart*)
Joseph Crehan (*Police Commissioner Salisbury*)
Lorin Raker (*Mr. Parkington*)
Jim Clark, Joyce Stuart, Carl Anders, Gabrielle Windsor, Paula Gray, Larry Wyle (*Students*)
John Hamilton (*Prof. Cushman*)
Beatrice Roberts (*Nurse*)
Charles Wagenheim (*Pawnbroker*)
Mary Anne Bricker (*Dorothy Obringer*)
Peggy Converse (*Mrs. Obringer*)
John Gallaudet (*Detective Guarding the Scott House*)
Alan Foster (*Jeweler*)
Danny Jackson (*Newsboy*)
Unconfirmed:
Martin Skelly (*Cab Driver*)

"Look at my face!" A Release History of The Brute Man

By Dr. Robert J. Kiss

Horror held sway for years at Universal City, but in 1945 its reign ended with a whimper, and Universal dumped *The Brute Man* on PRC like a supermarket dumping its past-its-sell-date hamburger.

No early parole for the Universal Creeper

Following the July 30, 1946, formation of Universal-International, the newly merged companies' president William Goetz implemented a lofty policy of no longer issuing B movies or serials in order for the studio to focus on "prestige" output. The following month's outright sale of the "old" Universal Pictures production *The Brute Man* to Poverty Row producer-distributor PRC thus constituted an advantageous deal for both parties: It allowed U-I to divest itself of an exploitation-minded 58-minute picture that was entirely out of step with its new ambitions, while PRC gained a competently made, fully edited and scored feature that fit well with its established expertise in supplying lower-tier houses with roughly hour-long product.

One should not, however, underestimate just how close Universal had come to unleashing *The Brute Man* on moviegoers under its own banner. During the two weeks from July 6 to 20, 1946, the title was listed in trade publications as an imminently forthcoming August 23 release from the studio, bearing the Universal scheduling code #547. Moreover, Universal had already created a complete portfolio of campaign and publicity artwork for the release. (This was also handed over to PRC.) In the case of National Screen Service–issued stills, lobby cards and posters, the only alteration made to the designs involved substituting

It seems like every one of Universal's 1940s monsters felt compelled to have its picture taken with this pedestal and against this swirl-texture stucco wall. Today it's Rondo's turn.

the Universal name and logo with those of PRC. A new purple-colored PRC pressbook for the film was created as well, although it's evident that a substantial number of green-colored Universal pressbooks, rather than being pulped, were sent out to theaters and exchanges too. Consequently, one in every 25 first-run engagements of PRC's *The Brute Man* during 1946 and 1947 ended up being advertised in newspapers with Universal-branded ad mats that included the words "A Universal Picture" and the Universal globe logo!

U-I meanwhile plugged the gap in its release schedule by reassigning the August 23 release date and scheduling code #547 to one of a string of J. Arthur Rank–controlled British "prestige pictures" to which it had acquired the U.S. distribution rights – namely, the portmanteau horror *Dead of Night*. Shorn of two of its five stories in order to streamline its running time down from 103 to 77 minutes, the film picked up plaudits from broadsheet critics, but still proved a somewhat tough sell to general audiences on account of the negligible U.S. marquee value of its all-star British cast. Tellingly, when a handful of movie theaters around the nation elected to pair U-I's *Dead of Night* with PRC's *The*

Brute Man as a first-run double bill between December 1946 and February 1947, each picture was equally likely to play as either the top or bottom half of the bill.

PRC, the dedicated underperformer

Trade magazine *Boxoffice*, in its November 9, 1946 and November 15, 1947 editions, tabulated the "average" first-run performance of some 652 features (excluding Westerns) released between fall 1945 and summer 1947, drawing on data from 21 major U.S. cities, as well as from mid-sized cities and small towns. According to these statistics, *Dead of Night* had grossed a just-above-average 102%, while *The Brute Man* had underperformed slightly at 95%.

In real terms, the outcome looked rather different, since *Boxoffice*'s "100 percent average" benchmark for determining success was at once an illusory and misleading figure, arrived at simply by averaging out the box office yield of major, minor and Poverty Row studio product – as if high-end, middle-of-the-road and lower-echelon manufacturers in *any* industry could be meaningfully compared in such a one-size-fits-all manner. Or, to put it another way: Who in their right mind would attempt to measure the success of a lavish, big-budget MGM Technicolor musical and a barely–hour-long Monogram or PRC black-and-white cheapie on a single scale, when the degree of investment in production and publicity, and the type and extent of business required for each to turn a profit, were clearly utterly disparate?

Box Office Digest of November 9, 1946, published an illuminating list with regard to what *really* constituted "average" box office business for different studios' output during the first three quarters of 1946, which it is worth reproducing here:

Paramount	19 releases	155%
Warner Bros.	15 releases	152%
MGM	22 releases	149%
United Artists	13 releases	143%
20th Century–Fox	25 releases	125%
RKO-Radio	26 releases	124%
Universal	34 releases	106%
Columbia	31 releases	99%
Republic	24 releases	88%
Monogram	23 releases	83%
PRC	14 releases	83%

Reconsidering the 102% gross scored for Universal by *Dead of Night*, one can see that this in fact represented a slightly less-than-average return once relativized in terms of the 106% norm for the studio. In the same issue of *Box Office Digest*, meanwhile, a predicted box office performance of 85% for the still-unreleased final Rondo Hatton feature was described with the statement, "PRC should do right well with *The Brute Man*," a comment which only makes sense after one realizes that 83% was the norm for the studio's releases. The proven 93% performance of Edgar G. Ulmer's 86-minute melodrama *Her Sister's Secret* – a veritable mega-production by PRC standards – was in turn declared "one of [its] biggest box office successes in a long time." Thus, *The Brute Man*'s ultimate 95% gross, as reported in the November 15, 1947, edition of *Boxoffice*, represents a figure that was some 14% above the studio average in real terms, and unequivocally a commercial success for PRC.

Accordingly, the seemingly contradictory assessments of advance reviewers in *Variety* and *The Hollywood Reporter* – who respectively pegged *The Brute Man* as "suitable only for lower dualers" and as a release that would "do handsomely for PRC" – may not be quite so at odds as they initially appear. For while the kind of flashy multi-venue openings at big city premiere houses which are popularly associated with first-run releases play only the scantest role in *The Brute Man*'s theatrical history, its release through PRC nonetheless highlights how a Poverty Row operation was able to clean up at the box office – relative to its own expectations – by distributing the picture in a gradual, workmanlike manner to mostly sub–thousand-seat lower-rung venues that were typically overlooked by first-run bookers, including second-run, revival, repertory and African-American theaters.

The October 1946 general release that never was

PRC's president, Harry H. Thomas, first announced the newly acquired *Brute Man* as part of the company's 1946-47 release program at its Atlantic City sales convention on September 5, 1946. By September 19, an unrealistic release date of October 1 had been affixed to the title in the context of a widely published schedule for PRC's forthcoming dozen releases for the final quarter of 1946. Although none of the dates in this schedule constituted anything more than "placeholders" designed to give a tentative outline of what was to come from the studio, they all wound up being endlessly repeated throughout the contemporary trade press – and equally ceaselessly regurgitated in film historical sources ever since.

In reality, *The Brute Man* would not be copyrighted (to PRC's parent company, Pathé Industries, Inc.) until October 13, and received its trade preview in New York on October 17. The slew of advance reviews that appeared between October 18 and November 9 in *Box Office Digest*, *Boxoffice*, *Harrison's Reports*, *The Hollywood Reporter*, *Motion Picture Daily*, *Motion Picture Herald*, *Showmen's Trade Review* and *Variety* were all based on this lone preview screening.

Among the aforementioned publications, only *Boxoffice* would go on (in its April 19, 1947, edition) to retrospectively adjust *The Brute Man*'s "street date" to November 2, 1946. However, this too was unduly optimistic. The film's earliest scattered – and decidedly low-key – openings had in fact taken place in the northeast and midwest during the *last week* of November. These included what may have been its *de facto* premiere, in the form of a two-day run commencing November 25 at the 500-seat Roxy Theatre in Meyersdale, Pennsylvania, where it served as the lower half of a double bill with Monogram's first-run *Wife Wanted* starring Kay Francis. It thereafter played for four days beginning November 29 at the 768-seat Viking Theater, a second-run house in Appleton, Wisconsin, where it again constituted the lower half of a double bill – this time headed by the second-run RKO Western *West of the Pecos* starring Robert Mitchum. To a great extent, PRC had started out just as it meant to go on, slowly and steadily supplying its latest release primarily to small-scale venues at which a first-run picture on the bill could in itself constitute a novelty.

A neverending first run, November 1946 to November 1947 (and beyond)

Significant numbers of local and regional first-run openings of *The Brute Man* continued in different sections of the nation over the next 52 weeks through the end of November 1947, with the period from March to May 1947 marked by a successive *increase* in bookings. Indeed, the overwhelming majority of the movie's first-run playdates fell in 1947, with no discernible interruption after PRC was subsumed within Eagle-Lion Films in August of that year. Only by December 1947 had new engagements fallen off to such an extent that the first run may effectively be considered to have concluded; although even then, a handful of theaters in small Southern communities such as Flomaton, Alabama (population 900), still screened *The Brute Man* specifically as a first-run attraction until as late as the end of February 1948 – more than two years after Rondo Hatton's death and fully 15 months since the earliest first-run engagements.

A good sense of PRC's cannily flexible approach, which allowed for *The Brute Man* to be shown in a wide array of different exhibition contexts, and alongside almost any co-feature, can already be gleaned from the following rundown of some of its quite disparate openings in major cities.

In Los Angeles, for a week beginning December 11, 1946, the film hitched a ride on the $19,500 box office success of a live entertainment bill headed by no lesser than Pearl Bailey and the former "Bronze Buckaroo" of all-black–cast singing cowboy movies Herb Jeffries at the 2420-seat Million Dollar Theatre, which at the time drew a predominantly African-American audience. In Minneapolis, meanwhile, a five-day booking from December 12 grossed $1800 at the downtown Aster Theatre, a 900-seat second-run house where it topped a double bill with the Columbia comedy *Blondie Knows Best*. On New Year's Eve, the 58-minute *The Brute Man* then commenced a four-day run playing in support of Monogram's 56-minute Johnny Mack Brown Western *Trigger Fingers* at Cincinnati's 1000-seat RKO Family Theatre, with holiday trade helping the pair to generate a healthy $1300 (or 118% of the house average).

Pearl Bailey, not *The Pearl of Death*. Los Angeles opening, December 11, 1946.

A selection of all–PRC bills added to the mix in 1947, including a two-week engagement with *Devil Bat's Daughter* at Chicago's 782-seat La Salle Theatre from January 10. Eye-grabbing horror artwork – which promised far more than either movie could deliver – assisted in the securing of ticket sales that were 20% higher than normal. This particular bill was subsequently rolled out to ten neighborhood houses across the city during the first week of March. In New York City, by contrast, the 54-minute Buster Crabbe Western *Overland Riders* was chosen as support for *The Brute Man* during its week-long debut appearance beginning January 21 at the 600-seat New York Theatre, a reissue house located at Broadway and West 43rd Street, where the duo successfully coined the venue's regular $6000 weekly aggregate. Back on the West Coast, phony swamp decor dominated in and around the lobby of the 2134-seat State Theatre on San Francisco's Market Street, as *The Brute Man* played for a week from May 13 in support of the hour-long Okefenokee adventure *Untamed Fury*

September 10 at the Translux Theatre, a revival and reissue house that flagged it up as the "FIRST BOSTON SHOWING" on a double bill with the not-quite-so-fresh-to-the-screen *Fog Island*.

A number of other cities first got to see *The Brute Man* as a standalone presentation supported only by selected shorts at small first-run houses that relied on a combination of heavy passing footfall and the exclusivity of their offerings to turn a profit. These included the "First N.O. Showing" at the 600-seat Center Theater in New Orleans for two days beginning January 29, 1947; the "1st Phila. Showing" at the 562-seat Capitol Theatre on Philadelphia's Market Street for a week commencing April 16, 1947; and the "First Greater Miami Showing" at the 887-seat State Theatre for three days from June 7, 1947.

Finally – and by way of a minor exception to PRC's standard approach – *The Brute Man* was also very occasionally afforded the opportunity to ride on the coattails of a major studio's well-publicized "low-end A" release at a big city premiere house. In both Detroit and St. Louis, this meant that the Creeper was joined by a bill-topping "crawler" in the guise of Warners' *The Beast with Five Fingers*. At Detroit's 3309-seat Broadway-Capitol Theatre, this combo played four times a day for two weeks beginning March 21, with the first week bringing in $16,500 (or 125% of the house average), which dropped to $12,000 (or 90%) during the second week. Not entirely accurately described as "a double horror-filled super-natural thrill show!" at the 3500-seat Missouri Theatre in St. Louis from April 9, this same bill grossed $14,000 (or 112% of the house average) in its first week, which fell off dramatically to roughly $8500 (or 68%) in its second week. The proprietors of the 2400-seat National Theatre in Louisville, Kentucky, appear to have realized that a "quick in, quick out" approach was best with such pairings of "low–A" and "B" product, and consequently scored a summertime smash of $11,000 thanks to their week-long engagement of United Artists' Basin Street musical drama *New Orleans* with *The Brute Man* in support from July 9 – and no chance of a holdover to drag the profits down!

To a certain degree, these various forms of play in major cities could be found replicated in communities of all sizes around the nation. Looking at a sample of 1200 theaters from coast to coast which showed *The Brute Man* in first run between November 1946 and November 1947 indicates that some 20% of engagements took the form of a standalone presentation. By far the most common way to have first experienced the movie, however – at a hefty 75% of engagements within

"And the Award for Most Misleading Artwork goes to…," Chicago, January 17, 1947.

starring Gaylord "Steve" Pendleton. When this same bill spent a week at the 550-seat Strand Theatre in Hutchinson, Kansas, from June 22, the ballyhoo stakes were raised even higher, with ads exhorting parents to "take the children to see the real live gator," purportedly the star of *Untamed Fury*, "alive and in person!" in the establishment's forecourt. Such varied "PRC doubles" continued through to *The Brute Man*'s final major city opening in Boston, with the film grossing an above-average $4000 over the course of a week's stay from

In first run at Boston's Translux revival house, September 10, 1947.

Crawly-creeper duo on the loose in Rochester, New York, March 13, 1947.

the sample – was on a double bill, with *The Brute Man* designated as the lower, supporting feature at two-thirds of such engagements. Less common forms of presentation included seeing the film alongside live entertainment, at 3.5% of engagements within the sample, or on a triple bill, which accounted for the remaining 1.5% of first-run engagements nationwide.

African-American audiences and venues

It is also apparent that *The Brute Man* received a noteworthy amount of play at predominantly – or in segregated states, exclusively – African-American theaters. With such venues frequently operating on limited budgets or otherwise restricted from acquiring first-run major studio product, low-priced Monogram and PRC releases consistently proved welcome, affordable fare. This had the consequence, at Monogram in particular, of these Poverty Row companies starting to take greater efforts to cast black actors in more sensitive, intelligent roles, and to ensure that they were featured in lobby card and poster artwork. The primary motivation here was assuredly financial – born of a desire to maintain or extend their market share at African-American venues – but the result was the production of pictures that would have been largely untenable at major studios, and which indeed received wide play in African-American neighborhoods. The most obvious example is Monogram's series of what are essentially eight interracial buddy movies starring Frankie Darro and Mantan Moreland, released between 1939 and 1941. African-American characters additionally got to stand out, and on occasion to demonstrate keener powers of reasoning than their white screen counterparts, in a number of Monogram horror films; key examples in this regard include Clarence Muse's character in *Invisible Ghost* (1941) and Mantan Moreland and Sybil Lewis' show-stealing comedy relief sequences in *Revenge of the Zombies* (1943).

Universal ad mat vacationing in Honolulu, June 4, 1947.

One wonders whether the *Brute Man* scene featuring little Dorothy, snappily asserting "Boogie-woogie *is* solid!" and referencing her "hot trumpet"-playing father, elicited some extra yuks at Harlem's Apollo Theater. Pictured: Peggy Converse, Jane Adams, Mary Ann Bricker.

As a feature that had merely been acquired by PRC, *The Brute Man* was obviously not subject to the same production considerations as the aforementioned titles. However, its usage at African-American houses unambiguously stemmed from the latter's long-established working relationships with PRC, and evokes the enigmatic – because woefully under-reported and under-researched – question of just how popular or commonplace Golden Age and Silver Age horror movies were with African-American audiences and at African-American venues. A tantalizing interview with Bela Lugosi conducted on the set of *Invisible Ghost* in late March 1941 suggests that a particularly strong following for the genre may have existed, with Harry Levette, entertainment columnist at Los Angeles' most widely circulated African-American newspaper *The California Eagle*, citing a "nationwide survey, made recently," according to which horror films were the third-favorite type of picture among black moviegoers. Lugosi in turn informs Levette that he "learned from fan mail" dating all the way back to *Dracula* that he had "many fans among them."

In the case of *The Brute Man*, some of its more readily identifiable engagements at African-American movie theaters include its March 5, 1947, opening on a PRC double bill with *Devil Bat's Daughter* at the Michigan Theatre on Chicago's South Side, with ads drawing attention to the additional presence of a "Negro News Reel" on the bill. Other houses elected to play *The Brute Man* alongside an all-African-American-cast feature, with known examples including a three-day run in support of *Dirty Gertie from Harlem U.S.A.* starring Francine Everett at the Harlem Theater in St. Petersburg, Florida, from September 29, 1947; and a two-day special engagement for Halloween 1947 at the Rialto Theatre in Trenton, New Jersey, with the Mantan Moreland feature *Tall, Tan and Terrific* (likewise featuring Francine Everett) serving as the bill's lower half. The racially divided entertainment pages of newspapers from segregated states also render the extent of *The Brute Man*'s deployment unintentionally visible, with three of the four separately listed "Negro theaters" in the *Miami Daily News* – the Ritz, the Harlem and the Lyric – showing the film between July and October 1947. The 542-seat Ritz had even employed it as a special stand-alone attraction over the Fourth of July weekend.

In the February 28, 1948, edition of *Motion Picture Herald*, there furthermore exists a rare piece of feedback that suggests multiple African-American audience members' enjoyment of the movie during a profitable two-day run at the New Ren Theatre in Yazoo City, Mississippi, on January 22-23, 1948 – so long as one is willing to fight one's way past the insensitive language and tone of white theater manager J.R. Revell: "I personally didn't think much of this but my dark skinned customers came out mumbling about the 'creeper,' so I guess they liked it. Doubled with *Fugitive from Sonora*. That's the combination it takes here. A good Western and a good mystery thriller. Business good."

With live entertainment

Nowhere was African-American patronage more evident, though, than at some of the 3.5% of showings nationwide which utilized *The Brute Man* as accompaniment to live entertainment.

At the previously referenced December 11, 1946, opening at Los Angeles' Million Dollar Theatre, the variety bill was split either side of the movie, so that audiences had already experienced Herb Jeffries singing "September Song," "Christmas Song," "Jump for

Joy" and his million-seller "Flamingo" prior to casting their gaze upon Rondo Hatton's physiognomy. Following his serial-killing antics on the screen, Pearl Bailey likewise appears to have slain the audience with renditions of "That's Good Enough for Me," "Row, Row, Row" and "St. Louis Blues" "with a new, bluish set of lyrics." *Billboard*'s reviewer rhapsodized: "Miss Bailey proves to be mistress of the clever lyric and smooth delivery. Her material is original and highly commercial, and her salesmanship leaves seat sitters whistling for more." Over three decades later, in April 1979, trampolinist Howard Krick, who also featured on the bill, affectionately recalled the show during an interview with Cathy Beckham of the *Salem* (Oregon) *Statesman Journal*, commenting: "Pearl Bailey sang following the showing of the film *Brute Man*. We did that four times a day for a week. I've never seen anyone keep time like Pearl Bailey did."

East of the Mississippi, *The Brute Man* likewise played in support of several of the nation's foremost popular musicians on the so-called "Chitlin' Circuit," a loose collection of venues that readily welcomed and headlined African-American acts during the era of racial segregation. These included a three-day stint at the 3880-seat State Theatre in Hartford, Connecticut, from May 16, 1947, at which the Mills Brothers quite literally "stopped the show" (according to the *Hartford Courant* reviewer) as they performed their #2 hit on the national juke box chart, "Across the Alley from the Alamo." They also showcased a number of their other recent recordings, such as "Dream, Dream, Dream," "Cielito Lindo" and "I'm Afraid to Love You," in addition to established favorites "Lazy River," "You Always Hurt the One You Love" and "Till Then." Two months later, *Variety* reported "better-than-average business" and "close to hefty returns" at Harlem's legendary Apollo Theater, with the first-run *The Brute Man* now supporting a variety bill headed by Illinois Jacquet and His Orchestra for a week from July 18, 1947. The publication's reviewer enthused: "Opener is a hot blues followed by 'Robbins' Nest' with Jacquet on solo. Arrangements leave plenty of room for improvising as in 'How High the Moon' where rhythm section tees off, then number fades into usual jammin'. 'Bottoms Up' is the blowoff and Jacquet does it up brown in torrid sax solo."

It's additionally worth observing that *The Brute Man* was selected as a special standalone attraction for Saturday, September 13, 1947, during the big gala opening week of business at the 850-seat art deco–style Hippodrome Theatre in the Jackson Ward neighborhood of Richmond, Virginia. The Hippodrome would swiftly es-

"It's a live! It's a live… spook show!" in Wilmington, California, March 28, 1947.

tablish itself as a further important Chitlin' Circuit venue.

In marked contrast to these entertainments fronted by "name" performers with a nationwide reputation, the live accompaniments to *The Brute Man* outside of African-American establishments fell much more in line with the ramshackle expectations that a PRC release might engender. Indeed, the only vaguely footnoteworthy variety line-up in this regard was a two-day engagement at the 1089-seat Strand Theatre in Elmira, New York (March 12-13, 1947), at which the movie played in support of a 45-minute performance of comedy and Western songs by local WENY radio stars the

Original Western Ramblers. Altogether more interesting were the array of spook shows that included the first-run *The Brute Man* as their "screen component," even though the earliest of these, on Friday, December 13, 1946, were decidedly homespun too, with the "Jinx Show" at the 1000-seat El Rancho Theatre in Victoria, Texas, for example simply daring patrons to walk under a ladder to enter the auditorium, and handing out prizes for the "biggest bad-luck story" and "unluckiest article" that they brought along to share. The theater's ad copy meanwhile maintained that (ten-months-dead) Rondo Hatton was "the new horror man who calls Boris Karloff 'Mama's boy.'" From February 1947, *The Brute Man* was repeatedly employed by several of the more professional touring spook shows, including Henry Valleau's "Zombie Show" ("Invisible Zombies on our stage"), Jack Baker's "Dr. Silkini's Asylum of Horrors" ("in person, Frankenstein monster, direct from Hollywood") and Arthur Bell's "Francisco and His Big Midnite Spook Frolic" ("Zemora the Restless Ghost – unhappy in his grave, he roams the theatre – may touch you!").

Tampa salutes its own, December 15, 1946.

Standalone engagements

The oldest known standalone showing of *The Brute Man* took the form of a special "pre–Christmas week" engagement at Tampa, Florida's 550-seat State Theatre, which ran for three days from December 15, 1946, with ad mats in newspaper listings columns altered to read: "Starring the Late Rondo Hatton, Tampa's Own Movie Star" – the latter epithet having been employed in the local press since the 1930s. Respectful advance write-ups of the engagement were carried in *The Tampa Daily Times* and *Tampa Sunday Tribune* under the respective headlines "Former Tampan Has Lead in Film at State" and "Tampa Movie Actor's Last Picture and Starring Vehicle Opens Today." When *The Brute Man* subsequently played on a double bill at neighborhood houses in the city from July 7, 1947, in support of the second-run Warners A-movie *Nora Prentiss* starring Ann Sheridan, Hatton was again billed as "Tampa's Own Movie Star."

The 20% of theaters from coast to coast that presented the first-run *The Brute Man* as a standalone may not have been anywhere near so reverential in their handling of the movie, but were otherwise broadly comparable to the State in Tampa, insofar as they tended to be sub–thousand-seat venues which ran the picture for between one and three days. The majority of these houses maintained a single-feature policy at all times anyway, either because they were located in what might be termed "one-theater towns" – that is to say, rural communities whose inhabitants had no immediately available alternative moviegoing options – or else because local exhibition chains effectively dictated such practice, as was particularly common throughout the state of Texas. When *The Brute Man* opened as a standalone for three days beginning April 13, 1947, at the 512-seat Palace Theatre in Abilene (a venue controlled by the Interstate Theaters chain), some original ad copy sought to convince patrons that they were hardly being shortchanged, since the movie represented "All the horror shows in one feature."

Double-bill engagements

PRC extended an exceptionally free hand to the 75% of venues which presented *The Brute Man* on a double bill, allowing them to pair it with almost any available first-run, second-run, third-run, repertory or reissue title that they cared to book. Consequently, it is perhaps unsurprising that, within the sample of 1200 theaters from coast to coast which showed the movie in first run, some 207 (!) different co-features were attested. One should not, however, conclude that exhibitors were afforded absolute *carte blanche*, since 31 of these co-features – accounting collectively for one-quarter of bookings – were PRC (or at later engagements, Eagle-Lion) releases. This indicates that PRC almost certainly offered special deals or incentives to theaters and chains that booked two of its titles at once, in turn giving the company the chance to "control" the box office at these establishments (rather than having to divide up profits with the distributor of the other feature on the bill). As with standalone engagements, two- and three-day bookings prevailed.

PRC's diversified approach meant that all of *The Brute Man*'s double-bill partnerships were limited to localized or merely scattered nationwide usage, with only two titles coming anywhere close to functioning as "regular" co-features: at 6% of double-bill bookings, though rarely encountered outside the midwest, *Devil Bat's Daughter*; and at 4% of bookings, in diffuse locations from Massachusetts to California between March and September 1947, *The Beast with Five Fingers*. Nine further horror titles – including Republic's *Valley of the Zombies*, Screen Guild's Cinecolor *Scared to Death* and Four Continents' *Frenzy* (a retitled, slightly abridged edit of Vernon Sewell's British-made *Latin Quarter*) – collectively made up for another 4% of double-bill engagements. Some acknowledgment should be made of the Friday the Thirteenth midnight show presented on June 13, 1947, at the Fox Redlands Theatre in San Bernardino, California, which – intentionally or otherwise – managed to create a double-acromegaly bill by pairing *The Brute Man* with PRC's 1944 entry *The Monster Maker*. This particular combo would turn up again at revival houses between 1948 and 1950, following Madison Pictures' reissue of *The Monster Maker*.

However, as much as it may pain our horror-fan sensibilities, an overwhelming 86% of first-run double-bill engagements took the form of so-called "balanced programs" comprising works of two distinct genres, which many in the trade believed held broader appeal than single-genre couplings. Thus, *The Brute Man*'s most prevalent double-bill companions were not Peter Lorre, Bela Lugosi or Rosemary LaPlanche, but rather – in order of frequency – Eddie Dean, Charles Starrett, William Boyd, Roy Rogers, Johnny Mack Brown, Jimmy Wakely, Gene Autry, Allan Lane, Wild Bill Elliott and Lash La Rue, in a large number of low-budget and reissue Westerns. Other widely used genres of co-feature included installments of crime and detective

Garishly irresistible ad to lure in the horror completists. Newark, New Jersey, March 26, 1947.

series, noirish psychological thrillers, new and reissue dramas, and comedies.

The following list comprises all 124 titles within the sample of 1200 theaters from coast to coast which served as the top half of a double bill with *The Brute Man*, indicating that they were regarded as holding greater pulling power, or simply being "of better quality," than the 58-minute PRC release. Longer running times abound, with the average length of these top-billed attractions some 79 minutes; there are 13 color productions; and a certain amount of major studio product is present, albeit often in second-run or reissue. The titles are arranged alphabetically, with the month mentioned in each case the earliest in which the pairing was attested. Underscored titles are PRC–Eagle-Lion releases.

June 1947 *Allegheny Uprising* (Claire Trevor; RKO reissue)

Mar. 1947 *Angel on My Shoulder* (Paul Muni; United Artists)

Sep. 1947 *Apache Rose* (Roy Rogers; Republic)

July 1947 *Backlash* (Jean Rogers; 20th Century–Fox)

Mar. 1947 *The Beast with Five Fingers* (Robert Alda; Warner Bros.)

Feb. 1947 *Belle of the Yukon* (Randolph Scott; RKO)

Aug. 1947 *Bells of San Fernando* (Donald Woods; Screen Guild)

Aug. 1947 *The Big Fix* (James Brown; PRC)

Feb. 1947 *Blind Spot* (Chester Morris; Columbia)

Mar. 1947 *Blondie's Big Moment* (Penny Singleton; Columbia)

Nov. 1947 *Border Feud* (Lash La Rue; PRC)

May 1947 *Boston Blackie and the Law* (Chester Morris; Columbia)

Mar. 1947 *A Boy, a Girl and a Dog* (Sharyn Moffett; Film Classics)

Jan. 1947 *Bringing Up Father* (Joe Yule; Monogram)

June 1947 *Carnival in Costa Rica* (Dick Haymes; 20th Century–Fox)

Feb. 1947 *The Cat Creeps* (Lois Collier; Universal)

Mar. 1947 *The Chase* (Robert Cummings; United Artists)

Aug. 1947 *City for Conquest* (James Cagney; Warner Bros. reissue)

Apr. 1947 *Cloak and Dagger* (Gary Cooper; Warner Bros.)

June 1947 *Code of the West* (James Warren; RKO)

Apr. 1947 *The Cowboy and the Lady* (Gary Cooper; Film Classics reissue)

June 1947 *Dangerous Millions* (Kent Taylor; 20th Century–Fox)

May 1947 *Decoy* (Jean Gillie; Monogram)

Mar. 1947 *The Devil Bat* (Bela Lugosi; Madison Pictures reissue)

Nov. 1947 *The Devil on Wheels* (Noreen Nash; PRC)

Apr. 1947 *The Devil Thumbs a Ride* (Lawrence Tierney; RKO)

May 1947 *The Devil to Pay!* (Ronald Colman; Film Classics reissue)

May 1947 *Dick Tracy vs. Cueball* (Morgan Conway; RKO)

Sep. 1947 *Dirty Gertie from Harlem U.S.A.* (Francine Everett; Sack Amusements)

Mar. 1947 *Down Missouri Way* (Martha O'Driscoll; PRC)

June 1947 *Easy Come, Easy Go* (Barry Fitzgerald; Paramount)

May 1947 *The Fabulous Dorseys* (Tommy and Jimmy Dorsey; United Artists)

May 1947 *The Falcon's Adventure* (Tom Conway; RKO)

Apr. 1947 *Fear in the Night* (Paul Kelly; Paramount)

Sep. 1947 *Framed* (Glenn Ford; Columbia)

Feb. 1947 *Gallant Journey* (Glenn Ford; Columbia)

Feb. 1947 *Gangs, Inc.* (Alan Ladd; PRC reissue)

May 1947 *Genius at Work* (Brown and Carney; RKO)

Apr. 1947 *The Ghost Goes Wild* (James Ellison; Republic)

June 1947 *Girl on the Spot* (Lois Collier; Universal)

July 1947 *Hard Boiled Mahoney* (Bowery Boys; Monogram)

Apr. 1947 *Heldorado* (Roy Rogers; Republic)

Oct. 1947 *Hollywood Barn Dance* (Ernest Tubb; Screen Guild)

May 1947 *Home in Oklahoma* (Roy Rogers; Republic)

Apr. 1947 *It Happened in Brooklyn* (Frank Sinatra; MGM)

July 1947 *Johnny O'Clock* (Dick Powell; Columbia)

Oct. 1947 *Killer at Large* (Robert Lowery; PRC)

May 1947 *King of the Wild Horses* (Preston Foster; Columbia)

Aug. 1947 *Lady Luck* (Robert Young; RKO)

Apr. 1947 *Last Frontier Uprising* (Monte Hale; Republic)

June 1947 *Lighthouse* (Don Castle; PRC)

Mar. 1947 *Little Iodine* (Jo Ann Marlowe; United Artists)

June 1947 *The Locket* (Laraine Day; RKO)

June 1947 *Lone Star Moonlight* (Ken Curtis; Columbia)

July 1947 *Love and Learn* (Jack Carson; Warner Bros.)

June 1947 *The Magnificent Rogue* (Lynne Roberts; Republic)

Jan. 1947 *The Man from Morocco* (Anton Walbrook; English Films)

June 1947 *The Man I Love* (Ida Lupino; Warner Bros.)

May 1947 *Margie* (Jeanne Crain; 20th Century–Fox)

May 1947 *Melody for Three* (Jean Hersholt; Astor reissue)

July 1947 *The Millerson Case* (Warner Baxter; Columbia)

June 1947 *Millie's Daughter* (Gladys George; Columbia)

May 1947 *Mr. District Attorney* (Dennis O'Keefe; Columbia)

Apr. 1947 *Moonlight and Cactus* (Andrews Sisters; Universal)

Nov. 1947 *Mother Wore Tights* (Betty Grable; 20th Century–Fox)

July 1947 *Murder Is My Business* (Hugh Beaumont; PRC)

July 1947 *My Brother Talks to Horses* (Jackie "Butch" Jenkins; MGM)

Feb. 1947 *My Darling Clementine* (Henry Fonda; 20th Century–Fox)

July 1947 *My Pal Trigger* (Roy Rogers; Republic)

May 1947 *The Mysterious Mr. Valentine* (William Henry; Republic)

July 1947 *New Orleans* (Arturo de Cordova; United Artists)

Feb. 1947 *Nora Prentiss* (Ann Sheridan; Warner Bros.)

Mar. 1947 *Northwest Trail* (Bob Steele; Screen Guild)

Apr. 1947 *One Exciting Week* (Al Pearce; Republic)

Sep. 1947 *The Perils of Pauline* (Betty Hutton; Paramount)

May 1947 *The Pilgrim Lady* (Lynne Roberts; Republic)

June 1947 *The Postman Always Rings Twice* (Lana Turner; MGM)

June 1947 *Practically Yours* (Claudette Colbert; Paramount)

June 1947 *Prairie Badmen* (Buster Crabbe; PRC)

May 1947 *Queen of the Amazons* (Robert Lowery; Screen Guild)

June 1947 *Range Beyond the Blue* (Eddie Dean; PRC)

Apr. 1947 *The Red House* (Edward G. Robinson; United Artists)

Jan. 1947 *Rendezvous with Annie* (Eddie Albert; Republic)

Apr. 1947 *Romance of the West* (Eddie Dean; PRC)

June 1947 *San Quentin* (Lawrence Tierney; RKO)

Dec. 1946 *A Scandal in Paris* (George Sanders; United Artists)

June 1947 *Scared to Death* (Bela Lugosi; Screen Guild)

May 1947 *Scarface* (Paul Muni; Astor reissue)

July 1947 *Shoot to Kill* (Russell Wade; Screen Guild)

Dec. 1946 *The Show-Off* (Red Skelton; MGM)

June 1947 *Silver Stallion* (David Sharpe; Monogram reissue)

Apr. 1947 *Sinbad, the Sailor* (Douglas Fairbanks, Jr.; RKO)

May 1947 *Somewhere in the Night* (John Hodiak; 20th Century–Fox)

June 1947 *Specter of the Rose* (Judith Anderson; Republic)

July 1947 *Stallion Road* (Ronald Reagan; Warner Bros.)

Aug. 1947 *Stanley and Livingstone* (Spencer Tracy; 20th Century–Fox reissue)

Mar. 1947 *Step by Step* (Lawrence Tierney; RKO)

May 1947 *The Strange Affair of Uncle Harry* (George Sanders; Universal)

Mar. 1947 *The Strange Love of Martha Ivers* (Barbara Stanwyck; Paramount)

June 1947 *Strange Triangle* (Signe Hasso; 20th Century–Fox)

June 1947 *Sun Valley Serenade* (Sonja Henie; 20th Century–Fox reissue)

Dec. 1946 *Sunset Pass* (James Warren; RKO)

Mar. 1947 *Suspense* (Belita; Monogram)

Apr. 1947 *Sweetheart of Sigma Chi* (Phil Regan; Monogram)

May 1947 *Swell Guy* (Sonny Tufts; Universal)

Mar. 1947 *Temptation* (Merle Oberon; Universal)

July 1947 *That Way with Women* (Dane Clark; Warner Bros.)

June 1947 *These Three* (Miriam Hopkins; Film Classics reissue)

June 1947 *They Were Expendable* (Robert Montgomery; MGM)

July 1947 *Three Little Girls in Blue* (June Haver; 20th Century–Fox)

Mar. 1947 *Three on a Ticket* (Hugh Beaumont; PRC)

June 1947 *Trail to San Antone* (Gene Autry; Republic)

June 1947 *The Trap* (Sidney Toler; Monogram)

May 1947 *Untamed Fury* (Gaylord "Steve" Pendleton; PRC)

"Towering" – beneath a swamp. San Francisco opening, May 13, 1947.

Mar. 1947 *Vacation Days* (The Teen Agers; Monogram)

Apr. 1947 *Vacation in Reno* (Jack Haley; RKO)

Dec. 1946 *Valley of the Zombies* (Robert Livingston; Republic)

May 1947 *Wake Up and Dream* (June Haver; 20th Century–Fox)

Nov. 1946 *West of the Pecos* (Robert Mitchum; RKO)

Apr. 1947 *The Westerner* (Gary Cooper; Film Classics reissue)

Feb. 1947 *White Tie and Tails* (Dan Duryea; Universal)

Mar. 1947 *The Wicked Lady* (Margaret Lockwood; Universal)

Nov. 1946 *Wife Wanted* (Kay Francis; Monogram)

Sep. 1947 <u>*Wild Country*</u> (Eddie Dean; PRC)

The next 20 double-bill co-features within the sample of 1200 theaters are arguably of greatest interest, inasmuch as they were used variously as either the top *or* bottom half of the bill when paired with *The Brute Man*. In other words: These movies were treated as being of just about equal value to – and essentially interchangeable with – the PRC release. Which, on the basis of the evidence below, seems to mean that, in the 1946-47 marketplace, Rondo Hatton's final feature was the horror equivalent of a PRC Eddie Dean Western, a Columbia Charles Starrett Western, or a Monogram Jimmy Wakely Western. Given that these were all long-running product lines and steady moneymakers for their studios, the comparison may not be quite so unfavorable or unflattering as it initially sounds. With regard to horror releases, meanwhile, it's impossible to overlook the fact (or to fail to savor the irony) that *Dead of Night* – the "prestige" picture which assumed *The Brute Man*'s place in U-I's new higher-minded release schedule – is included among these titles.

Feb. 1947 <u>*Born to Speed*</u> (Johnny Sands; PRC)

June 1947 *Child of Divorce* (Sharyn Moffett; RKO)

Dec. 1946 *Dead of Night* (Michael Redgrave; Universal)

Jan. 1947 <u>*Devil Bat's Daughter*</u> (Rosemary LaPlanche; PRC)

Feb. 1947 <u>*Driftin' River*</u> (Eddie Dean; PRC)

Feb. 1947 *The Fighting Frontiersman* (Charles Starrett; Columbia)

Jan. 1947 *Heading West* (Charles Starrett; Columbia)

May 1947 <u>*It's a Joke, Son!*</u> (Kenny Delmar; Eagle-Lion)

Apr. 1947 Law of the Lash (Lash La Rue; PRC)

Apr. 1947 Mr. Hex (Bowery Boys; Monogram)

July 1947 Out California Way (Monte Hale; Republic)

Feb. 1947 Rainbow Over the Rockies (Jimmy Wakely; Monogram)

Feb. 1947 Song of the Sierras (Jimmy Wakely; Monogram)

Feb. 1947 Stars Over Texas (Eddie Dean; PRC)

Apr. 1947 The Thirteenth Hour (Richard Dix; Columbia)

Dec. 1946 Trigger Fingers (Johnny Mack Brown; Monogram)

Feb. 1947 Tumbleweed Trail (Eddie Dean; PRC)

May 1947 Under Nevada Skies (Roy Rogers; Republic)

June 1947 West to Glory (Eddie Dean; PRC)

Jan. 1947 Wild West (Eddie Dean; PRC)

As for the question of what qualified as "less worthy" than *The Brute Man* during 1946-47, this final list of 63 titles comprises all those movies which played second fiddle to it on first-run double bills within the sample of 1200 theaters. No less than 30 of these films fail to crack the one-hour mark, and reissues of 1930s pictures, lesser studio and Poverty Row product all feature prominently – albeit with a few questionable lapses in judgment by local exhibitors, not least of which must be the first title on the list, a reissue of *The 39 Steps*. Devotees of Alfred Hitchcock will be relieved to learn that this bottom-heavy pairing was attested at only a single two-day engagement from February 12, 1947, at the 650-seat Weil Theater (now the H.J. Ricks Centre for the Arts) in Greenfield, Indiana. Perhaps the Weil's owners had read critic Bill Cope's advance review of *The Brute Man* in the Halloween 1946 edition of *Motion Picture Daily*, in which he made the very generous claim that director Jean Yarbrough "has injected into this Ben Pivar production an element of what is popularly known as 'Hitchcock' suspense" (!).

Feb. 1947 The 39 Steps (Robert Donat; independent reissue)

July 1947 Affairs of Geraldine (Jane Withers; Republic)

July 1947 The Bachelor's Daughters (Gail Russell; United Artists)

May 1947 Bar 20 Justice (William Boyd; Screen Guild reissue)

Feb. 1947 Beauty and the Bandit (Gilbert Roland; Monogram)

Mar. 1947 Betty Co-ed (Jean Porter; Columbia)

Dead of Night trounced by *The Brute Man* in Fremont, Ohio, February 24, 1947.

Dec. 1946 Blondie Knows Best (Penny Singleton; Columbia)

Nov. 1946 Borderland (William Boyd; Screen Guild reissue)

Jan. 1947 Colorado Pioneers (Wild Bill Elliott; Republic)

Mar. 1947 Cowboy from Lonesome River (Charles Starrett; Columbia)

July 1947 Criminal Court (Tom Conway; RKO)

Mar. 1947 Dangerous Money (Sidney Toler; Monogram)

July 1947 Dangerous Venture (William Boyd; United Artists)

July 1947 Dead Reckoning (Humphrey Bogart; Columbia)

May 1947 Don't Gamble with Strangers (Kane Richmond; Monogram)

Rondo "heads" the bill in Benton Harbor, Michigan, November 7, 1947.

Mar. 1947 *Durango Valley Raiders* (Bob Steele; Republic reissue)

July 1947 *Flaming Lead* (Ken Maynard; independent reissue)

Sep. 1947 *Fog Island* (George Zucco; PRC)

Apr. 1947 *Fool's Gold* (William Boyd; United Artists)

Mar. 1947 *Frenzy* (Derrick De Marney; Four Continents)

Nov. 1947 *Gunsmoke Ranch* (Three Mesquiteers; Republic reissue)

June 1947 *Hit the Saddle* (Three Mesquiteers; Republic reissue)

Feb. 1947 *Home on the Range* (Monte Hale; Republic)

Mar. 1947 *Jack London* (Michael O'Shea; United Artists)

May 1947 *The Killers* (Burt Lancaster; Universal)

June 1947 *Lady Chaser* (Robert Lowery; PRC)

Apr. 1947 *The Lady in the Morgue* (Preston Foster; Astor reissue)

Jan. 1947 *Landrush* (Charles Starrett; Columbia)

Oct. 1947 *The Last of the Mohicans* (Randolph Scott; Eagle-Lion reissue)

Mar. 1947 *The Lone Hand Texan* (Charles Starrett; Columbia)

May 1947 *Man from Rainbow Valley* (Monte Hale; Republic)

Oct. 1947 *Marshal of Cripple Creek* (Allan Lane; Republic)

June 1947 *The Monster Maker* (J. Carrol Naish; PRC)

Mar. 1947 *The Mutiny of the Elsinore* (Paul Lukas; Goodwill Pictures reissue)

Mar. 1947 *North of the Border* (Russell Hayden; Screen Guild)

Jan. 1947 *Overland Riders* (Buster Crabbe; PRC)

Feb. 1947 *Raiders of the South* (Johnny Mack Brown; Monogram)

June 1947 *Raiders of the West* (Bill "Cowboy Rambler" Boyd; Madison Pictures reissue)

Dec. 1946 *Rancho Grande* (Gene Autry; Republic reissue)

May 1947 *The Return of Frank James* (Henry Fonda; 20th Century–Fox reissue)

Aug. 1947 *Riding the California Trail* (Gilbert Roland; Monogram)

June 1947 *Rio Grande Raiders* (Sunset Carson; Republic)

Mar. 1947 *Santa Fe Uprising* (Allan Lane; Republic)

Apr. 1947 *Shadow of a Woman* (Helmut Dantine; Warner Bros.)

July 1947 *Shadows on the Range* (Johnny Mack Brown; Monogram)

Mar. 1947 *Sheriff of Redwood Valley* (Wild Bill Elliott; Republic)

June 1947 *Sioux City Sue* (Gene Autry; Republic)

May 1947 *Six-Gun Serenade* (Jimmy Wakely; Monogram)

July 1947 *Song of the Wasteland* (Jimmy Wakely; Monogram)

Jan. 1947 *The Stars Look Down* (Michael Redgrave; Film Classics reissue)

Dec. 1946 <u>Strange Holiday</u> (Claude Rains; PRC)

Oct. 1947 *Tall, Tan and Terrific* (Mantan Moreland; Astor)

July 1947 <u>Terror Trail</u> (Charles Starrett; Columbia)

Feb. 1947 <u>Terrors on Horseback</u> (Buster Crabbe; PRC)

Feb. 1947 *Three on the Trail* (William Boyd; Goodwill Pictures reissue)

Jan. 1947 <u>Thunder Town</u> (Bob Steele; PRC)

Aug. 1947 <u>Too Many Winners</u> (Hugh Beaumont; PRC)

May 1947 *Topper Takes a Trip* (Constance Bennett; Favorite Films reissue)

June 1947 *Trail Dust* (William Boyd; Screen Guild reissue)

Aug. 1947 *Valley of Fear* (Johnny Mack Brown; Monogram)

June 1947 *Vigilantes of Boomtown* (Allan Lane; Republic)

July 1947 *West of Dodge City* (Charles Starrett; Columbia)

July 1947 *Wild Bill Hickok Rides* (Constance Bennett; Warner Bros. reissue)

Triple-bill engagements

Finally, the 1.5% of first-run engagements that presented *The Brute Man* on a triple bill could be found exclusively in major cities where the PRC release was already being exhibited by way of a uniform double bill at multiple theaters. In a bid to stand out from these immediate competitors, a small number of venues added a (low-rent) third unit to their programs, thereby creating what essentially amounted to an "augmented version" of the local double bill. For example, with ten other Chicago houses playing the "PRC double" of *Devil Bat's Daughter* and *The Brute Man* during the first week of March 1947, the 1035-seat Imperial Theatre in the Near West Side sought to enhance the appeal of its otherwise identical line-up by appending the reissued Republic Gene Autry Western *Blue Montana Skies* to it. Likewise, when *The Brute Man* opened on a double bill with Monogram's Bowery Boys entry *Mr. Hex* at several neighborhood theaters in the Greater Los Angeles area during the second week of April 1947, the 640-seat Normandie Theatre in the Vermont Square neighborhood sought to offer that little bit extra by supplementing the pairing with the 58-minute PRC mystery *The Phantom of 42nd Street*; while the 600-seat Del Mar Theatre in the Pico-Robertson neighborhood – likely unintentionally – doubled the bill's Tom Neal quotient by "upgrading" it with Republic's 56-minute *Thoroughbreds*. Needless to say, such variant triple bills were for the most part unique to individual venues.

After the first run: gyrations and shudders

With the first-run *The Brute Man* having already been seen at second-run, third-run, repertory and reissue houses, so the film's second-run playdates swiftly filtered down to a yet lower rung of exhibition venues, including exploitation and burlesque theaters. As early as February 3, 1948, the Roseland in Omaha, Nebraska, was employing it as the third feature on a creaky exploitation bill that also comprised the 1932 goona goona breast-capade *Virgins of Bali* and Zita Johann's 1933 tumble onto Poverty Row, *The Sin of Nora Moran*. By Christmas 1949, the Garrick in St. Louis offered a flesh-filled festive frolic, running daily from December 23 through 26, that coupled PRC's *Untamed Fury* and *The Brute Man* with striptease shorts and the "In Person – Adults Only – Not a Movie" attractions of M'lle Fifi and Her French Models, in addition to Norita the Snake Dancer.

A not insubstantial number of "double horror show" engagements through to fall 1950 meanwhile "reunited" *The Brute Man* with a cavalcade of other Universal-produced titles, including its one-time Ben Pivar-Jean Yarbrough stablemate *She-Wolf of London* and Realart reissue prints of *Bride of Frankenstein*, *House of Dracula*, *The Mummy's Tomb* and *The Wolf Man*. From November 28, 1948, it furthermore played in support of the second-run *Abbott and Costello Meet Frankenstein* at the 856-seat Colonial Theatre in Sacramento, California. All-PRC horror bills continued to flourish too, not least at African-American theaters in the South, and variously paired *The Brute Man* with *Devil Bat's Daughter*, *The Flying Serpent* and (by way of its 1948 Madison Pictures reissue) *The Monster Maker*.

Beyond that, in April 1948, Pictorial Films Inc. of New York City announced its acquisition of the 16mm rights to 69 PRC and Eagle-Lion features including *The Brute Man*, which it distributed to non-theatrical and non-traditional theatrical markets from October of that year.

This period additionally witnessed *The Brute Man*'s first major non-domestic engagements. Although it had crept over the border to Ottawa, Canada, as early as March 31, 1947, Spanish-speaking nations to the south of the U.S. only gradually got to see the film from Au-

A Muncie, Indiana, theater's 1947 twin-bill of the drama *The Chase* (1946) plus *The Brute Man*, an "IDEAL PICTURE FOR ENTIRE FAMILY." Yeah…the *Manson* Family!

gust 12, 1948, on which date it opened at five theaters in Mexico City under the title *Rastro de muerte* (literally, "Trail of Death"). In Britain, *The Brute Man* was in turn picked up as one of a bulk lot of PRC features by Poverty Row mogul Edwin J. Fancey's New Realm Pictures. It was distributed through the company's Dublin office to theaters in Ireland from mid–April 1949, and then through its London office to venues throughout the United Kingdom from early June 1949. For its U.K. playdates, it frequently formed a double bill with *The Devil's Hand*, New Realm's dubbed edit of Maurice Tourneur's Faustian fantasy *La main du diable* (1943; U.S.: *Carnival of Sinners*) featuring new narration by Valentine Dyall, who was most familiar to British audiences of the day as "The Man in Black" on the long-running BBC radio horror series *Appointment with Fear*.

Onto TV with a whimper, before landing a knockout punch

The Brute Man came to television with next to no fanfare during the opening months of 1951. The first city to see it was Chicago, where it aired on station WENR (now WLS) at 8:30 p.m. on Monday, January 29. New York City followed, with the movie turning up in a Saturday, March 17, "Late Show Film" slot on WCBS at 11:15 p.m. It thereafter served as a piece of Friday the Thirteenth programming under the "Playhouse Nine" banner on WTOP (now WUSA) in Washington D.C., which went out at 11:30 p.m. on April 13; and reached Philadelphia over WPTZ – broadcasting from Plattsburgh, New York – as the "Mystery Hour" feature for Monday, May 17, commencing at 10:30 p.m. The earliest West Coast TV date came three days later, on May 20, during the course of a mood-lifting evening indeed for viewers of Los Angeles station KECA (now KABC) who saw *The Brute Man* get underway with his serial murders from 9:15 p.m., right in the afterglow of an 8 p.m. showing of the civil defense film *Atom Bomb Survival*!

After continuing to play to minimal attention in late-night and "owl" slots on further television stations around the country over the summer of 1951, *The Brute Man* was suddenly catapulted into public consciousness after the night of September 13, when actors Tom Neal and Franchot Tone got into a physical fight over the shared object of their affections, actress Barbara Payton, outside her Hollywood apartment. Neal hit the lighter, older Tone with such force that the latter was left unconscious, with a broken nose and fractured cheekbone, and his condition for a while listed as "serious." The unseemly drunken bout made front-page headlines nationwide, with numerous reports referencing the fact that Neal had once "starred" in an apparently aptly titled picture called *The Brute Man*. The resulting publicity was sufficient for the Woolner Brothers, Southern drive-in magnates, to immediately cobble together a "Battle of the Century" double bill pitting "Tom Neal – *The Brute Man*" against "Franchot Tone – *Dark Waters*," which debuted at their Drive-In Movies venue (later known as the Jeff Drive-In) in New Orleans on September 25.

By the time *The Brute Man* was rerun on WPTZ, serving Philadelphia, at 11 p.m. on Saturday, November 3, it had been promoted to the giddy heights of inaugural feature in the station's well-publicized new "TV Thriller" slot, which would keep on running into 1953 as a showcase for pre–1948 PRC and Monogram horror and mystery releases (see ad page 123). Likewise, the previously overlooked picture's New York rerun on WCBS at half past midnight on the morning of December 10 now merited the attention of Dorothy Kilgallen, who pointedly observed in her nationally syndi-

What a brew-t! On Philadelphia TV, November 3, 1951.

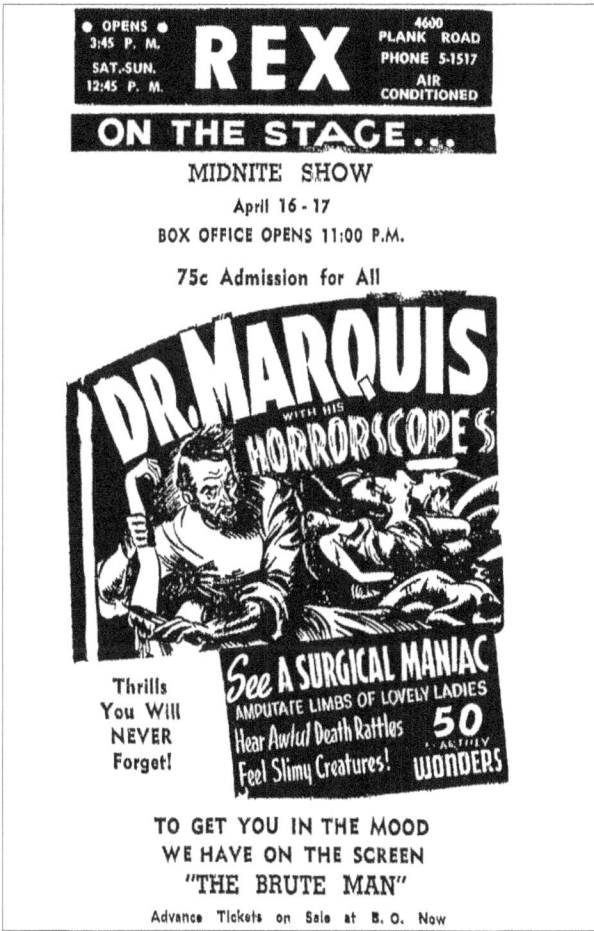

Serial killer seeks surgical slasher with view to short-term relationship in Baton Rouge, April 16, 1953.

cated column: "An old film of Tom Neal's is making the TV circuit. Its title: *Brute Man*." Entertainment reporter Harold V. Cohen of the *Pittsburgh Post-Gazette* had actually beaten Kilgallen to the zinger in his "Drama Desk" column of November 26, writing: "Appropriate title for the Tom Neal picture the Encore Theater will show on teevee Friday night: *The Brute Man*." However, the quality of the print furnished to station WDTV (now KDKA) was deemed to be "too bad," and so its place in the schedule was instead filled by the 1948 Eagle-Lion feature *The Cobra Strikes*.

Rondo gets you in the mood – and then goes retro

Interest in the Neal-Tone fisticuffs had already dissipated by 1952, without *The Brute Man* appearing to have truly caught the attention of televiewers and programmers on its own merits. The fact that prints supplied to some stations were either murky or damaged – as evidenced in an extreme form by the above example from Pittsburgh – cannot have helped. Wee-hours airings of the picture swiftly grew fewer and further between as the decade progressed, and from 1960, it was unusual for occasional local late-night broadcasts to take place in more than three or four different U.S. states each year.

A brief theatrical resurgence in early 1953 was meanwhile limited to distributor Howco's home state of North Carolina, where it deployed *The Brute Man* as support for an early run of its psychotronic sci-fi cheapie *Mesa of Lost Women*, commencing with a three-day engagement at the 500-seat Uptown Theatre in Durham on January 26. Further theatrical bookings during 1953-54 accompanied a newer breed of spook shows in the south-central and southeastern United States, promoted with pulp horror images that (not entirely truthfully) promised proto–*Blood Feast*–grade lashings of (comic-book) gore and ghoulishness. Playfully unrestrained ads for George Marquis' "Dr. Marquis with His Horrorscopes," in particular, practically dared audiences to "See a surgical maniac amputate limbs of lovely ladies – Hear *awful* death rattles – Feel slimy creatures," while at the same time emphasizing the presence of a movie on the bill with the lure: "To get you in the mood we have on the screen *The Brute Man*."

The Rondo Hatton picture was similarly the screen accompaniment of choice for spook show master and magician E. William Brundell during his spring-summer 1954 tour of Mississippi and Louisiana with "Brundell's Temple of Mystery," whose stage-based

Let's party like it's 1946! Halloween 1961 bill in Lubbock, Texas.

spectacles included "Satan's Daughter – Dracula's Trunk – Headless Monster." In promotional artwork, a hairy hand with pointed fingernails clutched at a stylized sign announcing an "Exciting Horror Show" "on the screen," which was further touted with the antimetabolic tagline: "A monster who lived to kill and who killed to live – *Brute Man*."

Other theatrical play from this point onward fell strictly within the realm of propping up the lower end of quadruple, quintuple and even sextuple bills at budget-conscious drive-ins. On February 5-6, 1954, this included a Dusk to Dawn Show at the 200-car Mount Vernon Drive-In in Mount Vernon, Illinois, comprising a marathon multi-genre mishmash of: [1] RKO's Tim Holt Western *Saddle Legion* (1951); [2] Specialty Pictures' reissue of the murder-by-lion crime drama *Caged Fury* (1948) starring Richard Denning; [3] the RKO-released British-made World War II musical drama *Lilli Marlene* (1951); [4] *The Brute Man*; [5] Eagle-Lion's insurance fraud crime drama *Assigned to Danger* (1948) with Gene Raymond; and [6] a second Jean Yarbrough–directed title in the shape of Monogram's World War II comedy *She's in the Army* (1942) featuring Veda Ann Borg. The venue pledged "free coffee and donuts to all who stay for the last picture" – which with temperatures of 30 degrees on the first night, falling to 27 degrees on the second, they most assuredly deserved, electric in-car heaters notwithstanding!

By 1961, all things that were old had again become new, with the dollar-per-carload Circle Drive-In in Lubbock, Texas, putting together a four-movie "Big Halloween Program" that sought to appeal to a generation of Monster Kids – or perhaps more specifically, Monster Teens – who had grown up with the likes of Screen Gems' "Shock!" television package of pre–1948 black-and-white horror and mystery flicks. Advertised in newspapers with what had in the interim become *retro* original 1940s ad mats, the murder-heavy "vintage" line-up took in Monogram's *Doomed to Die* (1940) and *Fear* (1946), as well as PRC's *The Brute Man* and – ending the bill on a somewhat lighter note – *The Panther's Claw* (1942). As late as October 1970, another Texas drive-in, the Meadowbrook in Fort Worth, was *still* making use of Rondo Hatton's final feature as part of its grab-bag pre–Halloween "4 Big Spook-er-ooos" bill, which presented – in reverse-chronological order – that year's Warner Bros. release of *Frankenstein Must Be Destroyed* (1969), Astor Pictures' *Frankenstein's Daughter* (1958), *The Brute Man* and Monogram's *The Ape* (1940).

After a prolonged dearth of television screenings, a small-screen incarnation of *The Brute Man* again became more readily available in November 1982, when Admit One released the movie on Beta and VHS. A wider rental launch on the Sony label in November 1985 was followed by a sell-thru release in March 1988.

Universal's discarded B, which had become PRC's reliable money-spinner, thereafter made its digital debut on the Image Entertainment DVD label in July 1999.

The Brute Man: Fun Facts

By Tom Weaver

 "Bilko's Vampire," a 1958 episode of TV's *The Phil Silvers Show*, includes a scene in which two Kruger Bros. Studio executives are in an office whose walls are decorated with (phony) monster-movie posters. They have the following conversation:

Exec #1: Tell me, how's the talent search for the new monster coming?

Exec #2: Nothin'. Nothin' so far.

Exec #1: Well, we gotta find somebody, Eddie. The public is tired of the old monsters. They want new faces, horrible new faces!

I note this because (1) a conversation very much *like* it *could* have taken place at Universal in 1944, and led to the Creeper's enlistment in the studio's army of monsters. And (2), because one of the posters hung behind the speakers is for *The Fifty Foot Midget* and it's dominated by artwork of Rondo Hatton in his Creeper clothes, standing hip-deep in skyscrapers (see photo above).

 Film historian William K. Everson featured a shout-out to Hatton in his 1964 book *The Bad Guys*, a tribute to movie villains and other varmints:

> Rondo Hatton certainly fits into the "brute" category [of movie villains] through a facial deformity that was rather tastelessly exploited in cheap horror films. Unfortunately, his literally Neanderthal face was accompanied by a listless acting style, and Hatton … found himself almost alone in the "freak" category insofar as Hollywood was concerned.

 In the *Brute Man* Production History chapter, I wrote that Hatton's average line in *House of Horrors* was 2.6 words. Lest any reader think I guesstimated that number…sad to say, no, I ventured

In the *Phil Silvers Show* episode "Bilko's Vampire," Rondo dominates the poster for the (non-existent) movie *The Fifty Foot Midget* (framed on the wall at the right).

deep into Get a Life Territory to get the exact word count. He has 32 lines, a total of 84 words, 84 divided by 32 is roughly 2.6. I think. Feel free to check my math:

1. Why?
2. Why are you good to me?
3. You know who I am?
4. *You* need *me*?
5. You ain't afraid of me?
6. For me?
7. You're my friend … shake.
8. Sure.
9. What is it?
10. Mud!
11. Stop yellin'.
12. No meat?
13. Yeah?
14. She screamed.
15. What's puppets?
16. You don't like the guy?
17. Sure.
18. You glad?
19. Good. Everybody happy.
20. Where does he live?
21. You happy?
22. They'd *better*.
23. It's pretty.
24. That girl took something.
25. Yeah.
26. You scared?
27. Is that bad?
28. Stop screamin'.
29. You'd let the police get me, huh?
30. Yeah?
31. C'mere.
32. *Shut up!*

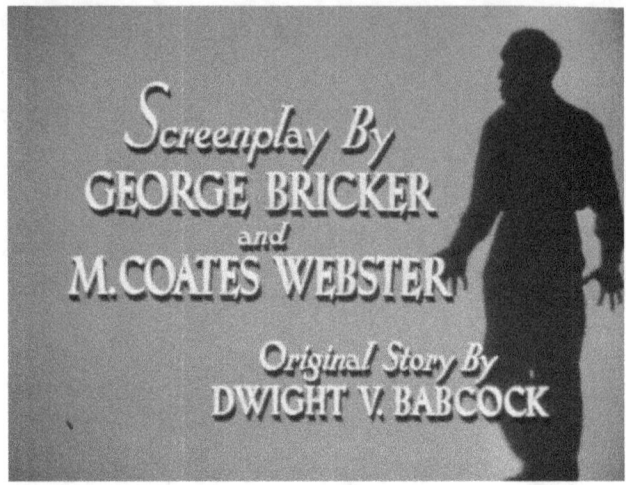

From the opening credits of *The Brute Man*: Rondo's shadow plus the names of the writers who concocted the Creeper's origin story.

The Man Behind the Creeper?: Both *House of Horrors* and *The Brute Man* were based on stories by Dwight V. Babcock (1909-1979), who also cooked up the idea of remaking *The Old Dark House* with Rondo, and co-wrote *The Jungle Captive*. Other Babcock screen credits that will impress Monster Kids, if no one else: *The Mummy's Curse*, some Inner Sanctums, *I Love a Mystery* movies and more. He got his start with detective stories in pulp magazines such as *Black Mask*.

A document from the *Brute Man* production files lists the estimated costs of various characters' wardrobes. It reveals that at some early point, Kirby Grant—the hero in Rondo's *The Spider Woman Strikes Back*—was penciled in for the role of Hal Moffat, i.e., the Creeper before his accident.

In the opening credits of both *House of Horrors* and *The Brute Man*, Rondo's name appears after all the other actors' names have been seen. He also gets special "And" billing on their posters. In the early days of Lon Chaney's Universal horror career, starting with *The Wolf Man* (1941), Lon got the same sort of treatment.

After the Creeper kills Joan Bemis, the *Transcript Journal* newspaper front-pages his crime with the headline **BACK BREAKER CLAIMS SECOND VICTIM**. But when Jimmy listens to the grocery store radio, the newscaster says, "The woman was murdered in the same way as the other four victims."

Actor Tristram Coffin was on the *Brute Man*'s Tenement Street set all day the first day of production, playing a police lieutenant whose men are trying to prevent the Creeper's getaway. But four minutes later, in the grocery store scene where Jimmy is glued to the radio, the Creeper's latest crime and successful getaway are described by a voice-only newscaster played by—Tristram Coffin!

House of Horrors was set in Lower Manhattan so it only makes sense that *The Brute Man* should also take place in Gotham; but at no point does anyone mention New York. And in *The Brute Man*, it doesn't "feel" like New York, because two Creeper killings are committed in tony-looking neighborhoods with trees and picket fences. If based in Manhattan, the Creeper would probably need a car for these sojourns to leafy suburbia.

Separated at birth? *The Detroit Times* (January 20, 1946) apparently can't tell our Rondo from Rhonda Fleming. Which Santa's lap would *you* rather sit in?

Did people ever actually live in waterfront "shacks," as the Creeper does in this movie? The Creeper's little hidey-hole has a **23** over the door, he calls it "23 Waters Street" in his grocery store note, and Jimmy beelines right to the place like he's been there, or other shacks like it, 100 times. But from what we see of the inside, it hardly looks habitable. In fact, its ceiling is the underside of the public boardwalk above, with spaces between all the boards and sunshine coming through the spaces to light the shack. Yeah, the Creeper's a prick, but you still hate to picture him there during a rainstorm—not to mention being at the mercy of every dog passing above!

As Mr. Haskins the grouchy grocer skims the front page of a newspaper, we see in an insert shot the headline **MAYOR CHARGES POLICE LAXITY IN CREEPER KILLINGS**. Another yarn has the attention-grabbing title **Meteorite Falls Near**

Baby. Apparently that funny article title was a favorite with the folks who prepared phony newspapers for Hollywood use: It turns up in many films, and as recently as the wacky disaster-movie spoof *Airplane!* (1980).

 The Brute Man's flashback scenes are just four minutes long, and yet Cliff manages to mention *five times* Hal Moffat's volatility: "Hal had a quick temper," "Hal's temper had made him a lot of enemies," "Knowing his temper, I seldom challenged him," "He was plenty angry because I'd outsmarted him, and he showed it," "You could never tell what he'd do when his temper flared." But after all that build-up, nowhere in the movie do we see the Creeper get visibly mad at *anything*. Yes he kills people, but never with any trace of anger, or *any* emotion.

 Stage 9's Collegiate Cafe set was used in two scenes, the opener where the Creeper appears out of the gloom of the night and peers in at astonished patrons, and the 1930 flashback with Cliff, Virginia, Hal and Joan. The two scenes were shot on the same day. What do you want to bet that some of the 1930 kids can also be seen as the modern-day (1946) kids, i.e., the same group of extras was used?

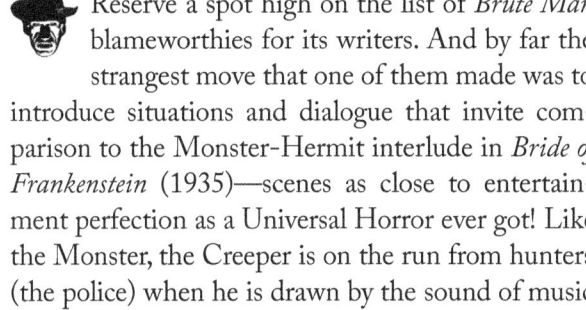 Reserve a spot high on the list of *Brute Man* blameworthies for its writers. And by far the strangest move that one of them made was to introduce situations and dialogue that invite comparison to the Monster-Hermit interlude in *Bride of Frankenstein* (1935)—scenes as close to entertainment perfection as a Universal Horror ever got! Like the Monster, the Creeper is on the run from hunters (the police) when he is drawn by the sound of music and takes refuge in Helen's apartment. The Hermit and Helen don't immediately mention their blindness; when they do, the lines and even the delivery are similar:

> **Hermit**: You must please excuse me, but I am blind.
> **Helen**: You see, I am blind.

The Hermit perceives that the Monster is bloody and exclaims, "You're *hurt*, my poor friend!"; Helen hears the Creeper groan and says, "Hal, you're *hurt*!" And both the Hermit and Helen imprudently latch onto the idea that this very strange intruder is a good candidate for future companionship.

There's also a scene in which the Creeper morosely examines his misshapen mush in a mirror, then

Home is where you hang your hat…and sometimes where you hide the body. The Creeper takes a cuppa-coffee break after a bit of dirty work in *The Brute Man*.

The grocer (Oscar O'Shea) and his delivery boy (Jack Parker) read the Creeper's note. You remember O'Shea as the Scripps Museum watchman menaced by Lon Chaney's Kharis in *The Mummy's Ghost* (1944).

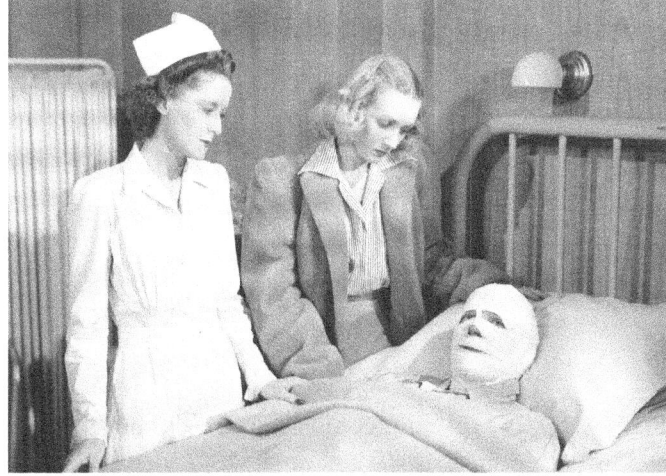

The plot sickens: Hal (Fred Coby) has put him*self* in the hurt locker (the lab explosion was his own fault), but he may already be plotting revenge against others. His nurse is Beatrice Roberts, *Flash Gordon's Trip to Mars*' (1938) Queen Azura.

When the Creeper enters Virginia's bedroom and she sees him in her dressing table mirror (top), Universal acolytes will recall a similar set-up in the studio's classic *Bride of Frankenstein* from a decade earlier (bottom).

breaks the glass with his fist. This calls to mind *Bride*'s scene of the Monster looking at his reflection in the surface of the waterfall pool, then lashing out at the image. (Also see the stills on this page.)

 Getting murdered was all in a day's work for Charles Wagenheim, the doomed *Brute Man* pawnbroker: The actor made a sideline career out of being choked and/or slain. Off the top of my head: Besides twice being liquidated by Rondo Hatton, in *The Jungle Captive* and *Brute Man*, he was fatally shot by George Zucco in 1940's *Dark Streets of Cairo*, fatally choked by Zucco in 1942's *Halfway to Shanghai* and throttled by Boris Karloff in 1944's *House of Frankenstein* ("*Now* will you give me my chalk?!").

In 1979, 84-year-old Wagenheim was found bludgeoned to death on the bedroom floor of his Fareholm Drive, Hollywood, apartment. When the foul deed took place, his wife Lillian was in the living room and the wife's practical nurse was downstairs in the laundry room—according to her (the nurse). In another movie-like development, Mrs. Wagenheim was an invalid, deprived of speech by a stroke a few years back, and she could not relate anything she may have seen or heard. Police briefly investigated the possibility that Wagenheim had been done in by the same person who had beaten aged actor Victor Kilian to death in his (Kilian's) apartment, a mile away, the same week; Wagenheim and Kilian had just appeared in "The Return of Stephanie's Father," an episode of TV's *All in the Family*.

But the slayings turned out to be unconnected: In June, the nurse, Stephanie Tonette Boone, 24, a prime suspect all along, was arrested on charges of murder and grand theft. She pleaded guilty to voluntary manslaughter and in January 1980 received an eight-year prison sentence: six on the manslaughter charge (*only six years*?!) and two tacked on as the result of her prior armed robbery and escape convictions. According to one newspaper account, "Investigators theorized she attacked Wagenheim with a table leg after he confronted her about stealing checks from him and converting them to her own use."

I Googled and tried to find her. Surely she wouldn't have talked with me, but it might have been fun to report whatever interchange we *did* have.

 In one Capt. Donelly office scene, he and Lt. Gates nonchalantly play gin rummy, their way of showing the visiting police commissioner and Mr. Parkington that they (Donelly and Gates) are satisfied with the progress of their Creeper investigation. Was this an in-joke on the part of one of the screenwriters? Ben Pivar produced *The Brute Man*; and according to Reginald LeBorg (director of several Pivar movies), when a Pivar production was coming along nicely, Pivar stayed in his office and played gin rummy. Veteran TV writer-producer Andrew J. Fenady writes in one of this book's appendices that Pivar's motto was, "If I'm sitting at my desk doing nothing, I know I've done my job."

Speaking of MacBride and Whitney, Pivar reteamed them as senior and junior cops in one of his next pictures, *Blonde Alibi* (1946).

 On pages 99 and 100, I speculated that the very high number of blown takes on *The Brute Man*

The last thing the Brute Man wants to do is hurt the pawnbroker. But it *is* on his list.

If Cliff and Virginia (Tom Neal and Jan Wiley) were Hampton U graduates, class of 1930, their grown-up characters should be in their 30s. But they (especially Neal) are made up to look eligible for senior discounts at the Collegiate Cafe.

was due to Hatton. I've examined the production paperwork on *The Jungle Captive* and *House of Horrors* and there were a lot less blown takes on those movies, possibly because those were better, healthier days for Rondo, and/or possibly because his dialogue in those pictures was kept to a minimum. As stated above, he had 32 lines in *House of Horrors* and the average line was 2.6 words. *The Brute Man* burdened the ungifted actor with many more lines (74) and longer lines, including a 13-, 15- and even a 21-word whopper that might have been beyond his capabilities at that point.

When Cliff shoots the Creeper, notice that actor Tom Neal — probably assuming that the gun is below the frame line — is pointing it toward the floor to Hatton's left. (Firing blanks at someone at close range is dangerous and, in at least one famous case involving an actor, has been fatal.) Hatton makes matters worse: After Neal fires past his left side, Hatton falls to the floor clutching at his right thigh.

After being made to look taller in *The Pearl of Death* and *House of Horrors*, Hatton is again a half-pint predator in *The Brute Man*, not much taller than the women, and seemingly shorter than the newsboy (see photo on page 215). But how can this *be*, when in *Brute Man*'s 1930 college flashbacks, the Creeper's earlier incarnation Hal Moffat towered over *every*body?

The last scene of the movie takes place in Capt. Donelly's office, with the detective telling Helen: "By the way, I have some news for you. I've been talking to certain people, and..." He looks up at Lt. Gates. "We... [*coughs*] *They* think you're going to *get*

At the end of *The Brute Man*, the implication is that Peter Whitney (right) may wind up with Helen (Jane Adams), to the dismay of Capt. Donelly (Donald MacBride).

that operation." The implication is that the two detectives are springing for the sight-restoring surgery, even though $3000 in 1945 is like 42 grand today, awfully steep for a coupla public servants.

But Universal paperwork related to Virginia's (Jan Wiley) wardrobe reveals that it was originally intended that she appear in this wrap-up scene, and this led me to wonder if one version of the script had wealthy Virginia ponying up for the operation. The synopsis in the *Brute Man* pressbook backs me up: It wrongly concludes with the line, "Helen is befriended by Virginia who promises to have her cared for by a famous eye specialist."

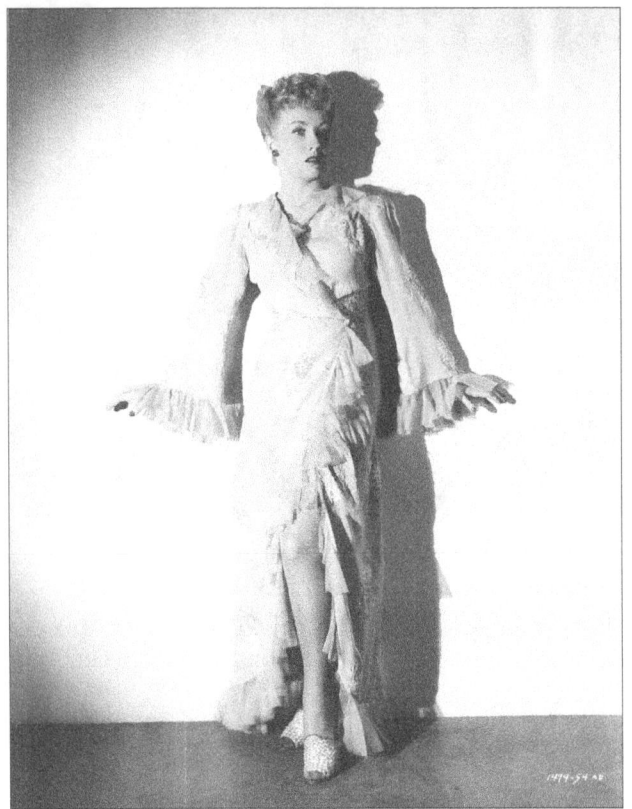

Soigné Jan Wiley co-starred in Universal's last two monster flicks pre–Universal-International and the monsters' exile: *The Brute Man* and *She-Wolf of London* (1946). She was also Dick Tracy's gal Friday, battling an invisible villain in *Dick Tracy vs. Crime, Inc.* 1941), and a gangster's sexy plaything in *The Strange Case of Doctor Rx* (1942).

Peter Whitney as *The Brute Man*'s Lt. Gates. Monster Kids may remember Whitney as the homicidal hillbilly twin brothers Mert and Bert in the hilarious *Murder, He Says* (1945); as the gorilla handler who appears part-ape himself in *Gorilla at Large* (1954), and, on TV, a wide array of oversized manimals.

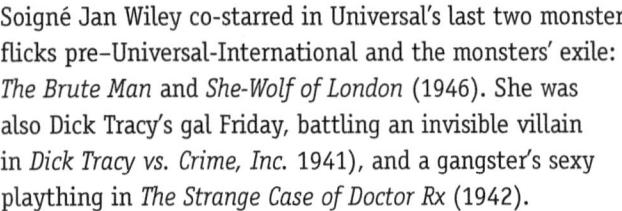 The *Brute Man* cast sheet shows that Rondo got a bit of star treatment: The Universal contractee had a dressing room (#119) with a phone (extension 490). (Jane Adams, another contractee, also had these luxuries; their co-stars, all "Outside Talent," went without.) The cast sheet lists Hatton's home phone as CR-1-2297. Yes, CR as in CReeper.

Donald MacBride was a stage and screen veteran with decades of experience, and in most (all?) of his *Brute Man* scenes, he does most of the talking. Peter Whitney, playing his sidekick, was twentysomething, practically a screen newcomer, and he has next to *no* dialogue. But both actors were paid the same amount, $1334. MacBride coulda used a better agent. Maybe Whitney's!

In other news from the salary world, Fred Coby got $500 for playing the younger, un-mutated version of the Creeper. Jan Wiley got $584 for her efforts, Tom Neal $1750. Read a lot more about Neal, including an interview with Tom Neal Jr., in "Scripts from the Crypt" #3, *Bride of the Gorilla*.

Speaking of Whitney, he stands out in the movie by standing a head taller than most of the rest of the players. This is Monster Kid heresy *but*: Whitney could and did play many brutish parts and I bet he'd have been a better choice for the Creeper role than monosyllabic little Rondo, whose one recommendation was that he was coyote ugly. By playing the Creeper in *House of Horrors* and *The Brute Man*, neither Hatton *nor* Whitney would have earned a niche in the temple where the names of Karloff, Lugosi *et al.* are consecrated—but I feel certain that Whitney's performances would *not* have been the embarrassments that Hatton's sometimes were.

The casting folks set aside a few dollars for a double for Hatton in a mirror-smashing scene and for Charles Wagenheim as the murdered pawnbroker. But watching the movie reveals that the players handled the action themselves.

Most of the *Brute Man* music is familiar to Monster Kids from past Universal Horrors. Thank goodness Universal put in the music before they sold the picture to PRC; imagine how much bleaker *Brute Man* would be with one of PRC's typically tuneless scores!

Early May 1946: a great time for New York horror fans. Rondo Rondo everywhere… but just one more to come.

During the opening credits, we hear a few *House of Horrors* bars before it segues into music from *The Invisible Man's Revenge* (1944). There's more *House of Horrors* music as the Creeper confronts Joan, as Virginia and the detective find Cliff's body, and at other spots. Drippy *Black Friday* (1940) music is heard over most of the drippy Creeper-Helen scenes, frequently enough that it qualifies as the "love theme" for this Beauty and the Beast combo. There's music from *The Wolf Man* as Jimmy delivers the groceries, as Jimmy peers at the Creeper through the sooty window and as Cliff shoots the Creeper.

From the "WTF?" Dept.: The slow, dreary *Black Friday* cue is again heard over the action scene at the end, as the Creeper's attempt to kill Helen is thwarted by the cops. Meanwhile, *Pearl of Death*'s ominous Hoxton Creeper theme is wasted on the shot of the Creeper sliding his shopping list under the grocery store door!

The Brute Man's Summary of Picture Cost, prepared on May 4, 1946, reveals that it was budgeted at $104,635; studio overhead raised this figure to $130,795. The movie ended up costing $96,530.86; the total with studio overhead, $120,663.62.

Macabre?, funny?, sad?, ironic?, all four? – *you* decide: Rondo made arrangements to travel to Tampa in February 1946 with his wife and his parents. The only changes to that plan: (1) the group left a few days ahead of schedule, and (2) poor Rondo was in a box.

Two weeks to the day after Rondo Hatton shed his mortal coil, *House of Horrors* made its debut: a Washington's Birthday weekend opening at the Rialto in New York City. According to researcher supremo Dr. Robert J. Kiss, the Rialto had earned itself the nickname "The House of Horrors" due to its long association with Universal chillers, and this allowed for some additional name-based ballyhoo for the opening. The reviewers for *The New York Post* and *PM* magazine were both savvy enough to mention that Hatton had recently died.

Rondo Hatton, April 22, 1894 – February 2, 1946. "For in that ~~sleep~~ creep of death, what dreams may come…"

I didn't get much food for thought out of Barry Brown's *Brute Man* synopsis-review in *Castle of Frankenstein* magazine, but it sure as shit increased my vocabulary:

> [The Creeper] is a profligate murderer, girt in sloven, gloomy attire, and inwardly indurated towards his former sweetheart when he sees that his ugliness repels her. [The] puerile plot and Hatton's lithoid acting style were enough to make the film a somniferous experience….

It Pays to Increase Your Word Power, Part Deux: *PM* magazine's 1946 review of *House of Horrors* called Rondo Hatton "prognathous."

Were Rondo Hatton's Creeper movies really so "boffo" at the box office that it made sense for producer Ben Pivar to call a later, unrelated horror movie *The Creeper* and invite confusion with them?

Exploiting his own medical misfortune, Rondo Hatton "wound up atop Universal's eroding heap of ticket-selling matinee monsters," according to Michael H. Price and John Wooley (*Forgotten Horrors 3!*). "Today, a sufferer would be likelier to parlay such a misery into a momentary recognition via tabloid television. Hatton's approach seems the more constructively entertaining, if not necessarily the more dignified."

 Un-Fun Fact: Rondo Hatton was the star of, and the title character in, *The Brute Man* but the Universal-prepared pressbook treats him like a redheaded stepchild. It spotlights Jane Adams and Tom Neal and ignores Hatton; in fact, its various news blurbs sometimes reduce him to "Also seen in the cast are…"–level insignificance. If the pressbook was prepared in February 1946 or thereafter, maybe this was the writer's way of avoiding mentioning that Hatton had died.

 I pity the fool who shelled out 50¢ ($12 today) to see *The Brute Man* because he was enraptured by the artwork of Jane Adams as a leg-baring floozy that dominates the poster (see page 106). I doubt that Adams' prim Blind Helen was a satisfactory substitute for guys lured in by the promise of hubba hubba.

 After the end of producer Ben Pivar's Universal days, he made three movies for Bernard Small Productions, and one of them has caused Monster Kids much confusion: 1948's *The Creeper*. Many horror fans probably tuned in to one of its years-later telecasts expecting the return of our favorite back-breaker; and a few early books on Hollywood Horrors declared that it *was* a Universal leftover from pre–U-I days and sold off to another distributor the way *The Brute Man* was. (Even the redoubtable William K. Everson made this assertion, in his *More Classics of the Horror Film*.) *The Creeper* was produced, directed and photographed by the three guys who did those jobs on *The Brute Man*, Pivar, Jean Yarbrough and George Robinson, respectively.

The facts are that *The Creeper* was made at the Motion Picture Center in March 1948 by Pivar and Bernard Small for 20th Century–Fox release. A whodunit in which a guy with a cat's claw for a hand dunit, this belongs on any list of Worst Hollywood Horror Flicks of the '40s…alongside *The Brute Man*.

 Some time in the mid–1940s, radio writer Joseph Ruscoll penned a whodunit script called "The Creeper," about a killer of women on the loose in "the Heights" in New York. Was Ruscoll ripping off the Creeper movies, or had he never *heard* of the Creeper movies? Who knows. The airwave Creeper concentrates on redheads but his heart isn't always in his work: At each crime scene, he uses his victim's lipstick to scrawl the message "For Heaven's sake, catch me before I kill more." The spine-tingler was first heard on the anthology radio series *Molle Mystery Theater* on

Rondo Hatton, Tampa Film Star, Plays Hollywood Horror Movie In Triplicate

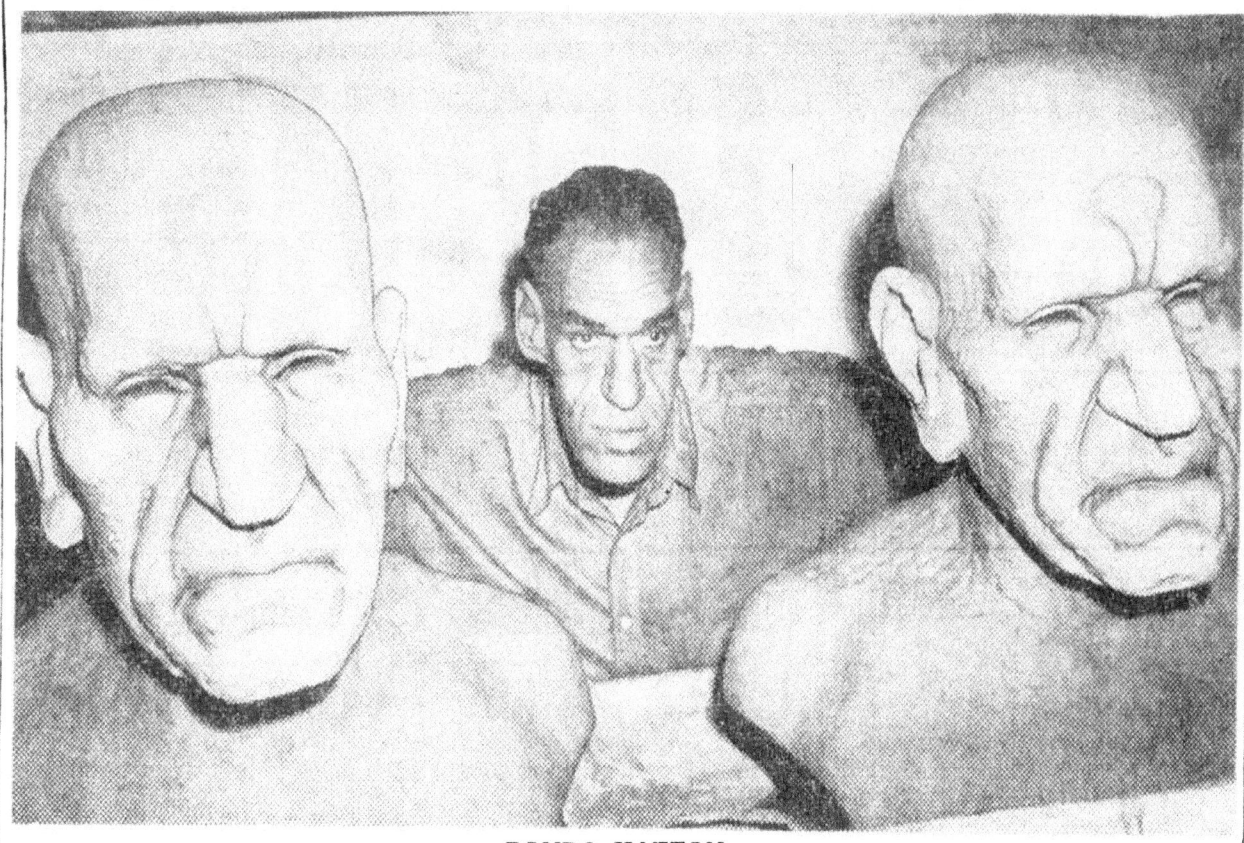

RONDO HATTON

Rondo Hatton, former Tampa newspaperman, who has learned to make the dread disease acromegaly an asset, will appear in triplicate in a new Hollywood chiller, "House of Horrors."

The new picture, based on a story of a mad sculptor, features the Tampa actor and two giant clay models of his head. Rondo plays "The Creeper" in the film.

As a student at Hillsborough High School and later at the University of Florida, Rondo won recognition as an honor student and an athlete and on two occasions was voted the most handsome boy in his class. In his Army uniform during World War I, Rondo gave the other men in his outfit stiff competition, his envious buddies admitted.

But the handsome young man, who entered as a private, was severely gassed and mustered out as a casualty—and a lieutenant. Army doctors did what they could, but the German's poison gas caused the development of acromegaly, which causes bones and tissues to grow although the stricken person already has attained normal growth. In Rondo's case it distorted his facial features.

In an effort to overcome his tendency to avoid people, Rondo got a job as a reporter at The Times and supplemented it with work at WDAE, The Times' station. Covering the filming of "Hell Harbor" here in 1929, Rondo met Henry King, the director, who gave the Tampan a job as an extra and was so pleased with his performance that he offered him a job in Hollywood.

Rondo took the director up on his offer about 10 years ago. He won critic's praise for his acting as a bodyguard in the Tyrone Power film "In Old Chicago." He has appeared as an extra in more than 100 films and recently has played leads in chiller films, such as "The Pearls of Death" and "Jungle Captive."

From the January 21, 1946, *Tampa Times*, probably the last article written about Rondo in his lifetime. You won't learn anything from reading it; it's included only because I like the part that says WWI doughboy Rondo "was severely gassed and **mustered** out"!

> **Lab kids burned**
>
> Two Bronx high-school students were burned on the face during a lab experiment gone awry Friday, cops said.
>
> The students, 15 and 17, were working on a project at Morris HS when they were burned, police said.
>
> They were taken to Jacobi Medical Center for an evaluation. — *Amanda Woods*

What New York school's chemistry lab will provide the Creepers of tomorrow? Answers only in *The New York Post* (October 2018)!

one-man crime wave who snaps his victims' spines and steals their bling, while in *The Brute Man*, poor Rondo competes in a slapstick boxing match for the $50 purse.

 In 2003, when Arnold Schwarzenegger was running for governor of California, Brian Lowry wrote a *Variety* story in which he recalled meeting and interviewing Ahhh-nold at a 1982 *Conan the Barbarian* press junket:

> I was a geeky (if somewhat thinner) sophomore at UCLA, reporting for the *Daily Bruin*. The actor puffed on a cigar and patiently endured a day of round-robin interviews.… He didn't even flinch when my pool partner suggested he'd be perfect to star in an autobiography of Rondo Hatton, the grotesque actor—deformed by a pituitary disease called acromegaly—who played the Creeper in films during the 1940s. I assumed Schwarzenegger didn't know who Hatton was, or he'd have torn the little guy's arms off.

March 29, 1946; the half-hour episode starred Charlotte Manson as a carrot-top with the jim-jams and, sounding very Tommy Udo–esque in his agitated moments, Richard Widmark as a likely suspect. Ruscoll's script was later performed on the series *Murder at Midnight* (syndicated, various dates across the country), *Murder by Experts* (July 23, 1949) and *The Chase* (January 25, 1953).

 For the ultimate in "From the sublime to the ridiculous…," someday make a home video double-bill of *The Brute Man* and Charlie Chaplin's "comedy romance in pantomime" *City Lights* (1931). In the latter, Chaplin's raggedy Little Tramp is devoted to a blind flower girl (Virginia Cherrill) and determined to get her the money for a sight-restoring operation, even though he knows this means that she will then see that the suitor she imagines to be wealthy is actually a vagabond. I have fun mentally mixing and matching some plot elements: I envision an alternate universe version of *City Lights* in which Charlie becomes a night-crawling

 Being a romantic *and* a *Honeymooners* fan, I like to imagine a happier ending for the Creeper and Helen. I see him calling on her at her home with a gift-wrapped box of Braille candy hearts, overcoming his shyness, pouring out his love to her like a modern-day Cyrano ("Oh, Hal!") and convincing her to share his off-the-grid, netherworld existence. And with a wave of his big hand toward Helen's piano and all her other belongings, he grins, "And wait'll you see how different this furniture looks, when it's in a 23 Waters Street apartment!"

"Hal, I *love* youuu…"
"Baby, you're the greatest!"

The Brute Man Reviews

Harrison's Reports: It belongs in the horror class of entertainment, and it has moments to recommend it to undiscriminating patrons who go in for this type of picture. Others, however, will probably find it tiresome, for it suffers from triteness in plot and in treatment.

New York Daily News (Wanda Hale): ★ (one star). [T]he least effective thriller that has been my misfortune to see.

New York Post (Archer Winsten): The basic idea is inspired by Rondo Hatton, a bit actor [with] a misshapen, enormous head and jaw.... It is his only fortune, for otherwise he is neither able to act or read lines with any degree of skill.... Just as clothes don't make a gentleman, so a face doesn't make both a villain and continuous thrills. All this picture has is a face, handicapped by encircling improbabilities.

Showmen's Trade Review: Story supplies a murder in every few feet of film and there is enough suspense in the 59 minutes of running time to entertain [chiller fans] in a very satisfactory manner.

Buffalo Courier-Express: [*The Brute Man*] is pretty silly. ...In particular is the sequence wherein police guard a house they know he will enter and the detective on duty is as obvious as a troop of soldiers on parade.

Motion Picture Herald (Mandel Herbstman): [A] taut little melodrama.... [T]he film utilizes the standard suspense-rousing devices, but in its category, it stands favorably.... Jean Yarbrough...keeps things moving briskly.

Variety (the first, and the more favorable, of its *two* reviews, published on October 18, 1946, after *Brute Man* was previewed at the Eagle-Lion studios): [A] chiller with more murders per reel than screen has seen in many a moon. ...[Its premise] leads to considerable suspense, set against a logically patterned plot. ...Photography by Maury Gertsman, in low key throughout, helps materially in retention of growing suspense. ... Hatton makes a most convincing brute man and lends all the menace role demands to the character.

Variety (its second review, October 23, after the movie's New York preview): Singularly unexciting meller is suitable only for lower dualers. ...Hatton's facial features, which run a close second to those of Frankenstein's monster, furnish the film's few chills. ...Producer Ben Pivar, long U's keeper of the Bs, has done little to make what may have been his last "B" to stand out from similar fodder.

Motion Picture Daily: *The Brute Man* is a better-than-average horror film that will satisfy both horror fans and the general theatre-goer. Director Jean Yarbrough has injected…an element of what is popularly known as "Hitchcock" suspense. [Hatton and Adams] turn in particularly effective performances.

Boxoffice: There is little suspense in the film as the audience knows all the time who commits the murders, but the frighteningly ugly features of Rondo Hatton … make for many spine-chilling scenes. …[T]he film also has its light and touching moments.

Walter Winchell: *The Brute Man* displays a listless frightmare that aims for the bogeyman and settles for the sandman.

Evansville (Indiana) *Press*: The late Rondo Hatton, ugliest man in pictures, and possibly in the United States, is the star of *The Brute Man*.…The picture apparently was intended to be a shocker, but is neither shocking or mysterious. It's just what the title implies—brutal.

Cleveland Plain Dealer: [T]he climax doesn't create any more noise than a one-inch firecracker.

Film Bulletin: Class C stuff as regards acting and production.… …Hatton's forbidding appearance and hollow voice will elicit shrieks from the youngsters, but a less-wooden performer might have created some sympathy for the misshapen brute.

Box Office Digest: It is a horror chiller of deepest dye, produced and directed by workmen who know their way around this field, containing sufficient of gore and shriek incitement to satisfy the most avid of fright fans, yet withal presented with a modicum of intelligence and capable playing.

CONTINUITY & DIALOGUE

On

"THE BRUTE MAN"

With
TOM NEAL
JAN WILEY
JANE ADAMS
DONALD MacBRIDE
PETER WHITNEY
FRED COBY
JaNELLE JOHNSON

And
RONDO HATTON
as the CREEPER

PICTURE NO. 1479
DIRECTOR - YARBROUGH

MAY 20, 1946

> Editor's note: We could not locate a script for *The Brute Man* and must use the movie's "Continuity & Dialogue" instead.

PICTURE NO. 1479
DIRECTOR - YARBROUGH
REEL ONE   PAGE 1

NO.	DESCRIPTION	DIALOGUE	

CONTINUITY & DIALOGUE

1. PART TITLE

   U N I V E R S A L
   "THE BRUTE MAN"
   P A R T
   1

2. FADE IN - TRADEMARK
   Whirling globe - words en-
   circling it -   MUSIC

   A UNIVERSAL PICTURE

   ...DISSOLVES INTO

   PICTORIAL ANIMATED MAIN TITLE

   UNIVERSAL
   Presents   "

   "THE BRUTE MAN"

   COPYRIGHT MCMXLVI BY
   UNIVERSAL PICTURES COMPANY, INC.

   ...DISSOLVES INTO

   With
      TOM NEAL
         JAN WILEY
            JANE ADAMS
               DONALD MacBRIDE
                  PETER WHITNEY
                     FRED COBY
                        JaNELLE JOHNSON   "

   ...DISSOLVES INTO

   CLOSE UP THE CREEPER
   As he comes on from b.g. - comes
   close to camera - staring off
   evilly - exits at side -
   Words over scene read -   "

            And
         RONDO HATTON
         as the CREEPER

   ...DISSOLVES INTO

NO.	DESCRIPTION	DIALOGUE

2. CONTINUED

      Screenplay By
     GEORGE BRICKER
         and
    M. COATES WEBSTER

       Original Story By
      DWIGHT V. BABCOCK

  ...DISSOLVES INTO

Director of Photography...
     ...MAURY GERTSMAN, A.S.C.
Film Editor......PHILIP CAHN
     Art Direction
JOHN B. GOODMAN - ABRAHAM GROSSMAN
Director of Sound.BERNARD B. BROWN
Technician........JOE LAPIS
     Set Decorations
RUSSELL A. GAUSMAN - EDWARD R. ROBINSON
  Gowns   Hair Stylist
VERA WEST   CARMEN DIRIGO
    Director of Make-Up
      JACK P. PIERCE
Dialogue Director.RAYMOND KESSLER

APPROVED BY MPPDA
Certificate No. 11369

THIS PICTURE MADE UNDER
JURISDICTION OF I.A.T.S.E.
AFFILIATED WITH AMERICAN
FEDERATION OF LABOR

  ...DISSOLVES INTO

     Produced
       by

    BEN PIVAR

  ...DISSOLVES INTO

     Directed
       by

  JEAN YARBROUGH

  ...FADE OUT

MUSIC

"

"

"

| NO. | DESCRIPTION | DIALOGUE | REEL ONE PAGE 3 |

3. FADE IN - CLOSE UP IN POLICE
    RADIO ROOM (NIGHT)
    Policeman talking into micro-
    phone -

    MUSIC

    POLICEMAN - Attention, all cars.
        Attention, all cars. General
        alarm.

    ...VERTICAL WIPE TO

    CLOSE UP IN POLICE CAR
    Two cops sitting in car, listen-
    ing to radio - driver speaks
    into mike - two men talk - driver
    starts car - drives off at side -

    MUSIC - MOTOR - SIREN

    POLICEMAN'S VOICE - Car Twenty-Two.
        Go to Seven-Thirty-Three Spring
        Avenue. It's a Three-Forty-One.
        That is all.

    DRIVER - Car Twenty-Two. We'll go.
        A Three-Forty-One?

    POLICEMAN - Yes. The man says
        murder.

    ...VERTICAL WIPE TO

    MED HIGH SHOT OF CITY STREET
    Cars passing - police car racing
    from b.g. - camera pans - police
    car passes camera - races down
    middle of street toward b.g. -

    MUSIC - SIREN

    ...VERTICAL WIPE TO

    CLOSE VIEW IN BUSHES
    The Creeper comes on past camera
    - slumps behind bushes - turns -
    looks off - exits -

    MUSIC

    ...VERTICAL WIPE TO

    PAN SHOT OF INTERSECTION
    Police car skids around corner
    - exits at side -

    MUSIC - SIREN

4. CLOSE UP MOVING SHOT THE CREEPER
    As he stalks along - eyes staring
    off -

    MUSIC

    ...VERTICAL WIPE TO

| NO. | DESCRIPTION | DIALOGUE | REEL ONE PAGE 4 |

4. CONTINUED.

   SHOT OF CITY STREET
   Police car races past -   MUSIC - SIREN

5. CLOSE UP THE CREEPER
   As he comes on close to camera   MUSIC
   - stops & looks about, his face
   evil & set - looks off -

6. MED LONG SHOT UNIVERSITY BUILDING   "

     ...DISSOLVES INTO

   CLOSE UP ON WALL
   Plaque reads -   "

     HAMPTON
     UNIVERSITY

7. LARGE CLOSE UP THE CREEPER
   Turns & looks off -   "

8. HIGH CAMERA SHOT IN BALLROOM
   Students standing about - looking off - large banner near   "
   camera reads -

     VICTORY
     DANCE
     TONIGHT

9. VIEW IN BALLROOM
   Students dancing - others sitting "
   about at side of room drinking -

10. LARGE CLOSE UP THE CREEPER
    Looking off, his face evil -   "
    camera dollies back before him
    as he moves down street -

11. CLOSE MOVING SHOT ON CREEPER'S
    FEET
    As he walks along -   FOOTSTEPS - AD LIB NOISES

12. CLOSE UP MOVING SHOT THE CREEPER
    As he walks along, his face grim
    & set -   FOOTSTEPS - MUSIC

13. SHOOTING THROUGH WINDOW OF
    COLLEGIATE CAFE
    Two girls & boys sitting at
    table next to window - other   MUSIC
    students standing, sitting &
    dancing in b.g.

| NO. | DESCRIPTION | DIALOGUE | REEL ONE PAGE 5 |

14. CLOSE UP MOVING SHOT THE CREEPER
    As he stalks along - almost
    exits past camera -   MUSIC - FOOTSTEPS

15. MED CLOSE SHOT EXT. CAFE
    Students inside celebrating -
    Creeper comes on past camera
    & stands at window, watching   MUSIC
    students - girl sitting at table
    near window reacts as she sees
    Creeper - others react as they
    turn & see him -

16. LARGE CLOSE UP THE CREEPER
    Glaring off hatefully -   "

17. CLOSE PAN SHOT EXT. CAFE
    On the Creeper as he walks along
    past students staring through   MUSIC - FOOTSTEPS
    window at him - he exits at side -

18. CLOSE UP MOVING SHOT THE CREEPER
    Follows camera as it dollies back   "   "
    along street - almost exits at
    side -

    ...DISSOLVES INTO

    CLOSE MOVING SHOT ON CREEPER'S
    FEET (CRANE SHOT)
    As he walks along past picket   MUSIC - FOOTSTEPS
    fence to driveway - camera tilts
    up, bringing Creeper into scene   AD LIB NOISES
    as he stops before lighted house
    - camera cranes back & up as
    Creeper takes cover behind shrubs
    along driveway as doors of house
    open - Joan & guests come out on
    to porch - cross toward car in
    driveway -

                                           MEN & WOMEN TALK AD LIB.

                                           MAN - Swell party, Joan. Thanks a
                                              lot.

                                           TALKING AD LIB.

19. MED SHOT EXT. HOUSE
    Joan & guests moving down steps
    of house - camera pans as they   MUSIC - FOOTSTEPS
    cross to car - talk - men & women
    start to get into car -   AD LIB NOISES
                    (Continued)

| NO. | DESCRIPTION | DIALOGUE | REEL ONE PAGE 6 |

19. (Continued)

MAN - Thanks, Joan. It was just like old times.

WIFE - Yes, the old crowd and everything.

MAN - And good old Hampton's still on the winning side.

GIRLS LAUGH AD LIB.

WIFE - You're right.

SECOND GIRL - Don't forget. We're having lunch tomorrow.

JOAN - Oh, yes. One o'clock at the Carlton. I'll be there.

GIRL - Right.

MEN AND WOMEN AD LIB GOODNIGHT.

20. HIGH CAMERA SHOT EXT. HOUSE & GROUNDS
Creeper watching from cover of bushes near f.g. as Joan's guests get into car in driveway - drive off - Joan waves - turns toward house - stops as Creeper speaks harshly -

MUSIC - MOTOR

AD LIB NOISES

GUESTS AD LIB GOODNIGHT.

JOAN - Goodnight. I'm so glad you came. Do come back soon.

GUESTS AD LIB - We will. Goodnight.

CREEPER - Joan!

21. CLOSE UP JOAN
Turns to camera - looks about - puzzled - speaks -

MUSIC - MOTOR

JOAN - Who is it?

22. CLOSE UP IN BUSHES
Creeper watching off, his face almost hidden in the shadows - speaks -

MUSIC

CREEPER - It's me. Hal Moffat.

| NO. | DESCRIPTION | DIALOGUE | REEL ONE PAGE 7 |

23. CLOSE UP JOAN
    Surprised - speaks - comes close
    to camera & stops -   MUSIC

                                                 JOAN - Hal Moffat?

24. CLOSE UP IN BUSHES
    Creeper's face in shadow -
    speaks as he comes forward -
    light falls across his face,   MUSIC - AD LIB NOISES
    revealing his ugliness - he
    stops - stares off - grim -

                                                 CREEPER - Hello, Joan.

25. CLOSE UP JOAN
    Staring off - scared - backs   MUSIC
    away as she speaks -

                                                 JOAN - You're not Hal Moffat?

26. CLOSE UP THE CREEPER
    Staring off - speaks shortly -   MUSIC

                                                 CREEPER - Yes.

27. CLOSE UP JOAN
    Terrified - staring off -   MUSIC

28. CLOSE UP THE CREEPER
    Comes forward slowly & menac-   "
    ingly -

29. CRANE SHOT IN YARD
    Joan backs away as The Creeper
    moves through shrubbery & across   MUSIC - FOOTSTEPS
    driveway toward her - camera
    cranes down past him as she moves
    toward steps - horrified -

                                                 JOAN - No! Stay away from me.
                                                 CREEPER - I won't hurt you.
                                                 JOAN - No! No! Stay away.

30. LARGE CLOSE UP THE CREEPER
    Moves close to camera, his   MUSIC
    face bitter & grim -

                                                 JOAN O.S. - (SCREAMS)

| NO. | DESCRIPTION | DIALOGUE | REEL ONE   PAGE 8 |

31. CLOSE SHOT JOAN (CRANE SHOT)
One hand to her mouth as she
screams - camera moves up close   MUSIC
- she drops out of sight below
camera - camera cranes up to
second floor of house -

                                JOAN - (SCREAMS)

...DISSOLVES INTO

MONTAGE

CLOSE MOVING SHOT OF CREEPER'S
FEET
As he walks along past picket
fence - newspaper comes on super-
imposed over b.g. shot - headline   MUSIC
reads -

    BACK BREAKER CLAIMS SECOND VICTIM

camera moves down close to column
- subheading reads -

    SOCIALITE JOAN BEMIS
    MEETS SAME FATE AS
    PROFESSOR CUSHION

    POLICE PUZZLED AS TO
    MOTIVES FOR CRIMES

b.g. shot changes to close up of
The Creeper -

...DISSOLVES INTO

CLOSE UP POLICE RADIO ROOM
Policeman sitting at desk - talks
into mike - various scenes come   MUSIC
on superimposed over b.g. shot -

    Policemen running past camera
    Police car racing along

...DISSOLVES INTO

Various shots superimposed one over
the other showing:

    Police start of hunt
    Policemen on motorcycles & cars
    Close up The Creeper   (Continued)

| NO. | DESCRIPTION | DIALOGUE | REEL ONE   PAGE 9 |

31. (Continued)
    Police car skidding around
       corner
    Creeper's feet moving along
    Police inspection at border
    Moving shot of Creeper's
       feet

END OF MONTAGE

   ...DISSOLVES INTO

CLOSE SHOT IN POLICE RADIO ROOM
Announcer talks into mike -   MUSIC

                        ANNOUNCER - Attention, all cars,
                        District Seventeen. All cars,
                        District Seventeen. The Three-
                        Forty-One suspect mentioned in
                        broadcast Number Nine is re-
                        ported surrounded in Woddel
                        Street seven hundred block.
                        Move in.

   ...VERTICAL WIPE TO

PAN SHOT SIDE OF TENEMENT STREET
Creeper running on at side,
looking back over his shoulder   MUSIC - FOOTSTEPS - SIREN
- stops at alley - moves about
- frantic - runs down alley
toward b.g. & exits -

32. MED HIGH SHOT END IN ALLEY
Creeper running on near camera
- stops - looks about - blocked   FOOTSTEPS - SIREN
- goes to door at side - finds
it locked -

33. VIEW OF SUBURBAN STREET
Police car coming on in b.g. -   SIREN
races down street & exits near
f.g. -

34. LOW CAMERA SHOT OF BUSINESS CORNER
Camera pans on police car as it
skids around corner - exits near   SIREN - AD LIB NOISES
camera - other police car comes
on around corner - exits near
camera -

35. MED HIGH SHOT IN END OF ALLEY
Creeper at door - finds it locked   SIREN
- exits at side -

NO.	DESCRIPTION	DIALOGUE
36.	PAN SHOT EXT. TENEMENT STREET On police car as it drives up to alley & stops - people standing about watching - curious - cops get out of car - other police car drives on - cops get out & move toward entrance of alley -	SIREN - DOOR - FOOTSTEPS
37.	SIDE IN ALLEY Creeper coming on at side near f.g. - stops - looks up - steps up onto barrel as he starts to climb up fire escape -	FOOTSTEPS - SIREN

TALKING AD LIB O.S. |
| 38. | MED SHOT EXT TENEMENT STREET Cops & plainclothesmen getting out of cars - gather about on sidewalk in alley entrance - onlookers gather about - | FOOTSTEPS

TALKING AD LIB. |
| 39. | MED SHOT UP TO SIDE OF BUILDING Creeper gets up onto fire escape landing - starts up steps to third floor - | AD LIB NOISES |
| 40. | INT. ALLEY NEAR ENTRANCE Police & plainclothesmen coming on - stop - cops talk - some start to push onlookers aside - others start down alley toward b.g. - | FOOTSTEPS |

LIEUTENANT - Now keep everybody back.

COP - All right. Everybody back here.

LIEUTENANT - He's in here somewhere.

COP - All right. Let's get back here.

| 41. | SHOOTING STRAIGHT DOWN FIRE ESCAPE - Creeper ascending fire escape from landing below - comes close to camera - | PIANO - FOOTSTEPS |

REEL ONE PAGE 10

| NO. | DESCRIPTION | DIALOGUE | REEL ONE   PAGE 11 |

42. SHOOTING TOWARD ENTRANCE IN ALLEY
    Cops moving down alley toward f.g. –

    PIANO – FOOTSTEPS

    TALKING AD LIB

43. MED CLOSE SHOT UP TO FIRE ESCAPE LANDING
    Creeper climbing onto landing – stops at window on landing – listens – looks off –

    PIANO – FOOTSTEPS

44. VIEW IN ALLEY
    Cops coming toward f.g. – plainclothesmen exit at side – one starts up steps at side as others exit past camera –

    "   "

45. MED SHOT UP TO LANDING
    Creeper on fire escape landing looking down – turns to open window on landing –

    MUSIC – FOOTSTEPS

46. CLOSE UP INT. WINDOW
    Creeper pushes curtains aside from outside window – camera pulls back & pans as he steps into darkened room – softly lowers window –

    PIANO

47. VIEW IN END OF ALLEY
    Cops moving about searching – one tries door at side –

    PIANO – FOOTSTEPS
    AD LIB NOISES

48. CLOSE VIEW SIDE IN BEDROOM
    Creeper standing at window – looking out – turns slowly – camera pulls back & pans as he moves slowly across room to open door of living room – looks off – sees –

    PIANO

49. SHOOTING THROUGH OPEN DOOR INTO LIVING ROOM
    Creeper standing at door near camera – watching Helen playing piano b.g. – she stops playing suddenly – listens – Creeper steps back behind doorway out of range as Helen rises from piano – comes slowly into bedroom – speaks – fumbles for light on wall by door –

    PIANO – FOOTSTEPS

(Continued)

| NO. | DESCRIPTION | DIALOGUE | REEL ONE   PAGE 12 |

49. (Continued)
turns to Creeper as he speaks
harshly - they talk - she turns
back into living room -

        HELEN - Who is it?

        CREEPER - Don't turn on the light.

        HELEN - Who are you? What do you
          want?

        CREEPER - Keep quiet.

        HELEN - If you're a burglar, I'm
          afraid there isn't much here
          for you to steal.

50. CLOSE VIEW SIDE IN LIVING ROOM
Helen coming from bedroom,
followed by Creeper - camera
pans - they stop near camera -
she turns to him - puzzled but
unafraid - he puzzled - they
react to sounds - camera pans
as he crosses back to bedroom
- exits - comes down behind him -

        PIANO - FOOTSTEPS

          KNOCKING

        CREEPER - I'm not a burglar.

        HELEN - Then what do you want?

        CREEPER - You're not afraid of me?

        HELEN - Well, I'm a little nervous,
          I guess. But why should I be
          afraid of you?

        CREEPER - There they are.

        HELEN - Who?

        CREEPER - Some men.

        HELEN - Are you in trouble?

        CREEPER - Yes. They're after me.

        HELEN - Go into the bedroom. Do
          as I say.

| NO. | DESCRIPTION | DIALOGUE | REEL ONE PAGE 13 |

51. MED CLOSE SHOT IN ROOM
Helen looking off - turns - camera pans as she crosses to door - opens it - steps back - stares off blindly as men pass her - one stops - they talk - cop exits at side -

MUSIC - DOOR - FOOTSTEPS
KNOCKING

HELEN - Just a minute. Yes?

PLAINCLOTHESMAN - Have you seen a man around here?

HELEN - Why, no, I haven't seen anyone.

PLAINCLOTHESMAN - Take a look in there.

52. CLOSE UP IN BEDROOM
Creeper standing in window - climbs outside on the fire escape landing & exits -

MUSIC

53. CLOSE UP IN BEDROOM
Door opening - cop enters - turns on light - moves around - almost exits into living room -

MUSIC - CLICK OF SWITCH

54. VIEW INT. LIVING ROOM
Helen standing near f.g. - facing plainclothesman & camera - cop comes from bedroom at side - other cop comes forward from b.g. - stops - listens as Helen & plainclothesman talk - react - listen - plainclothesman exits at side -

MUSIC - SHOT - DOOR

POLICEMAN - There's no one in there.

PLAINCLOTHESMAN - You sure you haven't seen anybody?

HELEN - Yes, I'm sure.

MAN O.S. - There he goes.

TALKING AD LIB.

PLAINCLOTHESMAN - Come on.

| NO. | DESCRIPTION | DIALOGUE | REEL ONE PAGE 14 |

55. SIDE IN LIVING ROOM
Helen standing at door - staring off blankly as plainclothesman & two cops pass her & exit outside - camera pans as she closes door - camera pulls back as she comes into room - bumps into piano - fumbles for piano bench - sits - stares off into space as she starts to play - camera moves up close to Helen, revealing her blindness -

   ...DISSOLVES INTO

MUSIC - SHOT - DOOR

| NO. | DESCRIPTION | DIALOGUE | REEL ONE PAGE 15 |

55. CONTINUED

MED SHOT EXT. GROCERY STORE
(NIGHT)
The Creeper coming on at side -
takes note from pocket & shoves
it under door - looks about -
exits at side -

   ...DISSOLVES INTO

EXT. GROCERY STORE (DAY)
Man & woman pass close to camera

   ...DISSOLVES INTO

MED CLOSE SHOT IN GROCERY STORE
Jimmy sitting behind counter
listening to small radio - camera dollies up to Jimmy - he
interested - looks off - startled

MUSIC - FOOTSTEPS

"   "

NEWSCASTER'S VOICE - The woman was murdered in the same way as the other four victims. Authorities have issued a warning to all citizens to be on the look-out for this fiend. As far as the police know, he only appears at night. He is a large, heavy-set man - usually wearing a black coat and hat. Descriptions of the Creeper have been submitted to headquarters, but these vary to such an extent that it's hard to give an accurate picture of the man's face. When last seen, he was on a tenement roof top near the waterfront. And now turning to the other news of the day --

HASKINS O.S. - Jimmy!

56. MED CLOSE SHOT IN STORE
Jimmy behind counter - turns off
radio as Haskins comes on to him
on near side of counter - puts
hat on counter as he speaks
gruffly to Jimmy - takes off
coat - Jimmy exits at side -
camera pulls back as Haskins
comes forward - sees note on
counter - reads note -

CLICK OF SWITCH
FOOTSTEPS
AD LIB NOISES

(Continued)

| NO. | DESCRIPTION | DIALOGUE   REEL ONE   PAGE 16 |

56. (Continued)

JIMMY - Mornin', Mr. Haskins.

HASKINS - Leave that radio alone! Sweep up the place! You're getting paid to work - not to entertain yourself!

JIMMY - Okay. Say, that Creeper guy murdered somebody again last night.

HASKINS - Oh, murders, detectives, gangsters -- That's all you think about! Get the broom!

JIMMY - Okay.

57. CLOSE UP WRITTEN NOTE
Held in Haskin's hands - reads -

    Send a loaf of
    bread - a can
    of beans - some
    potatoes and a
    can of coffee
    over to
        23 Waters St

      Thanks

58. PART TITLE   U N I V E R S A L
                        "THE BRUTE MAN"
                        END OF PART
                             1

MS - ib

PICTURE NO. 1479
DIRECTOR - YARBROUGH
DIALOGUE REEL TWO PAGE 1

NO. DESCRIPTION

CONTINUITY & DIALOGUE

1. PART TITLE

U N I V E R S A L
"THE BRUTE MAN"
P A R T
2

2. CLOSE UP IN GROCERY STORE
Haskins, standing close to camera, reading note - speaks - camera pans over slightly as Jimmy comes on from side holding broom - talk - camera pans and dollies up as Haskins goes to counter in b.g. - speaks angrily as he picks up paper sack - puts groceries into it as he talks - camera pans as Jimmy moves down counter - picks up bag of groceries - Haskins furious - Jimmy glares at Haskins - Haskins watches as Jimmy exits at side -

FOOTSTEPS
AD LIB NOISES

HASKINS - Jimmy!

JIMMY OS. - Yeah?

HASKINS - Where'd this come from?

JIMMY - Somebody stuck it under the door.

HASKINS - (GRUNTS)

JIMMY - Don't you think it's kind of funny, sticking a note under the door?

HASKINS - No and don't go tryin' to make a mystery out of it. Somebody probably too busy to pick up the stuff.

JIMMY - It could be The Creeper.

HASKINS - Creeper, Creeper, Creeper. You give me the creeps

(Continued)

NO.	DESCRIPTION	DIALOGUE REEL TWO PAGE 2
2.	(Continued)	JIMMY - Well, he could be. That'd be a swell reason why he wouldn't want to see anybody or come out 'cept at night.

HASKINS - You just gotta delivery these groceries and don't forget the money. A dollar and a quarter.

JIMMY - Okay but I still think it might be--

HASKINS - I know, so he's The Creeper. Well you just creep along with that--I mean, hurry up with that stuff and then get back here and do the rest of your work.

...DISSOLVES INTO

MED. LONG SHOT OVER WATER TO VIEW OF WATER FRONT STREET
Jimmy moving along on street - carrying bag of groceries - he moves down ramp to lower level -

FOOTSTEPS
MUSIC

3. PAN SHOT EXT. WATER FRONT SHACKS
On Jimmy as he moves along - stops outside shack - numbers over door read -

23

Jimmy knocks on door - puts groceries down near bottom of door - door is opened slightly from inside - The Creeper's hand hands money to Jimmy - Jimmy tries to peek into shack as door is closed quickly - Jimmy looks around curiously - camera pans as he moves along to ramp - sees other shack - Jimmy steps from ramp into shack -

KNOCK
MUSIC
DOOR
AD LIB NOISES

CREEPER'S VOICE - Leave it outside. How much?

JIMMY - A dollar and a quarter.

CREEPER'S VOICE - Go a way.

NO.	DESCRIPTION	DIALOGUE	REEL TWO PAGE 3
4.	CLOSE UP EXT. DOOR OF SHACK Door is opened from inside - The Creeper looks out cautiously - picks up bag of groceries - closes door from inside -	DOOR MUSIC	
5.	CLOSE UP AT CORNER OF SHACK Jimmy peering in through grimy window - tries to wipe away soot -	MUSIC	
6.	CLOSE UP PAN SHOT IN THE CREEPER'S SHACK On The Creeper as he moves to table - puts down sack of groceries - takes out articles - looks at them - Jimmy partly visible at window in b.g. as he peers in from outside - tries to rub away soot -	MUSIC AD LIB NOISES	
7.	LARGE CLOSE UP THE CREEPER (ANGLE) Looks off out of corner of his eye - tense -	MUSIC	
8.	CLOSE UP INT. GRIMY WINDOW Jimmy partly visible through window as he tries to peer into room from outside - rubs window with his fingers - looks in -	MUSIC	
9.	LARGE CLOSE UP THE CREEPER (ANGLE) Looking off from out corner of his eye - tense - starts to exit at side -	MUSIC	
10.	CLOSE UP PAN SHOT THE CREEPER Jimmy watching from window in b.g. as The Creeper comes forward - moves into other part of shack - camera pans excluding window - The Creeper stops - tense -	MUSIC	
11.	LARGE CLOSE UP THE CREEPER Watching off out of corner of his eye -	MUSIC	

| NO. | DESCRIPTION | DIALOGUE | REEL TWO   PAGE 4 |

12. CLOSE UP INT. GRIMY WINDOW
    Jimmy watching into room
    from outside -   MUSIC

13. CLOSE UP THE CREEPER
    His back to camera - moves
    slowly toward loose boards
    in wall - swings them aside -   MUSIC
    steps outside -   AD LIB NOISES

14. CLOSE UP AT DOORWAY
    The Creeper comes on slowly -
    looks off intently -   MUSIC

15. LARGE CLOSE UP JIMMY (SIDE)
    Peering through clean spot
    of window -   MUSIC

16. CLOSE UP THE CREEPER
    Watching off intently - raises
    his hands menacingly - camera
    pans as he stares off - moves
    slowly across - almost exits
    at side -   MUSIC

17. LARGE CLOSE UP JIMMY (SIDE)
    Unaware of his danger - peering
    intently through window - The
    Creeper's hands come on slowly
    from side - one hand covers
    Jimmy's mouth - Jimmy tries to
    free himself - is pulled off
    scene -   MUSIC

                                          JIMMY -(MUTTERS AD LIB)

    ...VERTICAL FEATHER WIPE TO

    CLOSE UP IN STORE
    Mrs. Hart standing on near side
    of counter - Haskins on far side
    taking money from cash register -
    hands it to her - speaks - he
    looks around anxiously - she exits
    at side with groceries - Haskins
    looks off - shakes his head as he
    speaks - camera pans over and
    tilts up to clock on wall b.g. -   AD LIB NOISES
    hands indicate ten minutes after
    ten -

                                          (Continued)

| NO. | DESCRIPTION | DIALOGUE | REEL TWO PAGE 5 |

17. (Continued) HASKINS - Thank you, Mrs. Hart. That boy!

18. CLOSE UP TO OPEN DOOR OF STORE
Haskins behind counter in b.g. -
Mrs. Hart coming forward to door -
stops - speaks to Haskins - Mrs.
Hart comes forward and exits at
side - camera dollies into store -
moves up to counter as Haskins looks
about - worried - looks down at   FOOTSTEPS
newspaper on counter - picks it up -   MUSIC STARTS
looks at headlines - startled -

MRS. HART - You'll send Jimmy over with the rest of that order, won't you, Mr. Haskins?

HASKINS - Yes, I will if he ever gets back from that errand I sent him on. He's been gone nearly two hours.

MRS. HART - Well, that's the boy for you. These days they can't seem to keep their minds on their work. Good day, Mr. Haskins.

HASKINS - Good day, Mrs. Hart.

19. CLOSE UP NEWSPAPER
Headlines read -

   MAYOR CHARGES POLICE LAXITY
      IN CREEPER KILLINGS
   ———
   POLICE COMMISSIONER PUTS CAPT. DONNELLY
         OF HOMICIDE ON SPOT   MUSIC

camera moves down close to
column head -

20. CLOSE UP IN STORE
Haskins staring at newspaper -
thoughtful - looks off -   MUSIC
rubs his chin -

   ...DISSOLVES INTO

| NO. | DESCRIPTION | DIALOGUE | REEL TWO PAGE 6 |

20. CONTINUED

    CLOSE UP EXT. DOUBLE DOORS
    Lettering on doors reads -

        CAPTAIN   HOMICIDE
      M.J. DONELLY   BUREAU

    CAMERA pulls back as Gates comes   MUSIC
    on from side to door - opens   DOOR
    door - goes into office -   FOOTSTEPS

21. PAN SHOT IN OFFICE
    On Gates, closing office door,
    as he hurries across office -
    camera brings Donelly into
    scene seated behind desk at
    side - Gates speaks cheerfully   MUSIC STOPS
    - Donelly questions him -   DOOR
    Donelly reacts as Gates speaks   FOOTSTEPS
    - camera pans Gates across
    office to door, excluding
    Donelly - stops at door -

GATES - Good morning, Captain.

DONELLY - What makes you think it's good? Or does that beaming puss of yours mean that you have some good news?

GATES - Uh uh. Bad news. It's on the way. I just saw Commissioner Salisbury parking his car outside. The Mayor's secretary is with him. Just thought I'd let you know -- give you at least two minutes to think up a good story.

DONELLY - Hold it. Lieutenant.

22. CLOSE UP IN OFFICE
    Donelly seated at desk in f.g.
    facing door in b.g. - Gates standing at door - Gates turns and
    comes slowly forward as Donelly
    rises, moves around desk to Gates -   FOOTSTEPS
    camera angles around and moves   DOOR
    up as the two talk - Donelly
    speaks sternly -

                (Continued)

NO. DESCRIPTION   DIALOGUE   REEL TWO PAGE 7

22. (Continued)
    Donelly reacts as he looks off
    -- yells at Gates -- Gates
    confused --

                                DONELLY - Come back here.

                                GATES - Who, me?

                                DONELLY - Yeah, you. After all,
                                    I assigned you to the Creeper
                                    murders, and I need a partner in
                                    this little game of buck passing.
                                    By the way, just what have you
                                    done toward apprehending the
                                    murderer?

                                GATES - Are you kidding? You know
                                    what we've done. We're operating
                                    the biggest drag net in the
                                    history of crime in this city.

                                DONELLY - Well, it isn't big enough.
                                    You haven't caught the Creeper
                                    yet. Uh -- I want every avail-
                                    able man in the Homicide Bureau
                                    put to work on this case imme-
                                    diately.

                                GATES - Now, wait ----

                                DONELLY - I don't want excuses.

23. CLOSE PAN SHOT IN OFFICE
    On Commissioner & Parkington
    as they move across office -
    camera pulls back and pans bring-
    ing Gates and Donelly into scene
    at side - Donelly yelling at
    Gates - he stops suddenly as
    he sees Commissioner & Parking-
    ton -

                                DONELLY O.S. - I want the Creeper
                                    in jail within twenty-four hours.
                                    (ON SCENE) Or there'll be some
                                    changes made around here. Uh --
                                    Good morning, Commissioner.
                                    Good morning, Mr. Parkington.

                                COMMISSIONER - Good morning.

                                PARKINGTON - Good morning, Captain
                                    Donelly.

                                DONELLY - You're looking fine,
                                    commissioner.

| NO. | DESCRIPTION | DIALOGUE | REEL TWO PAGE 8 |

24. CLOSE UP DONELLY, COMMISSIONER & PARKINGTON
Donelly facing other two as they talk - Commissioner angry - Donelly stalls -

DONELLY - And how's the missus? I trust she's feeling as good as you look.

COMMISSIONER - She's not. She's scared to death -- like every other woman in town, since wholesale murder has the police department stymied!

DONELLY - I presume you refer to the Creeper murders.

COMMISSIONER - You presume right! I've come here to find out why a killer can terrorize an entire city --

25. CLOSE UP DONELLY
(Over shoulders of Commissioner & Parkington) Donelly stalls -

COMMISSIONER - -- while the Police Department twiddles it's thumbs.

DONELLY - Oh, well now I wouldn't exactly call what we were doing thumb-twiddling, Commissioner.

PARKINGTON - Then just what would you call it, Captain?

26. CLOSE UP DONELLY, COMMISSIONER & PARKINGTON
Donelly facing side - Donelly tries to stall - Parkington speaks firmly -

PARKINGTON - His Honor, the Mayor, would like to know.

DONELLY - Now if you gentlemen will please sit down, I'll try to bring you up-to-date on The Creeper.

(Continued)

| NO. | DESCRIPTION | DIALOGUE | REEL TWO | PAGE 9 |

26. (continued)

PARKINGTON - We are up-to-date on The Creeper. We know that you haven't arrested him and His Honor, the Mayor, delivered an ultimatum to Commissioner Salisbury this morning. He demanded action within twenty-four hours.

27. CLOSE SHOT IN OFFICE
Donelly, Commissioner, Parkington and Gates standing - Parkington and Commissioner speak threateningly - Donelly points finger at Gates as he passes the buck -

PARKINGTON - If none is forthcoming he'll ask for the Commissioner's resignation.

COMMISSIONER - And I'm telling you, Donelly, if you don't turn up something to quiet public opinion before tomorrow, your job won't be worth a plugged nickel.

DONELLY - Exactly what I was telling Lieutenant Gates--

28. CLOSE UP GATES
Looking off - speaks firmly - catches himself -

DONELLY O.S. - --when you came in. Wasn't I, Lieutenant?

GATES - Yes, sir, you were. And I'll pass the bu--the word right on down the line till every man in the department knows exactly where this thing stands. You can depend on me, gentlemen.

29. CLOSE SHOT IN OFFICE
Parkington questions Commissioner - the two glare at Gates and Donelly - camera pans over and dollies up excluding Donelly and Gates as Commissioner

DOOR
FOOTSTEPS

(Continued)

| NO. | DESCRIPTION | DIALOGUE | REEL TWO PAGE 10 |

29. (Continued) and Parkington hurry to door - open it and exit closing door after them -

    PARKINGTON - Very well. Shall we go, Commissioner?

30. CLOSE VIEW IN OFFICE
Gates moves toward Donelly - camera dollies up as they shake hands - grin - Donelly answers phone - reacts - annoyed - hangs up - camera pans over and dollies up as the two move across office - Donelly talks as he takes hat from rack - Gates opens door - Donelly and Gates exit closing door after them -

    DOOR
    FOOTSTEPS
    PHONE RINGS
    CLICK OF RECEIVER

    GATES - How'd I do?

    DONELLY - Great. We're still a good team. (INTO PHONE) Homicide. Captain Donelly speaking. Huh? Okay, okay, we'll look into it. Everybody in town's got Creeperitis.

    GATES - Some grocer down near the water front. He thinks The Creeper might have knocked off his delivery boy. The kid's been away from the store for three hours. We'll just have time to get down there before lunch.

...DISSOLVES INTO

CLOSE UP IN WATER FRONT SHACK
The Creeper standing at stove stoking fire - camera pans over and tilts down to Jimmy's body, covered with gunny sack, lying on floor -

    MUSIC
    AD LIB NOISES

31. MED. LONG SHOT TO WATER FRONT
Police car comes on from side at top level of water front -

    AD LIB NOISES
    MUSIC

| NO. | DESCRIPTION | DIALOGUE | REEL TWO   PAGE 11 |

32. CLOSE UP IN SHACK
The Creeper standing near stove -
looks up startled as he hears
car pass on water front street
overhead - he hurries toward
door b.g. - peers out through
cracks -

    MUSIC
    AD LIB NOISES
    MOTOR

    GATE'S VOICE - Here's Number Twenty-three, Donelly.

33. MED. LONG SHOT TO WATER FRONT
Gates moving along street to
ramp - Donelly looking about
at buildings - the two start
down ramp to water front shacks -

    FOOTSTEPS
    MUSIC
    AD LIB NOISES

34. PAN SHOT IN SHACK
On The Creeper as he moves quietly
from door across room - picks up
his hat and puts it on - goes to
loose boards in wall - swings them
aside - steps through them into
other room -

    MUSIC
    FOOTSTEPS

35. CLOSE UP PAN SHOT GATES & DONELLY
As they move along ramp to door
of The Creeper's shack - Donelly
knocks - the two exchange puzzled
look - Donelly tries door - finds
it locked -

    MUSIC
    KNOCK
    FOOTSTEPS
    AD LIB NOISES

36. VIEW INT. SHACK
Room is empty - coffee pot on
stove - door in b.g. is rattled
from outside -

    MUSIC
    RATTLING NOISE

    DONELLY'S VOICE - Come on, open up in there.

37. CLOSE SHOT EXT. SHACK
Donelly and Gates shrug -
both take hold of door - force
it open - stoop as they start
to enter -

    MUSIC
    AD LIB NOISES

38. VIEW IN SHACK
Donelly, followed by Gates, entering
through door b.g. - look around -
Donelly comes forward to stove -
sees coffee pot - Gates exits at
side -

    MUSIC
    FOOTSTEPS

| NO. | DESCRIPTION | DIALOGUE | REEL TWO PAGE 12 |

39. VIEW OF PILINGS UNDER RAMP
The Creeper coming on slowly
from behind wall - makes his
way carefully across pilings -

                                                       MUSIC
                                                       AD LIB NOISES

40. VIEW IN SHACK
Donelly close to camera - Gates
standing beside Jimmy's covered
body in b.g. - Donelly turns as
Gates speaks - Donelly goes toward
Gates - camera dollies up as he
crouches beside body - gets to
his feet as Gates speaks - they
look around - Donelly gives orders -
Gates exits at side - camera tilts
down as Donelly bends over, opening
drawer of table - looks in it - looks
at clothes hanging in alcove - camera
pans and moves up as he goes to crate
fastened on wall as cabinet - mirror
on front of crate - Donelly looks at
himself in mirror - opens front of
crate - reacts as he sees clippings -
picks them up and looks at them -

                                                       MUSIC
                                                       AD LIB NOISES
                                                       FOOTSTEPS

GATES - Look! The Creeper again.

DONELLY - Yeah and from the looks
    of that coffee pot he can't
    be far away. Round up some
    men and start combing the
    neighborhood. I'll have a
    look around here.

GATES - Okay.

41. CLOSE UP NEWSPAPER CLIPPING
Printing reads -

        POPULAR TRIO
  (Cut of Clifford, Virginia)
  (& Hal in their college days)
  Clifford Scott, Virginia Rogers and
        Hal Moffett
  Three prominent members of the Senior
  Class of Hampton University.

                                                         MUSIC

42. CLOSE UP IN SHACK
Donelly studying clippings - smiles
grimly - looks at other clippings -
thoughtful -

                                                       MUSIC
                                                       AD LIB NOISES

| NO. | DESCRIPTION | DIALOGUE | REEL TWO PAGE 13 |

43. MED. CLOSE PAN SHOT OF PILINGS
    UNDER RAMP
    On The Creeper as he slowly makes
    his way along at edge of pilings -   MUSIC

44. MED. CLOSE SHOT TO RAMP
    Policeman, followed by Gates,
    hurrying along ext. shacks to
    ramp - Gates watches as policeman
    peers into shack next to The
    Creepers - camera pans over as
    Gates moves part way up ramp,
    bringing The Creeper into scene
    crouched on pilings under ramp -
    policeman follows Gates - they   FOOTSTEPS
    stop at spot above The Creeper's   MUSIC
    hiding place - look about -

45. CLOSE UP DOWN TO THE CREEPER
    Crouched on pilings - looks up -
    camera tilts up and pans over
    slightly to Gates and policeman
    standing on ramp - talking -   MUSIC

    GATES O.S. - I'm going to call
        Headquarters for more men-
        (ON SCENE) we'll give the whole
        district a house to house
        canvass.

46. MED. SHOT OF RAMP AND PILINGS
    The Creeper crouched on pilings
    under ramp - policeman watches as
    Gates hurries up ramp and exits   MUSIC
    at side - policeman looks around -   FOOTSTEPS
    The Creeper moves backward beneath
    ramp -

47. PART TITLE   U N I V E R S A L
                          "THE BRUTE MAN"
                          END OF PART
                              2

RA/vh

PICTURE NO. 1479
DIRECTOR - YARBROUGH
REEL THREE PAGE 1

NO.	DESCRIPTION	DIALOGUE	

CONTINUITY & DIALOGUE

1. PART TITLE

    U N I V E R S A L
    "THE BRUTE MAN"
      P A R T
        3

2. CLOSE UP TO PILINGS UNDER RAMP
The Creeper crouched on pilings - watching off -
Newspaper comes on from side, superimposed over b.g. shot - b.g. shot dissolves out - headlines of paper read -

    MUSIC
    AD LIB NOISES

  GROCERY BOY SLAIN BY THE CREEPER!
    Had Delivered Food
     To Monster's Shack
      On Waterfront

Other newspaper falls on over scene - Headline reads -

  CREEPER MURDERS TERRORIZE CITY

Camera moves down close to sub-head - reads -

    MUSIC

    CITIZENS CLAMOR
    FOR ACTION ON
    UNSOLVED CRIMES

Camera pulls back as other newspaper falls on over scene - Headlines read -

BOY MURDER CLUES MAY LEAD TO CREEPER
    WATERFRONT SHACK
    TELLS MUTE STORY
    OF DEPRAVED LIFE

    MUSIC

  ...DISSOLVES INTO

VIEW EXT. SCOTT MANSION (NIGHT)
Squad car pulling to a stop before porch - Donelly & Gates get out on far side - go up steps of porch - cross porch to door -

    MUSIC - DOOR

| NO. | DESCRIPTION | DIALOGUE | REEL THREE PAGE 2 |

3. CLOSE UP EXT. FRONT DOOR
Donelly knocks on door with
knocker - Gates watching -
door is opened - Clifford Scott
steps forward - Donelly questions
Scott - talk - Scott steps backward into hall -

                  MUSIC STOPS
                  KNOCK
                  DOOR
                  FOOTSTEPS

DONELLY - Good evening.

SCOTT - Good evening.

DONELLY - Are you Mr. Clifford Scott?

SCOTT - Yes.

DONELLY - Captain Donelly, Homicide
    Bureau -- and Lieutenant Gates.
    Mind if we come in?

SCOTT - Not at all. Come right in.

DONELLY - Thank you.

4. VIEW OF HALL
Scott steps aside - Donelly
& Gates step into hall, taking
off their hats - Scott closes
door - they talk - Scott gestures
- he comes forward, exits past
camera - Donelly & Gates put
hats on chair - come forward -

                  FOOTSTEPS
                  DOOR

SCOTT - What can I do for you,
    gentlemen?

DONELLY - I believe you can give us
    some important inforamtion, if
    you will.

SCOTT - I don't know what this is
    all about, but I'll be glad to
    help any way that I can. Shall
    we go into the living room?

DONELLY - Thank you.

5. VIEW INT. LIVING ROOM
Virginia Scott seated in f.g.
- rises as Scott, Donelly and
Gates come forward from hall
b.g. - camera moves up as Scott
makes introductions - talk -
Scott & Virginia puzzled -

                  FOOTSTEPS

         (Continued)

| NO. | DESCRIPTION | DIALOGUE | REEL THREE PAGE 3 |

5. (Continued)

VIRGINIA - What is it, Clifford?

SCOTT - I don't know yet, dear. These gentlemen are from the Police Department. They say they'd like to ask me some questions. Captain Donelly, Lieutenant Gates -- my wife.

VIRGINIA - How do you do?

GATES - How do you do?

DONELLY - You can help us, too, Mrs. Scott.

VIRGINIA - I?

DONELLY - Yes. I take it you've read about the murders committed by a characters the newspapers call the Creeper?

VIRGINIA - Why, yes.

6. LARGE CLOSE UP DONELLY
Watching off intently - speaks -

DONELLY - Well, we stumbled onto something this morning which leads me to believe you can help us identify him.

7. CLOSE UP SCOTT & VIRGINIA
Both startled - she speaks - incredulous -

VIRGINIA - You mean it's someone we know?

DONELLY O.S. - I think so.

8. CLOSE SHOT GROUP
Four standing as before - all grim - Donelly questions the Scotts -

DONELLY - What was you class at Hampton University?

SCOTT - Nineteen-thirty.

DONELLY - You were in that class, too, weren't you, Mrs. Scott?

(Continued)

| NO. | DESCRIPTION | DIALOGUE REEL THREE PAGE 4 |

8. (Continued)

    VIRGINIA - Yes.

    DONELLY - And you had a classmate named Hal Moffat? Remember him?

    SCOTT - He was a good friend of ours.

9. LARGE CLOSE UP DONELLY
Grim - speaks -

    DONELLY - We have an idea that Hal Moffat is the Creeper.

10. CLOSE UP SCOTT & VIRGINIA
Stunned - speak -

    VIRGINIA - Hal!

    SCOTT - No, he couldn't be.

11. CLOSE SHOT GROUP
Donelly takes pack of clippings from inside coat pocket - shows one to Virginia & Scott -

    AD LIB NOISES

    DONELLY - We found this in his shack -- among some of his other things. He apparently had been keeping it for some time.

12. CLOSE UP NEWSPAPER CLIPPING
Headlines & caption read -

    POPULAR TRIO

  (Cut of Scott, Virginia &)
  (Hal in their college days)

Clifford Scott, Virginia Rogers and Hal Moffat, three prominent members of the senior class of Hampton University.

    SCOTT O.S. - I remember when this was taken -- it was right after a football game.

13. CLOSE UP SCOTT & VIRGINIA
Smile reminisently as they look at clipping - talk -

    VIRGINIA - Yes. It was the day Hal almost won the game single-handed.

171

| NO. | DESCRIPTION | DIALOGUE | REEL THREE PAGE 5 |

14. LARGE CLOSE UP DONELLY
Speaks - grim -

    DONELLY - Two people from that college were killed by the Creeper -- Professor Cushman --

15. CLOSE UP SCOTT & VIRGINIA
Unhappy - lock down - he speaks -

    DONELLY O.S. - -- and a woman named Joan Bemis.

    SCOTT - We knew Joan quite well.

16. LARGE CLOSE UP DONELLY
Speaks -

    DONELLY - I thought you might have. When did you last see Hal Moffat?

17. CLOSE UP SCOTT & VIRGINIA
he turns to her - they talk -
Scott tries to explain - camera
dollies up very close to Scott
as he talks - remembering -

    SCOTT - We haven't seen him for years.

    VIRGINIA _ No. He just disappeared.

    DONELLY O.S. - Disappeared.

    SCOTT - Well, none of us have seen him since his last year in college. You see, something happened to Hal.

    DONELLY O.S. - What?

    SCOTT - He was probably our best friend. In his last year at Hampton, he was Captain of the football team.

...DISSOLVES INTO

(RETROSPECT SEQUENCE)

HIGH CAMERA PAN SHOT OF FOOTBALL
FIELD
Game in progress - camera pans
as Hal catches pass - races down
field toward end zone - other
players following -

    CHEERING

(Continued)

| NO. | DESCRIPTION | DIALOGUE | REEL THREE PAGE 6 |

17. (Continued)

SCOTT'S VOICE - In the final game of the season we were playing Rensler for the conference championship. The sports writers picked Hal for all American honors. And if they had any doubt about it--

18. CLOSE HIGH SHOT OF FIELD
Camera tilts up as Hal, carrying ball, runs into end zone making touchdown - he looks around proudly -

LOUD CHEERING AD LIB:

SCOTT'S VOICE - --the game he played against Rensler won their votes. Hal had a quick temper--

19. LONG SHOT TO GRANDSTAND
Jammed - fans waving and cheering wildly -

LOUD CHEERING AD LIB:

SCOTT'S VOICE - --but it certainly paid off on the foot--

20. HIGH SHOT PART OF GRANDSTAND
Fans cheering and waving wildly -

LOUD CHEERING AD LIB:

SCOTT'S VOICE - --ball field. He was--

21. CLOSE SHOT TO GRANDSTAND
Joan, Scott and Virginia standing - cheering and waving wildly -

LOUD CHEERING AD LIB:

SCOTT'S VOICE - --all over the place, blocking, backing up his line, passing Rensler dizzy.

22. CLOSE UP PART OF SCOREBOARD
Arrow indicates fourth quarter -

(Continued)

NO.	DESCRIPTION	DIALOGUE REEL THREE PAGE 7
22.	(Continued)	CHEERING AD LIB:

SCOTT'S VOICE - And up to the fourth quarter had scored three--

23. CLOSE UP ON PART OF SCORE BOARD
Clock indicating minutes to play - arrow points to 5 -

CHEERING AD LIB:

SCOTT'S VOICE - --touchdowns in brilliant broken field runnings.

24. LONG SHOT TO END ZONE OF FIELD
Camera pans slightly as Hal kicks ball for conversion - makes it -

CHEERING AD LIB:

SCOTT'S VOICE - Three times he converted for extra points.

25. CLOSE SHOT SCOREBOARD
Reads -

    Rensler   Hampton
      7   21

4th. quarter

   5 minutes to play
   First Down

R has ball - 10 yds. to go

CHEERING AD LIB:

SCOTT'S VOICE - The score stood: Hampton twenty-one, Rensler seven.

26. LOW CAMERA SHOT OF HAL
Man's fingers holding football in upright position close to camera - Hal steps backward ready to make kick -

CHEERING AD LIB:

| NO. | DESCRIPTION | DIALOGUE | REEL THREE | PAGE 8 |

27. LONG HIGH PAN SHOT OF FIELD
Hal kicks off - players move down field - man with ball is tackled in center of field -

LOUD CHEERING AD LIB:

28. HIGH SHOT PART OF GRANDSTAND
Fans cheering wildly -

CHEERING AD LIB:

29. HIGH CAMERA PAN SHOT OF FIELD
Game in progress - ball is passed to Rensler man - he passes ball to other player -

CHEERING AD LIB:

SCOTT'S VOICE - Hal's temper had made him a lot of enemies.

30. LOW CAMERA SHOT OF FIELD
Hal intercepts nearby opponent - Hal exits at side -

CHEERING AD LIB:

31. MED. HIGH PAN SHOT OF FIELD
Players follow Hal as he races down field with ball - side steps opponent -

CHEERING AD LIB:

SCOTT'S VOICE - But this year everyone was his friend. He was one one of the best players Hampton--

32. MED. HIGH PAN SHOT OF END ZONE
Players racing after Hall as he runs into end zone - opponent tries to tackle him -

CHEERING AD LIB:

SCOTT'S VOICE - --ever produced.

| NO. | DESCRIPTION | DIALOGUE | REEL THREE | PAGE 9 |

33. HIGH SHOT DOWN TO END ZONE
Hal evades tackler as he runs
into end zone - touches ball
making touch down -

    LOUD CHEERING AD LIB:

    SCOTT'S VOICE - And we were proud of him.

34. CLOSE UP PART OF SCOREBOARD
Hand indicating minutes left
to play - points to 0 -

    LOUD CHEERING AD LIB:

35. CLOSE UP TIMEKEEPERS
Men looking at watches - one
man fires gun into air indicating   SOUND OF SHOT
end of game -

    LOUD CHEERING AD LIB:

36. HIGH SHOT OF GRANDSTAND
Fans get to their feet -
cheering and waving wildly -

    LOUD CHEERING AD LIB:

37. CLOSE HIGH SHOT DOWN TO FIELD
Camera tilts down following
Hal as he comes forward grinning
proudly - almost exits beneath
camera -

    LOUD CHEERING AD LIB:

    SCOTT'S VOICE - Hal and I were very close friends. There was only one catch to it.

38. CLOSE UP SCOTT AND VIRGINIA
Smiling and cheering wildly -
his arm about her - Scott
looks off -

    CHEERING AD LIB:

    SCOTT'S VOICE - We were both in love with Virginia and to complicate matters--

| NO. | DESCRIPTION | DIALOGUE | REEL THREE PAGE 10 |

39. CLOSE UP JOAN
Grinning happily as she watches
off - she turns - exits at side
as Scott comes on from side -

          LOUD CHEERING AD LIB:

          SCOTT'S VOICE - --Joan Bemis was
             madly in love with Hal. We
             were going to celebrate that
             night--

    ...DISSOLVES INTO

MED. CLOSE SHOT EXT. COLLEGIATE
CAFE (NIGHT)
College crowd seen through window
of cafe as they dance in b.g. -
two girls come on from side - go
into cafe - camera dollies up   MUSIC
slowly to window -

          TALKING AD LIB:

          SCOTT'S VOICE - The four of us.
             I had a date with Virginia
             but Hal did a little con-
             niving. He picked her up
             in his car and didn't arrive
             until the evening was half
             over--

    ...DISSOLVES INTO

CLOSE UP IN BOOTH
Joan and Scott seated on either
side of table - both looking
dejected - table set for four -
kids in b.g. dancing - Joan and
Scott look around - annoyed -
Virginia and Hal come on from
side - Scott jumps up as Hal
speaks - Scott reaches for
Virginia - Hal steps between
the two - puts his arms around
Virginia - dances her toward   MUSIC
b.g. - Scott glares off -   AD LIB NOISES
sits at table -

          TALKING AD LIB:
           (Continued)

| NO. | DESCRIPTION | DIALOGUE REEL THREE PAGE 11 |

39. (Continued)

SCOTT'S VOICE - Leaving Joan and me to amuse ourselves by staring at each other across the table. Of course he had a story ready when they did get there. He always had a story and knowing his temper, I seldom challenged him.

VIRGINIA - Hi.

HAL - I'm sorry we're late, folks, but had some car trouble and couldn't seem to find out what it was. Then all of a sudden it started, just like that. You know how it is, Cliff, old boy.

SCOTT'S VOICE - Hal did the scoring again. Just like he did on the field that afternoon.

...DISSOLVES INTO

CLOSE UP IN HAL'S AND SCOTT'S COLLEGE ROOM (NIGHT)
Hal and Scott seated across from each other at table - studying - Scott eyes Hal curiously -

SCOTT'S VOICE - Hal and I were roommates. He was the athlete and I was the scholar. I used to help him a lot with his studies. It's an old college custom, keeping football stars eligible to play.

40. CLOSE UP HAL
Studying industriously - leans back in chair - looks off - thoughtful - smiles as he speaks - looks down -

SCOTT'S VOICE - It wasn't because Hal was dumb. He was just too impatient to study hard. On the football field he got action quick but you can't
(Continued)

NO.	DESCRIPTION	DIALOGUE　　REEL THREE　PAGE 12
40.	(Continued)	SCOTT'S VOICE (CONT'D) - stiff arm your way through a flock of chemistry problems.
		HAL - Yeah, I've got a very heavy date with Virginia right after chemistry class and boy, have I got plans.
		SCOTT'S VOICE - Hal did some boasting--
41.	CLOSE UP SCOTT Looking off thoughtfully - takes papers as Hal's hand comes on holding out papers - Scott starts to look over papers - shakes his head - marks on paper -	
		SCOTT'S VOICE - And I did some thinking. Then he made the mistake of asking me to check his chemistry answers. I saw a chance to keep him from having that date with Virginia. His answers were right but I fixed that. I gave him a set of wrong ones and he memorized them very carefully for the verbal quiz scheduled for the next day.
	...DISSOLVES INTO	

| NO. | DESCRIPTION | DIALOGUE | REEL THREE PAGE 13 |

41. (CONTINUED)

   CLOSE UP SCOTT
   Facing camera as he recites
   chemistry formula -

   SCOTT - Hydrochloric acid, sulphuric acid and nitric acid --

42. VIEW INT. CHEMISTRY CLASSROOM
   Students facing Professor Cushman in b.g. - various chemistry articles and tables near windows b.g. - Scott standing at side - speaks -

   SCOTT - -- are all catalytic agents.

   CUSHMAN - Very good, Mr. Scott.

43. VIEW OF FRONT OF CLASSROOM
   Cushman in f.g. facing students - Scott sits in b.g. - Hal rises in second row - speaks - Cushman and students react - surprised - Scott amused - Cushman rises in f.g. - camera dollies up as he speaks - Hal stunned -

   AD LIB NOISES

   CUSHMAN - Uh, Mr. Moffat,

   HAL - Sulphuric acid, when combined with H-four-N-seven will form a solution of hydrochloric acid.

   CUSHMAN - You'd better remain after class, Mr. Moffat.

44. CLOSE UP HAL
   Stunned - looks off knowingly - a look of hate in his eyes -

   CUSHMAN - O.S. - You seem to have everything wrong today. Class --

45. CLOSE UP DOWN TO SCOTT
   Looking off apologetically - camera tilts up as he rises -

   AD LIB NOISES

   CUSHMAN O.S. - --dismissed.

46. CLOSE UP HAL
   Glaring off hatefully - students exiting from room in b.g. -

   AD LIB NOISES

   SCOTT'S VOICE - Hal realized that I had crossed him up.

| NO. | DESCRIPTION | DIALOGUE | REEL THREE PAGE 14 |

47. CLOSE UP HAL
Smiles apologetically - amused -

      SCOTT'S VOICE - He was accustomed to being a winner -- never a loser.

48. CLOSE UP HAL
Glaring off hatefully -

      SCOTT'S VOICE He was plenty angry because I'd outsmarted him, and he showed it.

49. VIEW INT. CLASSROOM
Students moving toward door in b.g. - Scott starts to exit - Hal looks at Cushman, behind desk b.g. -

      AD LIB NOISES

  ...DISSOLVES INTO

CLOSE SHOT SIDE IN CHEMISTRY LAB
Hal, wearing rubber apron, busy mixing various chemicals at table near window - Scott and Virginia seen thru window as they stroll on from side - they stop outside window before Hal - Hal looks up - sees them - glares hatefully at Scott & Virginia - Scott and Virginia exit at side -

      MUSIC STARTS
      AD LIB NOISES

      SCOTT'S VOICE - Professor Cushman put Hal to work on a difficult experiment that would keep him busy the rest of the afternoon. And just to needle him, I walked Virginia past the window. The look he gave us told me I'd better get away from there quick. You could never tell what he'd do when his temper flared.

50. CLOSE UP IN LAB
Hal holding test tube of chemical as he watches off - enraged - throws test tube to floor in his fury - chemical explodes in front of him - smoke and flames rise -

      (Continued)

| NO. | DESCRIPTION | DIALOGUE | REEL THREE PAGE 15 |

50. (Continued)
Hal puts his hands to his face
in agony - camera moves up as
he sinks to floor - clutching
his face -

    MUSIC
    EXPLOSION

    HAL MOANS.

...DISSOLVES INTO

VIEW IN HOSPITAL ROOM
Hal, his head & face wrapped
in bandages, lying in bed -
Virginia & Scott standing on
far side - Joan on near side
of bed - Nurse watching from
end of bed f.g. - camera dollies
up close, to Hal's head, excluding the others -

    MUSIC

    SCOTT'S VOICE - This time it brought
    tragedy. We visited him in the
    hospital, and tried to talk to
    him. But he wouldn't answer.
    Just lay there -- staring up at
    us. The doctors told us that
    the chemicals might effect
    certain glands and nerves, and
    if they did, his features would
    never be normal again.

(END OF RETROSPECT SEQUENCE)

...DISSOLVES INTO

CLOSE UP SCOTT
Looking off grimly - speaks -

    DONELLY O.S. - Then you haven't seen
    him since then?

    SCOTT - No. He left the hospital
    after several weeks, and just
    dropped out of sight.

51. CLOSE UP DONELLY
Seated - speaks -

    DONELLY - Did the doctors tell you
    anything else about him -- I
    mean about his mental state.

52. CLOSE UP SCOTT
Speaks -

    SCOTT - Oh, yes. One of them did say
    that Hal was pretty bitter when
    he left.

| NO. | DESCRIPTION | DIALOGUE | REEL THREE PAGE 16 |

53. CLOSE UP DONELLY
Nods - speaks -

    DONELLY - Yeah. A thing like that could very easily have affected his mind. And if he is the Creeper -- I guess that's what happened.

54. CLOSE SHOT IN LIVING ROOM
Scott standing beside Virginia, seated in chair - he looks down at her as she speaks -

    VIRGINIA - You mean he may have killed Professor Cushman just because he kept him after class that day?

55. CLOSE UP DONELLY
SPEAKS - shrugs -

    DONELLY - Possibly. A mental quirk can develop into an extreme case of paranoia. You say he was in love with you?

56. SHOOTING OVER DIVAN TO VIEW IN LIVING ROOM
Gates & Donelly seated on divan facing Scott and Virginia b.g. - Virginia looks down - embarrassed - Virginia rises as Gates and Donelly rise - she watches as the three men cross to side and exit -

    FOOTSTEPS

    VIRGINIA - Oh, I -- I don't know. I never took Hal very seriously because Clifford and I were in love with each other.

    DONELLY - I see. Well, thank you very much for the information you've given me.

57. VIEW IN HALL
Scott, Donelly & Gates come on from side - Scott opens door as Gates and Donelly pick up hats from take in f.g. - go to door - camera dollies up as Donelly speaks to Scott - Gates exits outside - Scott upset - Donelly exits outside - Scott closes door - thoughtful -

    DOOR - FOOTSTEPS

(Continued)

| NO. | DESCRIPTION | DIALOGUE | REEL THREE PAGE 17 |

57. (Continued)

DONELLY - Oh -- I'm going to have your place watched day and night for a while, Mr. Scott.

SCOTT - You mean -- he might come here?

DONELLY - Well, you never can tell what a man will do when his mind's affected. Better to be on the safe side. He might hold you responsible for what happened. After all -- you gave him the wrong answers.

SCOTT - Yes, I did.

DONELLY - Well, now don't let it upset you. We won't let anything happen. And you will explain to Mrs. Scott about my men covering the place? She might think they're prowlers.

SCOTT - Surely.

DONELLY - Good night.

SCOTT - Good night.

...VERTICAL FEATHER WIPE TO

CLOSE DOLLY SHOT THE CREEPER
(NIGHT)
As he walks along past buildings - stops - looks around - looks up - sees -   MUSIC
   FOOTSTEPS

58. SHOOTING UP TO WINDOWS OF HELEN'S APARTMENT
Lights seen through windows -   MUSIC

59. CLOSE UP THE CREEPER
Watching off - thoughtful - looks off - sees -   MUSIC

60. MED. SHOT EXT. PAWN SHOP
Lights on in shop - various articles on display in window -   MUSIC

| NO. | DESCRIPTION | DIALOGUE | REEL THREE PAGE 18 |

61. CLOSE UP THE CREEPER
    Looking off - thoughtful -
    starts to exit at side -   MUSIC

62. MED. SHOT OF SIDEWALK
    The Creeper moves slowly along   MUSIC
    and exits at side -   FOOTSTEPS

63. MED. CLOSE SHOT EXT. PAWN SHOP
    The Creeper comes on from side -
    stops at window - looks at   FOOTSTEPS
    articles on display -   MUSIC

64. CLOSE UP DISPLAY TRAY
    Various types of ornamental
    pins on tray - one shaped as
    butterfly in center of tray -
    camera moves down close to
    butterfly pin -   MUSIC

65. CLOSE UP THE CREEPER (SIDE)
    Looking into window of pawn shop -
    looks around - camera pans as he
    goes to door of shop - looks in
    through glass window of door -
    sees shopkeeper going to rear
    of shop - The Creeper opens door -
    looks up - startled - shopkeeper
    in b.g. speaks to The Creeper -
    shopkeeper exits into rear of shop -
    camera pans slightly as The Creeper
    goes to side - reaches off scene -
    picks up butterfly pin - fondles   DOOR
    it carefully - shopkeeper comes on   MUSIC
    in b.g. - speaks to The Creeper -   FOOTSTEPS
    camera dollies up and pans as The   TINKLE OF BELL
    Creeper goes toward counter in
    b.g. - shopkeeper moves around
    behind counter -

    SHOPKEEPER - Be right with you.
       See something you like,
       Mister?

66. CLOSE UP AT COUNTER
    Shopkeeper and The Creeper face
    each other across counter -
    Shopkeeper speaks as he sees pin
    in The Creeper's hand -

                    (Continued)

| NO. | DESCRIPTION | DIALOGUE | REEL THREE | PAGE 19 |

66. (Continued)

    SHOPKEEPER - That's a very fine piece, my friend, and very reasonable.

67. CLOSE UP SHOPKEEPER
Over The Creeper's shoulder - shopkeeper speaks - looks up - reacts as he looks at The Creeper's face -

    MUSIC

    SHOPKEEPER - You can have it for--

68. CLOSE UP THE CREEPER
Over shopkeeper's shoulder - The Creeper speaks -

    MUSIC

    THE CREEPER - What's the matter?

69. CLOSE UP SHOPKEEPER
Over The Creeper's shoulder - speaks hesitantly - scared -

    MUSIC

    SHOPKEEPER - Nothing - ah - I was just going to say that you can buy it for practically nothing.

70. CLOSE UP THE CREEPER
Facing camera and shopkeeper, partly in scene at side -

    MUSIC

    THE CREEPER - How much?

    SHOPKEEPER - To you--twelve dollars and a half.

    THE CREEPER - I'll take it.

71. CLOSE UP SHOPKEEPER
Over The Creeper's shoulder - reacts - startled as The Creeper starts to turn away -

    MUSIC

    THE CREEPER - I'll pay you for it tomorrow.

    SHOPKEEPER - I'm sorry. I don't do business that way.

72. CLOSE UP AT COUNTER (SIDE)
Shopkeeper and The Creeper facing each other across counter -

    (Continued)

| NO. | DESCRIPTION | DIALOGUE | REEL THREE PAGE 20 |

72. (Continued) The Creeper angry - The Creeper puts pin in his pocket - shopkeeper leans over counter grabbing for pin - The Creeper grabs shopkeeper by the throat - camera dollies up quickly to The Creeper's face as shopkeeper's hand claws at his collar - hand relaxes -

MUSIC
AD LIB NOISES

THE CREEPER - You don't trust me?

SHOPKEEPER - No. In my business it's - it's too expensive. Put it back or I'll call the police. Help! (OFF SCENE) Police! (MUTTERS AD LIB)

...DISSOLVES INTO

MED. SHOT EXT. TENEMENT BUILDING
The Creeper coming on from side - camera pans as he moves to front steps - looks around cautiously as he goes up steps to door - opens it and exits into building -

MUSIC

...DISSOLVES INTO

PAN SHOT IN HALL
The Creeper coming up steps at end of hall - camera pans as he comes along hall to door in f.g. - knocks - speaks - door is opened - Helen comes out - smiles - she steps backward into room - The Creeper starts into room -

DOOR
MUSIC
KNOCK
FOOTSTEPS

HELEN'S VOICE - Who's there?

THE CREEPER - It's me.

HELEN O.S. - Oh, I'm glad. (ON SCENE) Come in.

73. HIGH SHOT IN APARTMENT
Helen holding door for The Creeper as he enters - she closes door - comes forward to him - she smiles - speaks - he speaks gratefully -

DOOR
FOOTSTEPS
MUSIC

(Continued)

```
NO.    DESCRIPTION                    DIALOGUE       REEL THREE PAGE 21

73.    (Continued)                    HELEN - I was worried about you.
                                          I mean, those men who were after
                                          you.

                                      THE CREEPER - Thanks for helping
                                          me.  I brought you something.

                                      HELEN - Thank you.  What is it?

74.    PART TITLE              U N I V E R S A L
                                   "THE BRUTE MAN"
                                    END OF PART
                                         3

       RA/vh
```

Fifteen years after the Universal Horrors cycle kicked off with *Dracula* ("The story of the strangest Passion the world has ever known!"), it presented the story of perhaps the *second* strangest Passion: Rondo and Jane Adams in *The Brute Man*.

PICTURE NO. 1479
DIRECTOR - YARBROUGH
REEL FOUR   PAGE 1

NO.   DESCRIPTION   DIALOGUE

CONTINUITY & DIALOGUE

1.   PART TITLE   U N I V E R S A L
                                 "THE BRUTE MAN"
                                    P A R T
                                       4

2.   CLOSE UP CREEPER & HELEN
     Creeper, holding pin, facing
     camera - annoyed - they talk   MUSIC
     she staring off -

                               CREEPER - Don't you like it?

                               HELEN - I'm sure I do.

                               CREEPER - Why don't you look at it?

3.   CLOSE UP HELEN
     Staring off - speaks gently -   MUSIC

                               HELEN - You see -- I'm blind.

4.   CLOSE UP CREEPER & HELEN
     He facing camera - reacts - they
     talk - he puts pin in her hand   MUSIC

                               CREEPER - Blind?

                               HELEN - I thought you might have
                                       guessed it last night. What
                                       did you bring me?

                               CREEPER - Here.

5.   CLOSE UP HELEN
     Staring off - she lifts pin in-
     to scene - touches it gently   MUSIC
     with her other hand - she re-
     acts - pleased -

                               HELEN - Oo - it's beautiful! I can
                                       tell!

6.   CLOSE UP CREEPER & HELEN
     He facing camera - watches her
     with delight - she turns away -   MUSIC
     almost exits at side - he starts
     after her -

                               HELEN - Please - let's sit down.

7.   MED HIGH SHOT IN ROOM
     Creeper & Helen moving from f.g.
     to divan - she sits - speaks -   MUSIC
                          (Continued)

| NO. | DESCRIPTION | DIALOGUE | REEL FOUR PAGE 2 |

7. (Continued)

HELEN - Why were those men chasing you?

8. CLOSE UP THE CREEPER
Looking off - speaks -

MUSIC

CREEPER - They thought I'd done something - but it wasn't my fault.

9. CLOSE UP HELEN
Staring off - speaks - rubs pin with her fingers -

MUSIC

HELEN - Oh, I'm sure it wasn't. I don't know if I should accept this from you. You haven't even told me your name.

10. CLOSE HIGH SHOT IN ROOM
Helen sitting on divan b.g. looking up at the Creeper near camera - talk -

MUSIC

CREEPER - It's Hal.

HELEN - Oh - mine's Helen. Last night you seemed surprised because I wasn't afraid of you. What's wrong, Hal? Should I be afraid?

CREEPER - Everyone else is.

HELEN - Why?

CREEPER - I can't tell you.

HELEN - Do you want to be friends with me?

11. CLOSE UP THE CREEPER
Eager - speaks -

MUSIC

CREEPER - Sure. You're nice to me.

12. CLOSE UP HELEN
Staring off - understanding -

MUSIC

HELEN - And no one else is -- is that it?

13. CLOSE UP THE CREEPER
Looks down - looks up -

MUSIC

| NO. | DESCRIPTION | DIALOGUE | REEL FOUR PAGE 3 |

14. CLOSE UP HELEN
    Staring off - speaks - understanding -

    MUSIC

    HELEN - I think I understand. When you've been blind as long as I have, you learn to see through your senses. I can't explain it exactly, but you get a feeling about people when you meet them. You see a picture of them in your mind --

15. CLOSE UP THE CREEPER
    Listening -

    MUSIC

    HELEN O.S. -- not just what they look like - but what they really are.

16. CLOSE UP HELEN
    Speaking - staring off -

    MUSIC

    HELEN - You see them much more clearly than you do with your eyes. Maybe that's why they say looks are deceptive.

17. CLOSE UP THE CREEPER
    Looking down - thoughtful - looks up - speaks -

    MUSIC

    HELEN O.S. - Do you know what I mean?

    CREEPER - Yes - I know.

18. CLOSE HIGH SHOT IN ROOM
    Creeper near f.g. facing Helen on divan b.g. - they talk -

    MUSIC

    HELEN - I'd like to help you if you'd let me.

    CREEPER - You can.

    HELEN - How?

    CREEPER - Just let me come to see you.

    HELEN - Of course. I want you to. I'm alone most of the time - except when I give piano lessons.

| NO. | DESCRIPTION | DIALOGUE | REEL FOUR PAGE 4 |

19. CLOSE UP HELEN
    Speaks intently -

    MUSIC

    HELEN - I have such a good idea of you now.

20. MED SHOT SIDE IN ROOM
    Creeper standing - speaks harshly as Helen rises from divan - puts out her hand - she surprised - withdraws her hand - CAMERA pans as he crosses to door near camera - exits - she calls - camera dollies up as she comes to door - worried - fastens pin to her dress -

    MUSIC - DOOR

    FOOTSTEPS

    HELEN - But if I could touch your face, then --

    CREEPER - No - don't do that!

    HELEN - Why not?

    CREEPER - I don't want you to!

    HELEN - Hal! Hal!

    Background shot dissolves out as newspaper comes on superimposed over scene - headlines read -

        CREEPER SLAYS PAWNBROKER -
                      VANISHES

          Brutal Murder
           Apparently
            Without Motive

    Other newspaper falls on over scene - headlines read -

        MYSTERY IN PAWNBROKER MURDER

    Camera moves down close to subhead - reads -

          Robbery Not
           Motive Say
            Police

| NO. | DESCRIPTION | DIALOGUE | REEL FOUR PAGE 5 |

21. CLOSE UP NEWSPAPER
As it falls into scene - headline reads -

    MAYOR IN ULTIMATUM TO POLICE   MUSIC

Camera moves down close to
subhead - reads -

    Demands Capture of
    Creeper in 24 Hours
      "Or Else"

...DISSOLVES INTO

INT. POLICE STATION
Commissioner Salisbury & Park-   " DOOR
ington enter from b.g. - both
grim - camera pans as they come   FOOTSTEPS
forward to door of Donnelly's
office at side f.g. - open door

22. INT. CAPTAIN DONELLY'S OFFICE
Donelly sitting at small table -
Gates sitting on corner of table   " MUSIC
- playing gin rummy - Commission-
er & Parkington enter b.g. -
stride forward - grim - camera
dollies up to table - talk as
two men play - Donelly bland -
two men fuming - Donelly rises
- camera pans & dollies up as
he crosses to desk - Parkington   AD LIB NOISES
& Commissioner follow him -
protest - worried - eager -   DOOR
annoyed - turn & exit b.g. as
Donelly returns to game -
camera pans - Donelly & Gates
resume playing as they talk -
Gates jerks hand back as Donelly flicks ashes on it - reacts -

                                        DONELLY - Oh, good morning, Com-
                                          missioner. Good morning, Mr.
                                          Parkington. I thought you'd
                                          be dropping by about this time.

                                        PARKINGTON - So! You're sitting
                                        here playing gin rummy with an-
                                        other Creeper murder on the
                                        front page of the newspapers!

(Continued)

NO. DESCRIPTION	DIALOGUE REEL FOUR PAGE 5
22. (Continued)	DONELLY - I think better when I'm enjoying my hobby. I'm a pigeon fancier.

GATES (Chuckles)

COMMISSIONER - Now you listen to me, Donelly! We told you ---

DONELLY - I know. I know. You told me already that you wanted the Creeper arrested within twenty-four hours. Well, gentlemen - he's still at large. Now, I suppose the Mayor and yourself have decided to take over personally. No doubt you'll have the killer in custody in ten minutes flat. I'll just let the newspapers know that it's in your laps.

PARKINGTON - Now, just a minute, Captain. Let's not be hasty about this!

DONELLY - You don't mean/that His Honor, the Mayor, wouldn't relish the job? That you wouldn't like to take over?

COMMISSIONER - That's beside the point! The entire city is up in arms and the Creeper goes on killing people. Now, I'm a reasonable man, Donelly ---

DONELLY - I'm glad to hear it, Commissioner! Now that the pressure's off, I can let you know that we have the first definite clue as to the identity of the Creeper!

COMMISSIONER - Who is it?

PARKINGTON - Yes. Who - who is it?

DONELLY - I said clue, gentlemen! When I'm certain I'll give you the lowdown. And I believe it'll be soon. That's all I can tell you at the moment. Now, if you-'ll excuse me - I have Gates on a triple blitz. |
| (Continued) | |

| NO. | DESCRIPTION | DIALOGUE | REEL FOUR PAGE 6 |

22. (Continued) (2)

    GATES - Why didn't you let 'em know about the newspaper clippings?

    DONELLY - What? And have those publicity hounds filling the front pages with a lot of stuff that would scare the Creeper right out of town! (Grunts) Discard!

    ...VERTICAL WIPE TO

MED SHOT UP TO FRONT DOOR OF TENEMENT (NIGHT)
Man & woman coming out of tenement - camera tilts down as they descend to sidewalk & move on down street to b.g. - exit - Creeper standing at foot of steps - looks about cautiously - camera tilts up as he ascends steps to door of tenement - exits inside - closes door -

    DOOR - FOOTSTEPS

    MUSIC

    ...VERTICAL WIPE TO

CLOSE VIEW IN HELEN'S LIVING ROOM
Helen standing on far side of piano hearing Dorothy's lesson - Helen counts as Dorothy plays - metronome swings back & forth keeping time -

    METRONOME - PIANO

    HELEN - One and two and three and four and one and two and three and four --

23. INT. HALLWAY OF TENEMENT
Creeper coming along hall from stairs b.g. - stops & listens at Helen's door -

    METRONOME - PIANO

    HELEN O.S. -- and one and two and three --

24. CLOSE VIEW IN LIVING ROOM
Helen counting as Dorothy plays piano - camera pulls back bringing Mrs. Obringer into scene - sitting near camera - Dorothy finishes lesson - rises - Helen pleased - comes forward to Mrs. Obringer - all talk - Dorothy picks up her music as her mother rises - camera dollies up as all turn to door b.g. -

    METRONOME - PIANO

    (Continued)

| NO. | DESCRIPTION | DIALOGUE | REEL FOUR PAGE 7 |

24. (Continued)

HELEN - ---and four and one and two and three and four and. That's fine, Dorothy. Just fine. She's coming along very nicely, Mrs. Obringer. You'll be playing the classics before you know it.

DOROTHY - I don't wanna play that stuff. I wanna play boogie-woogie.

HELEN - Oh, you can play that, too - as a hobby, but first you must master the things that are solid.

DOROTHY - But boogie-woogie is solid. It really sends me.

MRS. OBRINGER - (CHUCKLES) Hush, Dorothy. Put your music away. We're going home now. She gets that from her father. He plays hot trumpet in the Firemen's Band.

HELEN CHUCKLES.

MRS. OBRINGER - Come along, Dear.

25. INT. HALLWAY
The Creeper standing at Helen's door - listening - hurries to recess in wall near camera - ducks out of sight as Helen's door opens - Dorothy, her mother & Helen come out into hall - talk - Dorothy & her mother start to top of stairs b.g. - camera pans & moves up close to Creeper as he watches off - exits at side -

PIANO - DOOR - FOOTSTEPS

MRS. OBRINGER O.S. - We'll see you next week at the same time. (ON SCENE) I'll see that she practices like you told her to, Miss Helen.

DOROTHY - I'll be right in the groove.

MRS. OBRINGER - Oh, Dorothy. Goodnight.

(Continued)

| NO. | DESCRIPTION | DIALOGUE | REEL FOUR PAGE 8 |

25. (Continued) (2)

HELEN - Goodnight.

26. CLOSE VIEW IN HELEN'S LIVING ROOM
Helen sitting at piano f.g. playing - door opens silently b.g. - Creeper enters - camera pulls back as he crosses into room and stands behind Helen listening - she stops playing, suddenly aware of him - she turns - smiles as she recognizes Creeper's voice - camera pulls back & tilts down as Creeper sits in chair nearby - they talk

PIANO - MUSIC

HELEN - Who is it?

CREEPER - Hello.

HELEN - Oh, it's you, Hal. I didn't hear you come in.

CREEPER - I didn't knock.

HELEN - Are those men after you again?

CREEPER - No. I was listening outside. When those people left I just walked in.

HELEN - Please sit down.

CREEPER - You make a livin' -- teachin' kids to play?

HELEN - Oh, yes - I manage to get along.

CREEPER - It's tough - doin' that - you bein' - like you are.

27. CLOSE UP HELEN
Staring off - speaks gently -

MUSIC

HELEN - I love music -- and I like teaching it to others. I don't find my blindness too much of a handicap.

28. CLOSE UP THE CREEPER
Sympathetic - speaks -

MUSIC

CREEPER - Won't you ever be able to see?

| NO. | DESCRIPTION | DIALOGUE | REEL FOUR   PAGE 9 |

29. CLOSE UP HELEN
    Wistful - speaks -

    MUSIC

    HELEN - The doctor told me a year ago that there might be a chance - if I had an operation.

    CREEPER O.S. - Why don't you do it?

    HELEN - It would be very expensive.

30. CLOSE UP THE CREEPER
    Looking off - thoughtful - speaks -

    MUSIC

    CREEPER - How much?

    HELEN O.S. - A lot of money. So much that I don't even think about it anymore.

    CREEPER - If you could see, you'd -

31. CLOSE SHOT IN ROOM
    Creeper seated near f.g. - Helen sitting on piano bench facing him - he rises suddenly - camera dollies up as she rises & faces him - puzzled -

    MUSIC

    HELEN - What were you going to say, Hal?

    CREEPER - Nothing.

    HELEN - What's wrong, Hal? Why don't you want me to see you?

32. CLOSE UP HELEN & CREEPER
    They talk - she puzzled - he bitter - she stops him as he moves away from her - he exits quickly to b.g. as she puts her hand up - turns to camera - disappointed -

    MUSIC - DOOR

    HELEN - Are you afraid?

    CREEPER - Yeah. I'm afraid.

    HELEN - But why?

    CREEPER - You'd know if you could see me.

(Continued)

| NO. | DESCRIPTION | DIALOGUE | REEL FOUR   PAGE 10 |

32. (Continued)

    HELEN - Well, if I'm not afraid of you now - why would I be if I could see you?

    CREEPER - You would be. Everybody else is.

    HELEN - Then it's probably just as well that I'm blind.

    CREEPER - Don't you have any idea how much that operation would cost?

    HELEN - Oh, the doctor said it would be two or three thousand dollars, at least.

    CREEPER - I'm going now.

    HELEN - Hal --

    CREEPER - Yes?

    HELEN - If you'd just let me touch your face, I'm sure that --

...DISSOLVES INTO

CLOSE UP SIDE IN ROOM
Creeper comes on at side - stops before mirror on wall -   MUSIC

33. CLOSE UP CREEPER
Standing f.g. - his face reflected in mirror - he rubs his hand over his distorted features - his face becomes grim & uglier - he raises one fist & smashes mirror to bits

    "
    CRASH OF GLASS

...FADE OUT

34. PART TITLE   U N I V E R S A L
    "THE BRUTE MAN"
    END OF PART
    4

MS - ib

PICTURE NO. 1479
DIRECTOR - YARBROUGH
REEL FIVE   PAGE 1

NO.	DESCRIPTION	DIALOGUE

CONTINUITY & DIALOGUE

1. PART TITLE
   U N I V E R S A L
   "THE BRUTE MAN"
   P A R T
   5

2. FADE IN - MED SHOT EXT. SCOTT
   HOME (NIGHT)
   Detective standing on porch -
   smoking cigarette - looks about   MUSIC
   - alert -

3. CLOSE UP THE CREEPER
   Looking off from cover of shrub   "

4. MED LONG SHOT OF HOUSE
   The Creeper crouched behind
   bushes f.g. - watching detective   "
   on front porch of house b.g. -

5. CLOSE UP THE CREEPER
   Watching off -   "

6. CLOSE SHOT DETECTIVE
   Puffing on cigarette - moves
   about - alert - flips cigarette   MUSIC - FOOTSTEPS
   away - camera tilts down as he
   strolls across porch past front
   door -

7. MED LONG SHOT OF HOUSE
   Creeper watching from cover of
   bushes f.g. as detective strolls   "   "
   across, past front door of house,
   & exits at side - camera pans as
   Creeper moves along behind bushes
   - runs quickly across open space
   toward side porch of house b.g. -
   stops at window & peers into
   house -

8. SHOOTING ALONG FRONT PORCH OF
   HOUSE
   Detective strolling from b.g.   "   "
   toward f.g. on porch of house -
   looks off past huge pillars at
   side - puts cigarette in his mouth
   - stops - looks off -

NO.	DESCRIPTION	DIALOGUE	REEL FIVE PAGE 2
9.	CLOSE SHOT SIDE OF HOUSE Creeper crouched below window - rises slowly & looks through window - sees -	MUSIC	
10.	SHOOTING THROUGH WINDOW OF LIVING ROOM Grand piano f.g. - Virginia in negligee crossing hall in b.g. - starts toward stairs -	"	
11.	CLOSE UP EXT. HOUSE The Creeper looking in window - turns away -	"	
12.	MED SHOT EXT. HOUSE Detective standing on porch near pillar - smoking cigarette as he watches about - turns & strolls past front door -	FOOTSTEPS - MUSIC	
13.	CLOSE UP BY HOUSE Creeper standing at window - looks toward b.g. - camera pans as he moves stealthily along side of house -	MUSIC	
14.	INT. UPPER HALL OF SCOTT HOME Virginia, wearing negligee, mounting stairs at far end of hall - camera pans as she comes forward down hall toward camera -	"	
15.	SHOOTING ALONG SIDE OF HOUSE Creeper making his way past porch furniture toward b.g. -	"	
16.	CLOSE SHOT TO PORCH DOOR Creeper coming on near camera - looks about as he stops before door - tries to open door - finds it locked - steps away - looks upward -	"	
17.	SIDE IN VIRGINIA'S BEDROOM Virginia entering from hall - switches on light - closes door - camera pans as she crosses room to dressing table - sits -	DOOR - SWITCH - MUSIC	

| NO. | DESCRIPTION | DIALOGUE | REEL FIVE PAGE 3 |

18. CLOSE SHOT THE CREEPER
    Looking upward - looks away -   MUSIC
    exits at side -

19. SHOOTING ALONG SIDE OF HOUSE
    Creeper coming forward along   "
    porch - tiptoes down steps near
    camera - camera pans as he stops
    at corner of house - peers around
    corner -

20. VIEW OF FRONT PORCH OF HOUSE
    Detective standing near pillars,   "
    lighting cigarette - looks
    about -

21. CLOSE UP THE CREEPER
    Looking off around corner of
    house - withdraws - camera pans   "
    as he moves stealthily along
    side porch toward b.g. -

22. SIDE IN BEDROOM
    Virginia sitting at dressing   "
    table - primping - looks at her
    nails - starts to buff them -

23. CLOSE SHOT EXT. WINDOW
    Creeper comes on - looks about
    cautiously - tries to open
    window - finds it locked -   MUSIC - FOOTSTEPS
    annoyed - camera pans as he
    moves to door - tries to open
    it - finds it locked - camera
    pans as he moves down steps of
    porch & exits -

24. VIEW OF FRONT PORCH
    Detective standing before front   "   "
    door, puffing on cigarette -
    strolls toward f.g. - he looks
    about - exits past camera -

25. CLOSE SHOT CORNER OF HOUSE
    The Creeper comes on - stops at   MUSIC
    corner of house & looks back -

26. SIDE PORCH OF HOUSE
    Detective strolling across porch   "
    at side of house b.g. - looks
    about -

| NO. | DESCRIPTION | DIALOGUE | REEL FIVE   PAGE 4 |

27. CLOSE SHOT CORNER OF HOUSE
    The Creeper looking off - turns
    - camera pans as he goes to   MUSIC
    cellar window - steps down into
    small pit before window -

28. CLOSE PAN SHOT ON DETECTIVE
    As he crosses past window - goes
    to door opening onto side porch   FOOTSTEPS - MUSIC
    of house - looks at it - goes
    down steps & exits along side of
    house -

29. CLOSE UP INT. CELLAR WINDOW
    Creeper backing through open
    window into cellar - closes win-   MUSIC - AD LIB NOISES
    dow - starts to step down at
    side near camera -

30. CLOSE SHOT CORNER OF HOUSE
    Detective comes on to corner of
    house, looking about - camera   MUSIC
    pans as he starts along toward
    cellar window -

31. CLOSE UP INT. CELLAR WINDOW
    The Creeper watching off - ducks
    back out of sight as he sees   "
    legs of detective passing out-
    side of window - camera dollies
    up & angles around - detective's
    legs exit - Creeper looks out
    window -

32. CLOSE SHOT SIDE IN CELLAR
    Creeper standing on box before
    cellar window - camera tilts down   "
    & pans as he climbs down boxes
    to floor - looks about cautiously
    as he goes to door b.g. - opens
    it - exits, closing door after
    him -

33. CLOSE UP AT DRESSING TABLE
    Virginia sitting near camera,
    her back to camera, buffing her   "
    nails - part of room is reflected
    in mirror before her -

| NO. | DESCRIPTION | DIALOGUE | REEL FI 3 PAGE 5 |

34. CORNER IN LOWER HALL
    The Creeper comes on - stops at corner - looks about - camera pans as he comes slowly forward past camera - moves down hall to foot of stairs - looks up stairs - camera tilts up as he ascends stairs slowly - almost exits -

    MUSIC

35. VIEW IN UPPER HALLWAY
    The Creeper coming on up steps at side - looks about - turns & comes slowly down hall toward f.g. - camera pans slightly - he stops at door of Virginia's room - takes hold of door knob -

    "

| NO. | DESCRIPTION | DIALOGUE | REEL FIVE PAGE 6 |

36. CLOSE UP BEFORE DRESSING TABLE
Virginia sitting f.g. with back
to camera - buffing her nails -
room & Virginia are reflected
in mirror over dressing table -   MUSIC
door opens b.g. - Creeper enters
- Virginia looks up, startled
& scared - camera tilts up as   FOOTSTEPS
she rises, turns & faces camera
- reacts - puzzled - realizes
who he is - he comes slowly to-
ward her -

          VIRGINIA - What --?
              O.S.
          CREEPER/- Hello, Virginia.

          VIRGINIA - Who are you?

          CREEPER O.S. - You don't remember
            me?

          VIRGINIA - No, I -- You're not -
            Hal?

          CREEPER O.S. - Yeah. I've changed
            a little since I last saw you --
            haven't I?

          VIRGINIA _ Your face --

          CREEPER O.S. - It frightens you,
            doesn't it?

          VIRGINIA - I can't believe it!

37. CLOSE UP IN ROOM
Virginia facing the Creeper -
he bitter as they talk - she   MUSIC
scared -

          CREEPER - This is what you and
            Cliff did to me!

          VIRGINIA - But we never knew!

          CREEPER - Yeah! You're afraid of
            me -- just like all the others!
            You've even got a detective
            outside now - to protect you
            from me!

          VIRGINIA - They insisted on guard-
            ing the house! They told us you
            were the Creeper - that you'd
            killed all those people -- Joan

(Continued)

| NO. | DESCRIPTION | DIALOGUE | REEL FIVE PAGE 7 |

37. (Continued)

    VIRGINIA (Cont.) - Professor Cushman and the others.

38. LARGE CLOSE UP THE CREEPER
Staring off - speaks grimly -

    MUSIC

    CREEPER - I need some money. A lot of money.

39. LARGE CLOSE UP VIRGINIA
Staring off - speaks - scared -

    MUSIC

    VIRGINIA - I'll do anything I can to help you - but we don't keep very much money in the house.

40. CLOSE UP IN ROOM
Creeper & Virginia standing, facing each other - he speaks - bitter - both turn & look off -

    HORN
    MUSIC - SOUND OF CAR

    CREEPER - Cliff's doing all right for himself. You've probably got a lot of jewels.

41. CLOSE UP ON FRONT PORCH
Detective watching off - speaks to Scott as he comes on - Scott apologetic - opens door & exits into house - closes door - detective exits at side -

    MUSIC - FOOTSTEPS
    DOOR - AD LIB NOISE

    DETECTIVE - Good evening, Mr. Scott.

    SCOTT - Hello. Sorry you have to stay out here.

    DETECTIVE - That's all right, sir. It's my job. Good night.

    SCOTT - Good night.

42. LARGE CLOSE UP THE CREEPER
Listening intently - looks off - speaks harshly -

    MUSIC

    CREEPER - Keep quiet!

43. CLOSE UP IN ROOM
Creeper facing Virginia - she speaks - he grim - gives her order - she calls off -

    MUSIC

    SCOTT O.S. - Virginia?

(Continued)

| NO. | DESCRIPTION | DIALOGUE | REEL FIVE PAGE 8 |

43. (Continued)

VIRGINIA - There's Cliff.

CREEPER - Tell him to come on up. Go on!

VIRGINIA - I'm up here, Cliff.

44. CLOSE VIEW IN HALL
Scott standing by table - looking up & off - speaks - almost exits past camera -

MUSIC

SCOTT - Okay, dear.

45. INT. UPPER HALLWAY
Scott running up stairs to landing b.g. - turns & comes down hall to door f.g. - camera pans - he stares into room -

MUSIC

46. INT. BEDROOM
Virginia standing near f.g. facing door at side b.g. - she holds out her hands to Scott as he enters room & crosses to her - Creeper hiding behind door - camera dollies up as Creeper moves toward Scott & Virginia - Scott whirls to face Creeper - she explains - Scott aghast - they talk - Scott turns & starts toward camera - she fearful -

" FOOTSTEPS

SCOTT - Hello, darling! What's the matter?

CREEPER - Hello, Cliff.

VIRGINIA - It's Hal.

SCOTT - Hal?

CREEPER - Yeah. It's been a long time, Cliff. I don't blame you for not recognizing me.

VIRGINIA - Cliff, they were right. He is the Creeper. He killed those people.

SCOTT - But why, Hal? What happened to you?

CREEPER - Look at my face.

(Continued)

| NO. | DESCRIPTION | DIALOGUE | REEL FIVE PAGE 9 |

46. (Continued)

SCOTT - Well - yes, but --

CREEPER - That's what happened to me -- thanks to you!

SCOTT - Why did you come here?

CREEPER - I need money.

VIRGINIA - I told him we'd be glad to do anything we could to help him.

SCOTT - Yes, of course.

VIRGINIA - Got those jewels of mine in the wall safe.

SCOTT - But -- All right. They're in here.

47. CLOSE MOVING SHOT IN BEDROOM
Scott & Creeper follow camera as it dollies back thru' room to wall - Virginia comes on & stands by as Scott removes picture from wall, revealing wall safe - Creeper watching - alert - Scott manipulates combination & opens safe - takes out small strong box - turns to camera - Creeper snatches box from Scott - Scott speaks - points off - Creeper hands box back to Scott - Scott follows camera as it pulls back, bringing desk into scene - puts box on desk - opens drawer - takes out key & unlocks box - removes papers from box, closes top - picks up box in left hand - reaches quickly in drawer & pulls out gun as he hands box to Creeper - Creeper raises box to strike - Scott fires & hits Creeper - camera dollies up as Creeper reacts - camera tilts down to floor as Creeper falls - clutches his thigh - Virginia's feet run past near him - Scott comes on past camera & starts to kneel by Creeper -

MUSIC - FOOTSTEPS

AD LIB NOISES

SHOTS

(Continued)

| NO. | DESCRIPTION | DIALOGUE | REEL FIVE PAGE 10 |

NO.	DESCRIPTION	DIALOGUE
47.	(Continued)	CREEPER - I'll take it.
		SCOTT - But it's locked. I keep the key in a desk drawer.
		CREEPER - I won't need a key.
		SCOTT - But, Hal, there's personal papers in it - things of no value to you but very valuable to me. I'd like to keep them if you don't mind.
		CREEPER - O.K. Unlock it. Remember I'm watching.
		SCOTT - Here's the jewelry. Put up your hands!
		CREEPER - You--
		SCOTT O.S. - Go downstairs & let the detective in.
48.	CLOSE UP DOWN TO FLOOR Creeper lying on floor, apparently unconscious - camera tilts up as Scott kneels beside Creeper - speaks gently - Creeper reaches up suddenly - grabs Scott - camera pans as The Creeper rolls Scott over on his back - grabs Scott by the throat - camera dollies up close to Creeper, his face distorted with rage -	MUSIC - AD LIB NOISES
		SCOTT - I'm sorry, Hal, but I had to.
		DETECTIVE O.S. - Mr. Scott!
49.	CLOSE SHOT EXT. FRONT DOOR Detective standing at door - calls - worried - tries to break in door -	MUSIC - AD LIB NOISES
		DETECTIVE - Mr. Scott!

| NO. | DESCRIPTION | DIALOGUE | REEL FIVE PAGE 11 |

50. SHOOTING UP STAIRCASE
    Virginia hurrying down the
    stairs - camera tilts down &
    pans as she passes camera -   MUSIC - FOOTSTEPS
    goes to front door - opens it
    - admits detective - they   SOUND OF DOOR
    talk - camera pans on detective
    as he hurries across hall -
    starts to run up stairs - Virginia
    runs on after him - starts up
    stairs -

    DETECTIVE - What's going on? I
        heard a shot.

    VIRGINIA - It's Hal Moffat. He's
        upstairs. My husband shot him.

51. PART TITLE   U N I V E R S A L
                         "THE BRUTE MAN"
                          END OF PART
                              5

MS - IB

PICTURE NO. 1479
DIRECTOR - YARBROUGH
REEL SIX PAGE 1

NO.	DESCRIPTION	DIALOGUE

CONTINUITY & DIALOGUE

1. PART TITLE

    U N I V E R S A L
    "THE BRUTE MAN"
    P A R T
    6

2. VIEW IN UPSTAIRS HALL OF SCOTT HOME (NIGHT)
Detective, followed by Virginia, runs up stairs and along landing to door in f.g. - Detective starts to enter bedroom -

MUSIC

3. VIEW INT. BEDROOM
Scott's body lying on floor in f.g. - Detective and Virginia entering in b.g. - look around - rush toward f.g. - camera tilts down as they kneel beside body - detective examines body - Virginia questions him - Detective rises, goes to b.g. and exits as she puts her head on body - sobs - heartbroken -

MUSIC
FOOTSTEPS

VIRGINIA - Cliff! --- No. (SOBS) No.

...DISSOLVES INTO

(M O N T A G E)

CLOSE UP IN POLICE RADIO ROOM
Announcer talking into mike -

MUSIC

ANNOUNCER - Calling cars forty-one and fifty-three. District Five. Cars forty-one and fifty-three. District five. Proceed at once to five hundred block, Cottage Grove Avenue. Investigate a three-four-one. Proceed with caution. This job is by the Creeper.

Shot remains superimposed over b.g. shot of city street - police cars racing along - camera pans -

SIREN

(Continued)

| NO. | DESCRIPTION | DIALOGUE | REEL SIX PAGE 2 |

3. (Continued)
    Shot in Radio Room dissolves
out as Large Close up of Micro-
phone comes on superimposed
and remains superimposed as   MUSIC - SIRENS
b.g. shot changes, showing another
phase of squad cars racing down
street -

    ...DISSOLVES INTO

SHOT OF INTERSECTION
Police car swerves around
corner - camera pans -

(END OF MONTAGE)

    ...DISSOLVES INTO

MED. SHOT EXT. SCOTT HOME (NIGHT)
Squad car pulling up before   MUSIC - SIREN
porch - man starts to get out -

    ...DISSOLVES INTO

VIEW IN BEDROOM
Policeman at side in f.g.
watching as Donelly traces
blood stains on rug to window
b.g. - Gates watching - Donelly
looks out window - comes forward
to Gates - camera dollies up   FOOTSTEPS
excluding policeman - Detective   AD LIB NOISES
comes on from side - speaks -
camera pans as the three hurry
to door to hall - exit -

    DONELLY - There's another one. Oh,
        yes. He's been hit all right.
        And maybe he's been hurt badly
        enough to slow him up.

    DETECTIVE O.S. - Captain Donelly?

    DONELLY - Yeah?

    DETECTIVE - We just got a flash on the
        radio -- they've traced him to
        the tenement district, over by
        Grant Avenue.

    DONELLY - Well, maybe --

    (Continued)

| NO. | DESCRIPTION | DIALOGUE | REEL SIX PAGE 3 |

3. (Continued) -2

                        GATES - Hey, you know what I think?

                        DONELLY - Yeah, I know.

...VERTICAL FEATHER WIPE TO

    VIEW IN TENEMENT ALLEY (NIGHT)
    The Creeper comes on slowly
    from side - leans against   MUSIC - AD LIB NOISE
    packing box -

4. CLOSE UP IN ALLEY
    The Creeper clutching his leg
    in pain as he leans against   MUSIC
    box - looks up -

5. SHOOTING UP TO FIRE ESCAPE &
    HELEN'S WINDOW
    Light shining from window -   MUSIC

6. CLOSE UP IN ALLEY
    The Creeper looking up -
    clutches his leg -   MUSIC

7. CLOSE VIEW PAN SHOT IN ALLEY
    On The Creeper as he limps
    along - stops beneath fire
    escape - steps up onto box as   MUSIC ·
    he hangs onto rail - starts   AD LIB NOISE
    to pull himself up onto fire
    escape -

8. CLOSE UP THE CREEPER
    Pulling himself up onto fire   MUSIC - AD LIB NOISES
    escape - looks about cautiously -

9. VIEW EXT. BUILDING
    The Creeper pulling himself onto
    fire escape - starts to exit   MUSIC - AD LIB NOISES
    at top of scene -

10. CLOSE UP THE CREEPER
     Camera pans slightly as he
     makes his way slowly & painfully
     around to front of ladder - camera   MUSIC - AD LIB NOISES
     moves up as he climbs up ladder -
     looks up - camera tilts up
     bringing window into scene -

| NO. | DESCRIPTION | DIALOGUE | REEL SIX PAGE 4 |

11. CLOSE SHOT OF FIRE ESCAPE
    The Creeper pulling himself
    along - looks about - scared -
    moves toward window of Helen's
    apartment -   MUSIC

12. VIEW AT SIDE IN HELEN'S BEDROOM
    (DARK)
    The Creeper starts to climb
    into room thru window b.g. -   MUSIC

13. CLOSE SHOT IN ROOM
    The Creeper climbing into room
    - he winces as he drags his
    wounded leg thru window - he
    looks off - camera moves up
    and tilts down to his feet,
    slowly blood from wound dripping
    on rug & his shoe -   MUSIC

14. SHOOTING INTO BEDROOM FROM
    DOORWAY
    The Creeper slowly limps his
    way across room toward camera -
    camera pans slightly as he leans   MUSIC
    against door jamb and looks off -
    calls -

    THE CREEPER - Helen!

15. VIEW IN HELEN'S LIVING ROOM
    Helen seated at piano in f.g. -
    The Creeper standing in bedroom
    doorway b.g. - Helen, startled,
    rises and goes toward The Creeper
    as he comes forward - camera
    dollies up to the two - she
    worried - he reaches in his
    pocket - takes out jewels wrapped
    in handkerchief - puts them in
    her hands - Helen examines   MUSIC
    jewels with her hand -   AD LIB NOISES

    HELEN - Oh, Hal, you startled me.
        You came in by the fire escape.
        Are you in trouble again?

    THE CREEPER: No. I brought
        something for you.

    HELEN - What is it?

    (Continued)

Blind Helen (Jane Adams) is pleasant to the Creeper (Hatton), so he wants to fund her sight-restoring operation. Don't tamper with success, Creep Man!

"Extree, extree, read all about it: If this little old Brute Man tries to steal a paper, I'll flatten him!" And by the end of 1945, kid actor Danny Jackson probably *could*.

| NO. | DESCRIPTION | DIALOGUE | REEL SIX PAGE 5 |

15. (Continued)

THE CREEPER - This stuff will bring enough for that operation.

16. CLOSE UP THE CREEPER AND HELEN
She facing camera - wide-eyed as she examines jewels with her fingers - The Creeper doubles up in agony - Helen reacts - speaks anxiously - he speaks - she stares off, frightened, as he turns and exits at side - she calls after him -

MUSIC

HELEN - Where did you get these?

THE CREEPER - (MOANS)

HELEN - Hal, you're hurt.

THE CREEPER - I'm all right. You have that operation right away.

HELEN - Hal, wait.

...DISSOLVES INTO

CLOSE SHOT IN JEWELER'S SHOP
(DAY)
Jeweler behind glass counter - Helen placing jewels on counter before him - he picks up several - looks at them - she closes her purse - he speaks - picks up velvet tray with jewels - camera pans excluding Helen as he crosses to curtained doorway to back room - he exits through curtains -

MUSIC

HELEN - I'd like an appraisal of these jewels.

JEWELER - Yes, ma'am. It'll take a few minutes. Will you care to wait?

HELEN - Yes, I'll wait.

REEL SIX   PAGE 6

| NO. | DESCRIPTION | DIALOGUE |

17. VIEW IN BACK ROOM
    Jeweler coming on from side
    with velvet tray and jewels -
    puts them on desk - picks up
    report - examines jewels as
    he compares them with report -

    AD LIB NOISES
    MUSIC

18. CLOSE UP TOP OF REPORT
    Printing and typing read -

    POLICE HEADQUARTERS

    DETECTIVE BUREAU - MATSON REPORTING
           ROBBERY DETAIL
    Time 10:30 P.M. Place Clifford Scott Residence

    Arrests _____

    Suspects ___ The Creeper

    camera tilts down to other part
    of page - typing reads -

    MUSIC

           GOODS STOLEN
      1 pr diamond earrings--shell
      1 pr diamond earrings--link
      1 aquamarine (blue) ring
      1 aquamarine (green) ring
      1 jewel bracelet--4 sapphires
      1 gold bracelet (band type) square
            cut ruby set in diamonds
      1 diamond and pearl bracelet

19. CLOSE SHOT IN BACK ROOM
    Jeweler comparing jewels to report -
    puts down jewels and report -
    picks up phone - dials - glances
    off - speaks quietly into phone -

    MUSIC
    AD LIB NOISES

                JEWELER - Operator, get me the
                          police.

    ...DISSOLVES INTO

    CLOSE SHOT IN DONELLY'S OFFICE
    Donelly seated behind desk - looking
    at jewels - Gates standing across
    desk from him - Helen standing at
    far end of desk - Donelly questions
    Helen - she troubled -

    MUSIC STOPS

              (Continued)

NO.	DESCRIPTION	DIALOGUE REEL SIX PAGE 7
19.	(Continued)	DONELLY - What did he say when he gave you these jewels?
		HELEN - He told me to sell them and use the money for an operation on my eyes.
		DONELLY - Didn't you think that was a little funny?
		HELEN - I started to ask him about them but he left before I had a chance.
		DONELLY - Don't you realize you can get yourself into a lot of trouble protecting a criminal.
20.	CLOSE UP DONELLY AND HELEN She facing camera and Donelly, seated close to camera - she, startled, speaks -	
		HELEN - A criminal!
		DONELLY - Well, I think you can call him that.
		HELEN - Oh, I can't believe it.
21.	CLOSE UP DOWN TO DESK Donelly, seated, facing camera and Helen standing close to camera - he questioning her -	
		DONELLY - Didn't you know the police were after him?
		HELEN - No.
		DONELLY - Not even that first night when they came to your room?
22.	CLOSE UP HELEN AND DONELLY She facing camera and Donelly - she troubled -	
		HELEN - I thought they were just some men. He never told me.

| NO. | DESCRIPTION | DIALOGUE   REEL SIX   PAGE 8 |

23. CLOSE UP DOWN TO DESK
Donelly facing camera and
Helen standing close to
camera - he looks down as
he speaks -

  DONELLY - No, no, I guess he
     wouldn't.

24. CLOSE UP DONELLY AND HELEN
She facing camera and Donelly
seated close to camera - she
speaks unhappily - she aghast
as Donelly explains - Gates
comes on from side - assists
Helen to chair -

  HELEN - I know he was in some sort
     of trouble but I didn't realize
     it was with the police. What
     has he done?

  DONELLY - Murder - at wholesale.
     He happens to be The Creeper.

  HELEN - The Creeper!

  GATES O.S. - Maybe you'd better
     sit down.

25. CLOSE UP HELEN
Tears in her eyes - she speaks
unhappily -

  HELEN - He was so nice to me. I
     just can't believe this about
     him.

| NO. | DESCRIPTION | DIALOGUE | REEL SIX PAGE 9 |

26. <u>M O N T A G E</u>

CLOSE UP HELEN
Stares off unhappily - newspaper
comes on superimposed over top
part of scene - headlines read -

GIRL TIPS OFF POLICE ON "CREEPER"

B.g. shot dissolves into Close
Up Moving Shot The Creeper's
feet as they walk along - Camera
moves down close to column head-
ing - reads -   MUSIC

      BLIND PIANO TEACHER
        GIVES DETECTIVES
         CLUE TO FIEND

Other newspaper comes on over
scene - headlines read -

  BLIND GIRL CONFESSES FRIENDSHIP
     WITH "CREEPER" KILLER   MUSIC

Other newspaper comes on over
scene - Headlines read -

BLIND GIRL TELLS ALL ABOUT "CREEPER"

Camera moves down close to column
heading - reads -

     STRANGE FRIENDSHIP
      AIDS POLICE IN
        MANHUNT

(END OF MONTAGE)

   ...DISSOLVES INTO

VIEW ON STREET CORNER (NIGHT)
General street activity - newsboy
standing on corner giving spiel -
man comes on past camera - buys   MUSIC _ STREET NOISES
paper -

                 NEWSBOY - Extra! Extra! Blind girl
                          confesses friendship with Creeper
                          killer. Read all about it. Blind
                          girl confesses --

| NO. | DESCRIPTION | DIALOGUE | REEL SIX PAGE 10 |

27. CLOSE UP THE CREEPER
Standing in alley watching off –
comes forward slowly –

    MUSIC - STREET NOISES

    NEWSBOY O.S. – Extra! Extra! Read all about it. Blind girl tells all about the Creeper!

28. CLOSE SHOT ON STREET CORNER
Newsboy in f.g. – yelling –
The Creeper comes on from side
to him – buys paper – camera
pans on the Creeper as he goes
to alley – The Creeper leans
against corner of building as
he reads paper –

    MUSIC - STREET NOISES
    FOOTSTEPS

    NEWSBOY – Extra! Extra! Get your late edition here. Blind girl tells all.

    THE CREEPER – Paper.

    NEWSBOY – Yes, sir. -- BLIND Girl (OFF SCENE) tells all. Read all about it. Get your paper here. Get your late edition. Blind girl tells all. (AD LIBS)

29. CLOSE UP HIGH SHOT THE CREEPER
He reading newspaper –

    MUSIC - STREET NOISES

30. LARGE CLOSE UP THE CREEPER
Looks up from newspaper –
hurt – a look of hatred in his
eye – exits at side –

    MUSIC - STREET NOISES

    ...DISSOLVES INTO

PAN SHOT SIDE OF STREET
On The Creeper as he walks along
– turns down alley toward b.g. –
limping –

    MUSIC

31. VIEW IN ALLEY
The Creeper coming along toward
camera – stops – looks around
cautiously – looks up & off –

    MUSIC

32. SHOT OF FIRE ESCAPE EXT.
TENEMENT BUILDING
Lights shining from Helen's
windows –

    MUSIC

| NO. | DESCRIPTION | DIALOGUE | REEL SIX PAGE 11 |

33. LARGE CLOSE UP THE CREEPER (DOLLY)
    Looking up and off - bitter -
    he follows camera as it dollies
    along -   MUSIC

34. VIEW AT END OF ALLEY
    The Creeper goes toward fire
    escape - steps up on barrel as
    he catches hold of rail -
    camera tilts up as he lifts
    himself up onto fire escape -   MUSIC

35. CLOSE SIDE SHOT EXT. BUILDING
    The Creeper pulling himself
    up onto fire escape - camera   MUSIC - AD LIB NOISES
    tilts up as he climbs ladder -

36. CRANE SHOT OF FIRE ESCAPE LADDER
    Camera cranes up with the Creeper
    as he slowly climbs the ladder -   MUSIC
    looks up hatefully -

37. CLOSE SIDE SHOT EXT. BUILDING
    The Creeper slowly ascending
    ladder - starts to exit at   MUSIC
    top of scene -

38. CLOSE SHOT OF FIRE ESCAPE
    The Creeper climbing into scene   MUSIC
    - moves toward Helen's
    window -

39. CLOSE SHOT CORNER OF DARK ROOM
    The Creeper climbs into room
    from fire escape - camera pans
    and dollies along as he moves   MUSIC
    slowly across room to open
    door - looks off -

40. SHOOTING PAST THE CREEPER TO
    VIEW OF LIVING ROOM
    The Creeper watching as Helen,
    with back to camera, plays
    piano in b.g. - unaware of the
    Creeper's presence - Camera   MUSIC
    dollies after the Creeper as
    he moves slowly thru doorway -

41. LARGE CLOSE UP DOLLY SHOT THE
    CREEPER
    As he moves slowly across   MUSIC
    room - staring off menacingly -

| NO. | DESCRIPTION | DIALOGUE | REEL SIX PAGE 12 |

42. CLOSE SHOT SIDE IN ROOM
Helen, with back to camera,
seated at piano - playing -
camera dollies up slowly behind   MUSIC
her -

43. CLOSE UP IN ROOM
Helen seated close to camera -
completely unaware of the Creeper
as he moves slowly toward her
from b.g. - he raises his hands   MUSIC
menacingly - stares at her -

44. CLOSE UP INT. DOOR
Is opened a crack from outside   MUSIC
as detective looks into room -

45. VIEW OF LIVING ROOM FROM OVER
PIANO
Helen continues to play as
The Creeper moves up stealthily
behind her, his hands raised
menacingly - cop rises into scene
from hiding place behind sofa
as other cop rushes on from side
- the two grab the Creeper by
the arms - Gates comes out of
closet b.g., holding gun ready -   MUSIC
Helen stops playing - Donelly   AD LIB NOISES
comes on from side - watches   FOOTSTEPS
as two cops drag the Creeper
off scene at side - Helen close
to tears - Gates exits at side
- Helen leans on piano - Donelly
eyes her sympathetically -

        DONELLY - I'll be with you in a
           minute.

46. LARGE CLOSE UP HELEN
Hand over her eyes - she leans
on her hand as she stares off -
tears in her eyes - camera
tilts down as she falls forward
on piano, sobbing - Donelly's   MUSIC
hand comes on - presses her
shoulder comfortingly -

        HELEN - (SOBS)

...DISSOLVES INTO

| NO. | DESCRIPTION | DIALOGUE | REEL SIX PAGE 13 |

46. CONTINUED

CLOSE SHOT IN DONELLY'S OFFICE
Helen seated on edge of desk -
Gates standing between the two -
they talk - she unhappy - they
try to comfort her - Gates smiles
as Donelly talks - Helen speaks
happily - Donelly picks up deck
of cards - starts to toy with it -
reacts as Gates speaks to Helen -
he smiles - helps her to her feet -
Gates escorts Helen off scene -
Donelly glares off - disgusted -
camera dollies up close to him -
speaks - riffles cards, letting
them fly in all directions -

MUSIC STARTS
AD LIB NOISES
FOOTSTEPS

DONELLY - That was a fine thing you did, Miss Paige, helping us trap the killer.

HELEN - I wonder how he feels about it. He trusted me - wanted to help me.

GATES - Don't let it get you. His mind had snapped.

DONELLY - After all, he was a pyschopathic killer. And by the way, I have some news for you. I have been talking to certain people and we - ah - (CLEARS HIS THROAT) they think you're going to get that operation.

HELEN - How wonderful.

DONELLY - You look tired. Why don't--

GATES - May I see you home?

HELEN - Oh, thank you.

DONELLY - Well, there goes my pigeon.

...FADE OUT

If I Can't Be Number One in Your Life, Then Number Two on You: The Creeper tries to kill Helen for "betraying" him. But Johnny Law is there to make sure that doesn't happen.

```
NO.    DESCRIPTION                    DIALOG           REEL SIX   PAGE 14
47.    FADE IN - PICTORIAL ANIMATED
       END TITLE                                       MUSIC

            THE END

          A Universal Picture

         ...FADE OUT

48.    PART TITLE                     U N I V E R S A L
                                      "THE BRUTE MAN"
                                        END OF PART
                                             6

       RA/vh
```

The BRUTE MAN Trailer Script

CONTINUITY & DIALOGUE

T R A I L E R

on

"THE BRUTE MAN"

With
TOM NEAL
JAN WILEY
JANE ADAMS
DONALD MacBRIDE
PETER WHITNEY
FRED COBY
JaNELLE JOHNSON

and
RONDO HATTON
as the CREEPER

JUNE 1, 1946

PICTURE NO. 1479
DIRECTOR - YARBROUGH

PICTURE NO. 1479
DIRECTOR - YARBROUGH
PAGE ONE

CONTINUITY & DIALOGUE

T R A I L E R

on

"THE BRUTE MAN"

1. MED. SHOT EXT. SCOTT MANSION
   (NIGHT)
   Word comes on over scene -
   reads -   MUSIC THROUGHOUT TRAILER

        WARNING!

   WORD exits - other words come
   on over scene and exit -

        A BRUTE
          KILLER
        IS ON THE
          LOOSE...

2. HIGH SHOT OF STREET
   Police cars parked in f.g. -
   detectives and men milling
   about ext. buildings b.g. -   SIREN
   others cars come on from side   SCREECH OF BRAKES
   - stop in f.g. - men get out -
   words come on over scene and
   exit -

        TERRORIZING
          A CITY...

3. CLOSE UP IN CORNER OF SHACK
   The Creeper standing looking
   into mirror on wall at side -
   Words come on over scene -
   read -

        HATING
        THE WORLD...
        and HIMSELF...

PAGE TWO

4. CLOSE UP MIRROR
   (Over the Creeper's shoulder)
   His reflection shows his
   distorted features - words over
   scene read: -

     HATING
     THE WORLD...
     and HIMSELF...

   Words exit - The Creeper's   SOUND OF BREAKING
   reflection shows his hatred as   GLASS
   he looks at himself - he breaks
   mirror with his fist -

5. CLOSE UP IN DONELLY'S OFFICE
   Donelly seated close to camera
   - Helen, the blind girl, stand-
   ing - stares off as she speaks -
   Donelly looks up at her - Helen
   aghast -

     HELEN - What has he done?

     DONELLY - Murder -- at wholesale.
      He happens to be "The Creeper".

     HELEN - The Creeper!

6. CRANE SHOT IN YARD
   Joan backs away as The Creeper
   moves thru shrubbery & across
   driveway toward her - camera
   cranes down past him as she
   moves toward steps - horrified -   FOOTSTEPS
   she puts hand to her mouth as
   she screams - she drops out of
   sight below camera - camera
   cranes up -

     JOAN - Stay away from me. No.
      No, stay away. (SCREAMS)

7. CLOSE SHOT IN BEDROOM
   Virginia standing at side watching as Scott turns toward the
   Creeper holding gun ready -
   camer moves up and angles around,
   excluding Virginia as The Creeper   SHOT - FALL
   raises jewel box to strike -
   Scott fires gun - bullet hits
   The Creeper in the leg - camera
   moves up as he reacts - camera
   tilts down as he falls to floor -
        (Continued)

PAGE THREE

7. (Continued)   SCOTT - Put up your hands.

                                 CREEPER - You --

8. CLOSE UP SCOTT
Bending over The Creeper, lying on floor, apparently unconscious - The Creeper reaches up suddenly - grabs Scott by the throat - camera pans as he rolls Scott over on his back - The Creeper's face contorted with rage - words come on over scene and exit -

         INDESTRUCTIBLE
           IN HIS
            MAD FURY...

9. VIEW IN ALLEY
Mob of policemen moving down alley from b.g. toward f.g. - some exit past camera - words come on over scene and exit -

         with TOM NEAL
           JANE ADAMS
            JAN WILEY and
         RONDO HATTON
      AS THE CREEPER in

10. CLOSE UP AT COUNTER IN PAWN SHOP
Shopkeeper and The Creeper facing each other across counter - shopkeeper reaches toward the Creeper - The Creeper grabs shopkeeper by the throat - camera dollies up close to The Creeper's face as shopkeeper's hands claw at his collar -   <u>MUSIC THROUGHOUT TRAILER</u>

        "THE BRUTE
           MAN"

    A
Universal
  Picture

   ra

"Storm Chaser!" - Rondo Hatton and the Great Miami Hurricane

The Great Miami Hurricane of 1926 carved its path of destruction, and then Rondo Hatton was among the *Tampa Times* staff members dispatched to the stricken area before the roads were even passable. He filed a series of rich "you are there"-style stories (September 21, 22, 24 and 25) describing the conditions in Miami and in the area south of West Palm Beach. As well as these reports (and some survivors' stories), Hatton also brought back photographs which ran in the *Times* on the 22nd. Here are his stories and some of the photos (they looked better in the paper than they do here; use your imagination).

Tampa Daily Times, September 21, 1926:

REFUGEES BRING STORIES OF TERROR FROM GALE ZONE

RESCUE CREWS PUSHING WORK IN ALL AREAS

61 White Bodies are Reported Found at Moore Haven.

**By RONDO HATTON,
Staff Writer of The Times**

Sebring, Sept. 21. – In this little city, one of the hubs for relief work extending into the hurricane-devastated areas around Lake Okeechobee, Fort Lauderdale, Hollywood and Miami, there exists today material for any type of story or play.

Tragedy, pathos and comedy stalk hand in hand as refugees from Moore Haven, Clewiston, West Palm Beach and even Miami continue to arrive.

Every new arrival has a story to tell.

There are stories of thrilling rescues, of death, of hunger, of thirst, of heartaches –

And there are stories that would be comical under circumstances not surrounded by so much tragedy.

But out of these stories told here on all sides, the most touching probably are the ones told by father, mother, son or daughter who has loved ones at Moore Haven, West Palm Beach, Miami and other places in the storm-swept area. There are hundreds of such cases here now, and the number is steadily growing as people from all sections of the state continue to arrive.

With relief operations placed on a systematic basis, the countryside adjacent to Lake Okeechobee in the Everglades today took further check of its toll from the wind and high waves cast up on the small cities nearby.

Clewiston escaped without casualties, according to the latest news brought here by refugees and relief workers. The town, however, suffered heavy property losses. Aviators who circled the lake region reported they were unable to find the town.

Moore Haven likewise is in ruins. Struck from the tremendous waves lifted from the lake by the hurricane, the little city of something like a thousand inhabitants seemed to have borne the brunt of the storm in the Okeechobee region.

61 Bodies in Morgue.

An Avon Park newspaper man reports that the bodies of 61 white persons had been recovered in the Moore Haven area and removed to temporary morgues. He said that it was believed that 200 other white persons were missing.

The full extent of the damage in the Okeechobee area cannot be estimated for at least a week, in the opinion of relief workers hurried to the section from neighboring towns. A protecting dike crumbled before the gale-swept water and the unleashed waves swept inland for miles, wreaking death and destruction in their paths.

Refugees are being sent out of the stricken area as fast as rescuers can locate them. approximately 800 have been accounted for to date.

Many persons were saved by volunteer workers who plied the countryside in boats.

At least six relief trains, dispatched from as many points, have arrived, and the little army of volunteer workers was reinforced today.

Undertakers who accompanied the relief workers have, in several instances, been forced to send back for additional chemicals. The Sebring chamber of commerce has taken charge of bodies which cannot be shipped from the district because of decomposition. These bodies will be buried at Moore Haven. Seven bodies were brought here last night.

The plight of the populace in the devastated area is described as pitiful by all returning relief workers or new arrivals of refugees. The living have no homes and hundreds lost their funds when their homes and effects were swept away.

These stories, together with reports that orders have been issued barring outsiders from the storm-swept area caused a pall of gloom to settle down over the hundreds of persons here seeking trace of lost loved ones.

Many of the little army who rushed here to seek relatives declare they will evade this order if possible. Their one thought is to get into the wrecked places and search for themselves.

"My son is out in that territory somewhere – I must get to him," said one grey-haired old man who came here in an effort to locate his boy. "He was returning from West Palm Beach the night the hurricane struck and we haven't heard a word from him."

His story is typical of those heard on all sides.

Assistance Is Needed.

"Moore Haven and the surrounding countryside needs water and dry clothing," is the plea brought here by Mrs. R.L. Cunningham, one of the refugees who arrived during the night.

Scores of injured, many of them children, were treated at the Community Temple at Hialeah.

"Tell the world that Moore Haven does need help," she said, contradicting rumors that no aid was needed there.

Gathered here today among the host of refugees fleeing the devastated Moore Haven area are three Tampans. They are Alvida Tilden, Alice Tilden and Alfred Tilden.

They tell a story of a miraculous escape.

Cast into the swirling waters during the height of the storm, Alfred was floating around, clinging for life to any stray bit of wreckage. Just as he was giving up hope, his father, who had become separated from him early in the storm, came floating towards him on the remnants of what had been the floor of some home. Alfred climbed aboard and together they escaped, later finding the other member of their party.

A story of how many of those caught in Moore Haven escaped while the hurricane raged was told by Ed Davis, a refugee.

"I was working in a drugstore in one of the brick buildings when the raging waters reached the place," said he. "All the people in reach hurried to the second floor of the building.

"There we remained huddled together until rescue workers took us away in boats.

"Scores of others were not so fortunate. Many took refuge on the second stories of wooden structures and were thrown helpless into the waters when the buildings collapsed.

"Many, however, were later rescued from house tops or picked up while clinging to bits of timber.

"But there were many – just how many, I do not know – who perished."

Tangled mass of twisted steel sown here is all that remains of Meteor docks, Miami.

A little girl here last night looked down at her feet and smiled at a patent leather pair of slippers which she drew from a heap that was piled in the lobby of the Nancesowee hotel.

The smile radiated from tear-soaked eyes caused by the death of a little brother in Moore Haven.

"Jimmie lost his life trying to save his bicycle," the girl said.

She had just arrived on a refugee train and had worn wet clothing and gone without food and water since Saturday night.

Miami Refugee Talks.

A merciless storm which borrowed nature's most destructive elements – high winds, rain and darkness – spent its fury upon a helpless, fear-stricken Miami at 1:30 o'clock in the morning, according to a story told me at Avon Park by Mrs. W.G. Langford, who had just returned from Miami.

Mrs. Langford and her nine-year old daughter, Zelda, arrived in Miami shortly after midnight Saturday morning. She went to visit her mother, but the mother had moved, however, before Mrs. Langford arrived.

Failing to find any trace of her mother, Mrs. Langford and her daughter went to the Hampton hotel on First street about a block from the Flagler hotel.

"Just as the taxicab stopped in front of the hotel the storm broke in full force," said Mrs. Langford. "I told the driver the storm is here now – we had been expecting momentarily.

"We went on into the hotel, the storm increasing in fury. We had hardly reached our room when the lights went out.

"Then there was a clashing of glass and rain poured in through the broken windows.

"I could hear the people running around frantically in the hotel. They were crying to one another. There were shouts from the street. I did not know what to do. I had my child and I was afraid to go out in the street, yet I was afraid to remain in the room. But I stayed on in the room, because it was on the ground floor.

"The night passed somehow – but it all seems like a horrible dream to me now. I lived a thousand years, I guess, before daylight came. I was scared to death – I could not find my mother – I did not know whether she was dead or alive – and I was afraid for Zelda. I didn't know what to do.

"Daylight came, and I looked out of the broken window, but I couldn't go out. The streets were covered with broken glass, pieces of houses and bricks.

"Store fronts were caved in and twisted, wrecked houses stood swaying in the gale that still raged. Water ran down the streets like rivers. Underneath some of the wrecked houses could be seen people who had been caught by falling debris.

"It was a mad bedlam. People didn't know what to do. They searched frantically for relatives. Others tried to escape – but they didn't know where to go.

No Food Obtainable.

"Saturday we only had two sandwiches and a small bottle of milk. I met a woman from Tampa who had gone without food since early Friday night. she was hunting madly for milk for her child.

"I walked around some, but everything was so badly torn up I couldn't go far.

"I came to some of the American Legion boys who were among the first rescue crews to get into action. I was hunting my mother, I told them, but none of them knew her.

"They told me of finding hundreds of people, whole families with their babies, crouched under palms in the park. The homeless and fear-mad people sought shelter anywhere they could find it. One woman had wrapped a shawl around her baby and had taken refuge under a small bush on one street.

"I saw men and women running around half clothed. They had lost all, clothes, jewelry – everything. One woman had on only a night gown and a raincoat. Saturday night they put a guard around Miami and wouldn't let any one out. People were frantic. I got out yesterday on the first bus. It seems we have been traveling a hundred years."

She was tired, her experiences and fatigue had been too much. "I am sorry," she continued.

"I am sorry, I can't tell you more. I – well I had to leave and I don't know whether my mother is alive or dead. It is dreadful."

Lakeport Wiped Out.

Meagre reports from Lakeport, a small town on the shores of Lake Okeechobee about 10 miles north of Moore Haven, state assistance is needed badly at that point. Dozens of persons are said to have been injured when a building in which the citizens took refuge collapsed during the height of the storm.

Five lives were lost, the reports state, and many of the injured are in serious condition. The entire village is reported as being destroyed.

A relief expedition, headed by Sheriff Hancock, is en route to the scene from Avon Park, going via Okeechobee.

Another relief expedition is going to the stricken village across the country via Venus and Palmdale.

Lakeport is a small fishing settlement of approximately 200 population.

The state drainage dike to the south of Lake Okeechobee is about 60 per cent damaged, estimates ranging around $200,000. Several miles of highway east of Canal Point is under water and the highway will be out of commission for several days.

Damage at Canal Point, Pahokee, Rita and Belle Glade on the eastern slopes of the lake, while serious, is not as great as at Moore Haven.

Fruit crops were damaged at least 50 per cent and conservative estimates are set at several hundred thousand dollars to growers.

The seven bodies brought here last night are being held awaiting word from relatives or friends. They have been partially identified as: A.E. Gable, a Mrs. Young, Susie Lee, Clara Bowseen, Lottie Howe and a Mrs. Shepherd.

The wind's doings in East Flagler street. See the overturned automobile and twisted steel-work in the right background.

Tampa Daily Times, September 21, 1926:

Pathos, Tears and Laughter Rule Miami in Storm Wake

By RONDO HATTON, Times Staff Writer

Miami, Sept. 22. – Optimism sparkled like a large jewel today against a background of pathos and tears in Miami's story of the hurricane.

Like tiny threads of a master's web, this undaunted spirit tended to give the coloring to Miami's rainbow promise as a "Magic City" – to rebuild and carry on.

Glistening under the rays of a summer sun, which broke through to shine down on an area of widespread demolition, Miami today was weaving a new web – a new city.

The machinery this morning was a bit slow in getting started. Long, anxious hours during the storm and the fatigue of labors after it had had its part, early Tuesday morning there was little signs of the life. Everyone moved with a leaden, lagging step. Humans stirred here and there among the wreckage. Like stray dogs, some prowler aimlessly shuffled about the streets. More human, others gathered in little groups here and there. Soldiers and policemen were prominent.

The sun rose higher and higher. Streets attracted more and more people. Automobiles increased. Scenes changed from an almost lifeless stillness to one of hectic, noisy activity. Miami was awake.

After the waters had receded on Flagler street, one of Miami's main thoroughfares. Note the timbers torn from various structures by the crisscross air currents.

Some Turning Back.

Leaving the city was an endless stream of cars. Some were leaving never to return, others going to come back later. Jack J. Williamson and family filled one of the outbound automobiles. He was en route to New Jersey. "I am coming back," he shouted to a group of bystanders as he waved them goodbye.

Nine o'clock found the downtown section humming with activity. Business was being carried on as usual – almost. Many stores and business places carried on behind improvised fronts of bits of the storm's wreckage nailed up to take the place of the plate glass windows and doors. Other merchants moved their wares out onto the sidewalk and used packing boxes for counters. Bread lines were in operation throughout the city.

Late arrivals got the surprise of their lives when they found they could get food. Restaurants and cafes did a flourishing business. There were plenty of groceries, meats, produce and other supplies on hand. There was some shortage just after the storm. This caused reports Sunday and Monday at points north of here that newcomers could not get food here.

Newcomers seemed more affected by the storm than those who went through it. The newcomer was shocked by the devastation and its toll of dead. The Miamian and others who went through it, had taken stock and made their plans for the future. They went to work, rebuilding houses not destroyed or erecting temporary shelter places. New roofs were going on rapidly. The city was dotted with clothes lines, sagging almost to the ground under weight of wet wearing apparel of every description, bed clothing, rugs, draperies and what not.

Gangs Clear Streets.

Gangs of laborers were clearing the streets of fallen trees and telephone poles. Undaunted by the huge network of fallen wires everywhere, utility company workers plunged into the herculean task of restoring order to that part of the general chaos.

There was a bedlam of noise. Huge trucks, carrying debris, speeded here and there with cut-outs open. Thousands of automobiles jammed and clogged the streets. There was the noise of breaking glass. The riveter's gun was popping in spots throughout the city. There were the shouts of foremen booming out orders to their crews. Newsboys shouted "read all about the storm."

And there was laughter.

It was a queer thing to the newcomer, who came – as all have come so far – expecting to find a sullen, saddened Miami.

Miami gives this answer, as couched in many of the residents' remarks:

"We had the storm. It is over. We are looking to the future now. We are going to rebuild and carry on."

The rebuilding work now underway, impresses one that they intend to do as they say.

Of course, there is general talk of the darker side of the hurricane. The resident knows what has occurred. The evidence is too plain for the newcomer to overlook. In Miami morgues, lay scores of identified bodies. There were also bodies yet unclaimed and unidentified. They were still finding more of the dead today. Searchers found 10 additional bodies along the Bay of Biscayne front.

Houses Crowded.

Idly watching downtown activities was John Henry, negro. He had been caught in the storm as it lashed Twelfth street. During its height he had sought shelter in one of the brick buildings. Everyone he went to was so crowded he couldn't get in. He remained outside and weathered the blow on the streets. He escaped unhurt. Just how, he doesn't know.

Royal Palm park today still held its attraction for residents and visitors. Huge barges, large and small boats lay on their sides, and left just where the storm passed on after throwing them there.

On Fifth street, near Northwest First avenue, a group of housewives, returning from their morning

Drug store at First street and First avenue, Miami, showing how the wind tore away the heavy metal awning, which fell to crush two men to death.

shopping, was gathering boards and bits of wreckage which it converted into a small bridge to cross the small rivulet flowing down the center of the railway tracks. The crowd finally got across without mishap.

Out along Second avenue an energetic merchant, too busy with customers to give his name, was carrying on his business over the top of packing boxes. His store lay in ruins behind him.

Prize fight fans had not let the storm dampen their ardor. Barney Adair, who is to appear in Tampa Friday night, walked along the street with a group of his admirers.

Injured Trek to Hospital.

Out in the Jackson Memorial hospital, Miami's city hospital and the largest there, there was an endless trek of injured to and from the place.

There was one bit of joy in the institution. In the maternity ward, Mrs. Fred Brown, 3485 Indiana avenue, hummed a low, crooning song to a wee son, born during the peak of the storm early Saturday. Mother and son were "doing nicely."

Over in the children's ward, another baby cried lustily. Rescuers had found him somewhere around the city in the wreckage. He escaped injury. He cried for mother and papa, but none could tell who they are or where they are.

Miss Mary Corbitt, acting superintendent, was directing first aid work and between times directing carpenters and others in repairing and cleaning up the entire hospital. The storm caught the institution filled almost to capacity. The winds and rains damaged two wings of the plant, greatly endangering lives of patients. Almost heroic work, however, enabled the nurses and volunteers to move patients to other quarters in various wings and thus prevented any casualties.

316 Are Sheltered.

A normal capacity of 316 patients, the hospital Tuesday sheltered 387 persons. This was somewhat a smaller number than of previous days, but despite the overcrowded condition nurses reported only six deaths there from among the hundreds of storm patients brought in.

In the negro ward, there were patients with every kind of injury from minor cuts to broken backs. One negro, crushed under his home when the storm smashed it, moved feebly to view hospital visitors. He mumbled something to a nurse. Before she could turn around to answer him, he was dead. The nurse nonchalantly pulled a sheet up over his face, but the movement did not escape the negro who had the next bed. His eyes told only too well his thoughts. He was too badly hurt to do what his eyes told he wanted to.

Back downtown, the early afternoon had brought more sight seers. Local ones were joined by hundreds of "curiosity seekers" from practically every part of the state. Many had rushed there by auto from New York and other points as far away as that. The majority, who wedged through guard lines, were hunting relatives. Quite a few, however, were the morbid curiosity seekers. These will find Miami a very inhospitable city.

Real Work Needed.

There is so much real work and aid to be done. Miami has no time for the idle curiosity seeker. Miami needs workers and helpers who are willing to don the overalls.

Late lunchers were munching sandwiches at the drug store or sandwich shop, as though they had never heard of a storm. Some were eating with one eye on the clock, others were trying to eat and watch pedestrians at the same time. Some food was wasted in the experiment.

The McAllister hotel was a temporary hospital. It was crowded with patients. Temporary hospitals were established also in other hotels throughout the city. These and the downtown Red Cross stations were significant in one side of the storm's toll.

Tampa Daily Times, September 24, 1926:

75 Say Tearful Goodbyes in Evacuating Moore Haven

Ejected Pioneers Look Longingly Over Waters to Places Where Once Stood Homes, And Which Now Is Charnel House

By RONDO HATTON.
Times Staff Writer

Moore Haven, (Via Messenger to Sebring), Sept. 24. – Seventy-five persons today tearfully answered the order to evacuate Moore Haven – 72 men and three women – the last of that hardy lot of pioneers who had withstood Saturday's hurricane in this one thriving village.

Here too, were dogs, cows, chickens, pigs, mules, horses. Today at noon these 75 humans were gathered on the dike almost in the heart of the town. The dike stands out like an island in this water-covered, wrecked and littered area. They were looking longingly out over the waters of the lake, over the debris and the gnarled, twisted wreckage sluggishly floating around or protruding above the waters.

To Continue Search.

The military will remain. They will continue the search for the dead – for bodies of men, women and children that have not been recovered. One hundred and twenty-eight bodies have been found. It is estimated that many more have not been recovered.

This now is one of the tasks of the militia. In addition they are to care for the stock, build roads and do other work, unless orders are changed at the last moment.

In the future – maybe two months, perhaps three – some of the residents may come back. By that time this stricken village may be a fit place for a human to live in. nature, which destroyed it, is expected to make it habitable with the aid of human work and chemicals. And so the chapter closes.

It is hard for you to picture the scene at Moore Haven. It is hard for you to understand what the disaster was. Picture a little village of between 1,200 and 1,500 persons huddled together in houses behind a narrow barrier of sand and rock. The barrier was supposedly a guard against Lake Okeechobee. The village was typical of its type with the usual small stores, hotels, homes, gardens.

Most Were Pioneers.

To understand the tenacity of these people and their fight for their homes, it must be remembered the majority were pioneers – hard-working, simple, kindhearted people who believed in this last of the country's frontiers. They had fought off storm, flood and starvation. They knew hardships. Last week – the story must go back that far – there was issued a warning of an approaching storm. Only a few accepted the warning and left their homes. The majority stayed.

And so last Saturday because they chose to stand ground, there are today's death list and today's evacuation.

Horrors of the storm have been told. The story today is the evacuation. A part of the story must attempt to describe Moore Haven as it remains.

You have the choice of three ways to enter the place. You can motor comfortably to within about three miles of the town. From this point, a filling station, you must wade, must use a boat or wait for one of the high bodied military auto trucks.

If you wade you must go through water anywhere from knee-deep to waist deep. You also take the chance of wandering off the roadbed and slipping into a hole over your head. If you use a boat, you must have a guide, who knows the drainage canals as you know your streets.

Knows Drain Canals.

He knows the alleys and passage ways through the high weeds, wrecked buildings and debris. He learned them in searching for the storm's dead. If you have authority to pass the military and can find room on one of the trucks, you may get through and you may not.

The trucks have pushed out big holes in the water-softened road beds. Thoughtful soldiers have staked out most of the holes. If the truck slips into a new hole you get out into waist deep water and help it out. Anyway, you get wet.

Out here in what is left of this storm devastated little village, there is passing today the final trek of a band of hardy pioneers who fought a gamely courageous brave, but losing fight against the elements.

This trek is a funeral march. It is the death of Moore Haven. These pioneers are giving up the homes they fought to make and save, but lost. They are evacuating Moore Haven.

Exactly a week ago today, these pioneers anxious-

Small yacht washed into Royal Palm park, a block off the bay. The man is standing on dry ground in front. The windows of the big hotel were blown out.

The Meyer-Kiser building, a 14-story structure, in Miami's heart now being dismantled due to damage, which it was feared might cause it to collapse. When this photograph was taken, the building, which was bent in the middle by the wind, was leaning five feet over the street. Photo taken back of police dead line, one block away.

ly scanned the skies overhead. Lake Okeechobee, on whose shores they build their homes, tossed its angry waves high upon the banks. The darkened skies, the menacing waters. These were signs the old-timers here understood. A storm was brewing. They had weathered other storms. They looked forward with hope now.

The day passed. Saturday broke cloudier and gloomier; a few residents scurried like frightened rabbits, before the storm. By afternoon the storm had changed into a hurricane. It rained. It poured. The wind blew harder and harder. The lake joined the fiendish elements. The waters rose higher and higher. By half past one the hurricane sweeping and lashing its way across the lake, hurled rain, lake and wind against Moore Haven. The result is history now.

Final Chapter.

Today for some marks the final chapter in Moore Haven's history. Fear of disease and pestilence yesterday prompted health and mility [military] heads to order evacuation. The military was rushed here immediately after the storm for rescue and guard work, so today the military are carrying out the death order.

Here is the order, posted yesterday upon a huge elm standing sentinel upon one of the dikes:

Moore Haven, Sept. 23

"To All Citizens of Moore Haven and Vicinity:

"Upon advice from state medical officers, Sheriff Richards has instructed the national guard troops to evacuate all citizens from the overflowed district of Glades county immediately.

"The S.S. Priscilla will be available Friday, Sept. 24, for transportation of citizens to railroad bridge at Ortona, from whence railroad transportation will be provided to Sebring or other nearby towns and any citizen desiring transportation will report to Moore Haven Lock No. 1.

"All citizens must evacuate (leave) at 12 o'clock, noon, Friday, Sept. 24, 1926.

"By order of

"COLONEL LOWRY."

Arrangements have been made to take care of all refugees at Sebring. Troops will remain on guard until the citizens are allowed to return to their homes.

Tampa Daily Times, September 25, 1926:

Horror and Comedy Paint Vivid Scenes of Flood Area

By RONDO HATTON. (Times Staff Writer.)

Sebring, Sept. 25. – Enjoying their first real relaxation after the tension and grief of days clouded by hurricane and death, survivors here last night related stories of horror, comedy and heroism born in the hurricane which swept from them all they possessed.

These stories were drawn from the last of the refugees brought out of the stricken Moore Haven district.

There is the story of L.P. Ray, fisherman, caught on Lake Okeechobee. The storm sank his boat. He swam, floated and battled the tossed waters for hours., when almost exhausted he drifted into shallow waters. He joined rescue parties later and helped at Lakeport and Moore Haven. Now after two years in the section, he is leaving it for good. He will move to Grand Ridge, Fla.

Then there is the story of Alfonso Deyeart and his son, Frank, of Lakeport. When the storm broke Deyeart was alone at home. Like nearly all others in the section who had been through previous floods, he did not think the flood would be any worse than the others.

The waters kept rising. Deyeart thought of his chickens and livestock. He waded around his home and after many trips carried over 100 chickens into one of his bedrooms.

Sees Waters Rise.

About this time, Frank came home. He drove the school bus between Lakeport and Moore Haven. They scanned the skies. They watched the water steadily rising. They realized that unless they got out and got out quickly they would probably drown like rats in a trap.

They rushed into the house and snatched what food and clothing they could. They waded through the water to the bus. Then they remembered the chickens and cows. Deyeart managed to get to his cow. He cut it free from its rope. He started to the house with Frank, but before they could reach it the waters snatched it up and twisted it to pieces. They swam back to the bus and climbed to its top. The waters kept rising. A section of the floor of their home drifted towards them. it came nearer and nearer. They made a desperate leap for it, almost missed, but managed to cling on. They floated around but 10 minutes when a huge wave struck their raft and turned it up almost endwise. Deyeart was knocked from the raft. He drifted one way, Frankie another on the raft. Deyeart attempted to reach the raft. The waves buffeted him. Time after time, he almost was within reach of the raft when the waves drove him back. He came near again and made a desperate grab. He barely caught and hung on when Frank twined his legs around him. They drifted for three hours when the raft finally stuck in shallow water.

Cow is Unhurt.

Too fatigued to move, the men lay still several minutes. In a while they struggled to their feet. Imagine their surprise when they saw within a few feet of them the sow unhurt, which Deyeart had cut loose three hours before.

He left the cow and started wading back towards the town. As they drew near they found August Van Brock and his family marooned on the top of their home. They made their way there and joined the party. All were hungry and tired. The men made their way through the water to Brock's store and found some canned goods.

Deyeart was one of the first settles in the Lakeport section. He left there today never to return, unless some means is provided to prevent a recurrence of last week's tragedy. He plans to go to Miami temporarily and work as a carpenter.

Recovery from the storm at Miami is rapid. Here is a downtown scene Monday [September 20, 1926], showing resumption of traffic.

Chris Hutchinson, 70-year-old farmer, clung to pieces of his home when it was torn to bits. Finally he was tossed upon the bank of the canal. He lay there all night. despite his experiences he is going to return to Moore Haven as soon as the waters recede.

The homes of E.A. Winslow, retired farmer and Moore Haven hotel proprietor, withstood the storm. Winslow escaped by remaining with the house. He is going back to Moore Haven as soon as they will let him.

A.J. Thielen and his family explained their escape as an act of providence. The waters tore their home from its foundation and it began drifting. Another house floated by. They clung to this and remained on its top until the storm passed.

Demand Safety.

Mr. Thielen is a farmer and has spent six years in Moore Haven. He wants to go back there but not until all danger is removed.

Mr. and Mrs. W.T. Holt and two children sought safety on the second floor of their home where they were held prisoners from Saturday morning until Sunday morning. Mr. Holt is a section master and helped operate the first rail motorcars used in rescue work. He has been busy rebuilding railway tracks. He lost everything.

"Glad I got my family out," he said, "I'm not whipped and I will go back as soon as they build new quarters for me."

Members of nine Lakeport families will always love cypress trees. These families took refuge on a high rim of the lake during the storm. The high waters forced them to cling to the limbs of cypress trees for safety.

H.D. Stewart, one of the survivors, declared only courage and trees prevented drownings.

L.L. Hooker is another saved by trees. He lost everything but his hope, he said. He is going back to his old home to live as soon as he can.

One Moore Haven family beat death in a grim race between their auto and the water. M.S. Chase, county superintendent of schools, put his wife and children hin his auto and started to leave when waters rushed in and wrecked the machine.

Gets Car.

He ran to a garage and got his old car and started again. They ran across another family marooned in a car drowned out by water. Chase hooked up a tow rope and dragged the other car out behind his own. He plans to return to Moore Haven.

C. Eugene Smith, partner in the Wainwright Chevrolet company, and family, had a terrifying experience.

Miami waterfront loss. Vessels washed onto shore. At bottom are yachts scattered through park.

With Mrs. Smith and his three children, one 20 months old, one five, and another seven, he stood on chairs until the waters drove them to table tops. The waters kept rising and Smith put the sewing machine on top of one table and chairs on another. He put his two little girls on top of the sewing machine while he and Mrs. Smith, with the baby stood on the chairs.

Driven inch by inch from the ground to the attic, N.S. Wainwright, former Tampan and now circuit court clerk at Moore Haven and family owe their lives to the fact the waters stopped rising when they did. Mr. Wainwright had six relatives in his home when the storm caught them. none of the party was lost.

Between 20 and 30 persons, including one Tampan, were saved by taking refuge on the second story of the Parkinson brick building. Miss Bertha Gram was the Tampan saved. She was in Moore Haven doing special work.

Ed Ciminger, farmer, escaped the storm which came while he was in Fort Myers superintending loading of vegetables. He obtained a taste of the storm in Fort Myers and rushed home to his family to find Mrs. Ciminger dead and four sons were saved. He will return to Moore Haven when the waters recede.

Home is Wedged.

The opportune wedging of his home between two others is believed responsible by Mr. Valaer, court attache, for the saving of his life and three others during the storm. The storm tore the Valaer home from its foundation and washed it a block away. In the home during this perilous ride were Mr. and Mrs. Valaer and two women roomers. The house finally was blocked and wedged tightly between two other houses.

Loel Lence waded with his family two blocks through waist deep water to the brick school house where they took refuge on the second floor with 16 others, including many children. Darkness caught them without light. Searching about the building they found some candles but none had a match. Another long search, one lone match was found in a child's desk. They struck the match with anxiety. Sixteen faces broke into smiles when the candle sent up its feeble light.

"Oxton 'Orror, I Called Him!"
The Screen Bow of Rondo Hatton's Hoxton Creeper
By Tom Weaver

Aptly titled, *The Pearl of Death* is the jewel in the crown of Universal's Sherlock Holmes series *and*, in fact, one of the studio's best '40s horror films.

With director Roy William Neill at his customary post at the helm, this Holmes adventure began production on April 11, 1944, and wrapped 18 working days later, on May 1. Forty-nine-year-old Rondo Hatton signed his contract ($350 a week on a one-week guarantee) on April 18 and was on Stage 6 at nine the next morning, along with Basil Rathbone and Nigel Bruce (as Holmes and Watson), Dennis Hoey (as Inspector Lestrade) and Miles Mander (as the Hoxton Creeper's master, Giles Conover). It was the first of three days spent photographing the scenes set at Dr. Boncourt's home, a suspense-packed nine-and-a-half minutes that caps the picture. The action that takes place in the doctor's anteroom and corridor was shot on the 19th. Late in the day, there was a trip to the back lot where, outside the St. Claire Home (built for Universal's 1927 silent *Uncle Tom's Cabin*), director Neill filmed the exterior scene of Conover and the Creeper (Mander and Hatton) arriving at Dr. Boncourt's house by chauffeured car and gaining access through the servants' entrance. (An unexpected touch: Archfiend Conover mounts the stairs to the house and, without stopping or even stooping, he reaches down to scratch the head of an appreciative cat.)

Rathbone, Mander and Hatton spent all of the next day, April 20, and most of the 21st, on the Boncourt Lab set. Amusingly, because Rondo did the movie's last scene first, the Hoxton Creeper paid the ultimate

Throughout *Pearl of Death*, you see the Hoxton Creeper as a back-lit silhouette, or from behind, or just his shadow (as pictured in top photo), and anticipation builds. Contrast that with the Creeper movies *House of Horrors* and *The Brute Man* where we see a big closeup of Rondo's mug during the opening credits, even before the movies start!

price for his crimes (Holmes shoots and kills him) before *committing* any crimes on film!

Hatton having now done the finale where the Hoxton Creeper's face is seen by viewers for the first time, all of his subsequent work was in the Creeper "build-up" scenes in which d.p. Virgil Miller's camera gives us partial glimpses of the maniac, photographs him from the back, in silhouette, etc. The same day that they wrapped up the Boncourt House scenes, the 21st, Hatton and Mander did the Conover's Bedroom scene where Conover taunts Naomi on the phone ("[The Creeper's] devotion to you is most touching!") with the shadow of the hat-wearing, cigarette-puffing Creeper cast on a wall behind him. The two actors were dismissed at 5:20.

Hatton had a day off on Saturday, April 22—his 50th birthday—while director Neill shot Holmes and Watson's visit to the plasterers' shop, and then the amusing 221-B Baker Street scene in which Conover (disguised as "Theophilus Kirby, Lord Farnsworth's uncle and biographer") drops in on Watson. A day of rest, Sunday the 23rd, and then Hatton returned to work. He was allowed to arrive at two in the afternoon, because his scene wasn't going to be shot until late in the day: on the Process Stage, the Creeper in the tonneau of Conover's limousine en route to Boncourt's. We see the shadow of his head (including his monkey-like profile) on a car window shade, and then his gloved hands stroking Naomi's vanity case.

Hatton had another day off and then worked for the last time on the 26th: the scene where the Creeper, observed only by a scared cat, enters the Sandeford home through a library window and gives Sandeford (Arthur Mulliner) an unsolicited spinal work-out.

Hatton was dismissed at noon that day, the actor leaving the lot unaware that he'd just spent a week making movie history: He had brought life to the Creeper, the final fiend in the Universal Classic Monster Pantheon.

Script Excerpts from *The Pearl of Death*

Brutish, powerful henchmen can be found in several of the Universal Sherlock Holmes movies—for example, Gubec in *Pursuit to Algiers* (1945) and Hamid in *Dressed to Kill* (1946)—but none got the horror movie–style build-up that *The Pearl of Death*'s Creeper did. This made me wonder if Bertram Millhauser's *Pearl* script called for that type of build-up, or if someone else (director Neill?) had the idea after the casting of Rondo Hatton, he of the "Face That Launched a Thousand Shits."

I got a-hold of a *Pearl* script (dated March 28, 1944) and it turns out that Millhauser did call for the frightening build-up; for this brute to have an "unspeakable" face; and for the "reveal" of that face to be held off until the final reel.

On the pages that follow are the *Pearl* script pages that describe Creeper appearances—and you'll notice a few differences between these script descriptions and the action that made it onto film.

#1 describes the Creeper's late-night invasion of Thomas Sandeford's home. In the movie, we see Sandeford walk through the archway curtains into the library and we watch as he's grabbed from behind by the silhouetted Creeper, who puts a hurtin' on Sandeford's third lumbar vertebra as the old man sinks to the floor. In Millhauser's script, Sandeford goes through curtains (and out of our sight) into the dining room, and we hear a cry. The camera then sweeps down to the floor and pushes into the dining room, "and we SEE Sandeford's slippered feet lifted into the air…." The remaining moments of the on-screen scene are also different from the script.

#2 is the scene where Conover, in his bedroom, takes a call from Naomi, who's phoning from Amos Hodder's Art Shop's stock room. In the movie, we see Conover plainly in this scene, but the script calls for him to be a silhouette. The script also specifies a wide shot so that we simultaneously see both the silhouetted Conover *and* the Creeper's shadow. Best of all: the script indicates that the Creeper is making a "soft, whimpering noise."

#3 is the shot of the Creeper riding in the back of Conover's limo, stroking Naomi's vanity case. In the movie, it's closed; in the script, he's exploring its contents.

And **#4** is the climax at Dr. Boncourt's. There are a number of small differences between script and screen; for instance, in the movie, we first see the Creeper's face in the anteroom, but in the script, we don't see it until he's breaking Conover's back in the lab: "An unspeakable face—under-lighted—like Frederick [sic] March as Mr. Hyde." In the movie, the Creeper stalks an armed Holmes but we don't see the detective fire; instead, we *hear* three shots as we watch Watson, Lestrade and two constables arriving at Boncourt's side door. The script calls for us to see Holmes shoot twice, the Creeper leaping high in the air both times and then dropping to the floor at Holmes' feet.

"PEARL OF DEATH" - CHANGES - 4/3/44

71

INT. SANFORD'S DINING ROOM - <u>NIGHT</u> - CLOSEUP - CURTAIN POLE AND METAL RINGS

As the curtain is swept back, the metal rings make a characteristic SOUND along the pole. TILT CAMERA DOWN - to PICK UP the SHADOW of the Creeper on the moonlit floor as he ENTERS. CAMERA PANS along floor, following the SHADOW until it stops stock still on the carpet. CAMERA PANS <u>AWAY</u> from the shadow. It crosses carpet to:

THE SEAT OF AN UPHOLSTERED CHAIR - CLOSE. A black cat is asleep on it. We SEE the sudden gleam of its eyes in the soft darkness. Now it jumps up - streaks OUT OF SCENE!

CAMERA PANS to a sideboard, laden with silver, a-gleam in the moonlight. It slides along the wall - CLOSE! - past a cabinet of china - PAST a plate rail on which are jugs and plates and little <u>plaster</u> figures. CAMERA stops on the little plaster figures, as --

SOUND: A DOOR OPENING somewhere, OFF SCENE.

178   MED. CLOSE - SHADOW OF CREEPER - ON CARPET - <u>NIGHT</u>

At the SOUND of the DOOR CLOSING - shadow darts across the carpet. CAMERA FOLLOWS SHADOW in its eccentric motion across carpet and up to <u>the curtains that hang across the archway into the hall</u>.

PUSH CAMERA UP CLOSE to the curtains that hang across the archway into the hall. Now the rubber-gloved hand of the Creeper comes up INTO SCENE and moves the curtains - ever so little! - as if the Creeper himself were peering through into the hall. SOUND: FOOTSTEPS on the hall stair.

179   INT. SANDFORDHALL - <u>NIGHT</u> - CLOSE MOVING SHOT

A man's slippered feet descend the stair. The bottom of his bathrobe flaps around his bare ankles. The lighting is <u>DIM</u> from a single, low-watt bulb in the hall above.

PAN CAMERA to show THOMAS SANDEFORD descending the stair, half asleep - his hair disheveled. He's a middle-aged man. He pauses at the foot of the stair, muttering:

              SANDEFORD
     Blast that cat! I'd swear I put
     her out!

180   OMITTED

181 ANGLE SHOWING CURTAINS ACROSS ARCHWAY IN FGD. - <u>NIGHT</u>

We are SHOOTING PAST the curtains of the archway, in CAMERA FGD. The curtains move - just a little! - and we know the Creeper is behind them, in the dining room!

Sandeford - paused at the foot of the stair - starts forward toward the curtains - and we realize he's shuffling toward his death. He fumbles along the wall beside the archway - nearer and nearer to the curtains all the time!

                SANDEFORD
        Where's that blasted switch...

He comes abreast of the curtains - and sees the slit of moonlight from the dining room beyond.

                SANDEFORD
        That's funny. I'm sure I drew
        those dining room curtains...

He goes through archway curtains into dining room. We HEAR a CHOKED CRY.

CAMERA SWEEPS DOWN to floor - pushes into dining room - and we SEE Sandeford's slippered feet lifted into the air -- we HEAR his CRY --

CAMERA PULLS BACK into the HALLWAY, and TILTS UP to curtains. There is a moment of awful silence - then Sandeford's body falls back through the curtains in a spinless heap and lies quite dead on the hall floor. CAMERA HOLDS on the curtains. They fall quiet.

SOUND: The CLICK of an electric switch in the dining room behind the curtains. Through the slit we SEE ELECTRIC LIGHT take the place of moonlight in the dining room. SOUND: CHINA SMASHING - one thing after another!

                                    DISSOLVE

182 THREE INSERTS. - NEWSPAPER HEADLINES

    (A)   TWO MORE MURDERS IN A SINGLE NIGHT!

    (B)   DEADLY WORK OF BACK BREAKER!

    (C)   MANIAC SLAYER STILL AT LARGE!

                                      DISSOLVE

240   INT. CONOVER'S BEDROOM - <u>NIGHT</u> - CLOSEUP CONOVER

just his head and shoulders, <u>in silhouette</u> - at telephone on desk. Very dim lighting, from a single lamp OFF SCENE. A cigarette lighter shows his face momentarily - then snaps out - as he speaks <u>quietly</u>:

      CONOVER
  Thanks, my dear. That's what I
  wanted to know. I shall start at
  once. Meet me in two hours -
  same place ... Eh?
    (chuckles)
  Of course he's here! He's right
  behind me...

CAMERA PANS from Conover's CLOSEUP to the wall. Silhouetted on the wall is the grotesque, enormous SHADOW of the Hoxton Creeper!

SOUND: A soft, whimpering noise.

259   EXT. SUBURBAN STREET - <u>NIGHT</u> - LONG SHOT

Conover's limousine comes tearing toward CAMERA.

260   CLOSE - ON DRIVER'S SEAT - MOVING LIMOUSINE - <u>NIGHT</u>

Conover is seated beside the driver - the one who drove the taxi on the street outside Harker's house. The curtain to the tonneau is drawn down behind their heads.

                    CONOVER
                  (low-voiced)
         Drive slowly. I shouldn't care
         to be picked up with our passen-
         ger in the back.

                    DRIVER
                  (slows down)
         He's pretty quiet back there.
         What's he up to?

Conover lifts the edge of the curtains - peers back into the tonneau - says:

                    CONOVER
         He has Naomi's vanity case.

261   CLOSE - ON BACK SEAT - MOVING LIMOUSINE - <u>NIGHT</u>

Naomi's vanity case lies open in the Creeper's hands. He is exploring the contents.

                                        DISSOLVE:

CLOSE - CONOVER

          CONOVER
You know who.
    (turns slightly -
     calls:)
Creeper!

PAN from Conover's CLOSEUP - to the gleaming curtains. The huge, shapeless shadow of the Creeper appears on the curtains, as he shuffles forward from the corridor door, across anteroom, toward the arch. And as the shadow advances, it becomes sharper all the time!

296   HEAD CLOSEUP - HOLMES

in shocked reaction to what he sees on curtains.

297   MED. WIDE - TOWARD CURTAINS - (HOLMES' ANGLE)

with Conover standing to one side - as the shadow of the Creeper comes ever closer - smaller and sharper - until it is just outside the arch! Conover halts it:

          CONOVER
Stay where you are. Listen carefully. Go to the living room - that door with the light over it. You know what to look for.

298   CLOSEUP - CONOVER

his gun on Holmes - his eyes on Holmes - but speaking to the SHADOW, just OUT OF SCENE:

          CONOVER
And if you come across Doctor Boncourt - pay him your respects.

299   CLOSE - HOLMES

as he stares off - realizes the desperate need to save Boncourt's life as well as his own!

300   ANGLE TOWARD CURTAINS

as the SHADOW of the Creeper recedes - grows larger - more diffuse - on his way to the living room door.

lc

301   CLOSE - HOLMES

   watching the shadow recede. Now he makes his bid!

                    HOLMES
                 (raised voice)
           You'll hang for this, Conover!
           Just as Naomi Drake will hang!

302   ANGLE TOWARD CURTAINS

   Still the shadow recedes - as Holmes' VOICE COMES OVER:

                    HOLMES' VOICE
           We caught Naomi Drake, you know!

   PAN DOWN to Conover - CLOSE - as he smiles and says:

                    CONOVER
           Too bad! That's her lookout.

                    HOLMES
                 (for the Creeper's ear)
           It was your fault, Conover - all your
           fault. Poor Naomi!

303   INT. ANTEROOM - CLOSEUP - CREEPER'S FEET

   moving across thick carpet to living room door.

                    HOLMES
                      (o.s.)
           I shouldn't let the Creeper know,
           if I were you.
                 (THE FEET STOP)
           He wouldn't like it, if he knew you
           let Naomi down.

304   INT. LAB - CLOSEUP - HOLMES

                    HOLMES
           He's crazy about Naomi, you know.
                 (glances at curtain)
           She's a very pretty girl, Naomi is!

305   CLOSE - CONOVER

                    CONOVER
           Trying to scare me? It won't work.
           You've got nothing on Naomi. She'll
           get off.

306   CLOSE - HOLMES

                    HOLMES
              (pounding on it)
        Oh, no, she won't. She lost her
        head, you see. When she found she
        was cornered, she grabbed up a big
        pair of shears and stabbed Doctor
        Watson!
              (glances at curtains)

307   INT. ANTEROOM - CLOSEUP - CREEPER'S FEET - NIGHT

                    HOLMES (o.s.)
        She'll hang for that, you know!
        And it's all your fault, Conover!
        You got her into this.

    The Creeper's feet turn - pigeon-toe back toward arch! -
    soundlessly over the thick-piled carpet.

308   INT. LAB. - NIGHT - CLOSE - HOLMES

                    HOLMES
        And you won't lift a hand to save her!
              (looks at curtain)

309   ANGLE TOWARD CURTAINS

    as SHADOW of Creeper comes ever closer - sharper!
    (Conover, with his back to the curtains, isn't aware
    of it!)

                    HOLMES' VOICE
        She'll hang by her soft white neck -
        and the trusties will put their hands
        on that pretty body of hers and throw
        it into quick lime!

    SOUND: A ROAR of grief and fury!

    Now the curtains are swept aside - a gorilla-like arm
    goes round Conover's neck - he SCREAMS - and drops his
    gun! Holmes dives for it --

310   CLOSE - ON FLOOR

    as Holmes darts down INTO SCENE - reaching under some
    article of furniture, for Conover's gun!

311	CLOSE - CONOVER - AND THE CREEPER!

For the first time we see the Creeper - over Conover's shoulder - as he drags Conover back through the curtains - and out of sight! (An unspeakable face - under-lighted - like Frederick March as Mr. Hyde.)

312	CLOSE - HOLMES

He recovers Conover's gun - rises - dashes toward curtains.

313	MED. ANGLE - AT CURTAINS

Holmes steps quickly toward the curtained arch - just as Conover, limp, spineless, falls through the curtains and onto the floor at his feet.

Holmes draws back, gun in hand.

A big oblong of light falls on the floor of lab. where the curtains have been flung aside. In this oblong of light falls the SHADOW of the Creeper, advancing on Holmes, as he retreats.

314	CLOSEUP - HOLMES

retreating - gun in hand.

     HOLMES
  Keep back!

315	CLOSEUP - CREEPER

The hideous face - dim against the light behind him - advances.

316	CLOSEUP - HOLMES

     HOLMES
    (retreating)
  Keep back, I tell you!

317	CLOSEUP - CREEPER

smearing past CAMERA

318	CLOSEUP - HOLMES

retreating. Now his gun speaks - once - twice ---

319   CLOSE - CREEPER

as he leaps into the air, clutching at his heart --

320   REVERSE - FROM ARCHWAY -

with Holmes' face in the light - and the Creeper's silhouette between him and CAMERA - as the Creeper leaps high - clutching at his heart - and falls at Holmes' feet. Just in time! For at this moment Holmes has brought up with his back against the dissecting table.

Rondo Hatton's The Old Dark House
Dwight V. Babcock's Story Idea

As promised on page 88, here is Dwight V. Babcock's story "The Creeper #2—Idea: *The House of Horrors*," dated December 8, 1944:

First establish The Creeper as a psychopathic killer who roams the countryside at night, visiting towns and villages in the vicinity of a bleak and lonely house. His true identity is not known, for whenever seen by people, they shrink from him in horror because of his appearance and, enraged, he kills them. but his method of murder is always the same: he breaks their backs with sub-human strength.

A reign of terror grips the community. The countryside is aroused and alarmed, but the authorities are helpless as they have no lead to the identity of The Creeper.

Then the storm – a flash flood – and people, travelers on the road, become marooned and are forced to ask shelter at the lonesome old house. Among them are the boy and girl leads who may (or may not) thus meet for the first time.

The door is opened by The Creeper, who frightens them by his appearance and at first refuses to allow them admittance. He warns them away – triers to get rid of them. We, as the audience, know he is the killer who has terrorized the community. But the marooned travelers, ignorant of their danger, insist on shelter in the house. When ordered to admit them by one of the owners, The Creeper sullenly obeys.

The Creeper is a servant in the house, and the family too is made up of weird and frightening characters, as in The Old Dark House – the fanatical old lady, her brother, the old dying man, and his crazy son who is kept locked in a room with The Creeper as his guard.

The Creeper, with the advent of outsiders, is now alarmed for fear his identity as the killer will be discovered. This alarm, and the consequent menace to the leads and others, is increased when the owners are questioned about him and he overhears. The visitors are naturally curious as to why the family keeps such a horrible creature as a servant and ask who he is, where he came from, and etc.

The already considerable horror of the house and tits occupants is increased by efforts of The Creeper, as he tries in various ways to frighten the visitors into leaving. But much as they would like to go, they are trapped by the flood and it is impossible for them to get away. The Creeper cannot kill as long as they remain in a group. But as various individuals are left alone, he becomes a real and frightening menace.

At one or more points in the story, the girl or girls involved are thus threatened. They are terrorized out of their wits. But The Creeper becomes fascinated with one girl, and is interrupted at the last moment before we learn whether his purpose is actually murder in her case or rape. This choice of objectives is, of course, only suggested by The Creeper's manner with this particular girl.

> Base the story on the situation and characters in *The Old Dark House* – The Creeper (Rondo Hatton) to play a part similar but more important than that taken by Karloff.

Facing page: A make-believe poster for the never-made Rondo Hatton-starring *Old Dark House* remake, created for this book by artist **George Chastain**. You can see many other examples of George's monstrous art and research posted on his Facebook timeline and archived in his Facebook albums: https://www.facebook.com/george.chastain.13

During the night, The Creeper succeeds in killing one or two of the visitors by breaking their backs. He then throws their bodies down the stairs. When they are found, it is at first thought that they have fallen and been killed accidentally. But the lead becomes suspicious of The Creeper's real identity, because the manner of death is the same as in cases of murder which have terrorized the nearby communities.

He confides his suspicions to the other men. Trapped by the storm and the flood, it is impossible for them to get away, but they agree to watch and attempt to overpower The Creeper.

In one of his efforts to frighten the unwelcome visitors away from the house where he has found sanctuary, The Creeper releases the crazy man who is in his charge. The rest of the family seem terrified, and succeed in frightening the visitors. The appearance of the family lunatic is played for suspense, as in The Old Dark House, and when he finally does appear he seems to be a harmless little fellow.

He pleads with the lead not to lock him up again. He says that The Creeper is a monster who beats him, and claims that he is not crazy but that the others in the house are persecuting him because he knows they conspired to murder another member of the family. The man seems rational, and is believed by the lead. The lead agrees to protect him from the other members of the family and to help him get away when they all can leave.

At this point, the visitors seem surrounded by evil and menace, trapped in a house filled with murderers. Later, after convincing them of his sanity, the crazy man shows a surprising reversal of form, and it becomes obvious that he is actually mad as a hatter. He goes through the knife routine with the lead (as in The Old Dark House), ending in the struggle and fall to his death from the balcony.

The Creeper is grief-stricken at the death of his charge, and then becomes enraged. This leads to the climax in which, going berserk and attempting mass murder, The Creeper very nearly succeeds in killing everyone in the house, but is finally subdued and overpowered.

Morning. The sun shines; the birds sing. The Creeper has been taken into custody (later to escape and commit further crimes). Their night of horror seems like a nightmare, now that daylight has come. The boy and girl go off, on their way, to start a new life together.

Hollywood's Strangest Love Story

An article on Rondo from the July 1946 issue of Pageant magazine.

You might have seen only his ugly face. *She* saw the beauty of soul behind it

Hollywood's Strangest Love Story

By Erma Taylor

Rondo died a few months ago—Rondo Hatton, the Creeper, Hollywood's most recent horror hero. He died too soon for most Americans to know his face or his work well. Or his story. His was one of the strangest careers in Hollywood and one of the most courageous. He didn't want the story told while he lived; but he'd want it told now. Particularly to maimed veterans of World War II.

For Rondo Hatton, the ugliest man in pictures, had the happiest marriage in Hollywood. And his wife, May, is one of the most beautiful women even the city of films has ever seen.

As I said, it's a strange story, a horrible story, and yet beautiful. Rondo was the horror star signed up by Universal to replace Boris Karloff. Perhaps you've seen him in *The House of Horrors* or *The Brute Man*. But did you know that what you shuddered at was Rondo's real face?

Rondo was used to people's staring at the grotesque mask he wore always. He'd had to get used to it, the last 20 years. His fellow workers in the studios were used to his ugliness, too, and he was the most popular actor on the Universal lot. Because, when you finally got past the face, you found there was a swell person underneath, without pretense and without bitterness. Rondo had suffered too much ever to hold such barriers between himself and any other human being.

His early life was as happy and normal as any boy's. His father was president of a Maryland girls' college, and Rondo was born in the infirmary there. But the petticoat influence was not permanent and football became the boy's consuming passion. Despite a scant 136 pounds, he became captain of his University of Florida team, and he was named quarterback on the 1913 All-Star Southern Eleven. And not just once but *twice* he was voted the handsomest boy in his class in his Florida home town of Hillsborough, where he lived during his high-school years. (I've seen his school annuals, and I can vouch that the collar ads have nothing Rondo didn't have then.)

But that was before the last war. The war brought on his affliction. The doctors call it acromegaly, a rare disease which causes enlargement of the bones of the head. The assumption is that Rondo's case was caused when he was gassed on the Western front. At any rate, ten of the past 28 years Rondo had spent in hospitals from Connecticut to California. His case has made Ripley's *Believe It or Not* column, and there are reams about it in medical books and reports. His face bones increased to nearly double their normal size, distorting his features into frightening proportions. His weight went up to 204 pounds, and much of the gain was in the extra bone and cartilage that deformed his face and feet, his head and hands.

In one series of operations his cheek bones were taken out and replaced with metal. The lower jaw grew out so far his lower teeth extended at least an inch beyond his uppers, and it required several more operations and four sets of teeth before Rondo could chew again. No number of operations, however, could wholly alleviate the appearance or the excruciating pain. For a long time he was blind, and the ache in his bones, he once said, was like a migraine headache all over his body.

Rondo was still young when he came home from an early hospital siege, and his parents did not recognize him. That was a special kind of excruciating pain. Former girl friends crossed the street for fear he'd ask for a date.

"Facing the people you knew, seeing the shock and pity and horror in their eyes—that's tougher than anything that ever happened at the front," he told me. "To any casualty, the hardest part of war is coming home."

At first he tried to achieve his original ambition of becoming a football coach. But his pain-racked body couldn't stand exertion. Complicating the physical strain was the emotional. It seemed that everyone he passed on the street made some remark. What hurt most was the furtive whisper, "I'd hate to meet him in the dark."

"Finally you get to where your only impulse is to hide, run away, stay out of sight in hospitals, forever!" It was an effort for Rondo to remember those days, but he continued. "However, you can't stand yourself for long, running away. It's the sympathy that gets you, most of all self-sympathy. It's an insidious poison that gets into your soul, as this thing I've got gets into your bones.

"In a veterans' hospital, you see so many guys so much worse off than you are that—well, if there's anything left in you, you quit feeling sorry for yourself."

So Rondo had a long talk with himself one day, and he decided the best thing he could do was the hardest thing he could think of—to face people, new people, all the time. That's exactly why he chose reporting as a career.

He got a job on a newspaper in Tampa and became a good reporter, the best known and liked in town. Finally he was made sports editor, and he thought he'd found his right niche. He was no longer vulnerable about his face. He thought this was happiness.

And then he met May. He was covering a masquerade ball for his newspaper, and he saw her sitting on a stairway, about to fall asleep. She was the dressmaker for the hostess, and she'd been up all the night before sewing costumes.

"She looked like a tired little angel," explained Rondo. "Angel" is the word everyone uses for May. Her blondeness is so pure and natural that her beauty is always a kind of shock in Hollywood, capital of bleached albinism.

It's easy to see why Rondo fell in love with her. And May had been married once to a handsome man; she had learned to value more than looks. Rondo's appreciation and devotion and his unfailing kindness were to her the miracle of miracles. After 11 years together, Rondo still felt May was an angel, and May still felt Rondo's love was a miracle.

They went to Hollywood in 1938. Rondo had had a siege with arthritis, one of the many complications of his case. In 1937 he couldn't even walk, and the doctors advised California. It was then that Rondo remembered film director Henry King.

Back in 1929 King and a Fox film unit had come to Tampa to make *Hell's Harbor*. Rondo was a reporter then, and his editor had assigned him to cover the event. King, always on the alert for interesting types, insisted on casting Hatton as a pirate, replete with a patch over one eye. Afterward King tried to persuade Rondo to come to Hollywood. Rondo figured Tampa was used to his face; there was no point in pushing his luck.

But now, nine years later, he was just out of a veterans' hospital and out of a job. Hollywood seemed as good a bet as any. If people would pay to be scared by his face, what had he to lose? He wrote to King.

The director was right. Rondo's face was different enough to be interesting. People didn't forget it, to be sure, but neither did the movies know exactly what to do with it. In his first three years in Hollywood Rondo was in 23 pictures, but they weren't even bread and beans. Till his 100th role, as the Creeper in the chiller *The House of Horrors,* Rondo paid the rent by reporting for the Inglewood *Daily News*. The Creeper made him. It brought in an avalanche of mail, and Universal signed him to a seven-year contract. When Boris Karloff left the studio, Rondo was made a full-fledged star. And then, last February, Rondo had a heart attack that ended his long fight forever.

But I doubt if he minded missing stardom. Rondo was first and foremost a war veteran; he'd spent his youth in the Army, and what should have been his best years in hospitals among the disabled. Even after he'd become a prominent actor he spent every spare moment among young veterans, making them laugh.

"Look at me, boys—you won't believe it, but I won a beauty contest once," he'd say. And then, when he'd amused them into forgetting themselves, Rondo put every ounce of sincerity and faith he had into—not a lecture, but a heartfelt sermon. Life was still good, he told them. There was still a job ahead for them to do. There was still happiness ahead for them, too.

And if Rondo hadn't been so modest, the best proof he could have offered was his own story: the miracle of a man with a face grotesque beyond belief, who had won and kept the devotion of the most beautiful wife in Hollywood.

MEDICAL MARVELS
Acromegaly, Gigantism, and Other Awesome Afflictions

RONDO HATTON—Acromegalic journalist, actor (5'11", 182 lbs. *); Apr 22 1894-Feb 2 1946. His horror & adventure films (1930-1946) include *Hell Harbor, In Old Chicago, Captain Fury, The Hunchback of Notre Dame, Chad Hanna, Tales of Manhattan, The Moon and Sixpence, The Ox-Bow Incident, Johnny Doesn't Live Here Any More, The Pearl of Death, The Princess and the Pirate, Jungle Captive, The Royal Mounted Rides Again, The Spider Woman Strikes Back, House of Horrors* and *The Brute Man.*

* info from his April 1942 Draft Registration Card

BRUTE-Y IS IN THE EYE OF THE BEHOLDER

   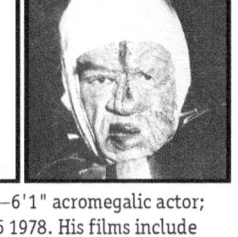  

MICHAEL BERRYMAN—6'2" actor afflicted with Hypohidrotic Ectodermal Dysplasia; born Sep 4 1948. His films include *Doc Savage: The Man of Bronze, One Flew Over the Cuckoo's Nest, The Hills Have Eyes* & sequel (r.), *Weird Science, Star Trek IV & V, The Guyver, Spy Hard, The Devil's Rejects, Army of the Damned*; TV: *The Fall Guy, Highway to Heaven, Star Trek: The Next Generation, Alf, Tales from the Crypt, The X-Files, Conan* and many more big and small screen roles.

HARRY WILSON—6'1" acromegalic actor; Nov 22 1897-Sep 6 1978. His films include *The Mad Genius, Dante's Inferno, Modern Times,* the *Flash Gordon, Batman & The Phantom Creeps* serials, *The Wizard of Oz, One Million B.C., Hold That Ghost, Brute Force, Macbeth, Unknown Island, A&C Meet J&H, Them!, Frankenstein's Daughter* (r.), *Some Like It Hot, Pocketful of Miracles, Robin and the 7 Hoods*; TV: *Alfred Hitchcock Presents, Peter Gunn, Johnny Staccato, Thriller, The Untouchables.*

AGOSTINO BORGATO—5'10" acromegalic actor born in Italy Jun 30 1871; died Mar 14 1939. He directed and acted in silent films in Italy and worked with many great stars and directors in Hollywood films including *The Eagle, A Woman of Affairs, The Show, Romance, The Maltese Falcon* ('31), *Murders in the Rue Morgue, A Farewell to Arms, Bird of Paradise* (r.), *Mad Love, Rose Marie, Maytime, Daughter of Shanghai, Swiss Miss, The Three Musketeers* ('39) and many others.

Don't just stand there—LURCH!

TED CASSIDY (Theodore Crawford Cassidy)— 6'9" acromegalic actor; Jul 31 1932-Jan 16 1979. Best known as Lurch (l.) on television's *The Addams Family*, and for his towering performances in a few films like *Mackenna's Gold* and *Butch Cassidy and the Sundance Kid*, and in many other TV shows including *The Man/The Girl from U.N.C.L.E., Lost in Space, Star Trek, The Beverly Hillbillies, I Dream of Jeannie, Tarzan, The Bionic Woman* and *The Six Million Dollar Man* (Bigfoot, bottom l.). He also did voices in hundreds of TV cartoons.

Every girl's crazy 'bout a shark-toothed man

RICHARD KIEL (Richard Dawson Kiel)— 7'2" acromegalic actor; Sep 13 1939-Sep 10 2014. Best known as Jaws (r.) in the James Bond films *The Spy Who Loved Me* and *Moonraker*; for other strong roles in films like *The Phantom Planet, The Magic Sword, Eegah, The Nutty Professor, The Human Duplicators, Brainstorm, The Longest Yard, Silver Streak, Pale Rider,* and *The Giant of Thunder Moutain*; and for TV shows like *Thriller, The Twilight Zone* (bottom r.), *The Man from U.N.C.L.E., Honey West, Gilligan's Island, The Monkees, I Spy, The Wild Wild West, Kolchak: The Night Stalker, Land of the Lost, The Fall Guy* and many others.

JACK O'HALLORAN—6'6" acromegalic heavyweight boxer, actor; born Apr 8 1943. Fought future champions Ken Norton & George Foreman before acting in films including *Farewell My Lovely* (1975, r.), *King Kong* (1976), *Superman I & II* (c.), *Dragnet, Hero and the Terror, The Flintstones*; and TV: *Cannon, Hunter, Knight Rider, Murder She Wrote, Morton & Hayes*, others.

ABE SIMON—6'4" acromegalic heavyweight boxer, actor; May 30 1913-Oct 24 1969. Fought Joe Louis for the heavyweight title twice. Films include *On the Waterfront* (r.), *Never Love a Stranger, Requiem for a Heavyweight*; TV: *Man Against Crime*, the Martin & Lewis *Colgate Comedy Hour*, others.

NEIL McCARTHY—6'1" acromegalic actor; Jul 26 1932-Feb 6 1985. Films include *Zulu, The Monster Club* (r.), *Clash of the Titans* (c.), *Time Bandits*; TV: *Danger Man, The Third Man, The Saint, The Avengers* (l.), *Catweazle, Z Cars, Doctor Who*, many others; stage: *Arsenic and Old Lace* (Karloff role).

DICK SUTHERLAND (Archie Thomas Johnson)—6' acromegalic actor; Dec 23 1881-Feb 3 1934. He played formidable brutes in silent films and early talkies starring Harold Lloyd, Laurel & Hardy, Lon Chaney, Greta Garbo, John Barrymore and many others: *Grandma's Boy, The Beloved Rogue, Uncle Tom's Cabin, The Battle of the Century, Don Juan, Tempest, The Viking, West of Zanzibar, Seven Footprints to Satan, Wild Orchids, Moby Dick, The Hoose-Gow, The Beast of the City, Chandu the Magician*.

  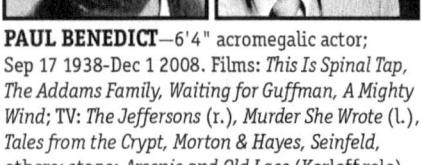  

PAUL BENEDICT—6'4" acromegalic actor; Sep 17 1938-Dec 1 2008. Films: *This Is Spinal Tap, The Addams Family, Waiting for Guffman, A Mighty Wind*; TV: *The Jeffersons* (r.), *Murder She Wrote* (l.), *Tales from the Crypt, Morton & Hayes, Seinfeld*, others; stage: *Arsenic and Old Lace* (Karloff role).

SALVATORE BACCARO—Acromegalic actor; May 6 1932-Mar 13 1984. Played many brutes in Italian horror films, westerns and comedies including *Man of the East, The Grand Duel, Deep Red, Frankenstein's Castle of Freaks, Blonde in Black Leather, The Beast in Heat* (r.), *Starcrash*.

IRWIN KEYES—6'1" acromegalic actor; Mar 16 1952-Jul 8 2015. Films include *Nocturna, Friday the 13th, Frankenstein General Hospital* (r.), *The Vampire Hunters Club, House of 1000 Corpses, Intolerable Cruelty*; TV: *Police Squad!, On the Air, The Jeffersons, Tales from the Crypt*, many others.

 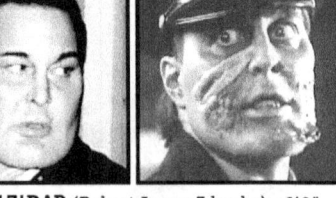   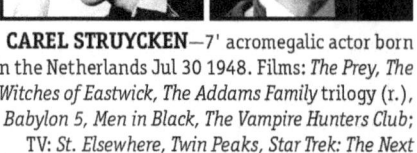

ROBERT Z'DAR (Robert James Zdarsky)—6'2" actor & rock musician afflicted with Cherubism; Jun 3 1950-Mar 30 2015. Best known for the title role in *Maniac Cop* and two sequels (r.); he played many other vicious brutes in scores of horror and action films from 1985 until his death.

RON PERLMAN (Ronald Francis Perlman)—6'1" actor with an unusual face that's perfect for brutal characters and monstrous makeup. Born Apr 13, 1950. Famous for *Hellboy* films (r.), *Cronos, Alien: Resurrection*; TV: *Beauty and the Beast, Sons of Anarchy*; voice work, much more.

CAREL STRUYCKEN—7' acromegalic actor born in the Netherlands Jul 30 1948. Films: *The Prey, The Witches of Eastwick, The Addams Family* trilogy (r.), *Babylon 5, Men in Black, The Vampire Hunters Club*; TV: *St. Elsewhere, Twin Peaks, Star Trek: The Next Generation & Voyager, Twin Peaks, Gotham*, others.

Lon Chaney's leg double pours the wine in *The Unknown*

PAUL DESMUKE—Born without arms April 25, 1876, in Texas, he became incredibly proficient with his feet, serving as a county justice of the peace, performing as a circus & sideshow attraction and in two films as an actor & stunt double. Desmuke perfected an amazing sideshow act, throwing knives at his wife Mae with his feet. He performed this and many other astounding feats for the A.G. Barnes Circus & Sideshow, for Zack Miller's 101 Ranch Wild West Show, and in Ripley's Believe It or Not Odditorium at the 1933-34 Century of Progress Expo in Chicago. "The Armless Wonder" died June 19, 1949.

Desmuke's special abilities won him the role of Lon Chaney's stunt double in Tod Browning's *The Unknown* (1927). When Lon's character "Alonzo the Armless" smoked cigarettes, drank wine or played a guitar with his feet, Paul doubled for Lon's talented toes in closeups (above) and stood in for him in long shots. Later, when he worked with A.G. Barnes show, he was billed as "Dismuki—The Man Who Doubled for Lon Chaney's Legs in *The Unknown*."

Again cast as an armless man in Erle C. Kenton's *The Sideshow* (1928), he shared the bill with Marie Prevost, Ralph Graves, "Little Billy" Rhodes, Steve Clemente (another well-known knife-thrower), and microcephalic Schlitze as "The Geek."

Paul Desmuke and his steadfast wife Mae. (Thanks to Dario Lavia for this discovery and the photo above)

AS IF THINGS WEREN'T BAD ENOUGH ON THE OLD PLANTATION! Two of brutal slavemaster Simon Legree's victims in Universal's silent film adaptation of *Uncle Tom's Cabin* (1927) had advanced cases of acromegaly, as shown in this photo of (l. to r.) Sambo (Dick Sutherland), Quimbo (Tom Amandares), and Uncle Tom (James B. Lowe). Sutherland was a white actor made up for the role, Lowe was black; Amandares has been a mystery man with this single known film credit—but his appearance explains why Rondo Hatton has been credited for this film, years before his first casting in *Hell Harbor*. See the last page of this chapter for more info on Tom Amandares.

  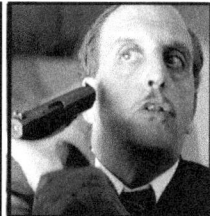

VINCENT SCHIAVELLI—6'4½" actor afflicted with Marfan Syndrome; Nov 11 1948-Dec 26, 2005. Films include *One Flew Over the Cuckoo's Nest*, *Amadeus*, *Buckaroo Banzai*, *Fast Times at Ridgemont High*, *Ghost* (c.), *Batman Returns*, *Lurking Fear*, *Tomorrow Never Dies* (r.) and others; TV: *The Corner Bar*, *Taxi*, *Fast Times*, *Star Trek: The Next Generation*, *Tales from the Crypt*, *Highlander*, *The X-Files*, *Buffy the Vampire Slayer*, many more.

THEY PLAYED CHARACTERS WITH ACROMEGALY IN A MOVIE

 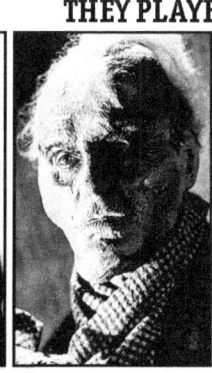

RALPH MORGAN as Anthony Lawrence in *The Monster Maker* (1944)

 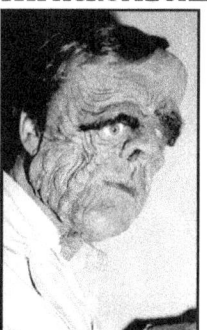

LEO G. CARROLL as Prof. Gerald Deemer in *Tarantula* (1955)

EDDIE PARKER as Paul Lund in *Tarantula* (1955)

MICHAEL BRENNAN as Tom Straker in *Doomwatch* (1972)

"TINY RON" TAYLOR as Lothar in *The Rocketeer* (1991)

"Rondo Haxton" (MARK GATTIS) as Gantok in a TV episode of *Doctor Who* (2011)

GIANTS OF THE GENRE

MATTHEW McGRORY—Acromegalic giant, actor (7'6", 317 lbs.); May 17 1973-Aug 9 2005. He first won fame as a guest on Howard Stern's radio show, then got bits in music videos and bigger parts in films including *Bubble Boy, Men in Black II*, Rob Zombie's *House of 1000 Corpses* and *The Devil's Rejects* (r.), *The Evil Within,* and Tim Burton's *Big Fish* (l.); TV shows: *Malcolm in the Middle, Charmed,* and *Carnivàle*.

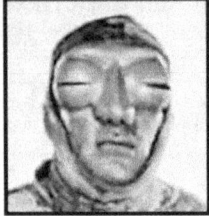
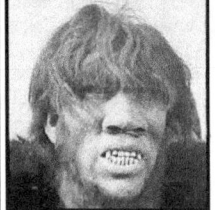
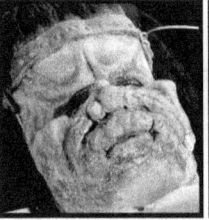

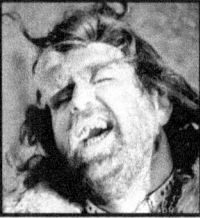

MAX PALMER—7'7", 499 lb. actor, pro wrestler, evangelist; Nov 2 1927-May 7 1984. He pursued an acting career from 1952-54 in films like *The Sniper, Invaders from Mars* (Mutant, c.) & *Killer Ape* (r.); TV: the Martin & Lewis *Colgate Comedy Hour, The Spade Cooley Show,* and *The Jimmy Durante Show*. He tried professional wrestling next, billed as Max Palmer or Paul Bunyan (105 matches, 1955-1960). He finally became an evangelist in 1963, preaching all over the US as "Goliath for Christ" until his death in 1984 from heart disease.

JOHN BLOOM—7'4" actor; Feb 19 1944-Jan 15 1999. Talked into big roles in movies by schlock filmmaker Al Adamson, he gave it a shot in *Brain of Blood, Dracula vs. Frankenstein* (The Monster, l.) & *Angels' Wild Women*. Bloom's other films include *The Incredible 2-Headed Transplant* (c.), *The Dark, The Hills Have Eyes II* (r.), *Runaway Train, Harry and the Hendersons* and *Star Trek VI: The Undiscovered Country*. He also appeared on TV shows like *B.J. and the Bear, Fame, E/R, Alice, Simon & Simon,* and *Guns of Paradise*.

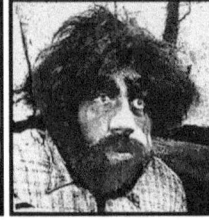
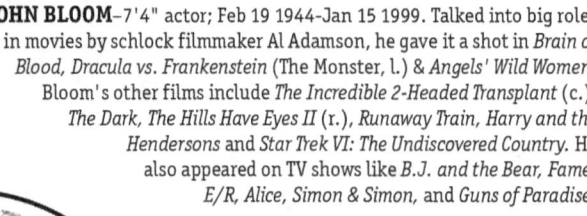

JOHN AASEN—7'2½" circus giant, actor; Mar 5 1890-Aug 1 1938. Played giants in silent and sound films from Harold Lloyd's classic *Why Worry?* in 1923 (l. & r.) to *Charlie Chan at the Circus* in 1936; his other films include silent comedy shorts with Charley Chase, W.C. Fields, Laurel & Hardy and Hal Roach's Rascals, and the sound features *Show of Shows, Freaks. Carnival* and *Bengal Tiger*.

JOHANN PETURSSON—Acromegalic circus giant, actor (7'4½", 359 lbs.). Born in Iceland Feb 9 1913, died there Nov 26 1984. He toured for decades as a circus & vaudeville attraction, billed as The Icelandic Giant, Nordic Giant Olaf, or Viking Giant (l.). He acted in three Danish films in the 1940s, *Prehistoric Women* (r.) in 1950, and *Carny* and the documentary *Being Different* (as himself) in the 1980s.

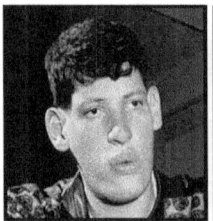
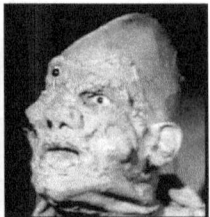

SAM BAKER—7', 300 lb. athlete, actor; May 4 1907-May 8 1982. He graduated from UCLA on a basketball scholarship, and played parts like *The Missing Link* (l.) and Hugo, the growling giant in *The Lost City* serial (r.), glad to get any work in the Depression. Better films include *The Thief of Bagdad, The Sea Beast, The Road to Mandalay, King of the Jungle, Les Misérables, Public Hero Number 1,* and *Steamboat Round the Bend*.

TSUNAGORÔ RASHÔMON (Zhuo Yi Yue)— Japanese pro wrestler, actor (6'8", 276 lbs.); Mar 20 1920-?. Alias: Iyaku Taku, Tak Yi-yak, Yiyue Zhuo. He acted in a few films from 1958 to 1965 including *The Geisha Boy* with Jerry Lewis (as a baseball player), Nagisa Ôshima's *The Sun's Burial,* and Akira Kurosawa's classic *Yojimbo* (Kannuki the Giant, above).

EDDIE CARMEL (Oded Ha-Carmeili)—7'6¾" acromegalic circus giant, actor, comedian; born in Tel Aviv Mar 16 1935, raised & died in the Bronx Jul 30 1972. He worked in sideshows, and as half of a stand-up comedy team, and made two films: *The Brain That Wouldn't Die* (r.) and a 1963 nudie, *50,000 B.C. (Before Clothing)*. "The Jewish Giant" is also remembered as the subject of a photo by Diane Arbus, taken at home with his parents.

MORE GIANTS OF THE GENRE

Two Silent Film Storybook Giants

Above left: JIM G. TARVER (James Grover Tarver)—7'3" circus giant, actor; Sep 17 1885-Jan 21 1958. Traveled with Ringling Bros. Barnum & Bailey Circus for 26 years, billed as The Tallest Man in the World (claiming 8'6"). Starred as The Giant in *Jack and the Beanstalk* in 1917.

Above center: JACK EARLE (Jacob Rheuben Erlich)—7'7½", 385 lb. acromegalic circus giant, actor; Jul 3, 1906-Jul 18, 1952. Supertall star of dozens of silent comedy shorts, he also played The Giant in Baby Peggy's *Jack and the Beanstalk* in 1924. He was hired by the Ringling Bros. circus because he was taller than their Tallest Man—Jim Tarver!

ANDRÉ THE GIANT (André Roussimoff)—7'4", 520 lb. acromegalic giant, pro wrestler, actor; born in France May 19 1946; died Jan 27 1993. He is fondly remembered for his zest for life, his career in the ring, and his larger-than-life performances in movies like *Conan the Destroyer, Micki + Maude, The Princess Bride* (r.); in TV shows like *B.J. and the Bear, The Six Million Dollar Man* (Bigfoot, l.), *The Fall Guy, The Greatest American Hero*, and *Zorro*; and in scores of wrestling videos.

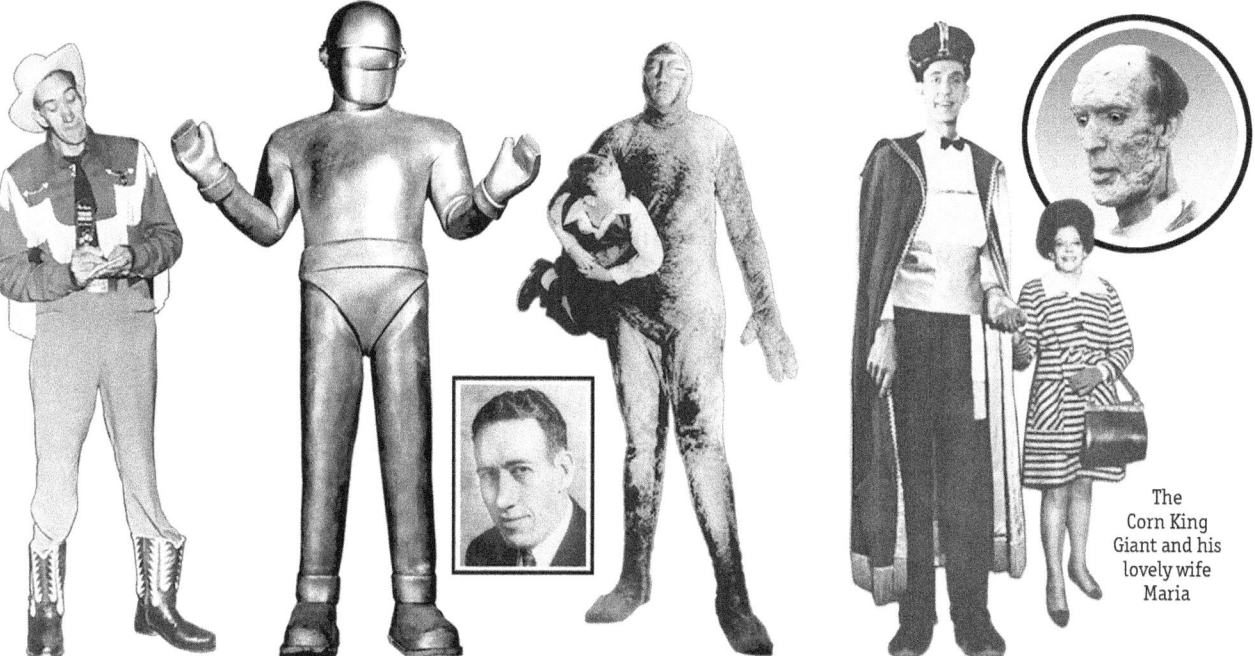

The Corn King Giant and his lovely wife Maria

LOCK MARTIN (Joseph Lockard Martin Jr.)—7'4" acromegalic giant, PR spokesman for Arden's Texas Pecan Ice Cream (l.), actor, kid show host; Oct 12 1916-Jan 19 1959. He was hired to play Gort (c.) in *The Day the Earth Stood Still* when he was spotted working as the doorman at Grauman's Chinese Theatre. Other films: *Lost in a Harem, Lady on a Train, Invaders from Mars* (Mutant carrying David, r.), *The Snow Creature*; TV: *Make Room for Daddy, Peter Gunn*, & *The Gentle Giant*, a children's show in Los Angeles.

HENRY HITE (Henry Marion Mullins)—7'6¾" acromegalic giant, actor, PR spokesman for Wilson's Certified Meat Corn King brand (l.); May 1 1915-May 26 1978. Films: *The Side Show Mystery* (1932 Vitaphone short), *New Faces of 1937* (Lowe, Hite & Stanley vaudeville act), and the 1965 Z movie *Monster a-Go Go* (Monster, circled), resuscitated on *Mystery Science Theater 3000* in 1993.

Ed Wolff in and out of characters

MORE AMAZING COLOSSAL GIANTS!

KEVIN PETER HALL—7'2½" actor; May 9 1955-Apr 10 1991. He won a basketball scholarship to George Washington University, where he majored in Theatrical Arts. He developed two-man musicals & nightclub acts with his friend & TV actor Jay Fenichel; big parts followed in films including *Prophecy* (mutant bear), *Without Warning* (Alien, l.), *Monster in the Closet* (Monster), *Harry and the Hendersons* (c.), *Predator I & II* (r.), *Big Top Pee-wee* and *Highway to Hell*; TV shows: *E/R, Night Court, The Dukes of Hazzard, Star Trek: The Next Generation* and *Harry and the Hendersons*. He contracted HIV from a blood transfusion and died of AIDS-related pneumonia.

ED WOLFF—7'4" circus giant, actor; Jul 2 1907-Jul 7 1966. Ed was one of the angry mob who killed Lon Chaney's *Phantom of the Opera* (1925), but he's better known for his inside jobs as Bela Lugosi's big ugly robot in *The Phantom Creeps* (l.), the human robot in *The Colossus of New York* (r.), the bug-eyed monster in *Return of the Fly*, and a few more big movie & TV roles.

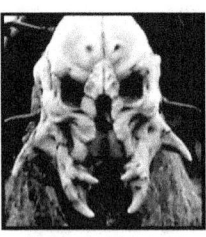  

NEIL FINGLETON—7'7½" athlete, actor; born Feb 18 1980 in Durham, England, died in London Feb 25 2017 of heart failure. He played basketball for UNC at Chapel Hill and Holy Cross before making it big in show business. His film work includes *X-Men: First Class, 47 Ronin, Jupiter Ascending,* and *Avengers: Age of Ultron* (motion capture actor & stunt performer); TV: *Doctor Who* (Fisher King in "Before the Flood," l.), *Game of Thrones* (Mag the Mighty, r., in "The Watchers on the Wall," and Giant Wight #2 in "The Dragon and the Wolf" and "Dragonstone").

  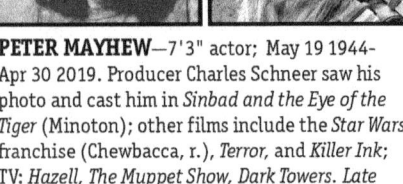   

PETER MAYHEW—7'3" actor; May 19 1944-Apr 30 2019. Producer Charles Schneer saw his photo and cast him in *Sinbad and the Eye of the Tiger* (Minoton); other films include the *Star Wars* franchise (Chewbacca, r.), *Terror*, and *Killer Ink*; TV: *Hazell, The Muppet Show, Dark Towers. Late Show with David Letterman, Glee, Breaking In.*

JOHN LEBAR—7'3" actor; his films include *Ordan's Forest* (short), *The Sickhouse, Prometheus* (Ghost Engineer, r.), *Jack the Giant Slayer* (Pantomime Giant), *The Lion Woman* and *Sherlock Holmes vs. Frankenstein* (announced; as The Creature). TV: *The League of Gentlemen, Lexx, Crooked House* and *Sherlock* (Golem, l.).

WILLIAM ENGESSER—7'3" athlete, actor; Feb 21 1939-Jun 20 2002. Played basketball for USC 1958-59. Films: *House on Bare Mountain* (r.), *Gator*; TV: *The Ghost Busters* (l.), *Isis* (Bigfoot), *Switch*. He was the first TV host of horrors on *Scream-In* in Cincinnati. He died in Pinson, Alabama, co-owner of BigFoot Auto parts.

THEY PLAYED MONSTROUS GIANTS IN '50S DRIVE-IN MOVIES

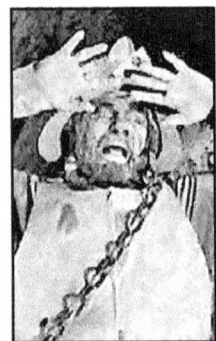 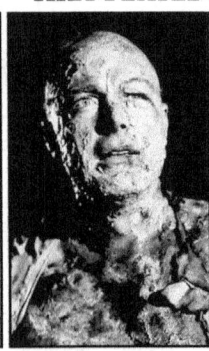  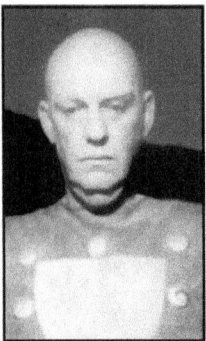  

BUDDY BAER Vargas in *Giant from the Unknown* (1958)

GLENN LANGAN Lt. Col. Glenn Manning in *The Amazing Colossal Man* (1957)

DEAN PARKIN Glenn Manning in *War of the Colossal Beast* (1958)

MICHAEL ROSS Space Giant in *Attack of the 50 Foot Woman* (1958)

CLEM ERICKSON Giant Man in *Jungle Jim in the Forbidden Land* (1954)

BELA LUGOSI Dr. Erik Vornoff in *Bride of the Monster* (1955)

CONSTANTINE ROMANOFF
(Friedrich William Heinrich August Meyer)
6'2", 197 lb. pro wrestler, actor born in Germany Aug 21 1881, died Feb 8 1969. Match data not yet available; alias: Jack Meyer.

BULL MONTANA (Luigi Montagna)
5'10", 251 lb. pro wrestler, actor born in Italy May 16 1887, died Jan 24 1950. 49 matches 1920-1933; alias: Louis Mantagna, Louis Montana.

Romanoff played tough brutes in American films from 1921-1951: *The Kid Brother*, *She Wanted a Millionaire*, *Chandu the Magician*, *Island of Lost Souls* (beastman), *Son of Kong*, *Dante's Inferno*, *Flash Gordon* (monkey man, left), *The Shadow*, *The Long Voyage Home*, *Terry & the Pirates*, *Hangover Square*, *The Vampire's Ghost*, *It's a Wonderful Life,* many others.

Italian champion wrestler Bull Montana's homely brutes were very popular characters in American silent and sound comedies and adventure films: *Treasure Island*, *Go and Get It*, *The Lost World*, *The Uneasy Three*, *Vanishing Millions*, *Show of Shows*, *Flash Gordon* (monkey man, right), *The Clutching Hand,* many more.

MONSTERS OF THE RING

Known wrestling career information from *Wrestlingdata.com*, "The World's Largest Wrestling Database" (research in progress)

 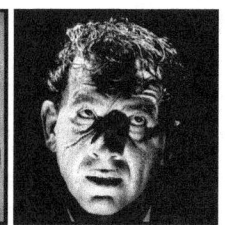 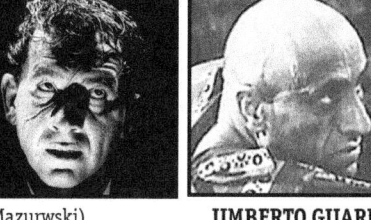   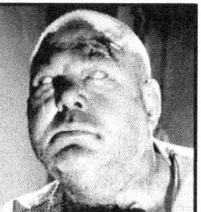

MIKE MAZURKI (Mikhail Mazurwski)
6'5", 240 lb. pro wrestler, actor born in Ukraine Dec 25 1907, died Dec 9 1990. 1347 matches 1932-63; alias: Mike Mazurski, Iron Mike. Films include *Dr. Renault's Secret*, *Murder My Sweet* (l.), *Dick Tracy* (r.), *Night and the City*, *Dark City*; TV: *The Munsters*, *It's About Time*, *Batman*, others.

UMBERTO GUARRACINO (aka **CIMASTE**)
Italian pro wrestler, actor; played monsters in silent films like *Il Mostro di Frankenstein* (third Frankenstein film, 1921), *The Island of the Lost* (beastman, r.), & *Maciste in Hell* (King of Hell). Personal and ring career details unknown.

ADY BERBER (Adolf Berber)—6'6¾", 330 lb. Austrian pro wrestler, actor; Feb 4 1913-Jan 3 1966. 106 matches 1939-62; alias: Adi/Adolf/Josef/Sepp Berber. Films include *Carnival Story*, *Lola Montès*, *Ben-Hur* (l.), *Dead Eyes of London* (r.), *The Return of Dr. Mabuse*, *The Strangler in the Tower*.

HANS STEINKE (Hans Hermann Steinke)
6'6", 275 lb. German pro wrestler, actor; Feb 22 1893-Jun 24 1971. 834 matches 1923-49; alias: Hans Brun, The German Oak. He made a few films in the '30s including *Island of Lost Souls* (tall apeman Ouran at right), *A Wrestler's Bride*, *People Will Talk*, *Nothing Sacred* and *The Buccaneer*.

HARRY EKIZIAN (Arteen Ekizian)—5'10", 251 lb. World Heavyweight Champion wrestler, actor, Armenian Genocide survivor; Sep 28 1901-Nov 16 1981. 578 matches 1927-55; alias: Ali Baba, the Terrible Turk, Ali Yumid, Harry Eikasian/Ekezian. Films include *Island of Lost Souls* (short apeman Gola at left), *Alice in Wonderland,* and W.C. Fields' *Man on the Flying Trapeze*, in which he picks up Tor Johnson and throws him completely out of the wrestling arena!

MORE MONSTERS OF THE RING

Known wrestling career information from *Wrestlingdata.com* (research in progress)

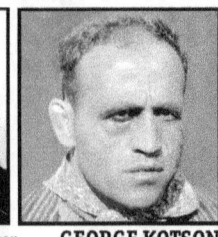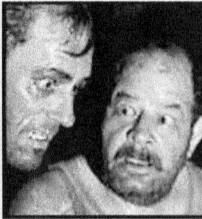

FRANK (Francis Charles) **MORAN**—6'1" pro boxer & football player, actor; Mar 18 1887-Dec 14 1967. Lost heavyweight title matches in 1914 & 1916; retired after 66 bouts (36 wins—28 KOs). Films: *Dante's Inferno, Mummy's Boys, Beware Spooks!, The Corpse Vanishes, Ghosts on the Loose, Return of the Ape Man* (r.), *The Man in Half Moon Street* and strong roles in dozens of other A & B movies, notably as one of Preston Sturges' stock players.

GEORGE KOTSONAROS—5'9", 199 lb. Greek pro wrestler, actor; Oct 16 1892-Jul 13 1933. 125 matches 1923-33; alias George Kotsonares. His menacing looks, broken nose and powerful build won him roles as brutes in silents & early talkies (some lost today): *Vanishing Millions, While London Sleeps, The King of the Jungle, The Wizard* (r.), *The Fifty-Fifty Girl, Street of Sin* (l.), *Beggars of Life*, others.

KALLA PASHA (Joseph T. Rickard)—5'7½" pro wrestler, actor born in Detroit Mar 5 1879, died Jun 10 1933. Ring data unknown; alias: Hamid Kalla/Kala Pasha, The Crazy Turk. He also played brutes in vaudeville & movies; debut film was Tod Browning's first starring Lon Chaney, *The Wicked Darling* (1919). Acted in scores of comedy shorts, *West of Zanzibar* (r.), *Tillie's Punctured Romance, Seven Footprints to Satan, Show of Shows*, others.

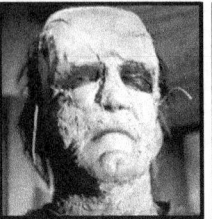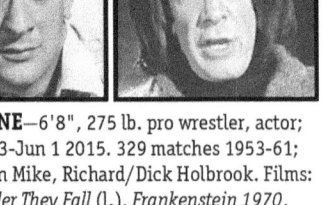

KIWI KINGSTON (Ernest Walter Kingston)—6'5" pro wrestler, actor; born in New Zealand in 1914, died 1992. Wrestling debut in 1939, retired 1970: 135 matches 1955-69; alias: Ernie/Kiwi Kingston. Made a big impression in Hammer's *The Evil of Frankenstein* (r.) and *Hysteria, They Came from Beyond Space*, and in documentaries as himself.

MIKE LANE—6'8", 275 lb. pro wrestler, actor; Jan 6 1933-Jun 1 2015. 329 matches 1953-61; alias: Tarzan Mike, Richard/Dick Holbrook. Films: *The Harder They Fall* (l.), *Frankenstein 1970, Valley of the Dragons, Ulysses Against Hercules*; TV: *The Outer Limits, The Monkees* (Frankenstein), *Batman, Monster Squad* (Frank N. Stein, r.).

IVAN LINOW (Janis Linaus)—6'4", 220 lb. pro wrestler, actor; born in Latvia Nov 21 1888, died Nov 21 1940. 121 matches 1918-1933; alias: The Cossack, Jack Linow/Lineau/Leon. Films: *The Red Dance, Black Magic, The Unholy Three* (l.), *Just Imagine* (r.), *The Shadow of the Eagle* (John Wayne serial), *The Black Room*, many others.

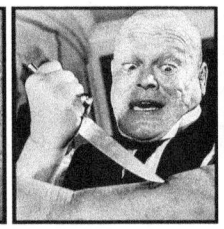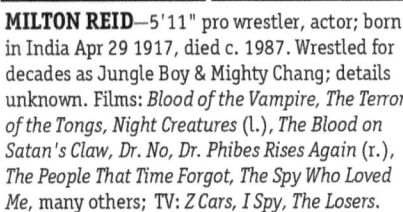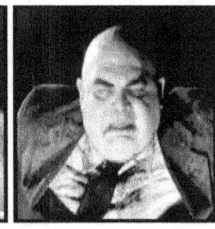

MILTON REID—5'11" pro wrestler, actor; born in India Apr 29 1917, died c. 1987. Wrestled for decades as Jungle Boy & Mighty Chang; details unknown. Films: *Blood of the Vampire, The Terror of the Tongs, Night Creatures* (l.), *The Blood on Satan's Claw, Dr. No, Dr. Phibes Rises Again* (r.), *The People That Time Forgot, The Spy Who Loved Me*, many others; TV: *Z Cars, I Spy, The Losers*.

ANTHONY QUINN (Antonio Rudolfo Quinn Oaxaca) 6'2" international star born in Mexico Apr 21 1915, died Jun 3 2001. Early boxing experience prepared him well for brutal, powerful roles in films like *Viva Zapata!, La Strada, Attila, Lust for Life, The Hunchback of Notre Dame* (r.), *The Savage Innocents, Barabbas, Requiem for a Heavyweight* (l.), *Lawrence of Arabia, Zorba the Greek*, and many other films & TV shows.

GEORGE "THE ANIMAL" STEELE (William James Myers)—6'1", 245 lb. pro wrestler, actor; Apr 16 1937-Feb 16 2017. 1604 matches, 1963-2000; alias: The Student. Films: *Ruthless People, Ed Wood* (as Tor Johnson, r.), others; TV: "The Animal" (l.) was a green-tongued wild man who chewed turnbuckles and hurled stuffing at his opponents—a monstrous wrestling superstar.

PAT McKEE (Forrest Robert Crandall)—210 lb. pro boxer, wrestler/referee, actor; Mar 24 1895-Jan 7 1950. 59 matches 1933-1948; alias: Pat Crandall. Films: *Fury, 3 Thin Man* movies, *Beware Spooks!, I Wake Up Screaming, Sullivan's Travels, Tales of Manhattan, Voodoo Man* (r.), *Hangover Square, Nightmare Alley*; serials: *Mandrake the Magician, Dick Tracy Returns, The Green Hornet, The Adventures of Smilin' Jack*; many others.

NAT PENDLETON—6', 200 lb. wrestler, actor; Aug 9 1895-Oct 12 1967. Won heavyweight silver medal in 1920 Olympics, then tried pro wrestling: 34 matches 1920-1932. Also played dozens of big brutes in films like *Blonde Crazy, The Beast of the City, Horse Feathers, The Sign of the Cross, Lady for a Day, I'm No Angel, The Thin Man, The Cats-Paw, The Great Ziegfeld* (l.), *Reckless, At the Circus, Buck Privates*, the *Dr. Kildare* series, *Scared to Death*, more.

THE MASKED MARVEL (Herman Munster)—7'3", 387 lb. gravedigger, wrestler; born c. 1815. Moonlighting as a masked wrestler, he lost all his matches because his opponents told him sob stories and he let them win. He quit the ring after magically winning a match—plus a $1000 safety award for clearing the arena instantly when a fire broke out—by removing his mask to announce it. TV: *The Munsters*, S1 E8, "Herman the Great."

EXTERMINATING ANGELS

Known wrestling career information from *Wrestlingdata.com* (research in progress)

 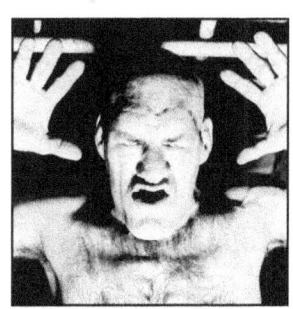

THE FRENCH ANGEL (Maurice Marie Joseph Tillet)
5'8½", 280 lb. acromegalic pro wrestler, actor; born in Russia to French parents Oct 23 1903, died Sep 4 1954 in Chicago. 483 matches 1940-1952; alias: The Angel, El Ángel Francés, Maurice Tillet. He was promoted as The World's Ugliest Man, but he got the nickname "The Angel" because he looked angelic as a child. He appeared in French films: *Dragnet Night, Princess Tam Tam, Carnival in Flanders* and *The Volga Boatmen*. He is alleged to be the model for the animated character Shrek.

THE SWEDISH ANGEL (Nils Phillip Olofsson)
6'6", 245 lb. acromegalic pro wrestler, actor; born in Sweden Oct 16 1906, died Feb 9 1974 in Utah. 957 matches 1933-1955; alias: Phil Olaffson/Olafson/Olson, Olaf Olson/Svenson/Swenson, Popeye Frankenstein, Popeye Olson/Swenson/the Swedish Angel. He became the second wrestling Angel following Maurice Tillet's great success in the US. Sole film credit: *Mighty Joe Young*.

A FEW OF THE OTHER MAT MONSTERS WHO USED THEIR BRAINS, BRAWN AND GOOD LOOKS TO CASH IN ON THE ANGEL BOOM

THE AMERICAN ANGEL
(Charles Marian Guy)
Self-styled ugliest pro wrestler;
1910-??
434 matches 1931-47;
alias: The Angel,
Pat Reilly, Pat Riley.

THE CANADIAN ANGEL
(Andre Vadnais)
6', 265 lb. acromegalic pro wrestler;
1914-??
49 matches 1941-44;
alias:
Andre Vadnais.

THE IRISH ANGEL
(Johnny Adams)
5'10", 215 lb.
self-styled ugliest pro wrestler; 19??-??
Match data unknown;
alias: John Adams,
Johnny Adams.

THE POLISH ANGEL
(Wladyslaw Frantiszek Talun)
6'8", 303 lb. pro wrestler, actor;
Oct 15 1909-Sep 15 1980.
748 matches 1938-60;
alias: Iron Man Talun, Goliath,
Walter/Wladislaw Talun, more.
Film: *David and Bathsheba*.

 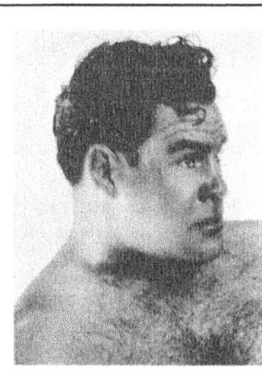 

THE SUPER SWEDISH ANGEL
(Tor Johnson, born Karl Erik Tore Johansson)
6'3", 387 lb.* pro wrestler, actor; born in Sweden Oct 19 1903, died May 12 1971 in California. 544 matches 1932-1954; alias: Thor Johnson, Tor Johansson, King Kong. His films include *The Canterville Ghost, Shadow of the Thin Man, Behind Locked Doors, Alias the Champ, Bride of the Monster, Carousel, The Black Sleep, The Unearthly, Plan 9 from Outer Space, The Beast of Yucca Flats, Night of the Ghouls*; TV: *Rocky Jones—Space Ranger, Peter Gunn, You Bet Your Life, The Man from Blackhawk, Bonanza*, others.

* Weight Tor told Groucho Marx on *You Bet Your Life*

THE *MIGHTY JOE YOUNG* STRONGMEN

Left to right, row by row:

SAMMY STEIN (Samuel Stein) breaks chain.
6', 200 lb. pro wrestler, NFL lineman, actor; Apr 1 1905-Mar 30 1966.
635 matches 1931-60. Dozens of other films including *The Lost Patrol,
Modern Times, The Long Voyage Home, Road to Morocco, Gentleman Jim,
Pittsburgh, Lost in a Harem, They Were Expendable, Fright Night* (3 Stooges).

"KILLER" KARL DAVIS (Karl T. Davis) bends crowbar.
6'2", 240 lb. pro wrestler, actor; Apr 16 1908-Jul 1 1977. 2063 matches 1925-57.
Other films include *The Lost Planet, Creature with the Atom Brain, Zombies of
Mora Tau*; TV: *Dick Tracy, Space Patrol, Alfred Hitchcock Presents*; many more.

RASPUTIN THE MAD RUSSIAN (Hyman Fishman) breaks chain on wrists.
235 lb. pro wrestler, actor; born in Massachusetts Jun 3 1912, died Sep 25 1976.
1269 matches 1935-58. One other film: *Friendly Persuasion*;
TV: "Requiem for a Heavyweight" on *Playhouse 90*.

"BOMBER" KULKY (Henry Kulkovich) lifts dumbbell with one arm.
5'11" pro wrestler, judo champion, actor; Aug 11 1911-Feb 12 1965.
723 matches 1934-53. Henry Kulky's other films include *Call Northside 777,
Alias the Champ, Red Planet Mars, Phantom of the Rue Morgue, Tobor the Great*;
TV: *Superman, The Lone Ranger, Topper, The Red Skelton Show, Hennesey,
Bonanza, Voyage to the Bottom of the Sea* and many more.

SLAMMIN' SAMMY MENACKER (Frank L. Menacker) rips phonebook in half.
Pro wrestler/commentator, actor; May 13 1914-Jan 7 1994. 616 matches 1936-76.
He appeared in five other films: *Alias the Champ, Always Leave Them Laughing,
Bodyhold, Abbott and Costello in the Foreign Legion,* and *The Wrestler*.

MAX THE IRON MAN (Ian "Mac" Batchelor) bends railroad spike in hands.
Legendary 6', 300+ lb. strongman, undefeated arm wrestler, LA bartender;
May 24 1910-Aug 10 1986. *Mighty Joe Young* is his only film credit.

"WEE WILLIE" DAVIS (William Grundy Davis) bends iron bar behind his neck.
6'5" pro wrestler/promoter, actor; Dec 7 1906-Apr 9 1981. 2151 matches 1930-61.
Many other films including *Shadow of the Thin Man, Arabian Nights, Ali Baba and
the Forty Thieves, Ghost Catchers, Pursuit to Algiers, Bowery Bombshell, Samson
and Delilah, The Asphalt Jungle, To Catch a Thief*; TV: *The Cisco Kid*.

MAN MOUNTAIN DEAN (Frank Simmons Leavitt) twists horseshoe.
5'11", 317 lb. pro wrestler, soldier, actor; Jun 30 1891-May 29 1953.
341 matches 1930-46. Other films: *Reckless, The Private Life of Henry VIII*
(Laughton's stunt double), *We're in the Money, Big City, The Gladiator*.

THE SWEDISH ANGEL (Nils Phillip Olofsson) breaks beam over his head.
6'6", 245 lb. acromegalic pro wrestler/trainer; born in Sweden Oct 16 1906,
died Feb 9 1974. 957 matches 1933-55. Sole film credit: *Mighty Joe Young*.

PRIMO CARNERA breaks metal armbands by flexing his biceps.
6'7", 263 lb. acromegalic Heavyweight Champion boxer, wrestler, actor;
born in Italy Oct 28 1906, died Jun 29 1967. Heavyweight boxing title 1933-34;
736 wrestling matches 1946-62. Other films include *The Prizefighter and the Lady,
Prince Valiant, Casanova's Big Night, A Kid for Two Farthings, Hercules Unchained*;
TV: The Monster in "Frankenstein" on *Matinee Theatre* (1954).

Known wrestling career information from *Wrestlingdata.com* (research in progress)

OTHER AWESOME BRUTES

    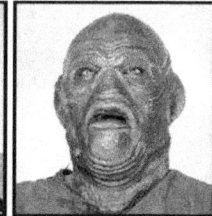 

KÁROLY HUSZÁR (Károly Hochstadt), aka **Pufi** (Fatty), **Charles Puffy**—actor born in Hungary Nov 3 1884; died in 1942 or 1943. He was a popular character from 1913-1938 in European and American slapstick comedies, and in major films like Fritz Lang's *Destiny* & *Dr. Mabuse: The Gambler* (l.), *Mockery* with Lon Chaney, *The Man Who Laughs* with Conrad Veidt, *The Blue Angel* with Marlene Dietrich—and two 1918 Hungarian films in which he is billed above Bela Lugosi. He and his wife died trying to escape the Holocaust; where it happened, in Japan or in a Russian labor camp, is disputed.

DON MEGOWAN—6'7" actor, athlete; May 24 1922-Jun 26 1981. His physical presence was equally imposing for hardbitten heroes, brutes and monsters. Films: *Prince Valiant*, *To Catch a Thief*, *The Creature Walks Among Us* (c.), *The Werewolf*, *The Story of Mankind*, *The Creation of the Humanoids*, *Tarzan and the Valley of Gold*, *Blazing Saddles*; TV: *The Lone Ranger*, *Davy Crockett at the Alamo*, *Cimarron City* (The Beast), *Tales of Frankenstein* (r.), *Cheyenne*, *The Beachcomber* series, *Rawhide*, *The Beverly Hillbillies* (as a TV cowboy werewolf!), *Get Smart*, *Kung Fu*, *Scream of the Wolf* and lots more.

  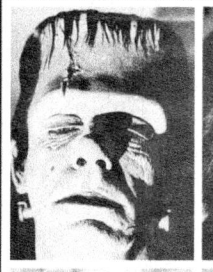   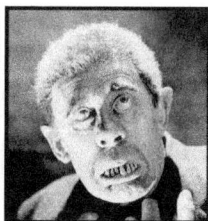

RICHARD ALEXANDER—6'4½" actor; Nov 19 1902-Aug 9 1989. Played hundreds of big tough guys in classic films like *The Cameraman*, *All Quiet on the Western Front*, *The Front Page*, *The Scarlet Empress*, *The Great Dictator*, *Modern Times*, *The Plainsman* and *The Ghost of Frankenstein*; in B-movies and serials like *Flash Gordon* (l.) & *SOS Coast Guard* (r.); and in TV shows like *Dick Tracy*, *Death Valley Days*, *Mike Hammer* and *Gunsmoke*.

WILFRED WALTER—British actor, playwright, WWII RAF squadron leader; Mar 2 1882-Jul 9 1958. Shakespearean actor with the Old Vic company and other theatre troupes. Films: *The Human Monster* (r.), *Lady in Distress*, *Night Train to Munich*, *Caesar and Cleopatra*, *No Highway in the Sky*; TV: British series & TV movies like *Rotten Row*, *Death of a Rat*, *The Monster of Killoon*, *The Clue of the Missing Ape*. Wilfred is sometimes credited as *Wilfrid* Walter.

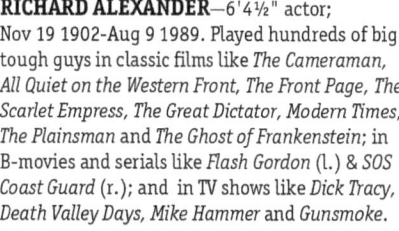

NOBLE JOHNSON—6'2" black actor, writer and producer; Apr 18 1881-Jan 9 1978. Played a wide range of different ethnic types in films from 1915 to 1950: *The Thief of Bagdad*, *The Mysterious Dr. Fu Manchu*, *Murders in the Rue Morgue*, *The Most Dangerous Game*, *The Mummy*, *King Kong*, *Son of Kong*, *She*, *Lost Horizon*, *Hawk of the Wilderness*, *The Ghost Breakers*, *The Jungle Book*, *Angel on My Shoulder*, *She Wore a Yellow Ribbon*, many others.

GLENN STRANGE—6'4" cowboy, musician, actor; Aug 16 1899-Sep 20 1973. He broke into films with the Arizona Wranglers cowboy band, performing in B-westerns. He played big brutes and good guys in hundreds of B-films, serials & TV shows, but his weatherbeaten face & hulking frame are beloved icons in '40s horror movies like *The Mad Monster*, *The Monster Maker*, *House of Frankenstein/Dracula*, *Abbott & Costello Meet Frankenstein* and *Master Minds*. In later years he worked mostly in TV westerns (*The Lone Ranger* villain Butch Cavendish, *Gunsmoke*'s Sam the bartender) but he revived Old Flattop 3 times: *The Colgate Comedy Hour*, *The Tex Williams Show*, & one of Don Glut's Monster Kid home movies.

HARRY CORDING—6' British actor; Apr 26 1891-Sep 1-1954. Played burly brutes in films: *The Black Cat* (r.), *Mystery of Edwin Drood*, *The Adventures of Robin Hood*, *Son/Ghost of Frankenstein*, 8 of the Rathbone Holmes series, *Tower of London*, *The Sea Hawk*, *The Hunchback of Notre Dame*, *The Wolf Man*, *The Mummy's Tomb*, *The Spider Woman*, *The Strange Door*, *Man in the Attic*, others; TV: *The Lone Ranger*, *Adventures of Wild Bill Hickok*, *Hopalong Cassidy*.

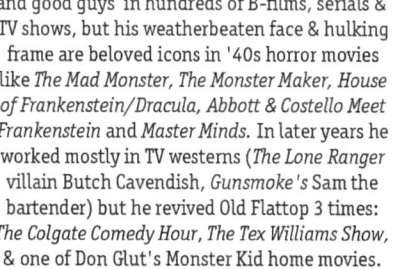

   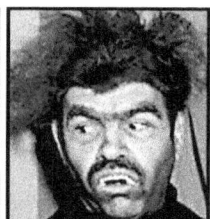  

DUKE YORK (Charles Everest Sinsabaugh)—Character actor in scores of features, serials and comedy shorts, and a few TV shows, from 1930 until his death by suicide; Oct 17 1908–Jan 24 1952. He is fondly remembered as Kala, King of the Shark Men in the *Flash Gordon* serial (#2 image above), and for his major roles in 10 Three Stooges shorts, mostly as brutes and monsters (#3, 4 & 5 above). His other films include *Island of Lost Souls* (#6 above), *Murders in the Zoo*, *The Three Mesquiteers*, *SOS Coast Guard*, *The Fighting Devil Dogs*, *Dick Tracy Returns*, *The Spider's Web*, *Topper Takes a Trip*, *Destry Rides Again*, *The Shadow*, *Terry and the Pirates*, *The Green Archer*, *Never Give a Sucker an Even Break*, *Shadow of the Thin Man*, *Saboteur*, *The Spoilers*, *Invisible Agent*, *Road to Rio*, *The Gunfighter*, *Winchester '73*, *The Red Badge of Courage*; TV: *The Lone Ranger*, *Adventures of Wild Bill Hickok* and *The Range Rider*.

MORE AWESOME BRUTES

JOE BONOMO—5'11½" body builder, physical culturist, publisher, film stuntman & actor; Dec 25 1901-Mar 28 1978. Joe's fabulous autobiography *The Strongman* discusses his contributions to classic horror films: doubling Quasimodo's long rope slide in Lon Chaney's *Hunchback*, handling the heavy lifting for Gemora's Gorilla in *Murders in the Rue Morgue* (c.), and playing several beastmen in *Island of Lost Souls* (r.). He brought heroic supermen & brutal dog heavies to life in dozens of serials, westerns, epics & action films from 1923-1936, then retired to manage his hugely successful businesses.

DAVID PROWSE—6'6" weightlifting champion, actor; Born Jul 1 1935. Bodybuilding publicity led to a bit as Frankenstein's Monster in the Bond spoof *Casino Royale*, big parts in Hammer films (*The Horror of Frankenstein*, l., *Frankenstein and the Monster from Hell*, *Vampire Circus*), *A Clockwork Orange*, *Jabberwocky*, *The People That Time Forgot*, and dream casting as Darth Vader (r., voiced by James Earl Jones) in the sci-fi trilogy *Star Wars*, *The Empire Strikes Back* & *Return of the Jedi*. TV: *Doctor Who*, *Space: 1999*, *The Benny Hill Show*, *The Hitchhiker's Guide to the Galaxy*, many others.

  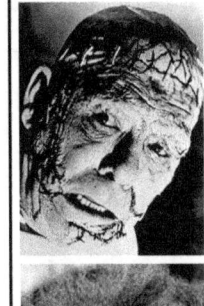 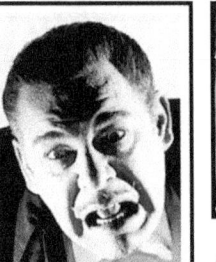 

TOM NOONAN—6'5" actor, writer, director; born Apr 12 1951. Films: *Gloria*, *Heaven's Gate*, *Wolfen*, *Manhunter* (l.), *The Monster Squad* (r.), *RoboCop 2*, *Mystery Train*, *Last Action Hero*; TV: *Tales from the Darkside*, *Monsters*, *The X-Files*, *Night of the Wolf*, *Damages*, *The Blacklist*, *Horace and Pete*, *Hell on Wheels*, *12 Monkeys*, many others.

ERNEST BORGNINE (Ermes Effron Borgnino)—5'9½" actor; Jan 24 1917-Jul 8 2012. Sadly better known for his TV sitcom *McHale's Navy* than for his Best Actor Oscar for *Marty* and other fine work, including terrific brutes in *From Here to Eternity*, *Bad Day at Black Rock*, *The Wild Bunch*, *The Devil's Rain* (l.), *Emperor of the North* (r.) and others.

 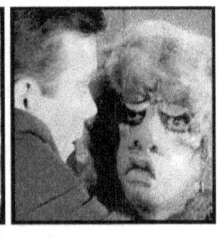 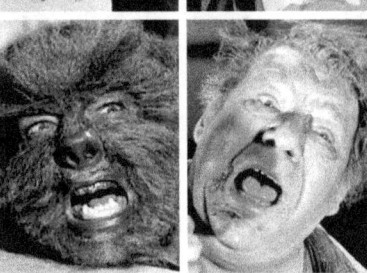  

NICK CRAVAT (Nicholas Cuccia)—5'4" acrobat, film stuntman, actor; Jan 10 1912-Jan 29 1994. 1930s acrobat partner of Burt Lancaster, worked with him in 9 movies. Films include: *The Crimson Pirate*, *The Story of Mankind*, *Phantom of the Rue Morgue* (Charles Gemora's gorilla double), *The Island of Dr. Moreau*; TV: *Davy Crockett at the Alamo*, *The Twilight Zone* (Gremlin, r.), others.

LON CHANEY JR. (Creighton Tull Chaney)—6'2" actor; Feb 10 1906-Jul 12 1973. There's no room to assess this genre giant, just enough to list some of his brute roles in films: *Undersea Kingdom*, *Secret Agent X-9*, *Of Mice and Men*, *One Million B.C.*, *Man Made Monster*, *Badlands of Dakota*, *Frontier Badmen*, *My Favorite Brunette*, *Captain China*, *The Black Castle*, *Passion*, *Big House U.S.A.*, *Indestructible Man*, *The Black Sleep*, *The Alligator People*, *Dracula vs. Frankenstein*; and on TV: *Bat Masterson*, *The Phantom*, *The Rifleman*, *Have Gun-Will Travel*, *Route 66*, *The Monkees*, many more.

MAX WAGNER—5'10" American actor, born in Mexico Nov 28 1901, died Nov 16 1975. Moved to California at the age of 10; bilingual, he acted in Spanish-language films & played Karloff's role in the Spanish version of *The Criminal Code* (l.). Played 400+ small parts as thugs & tough galoots in A & B films and TV shows, 1924-1975. He did a fine job as Sgt. Rinaldi (r.) in *Invaders from Mars*.

WALLACE (Fitzgerald) **BEERY**—5'11½" actor; Apr 1 1885-Apr 15 1949. Remembered for classic films like *The Champ* (l.), *Grand Hotel*, *Dinner at Eight* and *Treasure Island*, he was the world's highest-paid actor in the early 30s, a beloved character actor in 240+ films, 1913-1949. He was born to play homely brutes of some sort, starting with despicable ethnics in silents and winding up as lovable scalawags redeemed by adoring children to save the day at the end: *The Unpardonable Sin*, *Behind the Door*, *The Virgin of Stamboul*, *The Last of the Mohicans*, *A Blind Bargain* (r.), *Three Ages*, *Ashes of Vengeance*, *The Drums of Jeopardy*, *The White Tiger*, *The Lost World* (c.), *Beggars of Life*, *The Big House*, *Flesh*, *Viva Villa!*, *20 Mule Team*, *The Bad Man*, *Bad Bascomb*.

JACK PALANCE (Vladimir Ivanovich Palahniuk)—6'4" American actor of Ukrainian descent; Feb 18 1919-Nov 10 2006. He had experience as boxer "Jack Brazzo" and on stage (Brando's *Streetcar* replacement) before his film & TV career (1949-2004); his fearsome visage ensured many brutish roles in films like *Panic in the Streets*, *Sudden Fear*, *Shane* (l.), *Man in the Attic*, *Sign of the Pagan*, *Sword of the Conqueror*, *The Mongols*, *Barabbas*, *Contempt*, *Torture Garden*, *Alone in the Dark*; and on television: *Requiem for a Heavyweight*, *Alice Through the Looking Glass* (Jabberwock), *The Man from U.N.C.L.E.*, *The Strange Case of Dr. Jekyll and Mr. Hyde* (r.), *Dracula* (c.), *The Hatfields and the McCoys*, *Tales of the Haunted*, and many more.

THE FACE IS FAMILIAR

PRINCE VALIANT GIANT
Hal Foster's newspaper
comic strip, June 9. 1940

FRED GWYNNE
Kid-safe Karloff—Munsters
are GOOD for you

ABRAHAM LINCOLN
Portrayed by John Carradine
in *Of Human Hearts* (1938)

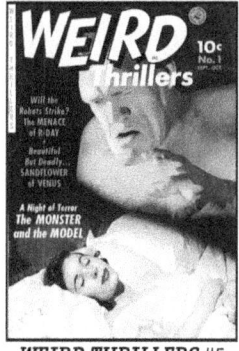
"POPEYE SWENSON"
Wrestler Phil Olofsson,
pre-"Swedish Angel"

WEIRD THRILLERS #5
Monster on 1951 comic
cover is *not* Rondo Hatton

MATT SMITH—11th
Doctor Who in the TV series;
54 TV episodes, 2010-2014

LOTHAR in Dave Stevens'
graphic novel *The Rocketeer:
Cliff's New York Adventure*

QUENTIN TARANTINO
Pulp affliction?
The Frightful Fate?

John Arcudi's **THE CREEP**,
a "defective detective," as
drawn by Gray Morrow

JOHN DIERKES
Lurch audition for *The
Addams Family* TV show

EASTER ISLAND STATUE
Aku-Akumegaly?

BRIAN THOMPSON
Why the long face?

H. P. LOVECRAFT
Weird Medical Marvel Tales?

LEBRON JAMES
Basketball case?

NAZI PROGRAM COVER
1937 Degenerate Art exhibit

MYSTERY MARVELS

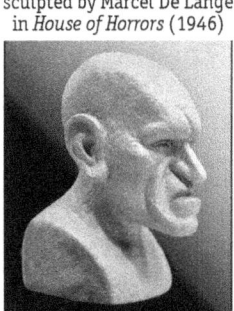
THE CREEPER BUST
sculpted by Marcel De Lange
in *House of Horrors* (1946)

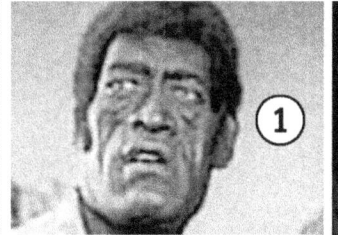

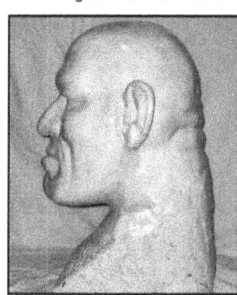
MAURICE TILLET
life cast of French Angel by
by Robert Manoogian Jr.

RONDO HATTON BUST
Classic Horror Award
sculpted by Kerry Gammill

TOM AMANDARES—Since we mentioned earlier that this "mystery man" appeared in the silent *Uncle Tom Cabin* (1), evidence that he's in at least two other films has surfaced: (2) as one of the Yakitch family of peasant farmers in Raoul Walsh's *The Red Dance* (1928); (3) as one of Ahab's crew in John Barrymore's 1930 sound version of *Moby Dick* (our thanks to Dario Lavia for this discovery). Now who are those two guys at top and bottom right?!

SHREK—ogre hero of CGI
animated film released by
PDI/Dreamworks in 2001

"He Made a Star Out of Rondo Hatton!"
Remembering Universal Producer Ben Pivar
By Andrew J. Fenady as Told to Tom Weaver

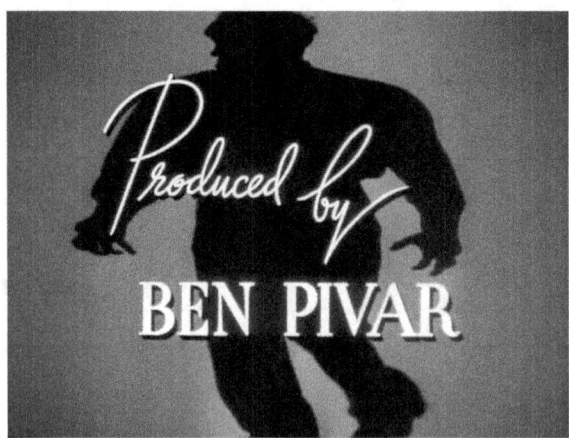

Pivar's name shares the screen with the Creeper's shadow.

Back in the 1950s, I was part of a very successful TV series called *Confidential File* with Paul Coates. There was never a program like *Confidential File* up to then, we were the precursor of *60 Minutes*. We did programs about homosexuals, about kid gangs, unwed mothers, "daytime whites" [blacks passing for white], the used car racket, the television repair racket.

We had been on the air for a couple of years, and won more than a couple of Emmys, when we made a deal with Guild Films to produce 39 nationally syndicated episodes, and Ben Pivar was brought in to produce those. [The show's topics] were all foreign to Ben, he didn't know anything about what the hell we were doing. This was not his genre. He had done horror stuff and adventure stuff over at Universal, where he'd been producing pictures for a good long time [from 1939's *Mutiny on the Blackhawk* to 1946's *Inside Job*].

Ben told me that the biggest shock of his Universal career...except for the time that they said they weren't going to pick up his contract and they let him go!...was when the head of production called him and said, "Ben, come on up to my office." He went there, and the head of production said, "Just sit down, because any minute now, your new leading man is going to come in, and I want to introduce you to him." Well, Ben was used to working with people like Lon Chaney Jr., Tom Neal, Turhan Bey, Dick Foran, [John] Carradine, people of that sort. So, okay, he was waiting to find out who it was. The secretary called on the phone and told the head of production, "He's here." "Send him in."

Ben started to get up to greet the man, before he saw him, and in came...Rondo Hatton! The head of production said, "Ben, I think we're going to do a series with Rondo. We'll try it out and see if the first one is good, and it *better* be because you're gonna produce it.

Behind-the-scenes on *House of Horrors*, producer Pivar has eyes for Joan Shawlee (a Hatton victim in that movie). Her hand is on star Robert Lowery's shoulder; Pivar's secretary Helen McLemore is on the left.

Andrew Fenady..." He was trying to play the big executive. He said, "Now, let me see here... Tell me, what is your salary?" I thought to myself, "Oh-oh. Here comes some bad news!" I said, "Ben, what are you tryin' to do, bullshit me? You got the budget there, you know how much money I make. Why do you ask me such a question?" He said, "Oh, yeah, yeah, yeah, I know. Well, I just called you in to tell you that from now on, while I'm here, your salary is *doubled*." I said, "*What*?" I think I was making $150 a week, something like that, maybe 125, and he doubled it! I said, "I haven't asked for a raise," and he said, "As far as I'm concerned, you're the most valuable man here next to Paul Coates." As I said, he kept a keen eye on *who* was doing *what*, he was always on top of everything.

He was not tall; he was short, as a matter of fact, probably 5'6", something like that. But he was a dapper sort of a fellow. Well-dressed. His clothes were probably a decade old, but he still wore them nicely-nicely. Full head of hair...graying. And he had a mustache, and I said, "Oh, you've got a military mustache, huh, Ben?" He said, "No, *noooo*! Ronald Colman!" [*Laughs*] Well,

He wasn't a tall man – in fact, he was quite short – and yet Ben Pivar easily made the leap from Universal's Keeper of the Bs to TV producer-director.

It's a series about the Creeper." That's how Ben found out that he was going to work with Hatton!

Ben told me that his big problem at Universal, always, was budget, budget, budget, "How much will it cost?!" They'd hand him the scripts and his job was to make sure they were shot as cheaply as possible. And he did a damn good job. His motto was, "If I'm sitting at my desk doing nothing, I know I've done my job." He was a strictly hands-*off* producer: On *Confidential File*, he did *not* get involved at all in any of the creative aspects, what our topics were going to be or where we were going to go or anything. But he knew *how* things should be done and he knew *who* should be doing *what*. And he didn't hesitate to fire somebody if he, Ben, thought a guy wasn't doing his job. And Ben did direct the interview parts of what we shot for the nationally syndicated episodes.

This I've never forgotten: Ben had been on *Confidential File* about three weeks when one day I was told he wanted to see me in his office. I went in there, and he had papers in front of him, and he said, "Yes, yes, yes,

It's been a spell since writer-producer-director Andrew J. Fenady's last movie-TV project, so he embarked on a new career—novelist—and quickly landed in the Western Writers of America Hall of Fame.

he didn't look like Ronald Colman to me!

Ben had a very, very successful and brilliant brother—do you know about Maurice Pivar? He was an editor, he was in charge of the editing department over at Universal. And on the side, if anybody wanted Maurice to take a look at a picture, he charged $1000 for comments. Not even written comments. They would go in the projection room, take a look at whatever the picture was, and Maurice would say, "Okay, cut the scene at the beginning, and cut such-and-such scene in the middle, and speed up the ending, and the music is lousy," and whatever the hell his comments were. He was very, very much appreciated and had a great reputation, Maurice.

Ben had ulcers. Two or three or four times a day, when he would get excited or try *not* to get excited, he had a bottle of Maalox or some damn thing, and he would drink a double dollop of that. And at times when he was sitting at his desk, his left elbow would *jerk* up, like it was trying to fly off, trying to fly away from him!

Ben was very light on his feet. He had a pal who was a professional dancer as well as an actor, named Alan Foster. When Ben came over to *Confidential File*, he brought Alan along, and we used him occasionally as an actor. Alan was Ben's pal, his associate, his stooge, call him whatever you want [*laughs*]. A very nice man. More than once, Alan and Ben would put on a little act. they danced in the office, without any musical accompaniment. They were like fugitives from vaudeville, for Christ's sake, they were show-offs, and they showed off that they could hoof. But *one* of 'em could hoof better than the other, and that was Ben! Ben had rhythm, he would dance better than the professional dancer did!

Ben was a family man, but I must tell you the truth, not a very good one. He had the roving eye. He had a very lovely wife, Judy, and a couple of kids, a boy and a girl, but after he left *Confidential File*, things didn't work out so well for them.

But as far as my relationship with Ben, I have to say that I'm very, very glad that I met him, because as far as I was concerned, he was a fine fellow. He was certainly a worthy relic of the Hollywood studio system of that time. I don't know whether he had creativity or not, but he did make a star out of Rondo Hatton. Albeit a *creeping* star!

Fears New and Old: The Postwar American Horror Film

By Gary D. Rhodes

Editor's Note: *The Brute Man* was one of the last horror movies to reach theaters prior to the start of a years-long horror drought. Well, that's what all The Books will tell you anyway. Gary D. Rhodes files this very different and far more accurate report on the visibility of horror flicks in the mid– to late 1940s. It was originally published in the 2014 book *Recovering 1940s Horror Cinema: Traces of a Lost Decade*.

Numerous historians of the American horror film have insisted that the genre came to a temporary close at the end of World War II, and some of them choose 1945 as a chronological endpoint for their books. Evidence for such a position rests largely on a perceived dearth of new horror film production in Hollywood in the late '40s.

While it is undeniable that during those years Hollywood produced few horror movies of the type popular between 1931 and 1945 (meaning a narrative concentration on monsters and/or mad scientists, and a reliance on film personalities such as Boris Karloff, Bela Lugosi and Lon Chaney Jr.), the traditional historical narrative remains fraught with enough misunderstandings to require a re-examination of the period.

To begin, it is important to consider the major shifts then underway in Hollywood. In the months following World War II, the American film industry achieved great economic success. According to film historian Thomas Schatz, "Hollywood enjoyed its best year ever" in 1946. The industry looked towards greater and greater profits, and why not? American troops returning home from Europe and the Pacific could only mean a significant increase for domestic movie ticket sales.

For the fiscal year ending on November 2, 1946, Universal reported the biggest profits in its lengthy history. Monogram's profits also increased to record levels. And by the end of the year, PRC—a company known for its Poverty Row output—had grown confident enough in its role in the marketplace to drop low-budget films from its program.

However, by the end of 1946, the American film industry began to undergo serious changes. Trade publications noted decreased movie attendance in early 1947, a problem that continued into the summer. All of this

As horror flicks petered out in the mid-40s, one "dying gasp" was *Strangler of the Swamp* with Miss America of 1939 Rosemary La Planche and, as the ghastly title goon, Charles Middleton.

Five-fingers exercise: Director Robert Florey watches as the ivories are tickled by the title character of *The Beast with Five Fingers* (1946).

came at a time of increasing operational and production costs at the studios. If 1946 became one of Hollywood's most successful years financially, 1947 would prove to be one of its worst, and it would set a trend that persisted for the rest of the decade.

What did that mean for the American horror film? In 1945, the situation appeared tenuous. On the one hand, in September 1945, *Variety* predicted that "balanced films" would replace movie "cycles."[12] But on the other hand, new horror film releases played in movie theaters throughout 1946, with the genre quite vibrant for well over a year after World War II. It would not be until 1947 that the numbers of new horror movies decreased dramatically. This was caused not the end of the war, but rather the subsequent changes in Hollywood.

The need to decouple a simplistic and parallel link between changes in the horror movie with the end of the war is important, but it alone does not account for two forms of growth that the genre experienced in the mid– to late '40s. One of these involved the massive reissue programs undertaken by various Hollywood studios that caused literally dozens of horror movies produced between 1931 and 1945 to return to movie screens in the late '40s.

The other issue the genre faced in 1945 and the years that followed had to do with the very meaning of the word "horror." Years earlier, certainly by the end of 1932, "horror" concretized as the film genre's name, much as other genres had one-word monikers like "musical" and "gangster." It served Hollywood quite well in the years that followed, representing a clear narrative tradition in the space of six letters and evoking the aforementioned kinds of film plots, characters and stars.

But that singular usage of the word "horror" became plural as the war came to an end, as journalists applied it first to cinematic images of the Nazi death camps and then to a number of adult-oriented fictional films featuring not the old monsters or actors, but instead suspenseful narratives featuring psychological themes. For the first time since its widespread usage in the early '30s, the boundaries of the term "horror movie" grew noticeably.

Re-examining the postwar American horror film with the use of primary sources allows for the construction of a different and more accurate historical narrative than has been offered in the past, introducing a necessary degree of revisionism to longstanding beliefs about the period from 1946 to 1950, an era during which movie theaters regularly screened horror movies that were both new and old.

Postwar Productions

In the late '40s, Hollywood did produce fewer horror movies of the type popular during the war, but their declining numbers did not begin with the surrender of Germany (May 8, 1945), Japan (August 14, 1945) or even with the calendar year 1945. By contrast, the horror movie continued unabated for the entirety of 1946. For example, during that year, American audiences saw:

 Monogram's *The Face of Marble* (released in January)

 PRC's *Strangler of the Swamp* (January), *The Flying Serpent* (February), *The Mask of Diijon* (March), *Devil Bat's Daughter* (April) and *The Brute Man* (October)

 Universal's *House of Horrors, The Spider Woman Strikes Back* (both March), *She-Wolf of London* and *The Cat Creeps* (both May)

 Republic's *The Catman of Paris* (April)

 Republic's *Valley of the Zombies* (May)

As the year came to a close, industry trade publications reviewed Warner Brothers' new film *The Beast with Five Fingers*. These movies were in addition to such horror comedies as Monogram's Bowery Boys feature *Spook Busters* (released in August 1946) and Columbia's short subject *A Bird in the Head* (released in April), as well as a number of horror films that had debuted in 1945 but still remained in general distribution, including Universal's *House of Dracula*.

Certainly it is true that changes to the horror movie and its audience were increasingly noticeable, but these had little if anything to do with the end of the war. Nor did they necessarily have much to do with ongoing attacks from parents and moral groups. For example, in late December 1945, a letter to the editor of *The Christian Science Monitor* described with alarm several young children becoming "hysterical" at a horror film screening, their older and "hardened" ten-year-old counterparts promptly ordering them to "shut up." The author proceeded to argue that exhibitors did not actually have to screen horror movies, and so it was the imperative of good citizens to make their complaints known. Otherwise, "horror on the screen will continue as long as we permit it to be profitable." A number of women in Columbus, Ohio, made similar complaints during early 1947, as did the Minneapolis Parent Teacher Association in 1947. But the American horror movie had proven resilient against such attacks since at least 1932.

Theater manager reports published in *Motion Picture Herald* from 1946 suggest something else was at work. For example, regarding *House of Dracula*:

> We say this is definitely our last horror film. There seems to be nothing gained by frightening the children away.
> – Winema Theatre, Scotia, California, May 4, 1946

> Used this for a Saturday midnight show and this is where it belongs. Wouldn't recommend it for any other time.
> – Sparks Theatre, Cooper, Texas, May 25, 1946

> About a year ago or so, a chiller-diller like this would be very good for our theatre, but today it is strictly [a] one-day showing and not any too good even for one day. The producers are making entirely too many chillers. Again we say when our patrons who like action, thrill and westerns don't buy chillers it's time for a considerable curtailment of this type of picture.
> – Fountain Theatre, Terre Haute, Indiana, September 28, 1946

At first, such accounts suggest that the horror movie was losing ground even with younger patrons who had frequented them during the first half of the decade,

When Dinosaurs Ruled the Loew Poli-Bijou, New Haven, Connecticut.

an argument that could be evidenced with the small number of such films released in 1947 (such as *Scared to Death*) and 1948 (such as *The Creeper* and *Unknown Island*).

Indeed, a survey of the film industry press in the late '40 seems to reveal more unmade horror movies than new product in release. Curt Siodmak, the screenwriter of such films as *The Wolf Man* (1941), and Lon Chaney Jr. attempted to start their own production company in 1948 to produce films featuring characters "more horrible than any yet seen on the screen." But nothing came of the venture. That same year, Film Classics announced that Boris Karloff and Bela Lugosi would costar in *The Strange Case of Malcolm Craig*, but the film was never produced. Lugosi also told one journalist that "there is enough material in the original novel [*Dracula*] for half a dozen pictures," but no studio produced any of them that year, or in the years that immediately followed.

Traditional horror film histories often seize upon Universal-International's *Abbott and Costello Meet Frankenstein* (1948) as key to the belief about the horror movie's postwar decline and even (temporary) death, in large measure because it paired popular monsters from earlier years with a film comedy team. Such a view was

Horror was on a Hollywood hiatus in the late 1940s, but not in the Three Stooges' "looniverse": Their fans were treated to the scare comedies *Crime on Their Hands*, *Who Done It?*, *The Ghost Talks*, *Shivering Sherlocks* (all pictured) and more.

not unknown in 1948 when the film was released. According to the *New York Star*:

> [I]t's heart-warming to see all our favorite monsters once more, each inexorably expressing his individuality, all at the same time. It's kind of like a class reunion. They look a little older now, and a little tired. Dracula seems to creak a bit with arthritis as he emerges from his coffin these days, and his bite has lost some of its depth.

Perhaps the damning phrase in this review is "once more," as if the subsequent disappearance of these monsters from the screen was a clear expectation.

Theater manager reports from across the U.S. were generally positive, except in cases where viewers interpreted *A&C Meet Frankenstein* as a horror film rather than a comedy:

> One of the best and most entertaining in the Abbott and Costello series. A good draw and a pleased audience.
> – Gray Theatre, Gray, Georgia

> A laugh riot from beginning to end. Liked by all. Did good midweek business.
> – The Gilbert, Okeechobee, Florida

> Just about their best, I reckon, and lots of people came to see them. We played a midnight preview on this which also drew well.
> – Eminence Theatre, Eminence, Kentucky

> Very good at the box office. A little too scary for the little ones, but the high school kids really enjoyed it.
> – Grove Theatre, Blooming Grove, Texas

> I wonder if it is worth it—all those howling kids, screams, and broken seats. Did an above average business, but it wasn't Abbott and Costello at their best. Had more walkouts on this than any picture we've ever played. This is the last "horror" picture we will ever book.
> – Williamette Valley Theatres, Albany, Oregon

> The shrieks and screams could be heard in the street. Small children jammed the foyer. Babies cried. Women scratched all the skin from their husbands' hands and the PTA descended in mobs, demanding to know why we played a "horror" picture on Saturday. If we get out of this one without bodily harm, we will be plain

lucky. Spent most of my time drying tears and allaying hysteria among the children. Wow!
– Shastona Theatre, Mount Shasta, California

As a result of such reactions, Universal-International planned more Abbott and Costello films (including the one that became *Abbott and Costello Meet the Killer, Boris Karloff* in 1949), but not any serious horror movies featuring Dracula, the Wolf Man and Frankenstein's Monster. The studio abandoned the old monsters, another apparent sign that the horror movie was under siege in the late '40s, even if its decline did not begin until 1947.

Reviving the Past

A poll of movie theater managers published in 1949 resulted in the following analysis: "There is small place for [horror movies] in most theaters, and the special horror shows and accompanying sensational advertising have given them a black eye. ...Most exhibitors think the zombies should be locked up in a closet and kept there." That same year, a poll of average Americans found men and women putting "horror, murder, gangster pictures first on their list of dislikes." Here seems to be an indicator as to why the numbers of new horror movies decreased from 1947 to 1950.

By contrast, after interviewing Lugosi in 1947, a Boston journalist told readers that the "studios are being swamped with requests for Lugosi and Karloff pictures." At first, given Lugosi's limited film output after World War II, it is tempting to view such a statement as nothing more than the actor's own wishful thinking and flair for publicity, channeled into the press thanks to a willing reporter. To be sure, Lugosi would have had little knowledge of how many letters the studios received on any subject.

That said, there seems to be a good deal of truth to the fact that many filmgoers in the late '40s did want to see horror movies, including a group that provided their key audience during the war and that may have well been underrepresented in the aforementioned polls: children. Perhaps some were frightened by horror movies, even when they were tempered with comedy from the likes of Abbott and Costello, but many still wanted to watch such films. And the simple fact is that they did get to see them. Moviegoers were in fact bombarded by a vast number of horror movies during the years 1947 to 1950. Some appeared in spotty releases, and some appeared only on spook show bills or at Halloween.

Even Boris Karloff got in a horror credit amidst the so-called "horror moratorium": Here's the King of Monsters with Lenore Aubert at the exclusive Lakeside Golf Club where *Abbott and Costello Meet the Killer, Boris Karloff* was on location for several days.

However, a large number of horror movies had major releases throughout the U.S. during those years. For example, they included at least 25 horror movies starring Bela Lugosi. Twenty-five, all in the space of just three years, even though Lugosi made only one new serious horror movie (*Scared to Death*) and only one horror comedy (*A&C Meet Frankenstein*) during the second half of the decade.

But none of these 25 Lugosi movies at movie theaters were new; they were all reissues. The back catalogues of studios like Universal and Monogram saturated theaters with old horror movies to the extent that they generally satisfied whatever demand existed for them, cheaply and efficiently. Put another way, why hire an actor like Bela Lugosi and produce a new horror film when an old one would fit the bill?

Reissues were particularly appealing to studios in 1947 and in the years that immediately followed. As previously mentioned, the high tide of Hollywood's economic success in 1946 receded rapidly. According to Thomas Schatz, "the American movie industry went into an economic tailspin and a sustained fall from social grace" during and after 1947. Box office receipts fell sharply due to declining attendance, with moviegoers spending an

In March 1947—the same month that one wire service article noted that ten "stock" film series, including "Frankenstein, Andy Hardy and Dracula," were "out of production"—Universal announced that they would reissue *Dracula* (1931) and *Frankenstein* (1931) on a double bill. It played Los Angeles in April of that year, and continued to appear on theater screens throughout the summer and autumn. The Roxy Theatre in Hinckley, Minnesota, reported, "Played this double feature one day to capacity business. It will scare them, especially *Dracula*." At a number of theaters, the dual bill played as a midnight show. At least a few theaters booked *Dracula* without *Frankenstein*.

The success of such reissues brought more of the same in 1948. That February, *The Hollywood Reporter* announced that the studios had scheduled 130 re-releases, the "greatest number of repeats for a single year's program in motion picture distribution history." The practice continued in 1949, despite warnings from some in the industry that reissues would eventually cause more problems than they solved.

Consider again the case of Bela Lugosi. Realart Pictures of New York City reissued many of his Universal films in 1948 and 1949. His Monogram films of the war era also returned to the screen. The following breakdown provides a partial list of the Lugosi films screened in the postwar era:

1947: *Phantom Ship* (aka *The Mystery of the Mary Celeste*, 1935), *The Human Monster* (aka *The Dark Eyes of London*, 1939), *The Devil Bat* (1940), *The Corpse Vanishes* (1942), *Ghosts on the Loose* (1943), *The Ape Man* (1943), *Return of the Ape Man* (1944) *The Body Snatcher* (1945)

1948: *Son of Frankenstein* (1939), *Black Friday* (1940), *The Wolf Man* (1941), *The Black Cat* (1941), *The Ghost of Frankenstein* (1942), *Voodoo Man* (1944)

1949: *Murders in the Rue Morgue* (1932), *The Raven* (1935), *Invisible Ghost* (1941), *Black Dragons* (1942), *Bowery at Midnight* (1942), *The Corpse Vanishes* (1942), *The Ape Man* (1943), *Frankenstein Meets the Wolf Man* (1943), *Ghosts on the Loose* (1943)

In this world of reissues, however, Bela Lugosi was not a special case. Many horror films starring Boris Karloff, Lon Chaney Jr. and others also appeared at American movie theaters during the same years.

While hardly helpful to the careers of individual Hollywood actors, the revival of old movies meant that

increasing percentage of their discretionary income on other kinds of leisure activities. The end result: The entire film industry felt great economic pressure.

At the same time, exhibitors perceived a shortage of new film product, something that led to a pronounced increase in the importation and distribution of foreign films. Many British films enjoyed great success at American theaters in the late '40s. In fact, England's Eagle-Lion purchased the low-budget American company PRC in order to gain greater access to the U.S. marketplace.

Along with obtaining product from other countries, studios realized that healthy profits could be had from reviving their own old films. It made good economic sense, at least in the short term. In April 1947, for example, *Motion Picture Herald* reported that seven of the 11 production-distributor companies—including MGM, Paramount, RKO, 20th Century-Fox, Universal, Warner Brothers and PRC—would release 29 "hit pictures" from previous seasons during the spring and summer of that year.

One studio executive noted that the "trend towards reissues [had] been brought about by the excessively high production costs which [had] practically doubled since 1941," adding that "the margin of profit from a reissue is sometimes even greater than that received from a new picture." Universal's vice-president agreed, deciding to re-release some of their back catalogue as double-feature packages.

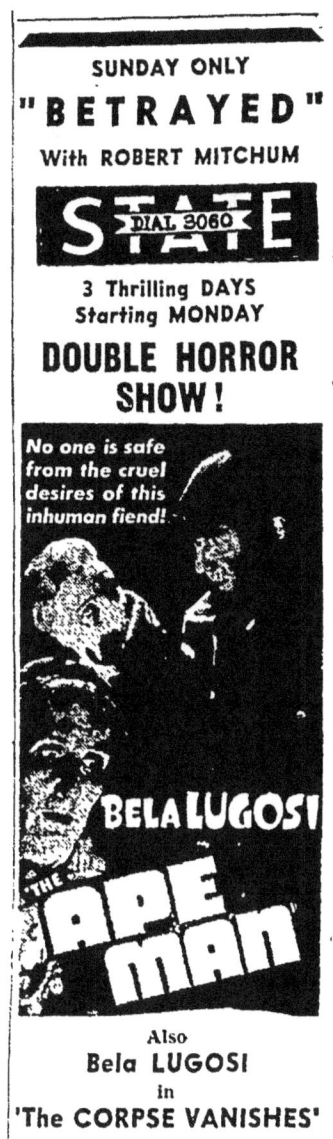

tion Picture Herald noted, audiences who viewed the Nazi films "have seen all the Four Horseman of the Apocalypse riding at last over the brink of a fetid hell."

Much of the American press labeled footage of the Nazi atrocities "Horror Films." A Gallup poll revealed that 60% of the American public believed the Nazi "horror films" should be shown in theaters. In St. Louis, for example, 81,500 persons attended 44 screenings, which had originally been scheduled for only 12 performances. And increased theater attendance occurred in numerous parts of the country when these particular "horror films" were screened.

Continued reports of similar "horror films" appeared in the press in 1946, including details of confiscated footage shot by the Nazis. In late February of that year, the *Los Angeles Times* described footage screened at Nuremberg:

> [Scenes of] German soldiers laughing while one of them swung an axe to behead helpless Yugoslavs, of S.S. men swinging corpses after hangings, and of ferocious dogs and starving hogs devouring other victims were shown today on [a] motion picture screen to the international military tribunal.

After mentioning such films as *The Cabinet of Dr. Caligari* (1919) and *Dracula* (1931), another journalist declared, "In all the grim record of man's inhumanity to man there is little to match the wholesale crimes of which the last batch of Nuremberg defendants now stand convicted." Such connections horror was a constant cinematic presence in the late '40s, a factor that has been largely ignored by historians who have generally (and incorrectly) equated the decline in new production with the genre's disappearance from theater screens.

Complicating the Present

Prior to the institution of reissue programs at Hollywood studios and companies, the genre grew thanks to the evolving use of the term "horror movie." Such complications began in the spring of 1945 during the final days of the war. The Allied liberation of German death camps resulted in many things, not least of which were terrifying non-fiction images. Public screenings of the film footage resulted in part due to General Eisenhower, who believed that Americans needed to see "what the enemy had done." As *Mo-*

Last of the Lewtons: 1946's *Bedlam*. The perspicacious producer and his team of directors were responsible for some of the 1940s' finest (i.e., most frightful) thrillers, the stuff that goosebumps are made of. Pictured: dialogue director Anthony Jowitt, director Mark Robson and co-stars Richard Fraser and Anna Lee.

between horror movies and the Nazi death camps continued as well. A 1947 *Daily Variety* article compared the experiences of an old man at Maideneck as being "like a movie of horror."

At roughly the same that audiences read about and saw the death camp footage, the film industry press began to describe yet another kind of new horror movie. In April 1945, *Variety* wrote that Universal—the key studio producing horror films from 1931 to 1945—would be using "psychological goose pimples" as the basis for a few of their new "chillers," rather than relying on the old "monsters." One year later, *The Hollywood Reporter* announced that "horror pix" were gaining "heavier adult patronage," adding that they were "winning universal appeal" thanks to bigger budgets and higher standards. Here the discussion centered not on films like *The Flying Serpent* or *Valley of the Zombies*, but on motion pictures of a different type, those that were more psychological or suspenseful.

Hollywood Reporter specifically cited such 1946 releases as RKO's *The Spiral Staircase* and *Bedlam*, the latter produced by Val Lewton and starring Boris Karloff. The trade also drew attention to Columbia's *The Walls Came Tumbling Down* (1946). In like fashion, *Daily Variety* told readers that 20th Century–Fox's *Dragonwyck* (1946) would gain a "ready audience among the horror film fans." Such an elastic understanding of "horror" could well have allowed *The Hollywood Reporter* to name other movies in general release during 1946, including Hitchcock's *Spellbound* (which premiered during the final days of 1945), Fox's *Shock* and Monogram's *Suspense*, as well as a number of foreign films that appeared on American screens, including the Swedish-made *The Girl and the Devil* and the British-made *Dead of Night* and *Frenzy*.

Others working in the industry also understood this expanded meaning of the word "horror." In 1946, for example, Curt Siodmak wrote, "Almost every melodrama contains scenes of horror, though the A-Plus producer would never accept that term for his million-dollar creation. When horror enters the gilded gate of top production, it is glorified as a 'psychological thriller.' But a rose by any other name…"

Even if some of those producers eschewed the word "horror," others did not. An article in a 1946 issue of *Liberty* magazine took pains to detail the different kinds of screen horror that existed, going so far as to say: "Horror can be a great many things, from the psychological thriller to the strictly monster tale. The witch scene in Disney's *Snow White* [1937] and the whale in *Pinocchio* [1940] were nothing but horror."

An industry trade publication offered a similar view in 1946:

> Henry Horsecollar, the horror fan, sat in the glum shadows of the film house, throbbing with suspense. Dracula had won a ghastly decision over the Wolfman and was prowling around to clamp a strangle hold on the Catman of Paris. Henry sat, spellbound, with his eardrums straining. He was waiting to hear the guy in the seat behind him start chewing another mouthful of popcorn.
>
> Psychological mysteries have been popping up all over the screen, and now comes the psychological western. Maybe the boys will chase each other in circles instead of going thataway. It will be a tough job to "psych" a horse. He has horse sense.

Surveying the upcoming season of releases in late December 1946, *Film Daily* told readers that there would definitely be "fewer psychological mysteries" on the screen the following year. While that prediction was true in many respects, trade publications continued to identify numerous suspense and mystery films as being "horror" movies or at least containing elements of that genre.

For example, *Daily Variety* told readers that Universal's *A Woman's Vengeance* (1947) "approximates the shudder thrills of a horror story." The same publication cited the "horror" elements in *Cry Wolf* (Warners, 1947). The following year, the *New York Journal-American* declared Paramount's *Sorry, Wrong Number* (1948) and Alfred

With monster movies out of vogue, spooky "psychological mysteries" picked up some of the slack. Left, Vincent Price as the haughty, haunted patroon in *Dragonwyck* (1946); Above, Edward G. Robinson is tormented by the skeletons rattling in his family closet in *The Red House* (1947)

Hitchcock's *Rope* (Warners, 1948) to be horror movies. Other such films in American theaters during this period included *Fear in the Night* (Pine-Thomas, 1947), *The Red House* (United Artists, 1947), *Inner Sanctum* (M.R.S., 1948), *Portrait of Jennie* (SRO, 1948), *The Spiritualist* (Eagle-Lion, 1948), *The Raven* (Westport International, 1948) and *The Woman in White* (Warners, 1948).

Many earlier American films had featured similar kinds of psychological mysteries and suspense themes, but it was only after World War II that the term "horror" became regularly used in both film trade publications and the mainstream press to describe them, a factor that became a part of popular culture. For example, in one of his 1949 acts, comedian Jack Carter included a bit needling the "psycho" and "horror" films.

Conclusion

No greater misconception exists about the history of the American horror film than the prevalent belief that such movies disappeared from theater screens when World War II came to a close. The year 1946 saw a large number of new horror film releases of a type similar to those popular from 1931 to 1945. While production of such movies did diminish greatly during the years 1947 to 1950, theaters regularly screened horror film reissues, as well as new kinds of "horror" movies ranging from non-fiction footage of wartime atrocities to fictional narratives focussed on suspense and psychological themes.

Releases of such films would continue in the 1950s, a period in which Hollywood did not recover from the economic problems that took hold in 1947 and which were in fact exacerbated by the ever-increasing popularity of television. Reissue programs continued, most notably a nationally distributed double feature of *Dracula* and *Frankenstein* in 1952. And the expanding boundaries of "horror" came to include a wealth of science fiction films that became extremely popular throughout the decade.

Writing about Howard Hawks' science fiction film *The Thing from Another World* (RKO, 1951), Walter Winchell told readers: "[P]reviewers say *The Thing* makes *Dracula* look like a petunia." Such a comment suggests a view that both films could be meaningfully compared, that they were part of the same category, the same genre.

Put another way, rather than viewing the horror movie as dying with the end of World War II and the reappearing in the '50s, we should see those years as part of an ongoing and evolving process. The horror movie changed during and after 1945, but it never disappeared from American theaters. Quite the opposite.

The Face That Launched the Rondo Hatton Awards
By David Colton

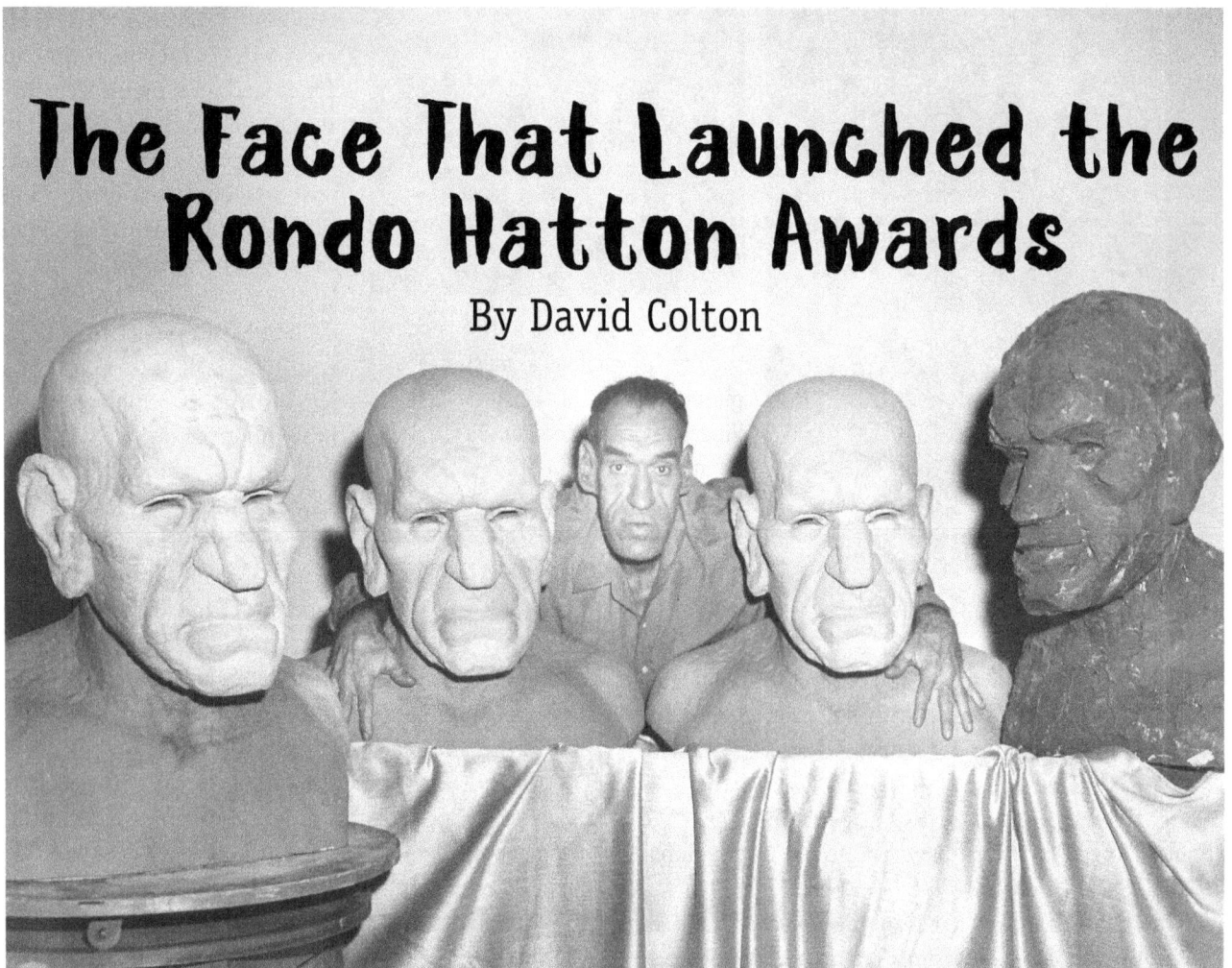

It's hard to imagine that a good-looking Florida high school student could, as an adult, end up being billed in movies as "The Creeper." It's even more unreal that this sadly disfigured B-movie villain would become the name and image for an annual award honoring the best and smartest in classic horror.

In horror as in life, redemption comes in many forms. That's exactly why the Rondo Hatton Classic Horror Awards, now (2019) headed into their 18th year, are as unforgettable as the *Brute Man* actor himself.

The award is known throughout monster fandom as the Rondo, a six-inch resin recreation of the giant bust of the Creeper created by a mad sculptor in *House of Horrors* (1946), one of Hatton's final films. More than 400 busts have been given out since the awards began in 2002. Talk about product placement!

Intended to recognize the best in classic horror scholarship, appreciation and enthusiasm, Rondos have gone to the likes of Ray Harryhausen, Ray Bradbury, Forrest J Ackerman, horror hosts Zacherley and Vampira, directors Guillermo del Toro, Peter Jackson, Joe Dante and John Landis, writer-editors Tim Lucas, Tom Weaver, Jovanka Vuckovic, Greg Mank, April Snellings and David J. Skal, and many others.

Voted on by thousands of fans in an online ballot every year, the Rondos have become the world's largest survey of the so-called "classic horror electorate."

Like Rondo Hatton himself, the origins of the Rondos are obscure.

Back in 2002, smoke and terror of 9/11 was still in the air; movies were available mainly at the video store; the Internet was up and running, but mostly on clumsy message boards and email. It was so long ago that AOL was still sending out discs.

It was there, on AOL, that a small group of classic horror fans gathered daily to discuss the monster movies of the 1930s and 1940s, including the near-forgotten films of Rondo Hatton. (The horror board was later to leave AOL and become today's Classic Horror Film Board.)

Inspired by the *Midnight Marquee* awards, called the Laemmles after the founders of Universal Pictures, we fans at AOL kicked around the idea of bestowing our own honors. What should these new awards be called? The Belas? The Karloffs? Too obvious. What about the Ravens? No, too Poe-centric.

Then someone suggested Rondo Hatton, whose misshapen likeness had been replicated as a wide-brimmed villain in the *Rocketeer* movie of 1991.

"Yeah!" one of us exclaimed in the days before emoticons. "The Rondos! He even had that bust in *House of Horrors!*" Calling our awards the Rondos sounded right, like the Oscars, the Tonys, the Emmys.

Still, it was only online chatter until a few days later when DC and Marvel comic book artist Kerry Gammill, a member of the AOL horror board, emailed me a detailed rendering of what the Rondo statuette could look like. "You could sculpt this?" I asked. "Let me try," he said.

We prepared a 14-category ballot and urged folks to vote online. We got back 198 emailed ballots, an amazing response we thought.

Rondo's first Movie of the Year was *Lord of the Rings: The Two Towers*; *Buffy* was Best TV Show; Best Convention was the Monster Bash; Best Book was *Heaven & Hell to Play With: The Filming of* The Night of the Hunter by Preston Neal Jones; Best Magazine was *Video Watchdog*; Writer of the Year was Tom Weaver (now editor of this *Scripts from the Crypt* series). Etc.

But the Rondos didn't go tactile until June 21, 2003, when we gathered in a crowded hotel room at the Monster Bash outside Pittsburgh waiting for Gammill to show up with the first-ever Rondos. He took one out of the box to gasps and applause. Gammill's elegantly sculpted Rondo Award perfectly channeled the Rondo Hatton bust from *House of Horrors*, as if a time portal had opened to 1946. His Rondo looked like the perfect prize: a true Brute Man.

Famed movie collector Bob Burns stared at his statuette and delivered the ultimate Monster Kid compliment: "What a thing," Bob said. "This Rondo is so cool!"

Since that day, Rondos have become highly prized, some mailed to winners as far away as Tokyo and Australia. Voting has expanded to almost 4000 a year, despite a clumsy ballot that requires cut-and-paste patience. It's gratifying to know that thousands of voters now know Rondo Hatton because of the annual awards.

Instead of a claustrophobic hotel room, we now hold a formal Rondo Awards ceremony at the WonderFest Convention in Louisville, Kentucky, every year. The ceremony includes live acceptances and videotapes

The Creeper just exercised his civic right to vote--in the yearly Rondo Awards, that is. Do you? You'd *better*! Check out rondoaward.com

from winners who couldn't make it. The award shows are always memorable, a mix of monsters, memories and tears.

We remember John Zacherle holding his Rondo high like a championship belt in 2007, saying that for all his acclaim, he had never won an award before. An ailing Forrest J Ackerman displayed his "Best Comeback" Rondo at the Ackermansion. Illustrator Basil Gogos received a standing ovation when he showed up to accept his Rondo in front of adoring fans.

Horror artist Bernie Wrightson, co-creator of Swamp Thing, explained at the Rondo 2008 ceremony that the Rondo symbolized a triumph over childhood ridicule.

"I'm just a kid who grew up in the '50s with Universal monsters on TV and reading EC Comics," he told the audience. "Like a whole lot of us, I was an oddball as a kid." He paused and held up the Rondo. "But now..." The crowd burst into applause.

Rondo Hatton's namesake award reaches deep into the Universal canon. While accepting his award, Donnie Dunagan, who played young Peter in *Son of Frankenstein* (1939) before going on to become a tough Marine veteran, told stories of sharing ice cream with Boris Karloff.

The Monster's real daughter, Sara Karloff, inducted into Rondo's Monster Kid Hall of Fame, recalled that when she discovered fandom, she thought that the "dealers room" was a casino. Victoria Price, the daughter of Vincent, said she never liked watching her father die in so many of his films, but felt finally like a true Monster Kid when she was inducted into the Hall of Fame.

A Roundup of Rondo Recipients

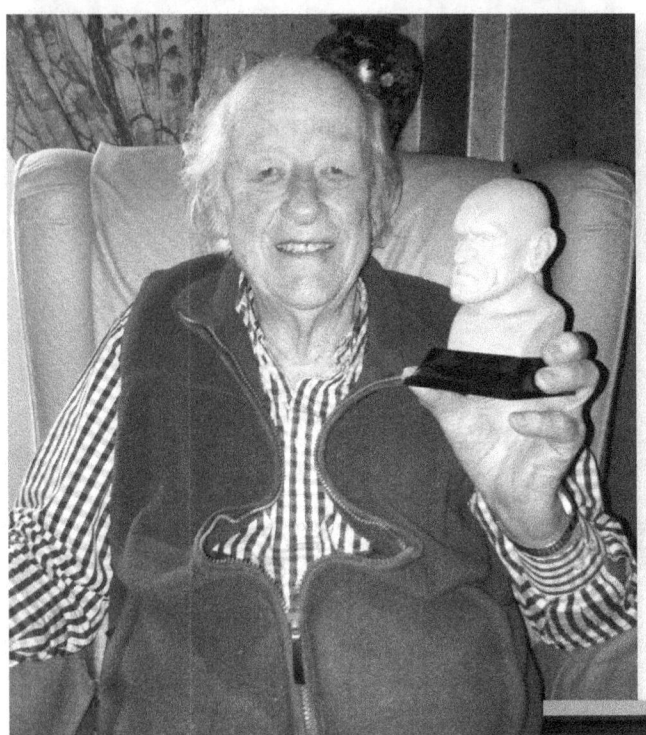

Bob Burns with his Best DVD Commentary Rondo.

Rondo Crosses the Pond!: Ray Harryhausen in London, showing off his Best Commentary Rondo.

Holding Rondos: Tom Stockman, who staged a St. Louis "Vincentennial" for Vincent Price in 2011; Rondo Hall of Fame inductee Julie (*Creature from the Black Lagoon*) Adams; and Tim (*Video Watchdog*) Lucas, winner for Best Writer. The onlooker is a multiple Rondo winner, TV horror host Dr. Gangrene.

Pioneering TV horror host Zacherley, a Rondo Hall of Famer.

Cortlandt Hull, whose relative Henry Hull starred in *WereWolf of London* (1935), broke down in tears as he introduced 92-year-old Ray Meyer, who sculpted several of the Aurora monster models in the 1960s. Illustrator William Stout was also tearful as he accepted his Hall of Fame honor.

In many ways, the Rondos are designed to honor those, like Rondo Hatton, who were rarely acknowledged for their work. They go mostly to those behind the scenes, those who study the monsters or make the monsters happen.

"We love being able to put a monster movie on TV every Sunday night," said Greg Nicotero, executive producer of *The Walking Dead*, holding two Rondos in 2015.

And then there was the time when an email arrived from alumni and students at Hillsborough High School in Tampa, Florida. Rondo Hatton was a 1913 graduate there, they wrote, a handsome football star before heading to World War I, returning with a mysterious condition that began to distort his face. Was there any way Hatton could receive a Rondo as a distinguished graduate?

The honor was long overdue. We're delighted to say that a 2017 Rondo is now on display at the school; see the photos on page 80.

Like any awards program, the Rondos have had their share of controversies. They can be susceptible to voting campaigns, *American Idol*–style, and the demographics don't always reflect the changing nature of the horror audience, although that happily is changing.

Some people object to the award altogether. They argue that using Hatton's grotesque image is disrespectful and even exploitive of his tragic fate.

We believe just the opposite. We think the awards not only keep the world of classic horror alive, but provide Rondo Hatton with the dignity and respect he did not always receive in life. At the beginning of every Rondo ceremony, a *House of Horrors* still is shown, overlaid with the following words:

> Dedicated to
> Rondo Hatton (1894-1946),
> the doomed character actor who
> never lost his monstrous pride.

David Colton, a former editor at *USA Today*, is a founder of the Classic Horror Film Board and administrator of the Rondo Hatton Classic Horror Awards. The Rondos can be found at rondoaward.com

The Brute Man: Pressbook

From the Ronald V. Borst Collection

PUBLICITY

Reveal Macabre Assassin In 'Brute Man' Shocker
(Review)

Movie patrons with an appetite for shuddery entertainment will find "The Brute Man," which opened yesterday at the .... Theatre, entirely satisfying to their palates.

The picture marks the return of "The Creeper," a terrifying human being of abnormal strength, who derives his macabre nickname from his habit of striking down his victims without warning.

Tom Neal, Jane Adams, Jan Wiley, Peter Whitney and Donald MacBride head a competent cast. Rondo Hatton has the title role.

Filled with suspense from the start, the story develops from an accident in a college chemistry laboratory which leaves a handsome young football player Hal Moffat, disfigured and embittered.

Tragic Transition

As the years go by, Moffat's mind becomes warped by the unsympathetic reaction to his forbidding appearance, arousing his hatred against all mankind and an obsession for revenge against those he blames for his condition.

After murdering two of his former campus associates, Moffat, fleeing from police, encounters a blind young piano teacher, played by Miss Adams.

The girl accepts him as a normal person and befriends him. Pathetically impressed by her lack of fear of him, the killer showers her with tokens of his abject devotion.

When he learns that an expensive surgical operation might restore the girl's sight, he applies the only means he knows—theft and murder—to obtain the necessary funds. His selfless action proves "The Creeper's" ultimate undoing—in a smashing climax.

Expertly directed by Jean Yarbrough and produced by Ben Pivar for PRC Pictures, "The Brute Man" lives up to this studio's high standard for mystery and horror thrillers. Photography by Maury Gertsman is geared to its melodramatic tone.

George Bricker and M. Coates Webster wrote the screenplay from an original story by Dwight V. Babcock.

'Brute Man' Is Shudder Drama
(Advance)

"The Brute Man," PRC's very much talked-about mystery horror film, comes .... to the .... Theatre. Tom Neal, Jane Adams, Jan Wiley, Peter Whitney, Donald MacBride and Rondo Hatton are headliners in the cast.

Plot of the new shocker deals with the bloody career of a demented killer, an ex-football hero who is disfigured in a laboratory accident. The assassin's friendship for a blind girl proves his undoing in the film's unusual ending.

Jean Yarbrough directed.

"THE BRUTE MAN," PRC's new sensational mystery-horror production, has Rondo Hatton (L), glamorous Jan Wiley and popular Tom Neal.

'Brute Man' Picture Tells Fabulous Murder Story
(Advance)

Shuddery suspense and breathtaking excitement are promised by PRC's offering "The Brute Man," mystery thriller due .... at the .... Theatre. Advance reports indicate that this film is one of the season's outstanding shockers. Tops among the players are Tom Neal; Jane Adams and Jan Wiley. Other notables in the roster include Peter Whitney, Donald MacBride and Rondo Hatton. The latter appears in the picture's title role.

In this film, moviegoers will again see "The Creeper," a sub-human killer who does his murdering in mysteriously gruesome fashion.

The story, said to be action-filled from the start, stems from the accidental disfiguring of a college football star. After years of brooding over his misfortune, the victim becomes demented and is plagued by an obsession for vengeance.

In more lucid moments, however, the maniac befriends a blind girl and commits a crime to finance an operation which may restore her eyesight. It is this dramatic situation which brings the picture to its crashing climax.

The character of the mad assassin is played by Rondo Hatton. It is described as one of the cinema's most gripping performances.

"The Brute Man," directed by Jean Yarbrough and produced by Ben Pivar, is based on an original story by Dwight V. Babcock. George Bricker and M. Coates Webster co-authored the screenplay. Maury Gertsman was the cameraman.

THE BRUTE MAN (1C)
Screen favorite Jan Wiley, appears in PRC's film, "The Brute Man."

Audiences Like Eerie Thriller
(Current)

Macabre thrills and eerie suspense are ingeniously combined in PRC's latest "The Brute Man," mystery horror film now at the .... Theatre. Seen in the cast are Tom Neal, Jane Adams, Jan Wiley, Peter Whitney, Donald MacBride and Rondo Hatton.

The original story by Dwight V. Babcock deals excitingly with the criminal career of an ex-gridiron hero who becomes a killer after being disfigured by acid during a laboratory experiment.

Highlight of the film is the performance of Rondo Hatton as the mad murderer. Lovely Miss Adams appears as a blind girl who finds herself accused as the assassin's accomplice.

Jean Yarbrough directed. The producer was Ben Pivar.

Crime Picture Has Jane Adams
(Current)

Colorless contact lenses were worn by Jane Adams for her blind girl role in PRC Pictures' "The Brute Man," now at the .... Theatre. The glasses, fitting directly over the eyeballs, assisted the actress in affecting the fixed stare of a sightless person.

Director Jean Yarbrough vetoed the original idea of Jane donning white lenses, similar to those Herbert Marshall had in "The Enchanted Cottage," and which produce a cloudy effect, on the grounds that they were "not glamorous."

Miss Adams' own orbs, a luminous blue, are among the most striking in Hollywood.

Actor Related To Noted Stars
(Current)

Movie actor Tom Neal, featured in PRC's release "The Brute Man," now at the .... Theatre is a cousin of Lionel, Ethel and Diana Barrymore. His mother was a niece of John Drew, one of America's greatest stage actors.

THE BRUTE MAN (1A)
Lovely Jane Adams is featured in PRC's exciting "The Brute Man."

Credits

PRC PICTURES INC.
presents
"THE BRUTE MAN"
with
Tom Neal
Jane Adams — Jan Wiley
Peter Whitney — Donald MacBride
and
Rondo Hatton
as
"The Brute Man"

Screenplay
by
George Bricker—M. Coates Webster

Original Story
by
Dwight V. Babcock

Director of Photography: Maury Gertsman, A.S.C.; Film Editor: Philip Cahn; Art Direction: John B. Goodman, Abraham Grossman; Director of Sound: Bernard B. Brown; Technician: Joe Lapis; Set Decorations: Russell A. Gausman, Edward R. Robinson; Gowns: Vera West; Hair Stylist: Carmen Dirigo; Director of Make-up: Jack P. Pierce; Dialogue Director: Raymond Kessler.

Directed
by
Jean Yarbrough
Produced by Ben Pivar
A
PRC PICTURE

Synopsis
(Not for Publication)

Hideously disfigured by acid, Hal Moffat (Rondo Hatton) ex-football hero, becomes a psychopathic killer known as the Creeper. He is befriended by a blind piano teacher, Helen (Jane Adams), who is unaware that Moffat is a ruthless murderer.

To obtain funds for an operation on Helen's eyes, the Creeper confronts his former college friend, Clifford Scott (Tom Neal), and the latter's wife, Virginia (Jan Wiley), and blames them for his plight. After confessing his identity, the Creeper strangles Scott and steals Virginia's jewels.

Helen unwittingly accepts the jewels to finance her operation and takes them to a jeweler for appraisal. Suspicious, the jeweler notifies the authorities and the horrified girl is informed that she is allegedly the Creeper's accomplice.

The Creeper, meanwhile, believes Helen has betrayed him and seeks vengeance. Detectives, however, anticipate his next move and he is trapped in Helen's home before she can be harmed.

Absolved of complicity in the Creeper's bloody career, Helen is befriended by Virginia who promises to have her cared for by a famous eye specialist.

Cast

The Brute Man	Rondo Hatton
Clifford Scott	Tom Neal
Helen	Jane Adams
Captain Donelly	Donald MacBride
Lieutenant Gates	Peter Whitney
Hal Moffat	Fred Coby
Virginia Scott	Jan Wiley
Joan Bemis	Janelle Johnson

2 Col. Ad Mat 201   30 lines

2 Col. Ad Mat 202   56 lines

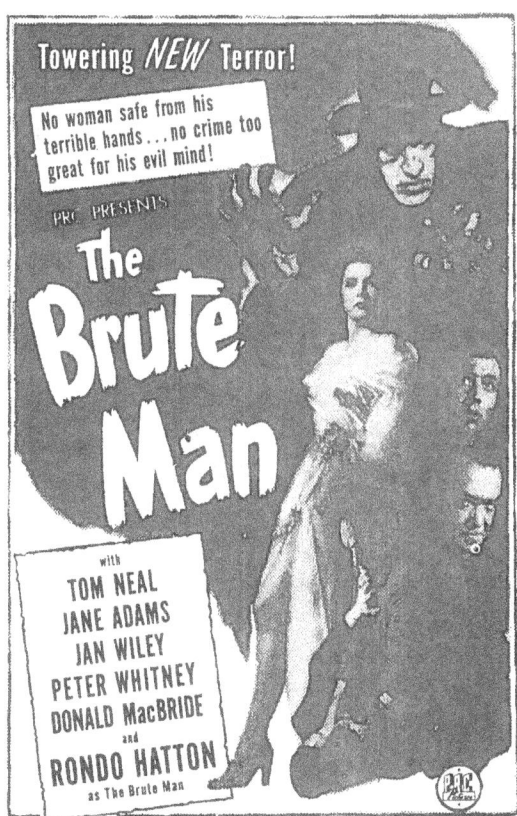

2 Col. Ad Mat 204   178 lines

1 Col. Ad Mat 105   78 lines

1 Col. Ad Mat 103   28 lines

FROM THE COLLECTION OF
John Antosiewicz

2 Col. Ad Mat 203   118 lines

Jane Adams Wins Leading Role in Horror Production
(Advance)

When screen actress Jane Adams entered the Hollywood handicap a few seasons ago, she was not a sure bet for "smart money." On the photogenic side, it's true, she had decided class. Her good breeding was an additional asset.

But the young actress, coming .... to the .... Theatre in PRC's film "The Brute Man," set an ambitious goal for herself. She wanted to become a dramatic actress. And that's reaching high in an industry where beauty is a surplus commodity, but the demand for girls able to play strong, meaty roles exceeds the supply.

Jane's maiden race before the cameras found her lined up beside half-dozen other new entries, all lovely but inexperienced like herself, in Walter Wanger's "Salome, Where She Danced."

Yet today, she has emerged a winner on the movie track, showing definite promise of realizing her ambition.

Not only did she outdistance the other maidens, but after several minor starts, Jane is now playing leads.

Her current picture, "The Brute Man," gives Jane the most difficult assignment of her career.

In this picture, directed by Jean Yarbrough, she portrays a blind music teacher innocently involved in a maze of crime.

Advance notices say that Jane gives an outstanding performance in the new thriller and other roles of equal importance are sure to follow.

Tom Neal, Jan Wiley, Peter Whitney, Donald MacBride and Rondo Hatton are seen with Miss Adams in the cast of "The Brute Man." Produced by Ben Pivar, the film is based on an original story by Dwight V. Babcock.

The screenplay was co-authored by George Bricker and M. Coates Webster.

THE BRUTE MAN (1B)

Tom Neal and Jan Wiley appear together in some of the vivid dramatic sequences of PRC Pictures' latest horror production, "The Brute Man," in which these two popular players are featured with Jane Adams, Peter Whitney, Donald MacBride and Hollywood's most colorful exponent of weird characterizations, the celebrated Rondo Hatton.

Tom Neal's Rise to Fame Thrills Motion Picture World
(Current)

Tom Neal's insistence on making a place for himself as a screen actor will never cease to surprise certain "false" friends—and an octopus he met at Papete. Tom is appearing currently in PRC Pictures' "The Brute Man" at the _____ Theatre.

The eight-armed sea monster, with whom he tangled while pearl-diving during a Tahitian vacation, offered even more stubborn resistence to his future career. To any future, for that matter.

As proof of having successfully overcome both factions' arguments, Neal has acted in half-a-dozen Broadway plays, and upwards of seventy-five motion pictures.

His latest movie is "The Brute Man."

Neal's original ambition, however, was not acting. It was the desire to become a millionaire!

As the son of a banker, now deceased, Tom had the advantage of extensive travel on this continent and in Europe, in addition to a sound education.

Born in Evanston, Ill., he attended prep school at neighboring Lake Forest Academy and St. Johns Military Academy, and later, Northwestern University. At college he joined Sigma Chi fraternity and played varsity football.

Tom's friend, screen star Rosalind Russell, was responsible for encouraging the young actor to try Hollywood where he has found so much success.

In "The Brute Man," Tom appears with Jane Adams, Jan Wiley, Peter Whitney, Donald MacBride and Rondo Hatton.

Jean Yarbrough directed the new murder mystery thriller and Ben Pivar was the producer. Dwight V. Babcock wrote the original story from which the screenplay, by George Bricker and M. Coates Webster, was prepared.

SHOWMANSHIP

BRUTE MAN TEASER

The menacing figure of The Brute Man is an effective piece of teaser art and can be used in several different ways. All the paper contains this figure and with a little additional art work it will be excellent as a hanger or a lobby standee. The huge body with outstretched arms creates a terrifying aspect and will get over the monster angle. Your sign artist can make up a drawing from the illustration which can be used for tack cards, paper streamers, newspaper teaser ads and for any other practical purpose. Even an animated display, with moving arms, can be made with very little trouble.

HE'S LOOSE!

Put across "the 'brute-man' is loose" angle as an advance bally by following the suggested lay-out and copy, using a heavy chain and broken handcuffs, as shown. Some signs should carry the 'Beware' warning, some should offer rewards for capture. Change them all during run of picture to "We have captured 'The Brute Man' . . . See him at the Rivoli."

USE RADIO SPOTS

Here's the kind of picture that lends itself effectively to radio advertising. Get "THE BRUTE MAN" on the air three or four days before your opening and spot your announcements before and after popular horror shows. Perhaps you can make a deal with local radio station to put on these spots in return for trailer advertising on your screen.

NO. 1 FIFTEEN SECOND STATION BREAK
ANNCR: (After Hideous Laughter) Lock your doors . . . ! Lock your windows . . . ! The screen's mightiest NEW monster of menace is on your trail . . . "THE BRUTE MAN." No evil too great for his terible brain! See "THE BRUTE MAN" for your most thrilling excitement . . . !

NO. 2 FIFTEEN SECOND STATION BREAK
ANNCR: (After Sirens, Pistol Shots, Crowd Yells) He's on the loose . . . He's coming your way . . . The screen rocks to the shock of this most towering terror . . . "THE BRUTE MAN" NEW thrills . . . NEW excitement! See "THE BRUTE MAN."

NO. 3 FIFTEEN SECOND STATION BREAK
ANNCR 1: (After Scream, Hideous Laughter) It's "THE BRUTE MAN."
GIRL: "THE BRUTE MAN"?
ANNCR 2: "THE BRUTE MAN."
ANNCR 1: Yes, the screen's mightiest NEW monster of menace is on his way to give you the thrill of your life . . . . !
ANNCR 2: See "THE BRUTE MAN."

STREET BALLY of huge man with padded shoulders and chest, securely chained and being led by uniformed "officer" with rifle, is a natural for this picture. It's simple, inexpensive and effective. Card copy: "We have captured 'THE BRUTE MAN' . . . see him at the Rivoli."

POSTER CUT-OUTS

The giant figure of the "Brute Man" in all posters was designed with an eye to seat-selling lobby cut-outs. It can be used in various sizes in lobby standees, on display boards and for marquee hangers. Select the size that suits your purpose and plant them freely around your theatre during the week ahead of your playdates.

Different combinations can be made by using blow-ups of the cast heads with the poster cut-out of the "Brute Man" as a background. A green baby-spot, focused on this figure from some distance away, will give added "horror-value." Top your display with copy as shown in illustration.

Page Three

Lobbies and Posters

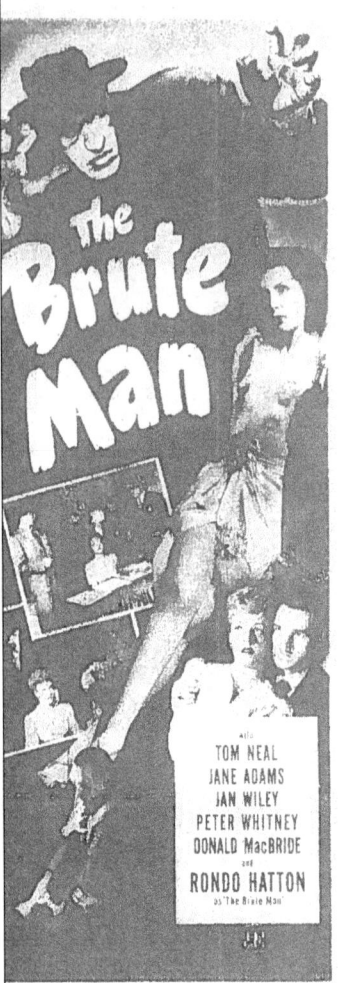

14x36 INSERT CARD

22x28

ORDER ACCESSORIES FROM YOUR
NATIONAL SCREEN
SERVICE EXCHANGE

ONE SHEET

THREE SHEET

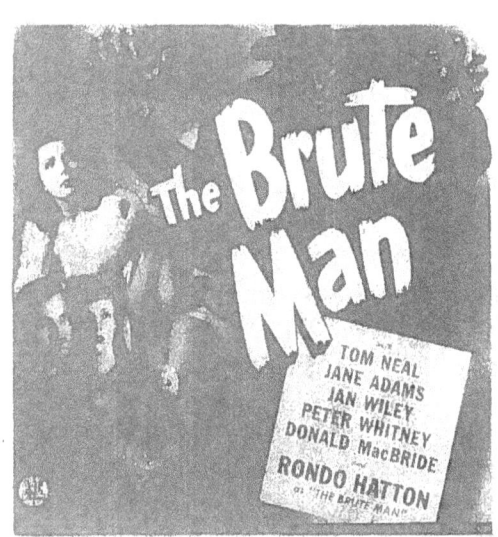

SIX SHEET

All gave some, some gave all

American Legion Post 5, 3810 West Kennedy Blvd. in Tampa, has the only privately owned American Legion cemetery in the country. Initially the Post was on Tampa's outskirts, but with the growth of the city, it's now located near a busy intersection. Post 5's website encourages motorists waiting for the stoplight to change to instead visit the cemetery and thank our departed veterans. From the website: "Lindell Motors is on one side, a strip mall on the other. The bone-white tombstones march toward a line of oaks. Still, this is sacred ground. Protected ground."

The year 2019 was the 100th anniversary of the founding of the American Legion, and on June 19, there were 60 or 80 attendees at a Post 5 luncheon in Rondo Hatton's honor. Many braved the heat and made a sojourn to his nearby grave, where a Rondo Hatton Classic Horror Awards bust was placed atop the actor's tombstone and photos were taken. But that part of the day's activities was necessarily brief, as attendees were sensibly eager to return to the air-conditioned indoors!

Two Rondo busts were donated to Post 5, one by Rondo Awards honcho David Colton and one by Tom Weaver. There was talk of affixing one to the top of Hatton's tombstone, but all involved sadly realized that it would soon be gone. So the former now has a home in a Post display cabinet, the latter near the Post's phone.

Endnotes

1. Many sources say that Rondo was voted "Most Handsome" in high school and that this is mentioned in his yearbook. There is no such notation. "Most Handsome" that year was Rondo's good friend Rex Farrior.
2. During the Prohibition era, a Tampa crime reporter probably never had to wait long for news: The battles between mob gangsters became so ugly that *Life* magazine called the city "the hellhole of the Gulf." According to a 2012 *Orlando Sentinel* article, Prohibition galvanized Tampa's underworld in the 1920s: "Through the city's port, bootleggers were able to import molasses and other materials to make illegal booze. … The sawed-off shotgun apparently was the weapon of choice for Tampa's version of 'goodfellas.'"
3. Immell reverted to her maiden name almost immediately following the divorce. Newspaper reports reflect that she remained in Tampa for a short time before she returned to Plattsburg, Missouri, where she married farmer Howard Thurman. After Thurman's death in 1980, Immell because active in local politics. Elizabeth Immell James Hatton Thurman died on March 7, 2000, at the age of 94.
4. Years later, when Rondo and his second wife Mae were in a Beverly Hills post office, a little girl saw Hatton's face and began to cry. Rondo was mortified, as was everyone else around. In an effort to dispel the discomfort, Mae suggested that same tried-and-truc solution: She nudged her husband and whispered, "Say 'Boo!'" He did, and everyone laughed.
5. John D. Kelton went on to become head of the psychology department at North Carolina's Davidson College. He died in 2013.
6. Hatton fans have producer Kevin Burns to thank for the modern-day availability of Fields' *Tales of Manhattan* sequence with its fleeting frames of Rondo. Plumbing the Fox vaults several decades ago, Burns unearthed it along with forgotten screen tests, extra footage from classic movies, a never-seen Betty Grable number from *I Wake Up Screaming* (1941) and much more. He turned all of this material into specials, most of which ran on American Movie Classics; one of them uses all the existing footage of Marilyn Monroe's never-finished *Something's Got to Give* (1962).
7. Probably Hatton was directed to do all these things: His character name is Gabe Hart, and in the novel, Gabe is one of the men appointed to whip the horses out from under the "rustlers." When Gabe refuses, another man explains to the posse ringleader that Gabe "can't stand to hurt anything. It would work on his mind."
8. The not-always-reliable Internet Movie Database adds two more 1942 credits to the Rondo résumé. Its castlist for Fox's *It Happened in Flatbush* (1942) credits him with an unbilled role as Baseball Game Spectator. Consider this a "definite maybe": At just past the 72-minute mark, an insert shot of several dozen excited fans features, just north of the center of the screen, a fellow who does look very much like Rondo would look … if Rondo had appeared in a distant shot, amidst a lively throng, wearing a hat, and with his face obscured by the shadow of the hat brim. *Is* it Rondo? The umpire hasn't yet made his call. Universal's 1942 Western *Sin Town* falls into the same category: The inclusion of Rondo's name on its IMDb castlist (credited with the role of Townsman) doesn't appear to be backed up by any primary sources. Watching this movie didn't yield a Rondo sighting or even a "*Might* be Rondo" sighting. Some sources include Fox's same-year *The Black Swan* among Hatton's credits. Since this rousing Rafael Sabatini swashbuckler was directed by Henry King, there's a chance this is legit, but try spotting him.
9. Republic asked Universal for permission to include figures of Frankenstein, Dracula, the Wolf Man and the Invisible Man in this scene. According to Jack Mathis' book *Republic Confidential Volume 1—The Studio*, Universal refused "on the grounds of considerable value impairment to the characters they had developed and exploited." Republic gave Rondo the character name "Hunchback" for *Sleepy Lagoon* but he's not hunchbacked in the movie. I wonder if the original plan, before Universal turned thumbs-down, was for Rondo's figure to represent Universal's Hunchback of Notre Dame. He *is* standing near a figure that looks like Universal's Phantom of the Opera.

10. Because of its "variety of topography and terrain," the Providencia Ranch, located north of Hollywood near Burbank, was in almost constant use during silent days, according to a 1930 *Los Angeles Times* article. After the coming of sound, it was in less demand because it was under the air routes of planes leaving from two big L.A. airports. Universal Horrors fans can get another look at it in *She-Wolf of London* (1946).
11. A completely dispensable "aside": When *The Jungle Captive* came to New York TV in the late 1950s, it was hosted by the immortal Zacherley, who habitually popped in and out of the movies he played. After Moloch pushes the morgue wagon off the cliff and it explodes into flames, TV viewers next saw a shot of Zach toasting marshmallows, presumably at the foot of the cliff. He cringes, mutters "Hey, what the heck are you doin' up there?!"—then looks up, sees who it is and waves: "Oh! Hiya, Creep!"

www.ingramcontent.com/pod-product-compliance
Lightning Source LLC
Chambersburg PA
CBHW082110230426
43671CB00015B/2656